Marketing

Longman modular texts in business and economics
●●●●●●●●●●●●●●●●●●

Series Editors
Geoff Black Win Hornby, Bob Gammie and Stuart Wall

Other titles in this series:

Introducing Human Resource Management
Margaret Foot and Caroline Hook

Business Economics
Win Hornby

Business Law
Ian Stirk and Helena McFarquhar

Management Accounting
David Wright

Financial Accounting
Christopher Waterston and Anne Britton

The Macroeconomic Environment
Andrew Dunnett

Business Information Technology
Geoffery Elliott and Susan Starkings

Marketing

·················

Elizabeth Hill & *Terry O' Sullivan*

LONGMAN
London and New York

Addison Wesley Longman Limited,
Edinburgh Gate,
Harlow, Essex CM20 2JE, England
and Associated Companies throughout the world

Published in the United States of America
by Longman Publishing, New York

First Published 1996, Reprinted 1997

ISBN 0 582 26255–0 PPR

British Library Cataloguing-in-Publication Data
A catalogue record for this book is
available from the British Library

Library of Congress Cataloguing-in-Publication Data

Hill, Elizabeth, 1960–
     Marketing / Elizabeth Hill and Terry O'Sullivan.
          p.   cm. –– (Longman modular texts in business and economics)
     Includes bibliographical references and index.
     ISBN 0–582–26255–0
     1. Marketing.   I. O'Sullivan, Terry, 1957– .   II Title.
III. Series.
HF5415.H5165   1996
658.8––dc20
                                                                                        96–3877
                                                                                        CIP

Set by 30 Stone Serif 9/12 pt
Produced by Longman Singapore Publishers (Pte) Ltd.
Printed in Singapore

Dedicated to our parents

Contents

Acknowledgements

We would like to take this opportunity to thank those individuals and organisations who have given us permission to use and adapt material for this book. Every effort has been made to trace the owners of copyright material, though in a few cases this has proved impossible and we apologise to any copyright holders whose rights may have been unwittingly infringed. We trust that in the event of any accidental infringement, the owners of the material will contact us directly. Special thanks are due to Clive Bayley, Kay Brandon, Jackie Church, John Newsome, Catherine O'Sullivan and Tom, Belle, Ollie, Ruari and Ned who have all, in their separate ways, been a lot of help.

The publishers would like to thank the following for permission to reproduce copyright material: Butterworth-Heinemann Ltd for the figure 'Key stages in conducting a survey' in *Creative Arts Marketing*, Hill, E., O'Sullivan, C. and O'Sullivan, T. (1995).

Trademarks

Introduction to marketing

Introduction

This chapter introduces the topic of marketing. It discusses the fundamental characteristics of firms which can claim to be marketing-orientated, examining the reasons for the growth of marketing in recent years and the problems associated with alternative approaches to doing business. The primary activities for which the marketing function is responsible are explained, and the contexts in which they can be usefully applied are also discussed. This chapter also sets the framework for the rest of the book, indicating how the various elements which comprise the discipline of marketing fit together, and introduces concepts that are explored in more detail in later chapters.

What is marketing?

Most people think they know what marketing is and what marketers do. Marketing has become widely synonymous with the ways in which organisations attract their customers and persuade them to buy products and services. The marketing department is seen as being responsible for launching new products, for generating good press coverage, for placing advertisements, for conducting research and for supporting the sales force. Marketing staff are expected to liaise with advertising agencies, to deal with customer complaints, to advise on product ranges and to arrange promotions. Such descriptions imply that the main function of marketing is to present an organisation and its products to its potential customers.

This, however, is by no means the whole story. Organisations who see their marketing activity as no more than a ploy to take them to their customers are missing the point altogether. The discipline of marketing is both broader and more meaningful than this. It is *a business philosophy that regards customer satisfaction as the key to successful trading and advocates the use of management practices that help identify and respond to customer needs.* An examination of some more definitions of marketing helps to clarify this. They tend to fall into two categories:

those that emphasise a philosophical dimension and those that focus on the more concrete managerial processes of marketing.

Marketing as a business philosophy

An organisation that adopts the concept of marketing as a philosophy sees the customer as the central driving force behind its activities, recognising that businesses only survive if they meet customer needs. In a free-market economy, consumers have a choice of what to buy, when to buy, and where to buy, as well as whether to buy at all. Therefore, to be successful at attracting consumers, the most logical starting point for an organisation is to identify what customers want and then to attempt to supply it more effectively and efficiently than the competition. To thrive in the long term, an organisation must meet customer needs over a period of time and make money from its transactions. The closer the fit between the customer's needs and what the organisation supplies, the more the customer is willing to pay and the more profits the business will generate.

To summarise, marketing as a business philosophy can best be defined as: '. . . the ability to create and keep profitable customers' (Brown, 1987).

▶ *Creating* customers requires an organisation constantly to monitor its environment to ensure that it recognises and acts upon the opportunities presented by the changing needs of its potential customers, so that they become actual customers.

▶ *Keeping* customers means that organisations must minimise or avoid threats to an established customer base, either from changes in existing customer needs or from competitor activities.

▶ *Profitable* customers are those who have the potential to generate revenues that will more than exceed the costs of the business. Organisations must ensure that they focus their attentions on profitable business rather than pursue any customers at any price.

DID YOU KNOW?
Although 'marketing' is a relatively young discipline which first developed in the US after the Second World War, the concept of marketing was first expounded in the UK in 1776 by Adam Smith in The Wealth of Nations:

> Consumption is the sole end and purpose of all production, and the interest of the producer ought to be attended to only so far as it may be necessary for promoting that of the consumer (Smith, 1993).

Marketing as a managerial function

Many definitions of marketing refer not specifically to the philosophy of marketing, but to the managerial processes that are inherent in 'creating and keeping profitable customers'.

> Marketing is the management process responsible for identifying, anticipating and satisfying customer requirements profitably (The Chartered Institute of Marketing, UK).

> [Marketing is] ... a social and managerial process by which individuals and groups obtain what they need and want through creating and exchanging products and value with others (Kotler and Armstrong, 1994).

Marketing is the process of planning and executing the conception, pricing, promotion and distribution of ideas, goods and services to create exchanges that satisfy individual and organisational goals (American Marketing Association, 1985).

These definitions help us to build up a picture of the role of marketing in an organisation. They portray marketers as facilitators, helping individuals to satisfy their needs and organisations to reach their goals. The task of the marketer is to arrange exchanges: usually customers' money in exchange for the organisation's products and services. A car manufacturer, for example, designs a range of models to meet the needs of its potential customers and requires them to pay a sum of money in exchange for the benefits that they will reap from ownership of their car. This is an example of a monetary transaction, but not all exchanges will be financial and the benefits sought by customers will not always be so tangible. A political party, for example, offers promises of prosperity and social harmony in exchange for the electorate's votes. A charity offers people clear consciences in exchange for their money or their time as volunteers.

These definitions of marketing also offer guidance as to how marketers should go about their task of facilitating exchange processes. Attention is drawn to the importance of researching customers' needs (identifying and anticipating needs). The creation of value is emphasised, indicating that marketers are responsible for developing products and services that offer sufficient benefits to induce customers to participate in the exchange process. Pricing is also mentioned, being an activity that assesses the value the customer places on the product and sets the terms under which exchange can take place. Promotion and distribution are both means by which the exchange process is made easier: promotion by raising awareness of products, services and the benefits they offer, and distribution by making them available in a convenient location for the potential customer.

The managerial function of marketing, therefore, goes way beyond the rather limited administrative activities suggested at the beginning of this chapter. It is an integrative function which helps match the needs of actual and potential customers with the goals of the organisation through desirable exchanges. Marketing management is:

> ... the analysis, planning, implementation and control of programs designed to create, build and maintain beneficial exchanges with target buyers for the purpose of achieving organisational objectives (Kotler and Armstrong, 1994).

The marketing concept

The definition of marketing, and the recognition that marketing is an integrative discipline that places the customer at the centre of the business, has led to the development of the 'marketing concept'. This concept highlights the importance of three key features that should be at the core of any organisation that claims to be marketing orientated.

Customer orientation

This is demonstrated when an organisation makes efforts to find out what its customers need and want before it decides what to produce and sell. This appears to be little more than common sense: if an organisation cannot sell its products, what is the point of producing them in the first place? In practice, though, organisations can easily become so preoccupied with manufacturing and its associated technologies that they lose sight of the changing needs of their customers and fail to see that they are not adequately meeting their needs. This leaves the door open for competitors to attract customers with products that suit their needs better, and leaves the organisation with products that are increasingly difficult to sell.

ACTIVITY **1.1**
••••••••••••

Holiday horrors

Although the number of tourists visiting Britain increased by five per cent in 1994, the average increase in visitor numbers across Europe was eight per cent, and since 1980 Britain's share of world tourist spending has declined from 5.6 per cent to 4.3 per cent. A recent survey by the London Tourist Board has indicated that one in four overseas visitors to London was dissatisfied with their accommodation. Foreign and domestic customers alike complain that service in British hotels is often poor, that rooms are overpriced, that resorts are shabby and that the people are unfriendly.

Based on your experience of holidays in the UK and overseas, make a list of ways in which your needs as a tourist could be better satisfied by:

▶ Hotels and guest-houses in Britain.
▶ Regional tourist boards.
▶ Local authorities.

Identify the barriers to implementing your recommendations and suggest ways in which these may be lowered.

Source 'A missed opportunity', 1995.

Integrated effort

This means that the different departments within an organisation should all be working together towards the common goal of satisfying the customer: marketing should be a company-wide orientation, not just the domain of the 'marketing' department. A key role of marketing is to build bridges between the needs of customers and the capabilities of the organisation. Unfortunately, the way in which many organisations are structured, the basis on which their managers are rewarded and the nature of some roles can militate against this. Look at the accountant's role, for example. Accountants are responsible for controlling the finance of a business as efficiently as possible and are keen to keep costs down. They are reluctant to sanction the holding of large stocks, as stocks tie up working capital. In other words, £100 worth of stock sitting on the shelf in the warehouse is a £100 that could be taken off the organisation's overdraft, thereby reducing interest payments. On the other hand, the sales manager will be keen to keep stock levels as high as possible, knowing that if a customer wants to buy a product but finds it temporarily out of stock, that customer is likely to find a competitor to buy from, and may never return. The dilemma here is how to set appropriate stock levels that optimise this inevitable trade-off between customer service levels and cost efficiency. Similar trade-offs occur in other departments too: production managers looking for economies of scale may resist product range extension; salespeople trying to generate commission may put their efforts into selling existing products as opposed to introducing new and better models; technical departments, encouraged to harness new technologies, may design products with features that have little value to customers. In these situations the function of marketing is to encourage compromises that create an optimal balance between the needs of the customer and those of the organisation.

ACTIVITY **1.2**

·············

Efficiency vs effectiveness

Efficiency is a goal that is hotly pursued by most organisations. It is concerned with producing products at minimum cost, so as to maximise profitability. It is sometimes dubbed 'doing things right'. Consequently, hardly a day goes by without announcements being made in the press about job losses being incurred to improve productivity and make companies more efficient. But marketing-orientated firms place their emphasis primarily on being effective. *Effectiveness* is concerned with satisfying the needs of the market, and 'doing the right things' in the eyes of the customer. Efficiency is a means of enhancing profitability rather than the primary means of achieving it.

Of course, the ideal is for a business to be both effective and efficient, in which case it will thrive. But there are three other categories firms can fall into:

	Effective	*Ineffective*
Efficient	1 Thrive	2 ?
Inefficient	3 ?	4 ?

1   What is the outlook for the firms that are efficient but ineffective (2), effective but inefficient (3), and neither effective nor efficient (4)?
2   Find examples of existing (or now defunct) businesses that fall into each of the four categories and explain the criteria on which you based your decision.

Goal focus

Organisations should only attempt to generate business from exchanges with customers that will help them to reach their own objectives. These objectives are commonly related to making profit, though some organisations such as charities, the health services, local authorities, educational institutions and arts organisations may espouse a wider range of objectives. One of the traps that firms often fall into is to expend so much energy chasing sales that profitability is overlooked. Sales forces, for example, may be given bonuses based on the sales revenues they generate, as opposed to the profit margins they make on those sales, thus tempting them to cut prices to get the business without worrying whether the deal makes any money for the firm. The second trap is to strive so hard to achieve the short-term organisational objectives, many of which are easy to measure, that people lose sight of the goal of long-term profitability. Take the example quoted by Brown (1987) of a UK brewery that was so keen to reach its objective of reducing tyre pilferage from its delivery vehicles that it included in its monthly accounts a measure of the amount of tyre tread incurred per thousand barrels of beer delivered. The result was to discourage managers from trading with otherwise profitable outlets, merely because they had unsurfaced delivery bays that could potentially damage the tyres! A similar scenario can be envisaged in the not-for-profit sector, for example in a theatre that is partly funded by the public purse and given the remit of encouraging new artistic work and encouraging audiences from across the social spectrum. If it becomes preoccupied with 'bums on seats' to generate its top-up revenue, and subordinates the requirements of the funding bodies to its internal daily targets, it will be in danger of losing its underpinning funding altogether.

CASE STUDY **1.1**
....

Morgan Cars

The Morgan Motor Company was founded by HFS Morgan in 1909. It is the world's oldest privately owned motor company producing the last coach-built car. Still actively managed by members of the Morgan family, the company is very much a family business where the whole workforce is committed to the success of the product. The tradition of craftsmanship has been passed down the generations and the atmosphere at the factory is that of one family with a strong community spirit.

Morgan owners are also regarded as part of the family, and visitors are welcome to come to see for themselves the loving care that is lavished on each new vehicle in production. A Morgan is generally bought as a second car by male drivers from all walks of life. The business is very much an international one, with demand coming primarily from the UK, the US and mainland Europe, particularly Germany.

The car itself is unique in design, conveying the image of a vintage 1930s sports car while incorporating engineering features that offer high levels of reliability, performance and safety. Many have tried to imitate this successful formula, but failed. Positive decisions have been made over the years to keep the character of the car intact, in spite of pressures to conform to more modern designs. It is quite literally a tailor-made vehicle, coming with a choice of 35,000 body colours and optional features which include authentic walnut fascia panels, leather upholstery, coloured hoods and badge bars. Changing vehicle legislation has led to other developments, and models for the US market now come complete with airbags, low speed bumpers and emissions refinements. This level of customisation is made possible by the existence of extensive waiting lists for the product, currently standing at six years; production volume is in the region of 500 vehicles a year. Despite this, the prices are considered to be extremely reasonable, starting at around £17,000 (1995).

In 1989, Morgan Cars was the subject of a BBC documentary in the 'Troubleshooter' series, presented by Sir John Harvey-Jones. He expressed some reservations about its highly labour-intensive production techniques, the desire to produce even small components in-house and the low price levels, given the high waiting lists.

Questions

1 How would you describe the business orientation of Morgan Cars?

2 Who do you think Morgan Cars competes with?

3 Sir John Harvey Jones asked the question 'Why don't you hike up the price, double production, send work outside, cut down on stocks and install modern machinery?' What would be your reply?

Sources Morgan literature; Ashton, 1994; Rhys, 1992; 'Family values', 1994/5.

The societal marketing concept

All of the discussion about the nature and role of marketing so far has assumed that the firm is responsible for satisfying the needs of individual consumers. What may be best for individuals, though, may not be best for society: individuals may like powerful cars with large engines, but the effects of the pollution they generate on air quality may be lethal to others; non-returnable bottles may be more convenient for consumers, but do not help to preserve natural resources and cause problems of waste management; more and cheaper beef-burger outlets may be demanded on the high street but if the grazing of the cattle to produce the beef requires the rain-forests to be cut down, then the environmental impact may be detrimental to many more people than those who enjoy the product. This has led to the development of a business philosophy called the Societal Marketing Concept, which advocates attempts to satisfy consumer needs in line with the objectives of the organisation as well as the needs of society. It has been adopted by a number of organisations who see their roles as balancing the interests of not just the firm and the individual, but also society as a whole. Resistance to this concept comes from those who argue that marketing executives are taking on the role of guardianship of public standards, which should be the role of democratically elected politicians. Nonetheless, organisations such as the Body Shop have proved that financial success and social responsibility are not necessarily mutually exclusive.

DID YOU KNOW?

Cynics suggest that firms who adopt the societal marketing concept have little more than self-interest at heart. Research by the Henley Centre for forecasting found that the percentage of shoppers influenced in what they buy by companies' records of social and environmental responsibility has risen from 52 per cent in 1981 to 64 per cent in 1994 (Sylvester, 1994).

CASE STUDY **1.2**

The Body Shop

Body Shop International, manufacturer and retailer of cosmetics, is synonymous with humanitarian ideals and social responsibility, and is often referred to as the embodiment of the societal marketing concept. Committed to recycling, opposing animal testing, dedicated to helping less developed countries and responsible towards employees, the company eschews any business practices associated with the 'hard-sell'. With no marketing department and no advertising, the company gives customers product information stressing health rather than a sales pitch promising glamour, and their leaflets explain the firm's opposition to animal testing and its recycling policy.

But is Body Shop merely following a social agenda, or is its approach grounded in enlightened self-interest? A damning article in *Business Ethics* (September 1994), subsequently much quoted in the press and causing ripples throughout the financial markets, implied that the company's image for insisting on natural ingredients and socially conscious business practices was being exaggerated for marketing purposes. Allegations were made of products being copied from an American store, of ingredients that are not as pure as customers believe and of promises made to franchisees that have not been kept. Other reports suggested that, while the Body Shop has campaigned against animal testing, it does not meet RSPCA guidelines.

The extent to which such accusations can alienate shoppers who are willing to pay premium prices to support the ethical stance of the company is as yet unclear, but many suspect that the reputation of the company is sufficient for it to weather the storm. The typical Body Shop customer distrusts traditional advertising and sales promotions and is loyal to companies believed to have a social conscience. So by adopting marketing practices that aim to build respect for the company's philanthropic approach and moving away from an emphasis on individual transactions, profitable long-term relationships have been developed.

The firm's social conscience has certainly done it no harm financially. Since it went public in 1984, its value on the stock market has risen by over 10,000 per cent and profits are predicted to grow by over 25 per cent annually.

Questions

1   To what extent does the Body Shop demonstrate its social conscience through its marketing mix?
2   Is the Body Shop competing in the cosmetics industry? Or which industry?
3   As the Body Shop has effectively proved that corporate philanthropy is a profitable strategy, why do so many other firms resist it?

Sources Jacob, 1992; Garfield, 1992; 'An image eroded', 1994; Bernoth, 1994.

The growth of marketing

The number and range of organisations having adopted the marketing concept in recent years can be attributed to changes in the social, business and economic environments and the growing complexities of doing business in modern industrial nations. Five factors have been instrumental in raising the importance of a marketing orientation in today's world.

More sophisticated consumers

Maslow (1970) suggests that each individual is motivated by a series of needs, which range from those that are most fundamental to all human beings, to those that are highly specific to each individual. (See Figure 1.1.)

People are motivated to satisfy their needs sequentially, only attempting to satisfy social needs, for example, when their physiological and safety needs have been met. In subsistence economies, a high proportion of the population will be striving to meet the lower level needs – for food, water, shelter and warmth – universal needs that are easy to identify and anticipate. In the Western world, though, consumers are increasingly in a position of having disposable income that is more than sufficient for supplying their basic needs. They are looking to

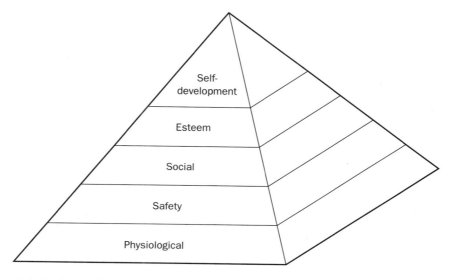

satisfy higher order needs, and the individuality of these needs makes it much more difficult for the producers of products and services to know exactly what to supply. Take motor cars as an example. A family looking to satisfy its social needs may be looking for a car that can carry two adults and two children in comfort, with room for the dog in the back and a roof-rack for luggage on holiday. On the other hand, the social needs of a teenager looking for a first car may be defined more by the need to build relationships with other young people and consequently the most 'sociable' vehicle would be a small sporty model with economic fuel consumption. Esteem needs may motivate some people to buy a vehicle offering them comfort and style on a grand scale, such as a Rolls Royce, while others may feel that their status is better reflected in the purchase of a vehicle with a reputation for speed, such as a Ferrari or a Porsche. Those who view cars as objects of intrinsic interest rather than means of transport may be seeking to satisfy self-development needs in their choice of car – they may choose a classic car, spend many a happy evening with their heads under the bonnet and only drive it to shows and owners' club rallies.

The key point here is that while it is easy to predict and supply lower order needs, the task of anticipating, identifying and satisfying the more complex and individual human needs, and matching them with the capabilities and objectives of an organisation is a complex and difficult one. A marketing orientation, putting customers at the centre of a business and making concerted efforts to find out just what they do want, is the approach most likely to encourage a successful match.

Greater competition

Firms are facing ever increasing competition from a number of sources:

▶ *International competition*: As global communication systems improve, the potential for organisations to supply customers from whom they are geographically remote increases dramatically. This poses both opportunities and threats for businesses: opportunities to search for customers abroad, but also threats from foreign competitors, eager to find markets where they can supply customers more effectively than the current domestic suppliers. Foreign firms may have certain competitive advantages, stemming from access to raw materials, from superior technologies, from lower costs (particularly those from low labour-cost countries) and even from a better understanding of customer needs, built up from experience in other parts of the world.

▶ *New technologies*: It is inevitable that from time to time new technologies will challenge and ultimately cannibalise existing industries. Described as a force for 'creative destruction' (Levitt, 1960), major innovation is increasingly likely to come from new classes of competitors emerging outside existing industries rather than from within them. Watchmakers have been overtaken by electronics firms as customers are wooed by the benefits of accuracy and reliability over craftsmanship. Printers are threatened by computer and copier manufacturers as customers demand flexibility and control over their publications. Genetic engineering may ultimately threaten the pharmaceutical industry as people increasingly attempt to avoid illness rather than cure it. As the speed of technological change gathers pace, organisations must adapt to survive, and recognise that the better they understand the needs of their customers, the better they can anticipate changes in demand and avoid extinction at the hands of these new competitors.

▶ *Imitators*: Although the law gives some protection to the originators of products through the granting of patents and copyright protection, whenever an organisation establishes a new product in a market and starts to gain business, competitors will be keen to attract a share of the new market. They will often launch 'me-too' products, adapted versions of the innovator's product, in an attempt to take a slice of the profitable new business for themselves. To gain ground they may use heavy promotional activity or price cutting tactics, thereby posing a serious threat to both the potential sales and profitability of the firm that introduced the product in the first place.

A marketing orientation is one defence against such tactics. The better an innovating organisation understands the motivations and buying habits of its potential customers, the more prepared it can be to take pre-emptive action and the better will be its defences against this form of competition.

CASE STUDY **1.3**

Cola-clones

Having spent decades fending off its arch-rival, Pepsi, in 1994 Coca Cola suddenly found itself under attack from a set of imitators in the form of Sainsbury Classic Cola and Richard Branson's Virgin Cola (sold through Tesco). Coca Cola, with about 80 per cent of the UK market, was the single biggest branded product in Britain, with sales of £411 million a year. With UK consumers drinking only half the average 300 drinks a year consumed in the US, the new entrants perceived an opportunity to take a significant share of the cola market away from Coke by encouraging increased consumption and attracting new customers with a very similar product.

Obtaining their supplies from an erstwhile obscure Canadian soft-drink bottler called the Cott corporation, the imitators based their marketing proposition on product quality (an American cola that tasted just like Coca Cola), price (a price that undercut the market leader) and packaging (a can that looked just like Coca Cola). The subsequent threat by Coke to take legal action if Sainsbury's did not make some changes to its look-alike packaging seemed to serve only to increase publicity about the new product launch and encourage people to try it.

The cola market is clearly divided into two segments: purchases made by shoppers as part of the weekly grocery run, mainly from supermarkets, account for 56 per cent of purchases, while impulse purchases from small outlets which are consumed on the spot account for the other 44 per cent. Twelve months after the imitators' attack, Coke seems to be holding its own in the second of these segments, but experiencing problems in the first. Despite a growth in the overall market of 18 per cent, industry estimates suggest that Coke's share of supermarket sales has fallen from 44 per cent to 32 per cent, while own-label sales have increased from 20 per cent to 36 per cent and Virgin is attracting nine per cent. Two more imitators have also jumped on the bandwagon – Safeway's Select and Woolworths' Genuine American Cola.

Perhaps Coca Cola has no reason to panic, though. 1994 was still the company's best year in recent history, with world-wide sales of 12 billion cases and profits running at $2.6 billion. The company still remains confident that the strength of its brand image will carry it through such turbulent times, even going so far as to express gratitude to the new supermarket brands for the way in which they are expanding the market. Nonetheless, it has reacted to the new threat in the UK by doubling its marketing budget and attempting to rekindle consumer interest in Coke's famous contour bottle – something its competitors will find harder to copy – and improving distribution through non-supermarket outlets, including office vending machines.

Questions

1 Should Coca Cola be concerned that cola is becoming a commodity?
2 What type of people seldom or never buy Coke? Could they be persuaded to, and if so, how?
3 How much are you likely to pay for:
   – A litre of Coke in the supermarket?
   – A glass of Coke in the pub?
   – A can of Coke from the corner shop?
   What does this imply about people's price sensitivity for Coke?

Sources Cowe, 1995; Buck, 1995; Mitchell, 1995; 'CopyCotting catches on', 1994.

Separation of production and consumption

In days gone by, if a man needed a new suit, he would go to a tailor who would take his measurements, offer him a selection of cloths, discuss appropriate styles and invite him to return for fittings as the garment was being prepared. With the coming of mass-production, such immediate contact between producer and consumer is lost. Cloth manufacturers will have to anticipate the fashion for forthcoming seasons, often years in advance of their sale on the high street. They will have to predict the popularity of raw materials, patterns and colours, and must understand the potential benefits of any new man-made fibres becoming available. Garment manufacturers are then responsible for choosing cloth, colour and styles on behalf of a large number of potential customers, who are unknown to them at the time the production decisions are made. They must decide how many of which sizes to produce, and in so doing will be making assumptions about the tolerance of their customers in buying garments that nearly fit but are not made-to-measure. Finally, retailers must assess which type, style and sizes of garment to stock to attract potential buyers into their stores. Chain stores may be making decisions for shops that are geographically very separate and whose average shoppers may be very different from each other.

In this process, unlike a visit to the tailor, the customer is not automatically consulted. Others are making decisions on his behalf. However, if he is unhappy with the decisions made by the cloth producer, the garment manufacturer or the retailer, he is in a position to take his business elsewhere, to others who can satisfy his particular requirements better.

The moral of this tale is that unless organisations make conscious, co-ordinated and consistent efforts to identify the changing needs of their potential customers, they are always in danger of missing vital signals from the market which would have been more evident had they had face-to-face contact with them during the buying process. A marketing orientation encourages contact with customers, in particular through market research.

More complex organisations

As firms increase in size, their staff usually become more and more distant from the end-user of the organisation's product. Two significant problems emerge as a result of this:

▶ *Conflicting demands*: In all but the smallest organisations, employees are likely to be more responsible to 'internal' customers – normally their bosses, or other departments for whom they perform a service – than to those who buy the organisation's products and services. From time to time, the demands of these internal customers will conflict with the needs of the real customer. Suppose, for example, in an attempt to maintain high quality standards, a fashion store's policy requires shop assistants to remove shop-soiled goods from display to be destroyed, and not to offer them at a discount. But then, after a long day's shopping, a customer finds the perfect dress in the store – the last one in her size. However, the previous person who had tried it on left a lipstick mark on it. The customer offers to purchase the dress, but asks for a 20 per cent discount. Organisations that have adopted the marketing concept will put into practice the principles of 'customer focus' and 'goal orientation' and will empower the shop-assistant to make a decision that will send the customer away happy, regardless of the rule book. Organisations whose own procedures are given precedence over responding to customer needs will gradually find themselves being labelled as bureaucrats and ultimately running out of customers!

▶ *Separation of ownership and control*: Employees tend to be less profit-orientated than owner-managers. If management fails to communicate effectively, the correlation in the minds of employees between serving customers, making profits and getting paid can be lost: in the short term, most employees will take home a wage-packet or salary cheque whether or not the organisation's customers are satisfied. Compare this with the self-employed person who knows that failing to meet customer needs equates with a reduction in take-home pay.

To overcome the problems that emerge from this, marketing orientated firms have started to design their organisational structures, their operating and communication systems, their remuneration packages, their staff appraisal and their training activity in such a way as to motivate employees to attend first to the needs of the customer.

DID YOU KNOW?

ABB Asea Brown Boveri is a multinational engineering company with an annual turnover of $30 billion. The chief executive believes that to be successful, big companies must learn to behave like small ones. So he reduced the size of his head office staff from 2,000 to 100, and divided the whole company into 1,300 autonomous businesses, each with full responsibility for its own destiny ('Crazy ways for crazy days', 1993).

Faster environmental change

There is more discussion of this in Chapter 2. However, it is worth noting here that the world is changing ever more rapidly and that if there ever was such a thing, a stable business environment is a thing of the past. New technology, as we have already seen, is making whole industries redundant. Social change is occurring as more of the world is educated at higher levels and demanding more and better products. The environmental movement is gaining pace and influence over business practices. Political change has ended the primary divisions between East and West and is encouraging the further integration of Europe. Economic influences are being felt globally rather than nationally, with events in Japan, the US and Europe affecting the world rather than just their own trading blocks. Firms that fail to integrate their own efforts in responding to changing customer needs in such a turbulent environment are in danger of being left behind in current markets and left out of new ones.

Alternative approaches to marketing

Looking at alternatives to marketing orientation, it is clear that they are becoming more and more difficult to justify.

Production orientation

Mass-production industries rely on economies of scale to reduce their unit costs and enable them to supply mass markets at prices that people can afford and that are simultaneously profitable to the organisation itself. The greater the number of units produced, the lower the cost per unit – known as productivity. If we assume that customers are primarily price-driven, then the reduction of price is an effective tool for generating new business and retaining existing customers. The temptation in industries characterised by economies of scale, therefore, is to become preoccupied with producing as much and as efficiently as possible without much thought as to whether customers want or need large supplies of uniform products. This is known as a production orientation.

As a rule of thumb, a production orientation can be considered as an appropriate short-term approach to business under two circumstances:

▶ *Shortage*: if customer demand exceeds what businesses can supply, prices in the market will be artificially high and competitors will be attracted by the high profit margins that can be generated. If a firm wishes to deter competitors it may seek to raise its own production levels so that there are fewer customers left for potential new competitors. Any that do choose to enter the market will have to undercut existing firms and operate on reduced profit, just to get a foothold.

▶ *High unit costs*: if the unit cost of producing an item is high then the prices that need to be charged to cover costs may deter customers and slow down or even prevent the growth of a potential market. Improved productivity and reduced unit costs may be brought about by concentration on increasing production, and this in turn may stimulate market growth.

CASE STUDY **1.4**

Krosno: troubleshooting and glassblowing

Under communist rule since the Second World War, Polish industry has grown up in a state-controlled economy. Factories were responsible for production and the state was responsible for distribution of the output as it thought best. The concept of a consumer was a remote one for the manufacturer. The customer was the state, end-user satisfaction was a low priority and there was no such thing as competition. Consequently, the collapse of the communist regime and the subsequent privatisation programme led to a rude awakening for Polish managers.

Krosno is a Polish glass manufacturer. It was one of the first five Polish companies to be privatised following the announcement that 200 companies were to be returned to the free-market environment to fend for themselves in 1991/2. It was a time of high inflation, high interest rates and high exchange rates in Poland, none of which are conducive to profitable trading. As part of the TV series 'Troubleshooter in Eastern Europe', the company was visited the following year by Sir John Harvey Jones. He found that the firm was already experiencing serious difficulties, many of which stemmed from its overriding preoccupation with production – an ethos left over from its previous role as a state-owned enterprise. An old and inefficient production line was being used to produce a seemingly inexhaustible supply of cheap drinking glasses, $1 million worth of which were sitting as stock in the warehouse because there was no market for them. Based on the saying 'if you're in a hole, stop digging!', Sir John recommended that the factory should close for three or four weeks while efforts were made to find markets for the product, but there was great reluctance by management to switch off the production line on the grounds that this would be inefficient. Another recommendation was that the firm should close down its production line permanently, and concentrate on low-volume high-value products, including hand-blown and stained glass, which were made at relatively low cost (due to low wage-rates) by skilled craftsmen and had the potential to be sold on world markets.

Questions ·

1 What type of activities might Krosno need to engage in if it is to become:
– More effective?
– More efficient?

2 What are the advantages and disadvantages of producing a low volume of specialised products for specialist markets?

3 What difficulties might firms in Eastern Europe face when trying to enter established Western European markets for the first time?

Source 'Troubleshooter in Eastern Europe', 1992.

DID YOU KNOW?

Henry Ford claimed to have invented the assembly line for the Model T after having calculated that it would enable him to set prices at levels that would attract millions of new car owners. However, his continued emphasis on productivity and cost minimisation, in particular his refusal to produce in colours other than black, were an opportunity eagerly seized by his subsequent competitors at General Motors who identified a demand for other colours and were more than happy to supply red as well!

DID YOU KNOW?

The Disney Corporation was confident that the more 'American' Euro Disney was, the better people would like it. But Europe refused to appreciate the experience of the theme park in the same way as the Americans. Rather than saunter around the park soaking up the atmosphere and taking advantage of the shops and restaurants, they headed straight for the rides and tried to experience as many as they could in the shortest possible time. The subsequent financial difficulties experienced by Euro Disney have been partly blamed on its failure to generate income from discretionary expenditure in the park (Langley, 1993).

Product orientation

Organisations that are product orientated define their businesses in terms of the products they sell, rather than the needs of their customers. As such, preoccupied with the addition of ever more intricate features, improving product quality or enhancing product performance or appearance, they often misunderstand the core benefits that their customers are seeking from their products. Manufacturers of video recorders are often seen as having fallen into this trap. Keen to outdo their competitors in terms of the numbers of functions that their equipment would perform, they lost sight of the difficulties faced by their customers in operating the increasingly complex technology. Simpler operating procedures were a much sought-after benefit and new, simpler control mechanisms were subsequently brought onto the market to help solve the problem.

Another symptom of product orientation is the failure to recognise that a product is becoming obsolete. By defining their markets and customers in terms of their products they may fall into the trap of 'marketing myopia' (Levitt, 1960) and fail to see the threat posed by product developments in other industries. Marketing history is littered with casualties from product orientation – the growth of the 'dry-cleaning' industry was halted by developments in fabric technology as well as domestic laundry equipment. People wanted clean clothes, not dry-cleaners. Slide-rule manufacturers have had no chance of survival up against the complex mathematical functions performed by computers and calculators at the touch of a button. People wanted simplicity and accuracy in their calculations, not slide rules.

Sales orientation

This approach assumes that customers will not be willing to buy sufficient of an organisation's products or services unless considerable effort is put into influencing them through persuasion and promotion. This is quite the contrary of a marketing orientation, which seeks such a close match between what the organisation is offering and what the customer wants that the product should virtually sell itself. A sales orientation considers the customer only after decisions have been made about what to produce, and this implies that the organisation is more interested in its own goals – converting products into sales revenues – than in satisfying customer needs and generating customer loyalty. (See Figure 1.2.)

As a result, a sales orientation can only prove effective in the short term, and then only if the organisation wishes to create customers but is not worried about keeping them. This may be the case in markets characterised by few repeat-purchases – items such as fitted kitchens, sets of encyclopaedias and double glazing, where the customer is unlikely to want the item again for a long while. The organisation does not have to consider the possibility of a repeat purchase and may decide that 'getting the sale' is more important than post-purchase satisfaction. Election campaigns are characterised by similar approaches: promises may be made that prove impossible to fulfil, but once elected a candidate needn't worry about getting votes for another five years.

In the long term, even if individual customers are not in a position to repurchase, by undermining the company's reputation they can be a powerful force

figure 1.2
**Marketing is NOT...
HARD SELLING!**

in damaging future sales. If they are dissatisfied with the products or services they were persuaded to buy, they are likely to spread the word and warn others not to make the same mistake. Research suggests that bad word-of-mouth travels far faster than good, with dissatisfied customers commenting on disappointments more than three times as often as satisfied customers comment on good experiences (Kotler and Armstrong, 1994).

The practice of marketing

As explained earlier, marketing is a philosophy that should underpin the business activities of an organisation, but it is also a managerial function that takes responsibility for the matching of customer needs with an organisation's products and services. The most fundamental tasks that fall to marketers are analysis, strategy, tactics and management.

Analysis

This helps organisations to answer the question 'where are we now?' Effective marketing requires that firms understand their current position and anticipate any changes that may affect their abilities to serve customers. Therefore, marketing-orientated firms are committed to gathering and analysing information from their environment and their customers to build up a picture of the opportunities and threats facing them in their markets and enable them to respond to them in appropriate ways.

Environmental scanning is undertaken to identify the forces that surround the buyer and the firm and are beyond the control of the organisation itself. Changes in legislation, for example, may render an existing product obsolete or encourage demand from customers who had previously had no need for a particular product. The arrival of foreign competitors may start a price war which a domestic firm with high costs may find very difficult to win. An increase in disposable income brought about by falls in the mortgage rate may lead to increased demand for luxury goods and better quality products. (Further discussion of this appears in Chapter 2.)

Buyer behaviour needs to be assessed so that firms have a good understanding of what makes their customers buy. It is a critical role of marketing to identify the buyers of their products and services, the decision processes that they go through in making their purchase choices and the way in which their personal motivations and attitudes, educational levels, social class, age and many other factors influence their buying decisions. Individuals wanting to go on holiday, for example, may be motivated by a need for a rest, a desire to make new friends or a wish to explore new places. Their choices are likely to be influenced by their age, their family commitments, their budget and even their susceptibility to sunburn. (Chapter 3 explains the concept of buyer behaviour in more detail.)

Marketing research is the process by which much of the information about customers and the environment is collected. The marketing function is responsible for identifying information needs, gathering data and systematically feeding information into the organisation to help it make better marketing decisions. Without marketing research an organisation has to make guesses about its customers – a dangerous stance to take if you think about the sheer diversity of opinions, tastes and preferences that are evident when we look at buyer behaviour. (Chapter 4 looks at the applications and implementation of marketing research.)

Strategy

Designing a marketing strategy is about setting the direction for marketing activity. As a result of thorough analysis, appropriate decisions can be made about the types of customers that the organisation wants to reach and the ways in which it will attempt to satisfy their needs.

Market segmentation recognises that not all customers for a particular type of product or service are looking to satisfy exactly the same needs, though there are likely to be some similarities between them and a number of common needs. It is a process in which marketers examine all the potential customers for a particular product or service and divide them into groups with similar characteristics or buying habits, with members of each group having similar product requirements. Take the holiday example given earlier. Segments can be identified in terms of holidays for young people, holidays for families with children, activity holidays for active adults (or children), cultural holidays for those interested in history, walking holidays for those wanting to explore, country retreats for those in search of peace and beach holidays for those in search of the sun, etc. The list is endless. The groups, or segments, with the closest match between their needs and what the organisation can potentially offer will form the basis for target marketing.

Target marketing decisions involve the organisation in deciding whether simply to address a single segment with their products, whether it is possible to offer the same products to a number of segments, or whether it needs a range of different products to meet the needs of different segments. Take holiday companies such as SAGA or Club 18-30. Their products are carefully targeted at the needs of different age segments. Others, such as Thomson, offer a wider range of holidays of a more general nature with a view to attracting a range of different segments with overlapping needs. Such decisions on target markets have a major impact on both the organisation's resources and customer perceptions of it. (A full discussion of target marketing appears in Chapter 5.)

Product positioning takes place when decisions have been made about target markets. The needs and wants of the various market segments to be served have to be translated into a tangible set of features which an organisation will design to give its products a unique position in the minds of both actual and potential customers, so that members of its target segments see it as offering advantages over competitor products. This requires not only that the products themselves are tailored to the needs of the targeted segment or segments, but that their price levels are in line with customers' willingness to pay, that the promotional activity used to communicate with customers about the products puts across an image that appeals to them, and that the distribution of the products makes them fully accessible to their key potential customers. In other words, the organisation must develop a marketing mix strategy that supports its products' positions in the market.

The *marketing mix* consists of those features of the organisation's activities that have a primary influence on sales: namely the product itself, price levels, promotional activity and distribution (also known as 'place', hence the four elements are often referred to as the '4 Ps'). At the strategic level decisions are made on a variety of issues:

▶ Which products should be targeted at which market segments?
▶ Should any new products be introduced?
▶ How high should prices be set compared with the competition?
▶ What do we need to communicate to our target markets?
▶ Could distributors be used to reach the customer more effectively than selling direct?

These strategic decisions (in other words, decisions that affect the future direction of the business) then form the basis for the formulation of marketing tactics, which should be designed to fine-tune the match between customer needs and what the organisation supplies.

Tactics

Marketing tactics are the specific activities undertaken to implement the marketing strategy. These build on the broad outlines given in the strategy by providing more detailed descriptions of precisely how the elements of the marketing mix should be developed.

Products and services have to be carefully designed to provide the characteristics sought by the target market segments. In implementing a product strategy, marketers must recommend the most appropriate tangible features, such as colour, style, size and functionality, but they must also look at some of the less tangible elements that make up the 'total' product in the eyes of the customer. For example, a customer thinking of buying a carpet is certainly going to be interested in its colour, pattern and durability, but might also be concerned about it being a 'good make', whether it can be delivered and fitted and whether it is possible to pay in instalments, so responsibility for creating brand image, appropriate packaging, associated services and other intangible aspects of what the customer buys also falls to the marketing function. (This is discussed further in Chapter 6.)

Price levels have strategic and long-term implications for an organisation as they are related to the image of the product and will partly determine the nature and strength of competition that a firm faces in the market. Price levels should be set as a reflection of the value that customers place on the product – not always easy to determine, particularly as different market segments may be willing to pay different amounts. Tactical decisions have to be made if sales are not to be lost due to the inevitable mismatches that will occur between prices set and customers' perceptions of the value of the product. Price discrimination may be appropriate, whereby certain buyers are charged more than others – if so, under what circumstances? Discounts may be required to attract less enthusiastic potential buyers – to whom should they be given? how much of a reduction? (These and other pricing issues are dealt with in Chapter 8.)

Promotion is the means of communicating with potential customers about an organisation and its products and services. Promotional strategy will determine what needs to be communicated and to whom, but tactical decisions then have to be made as to how that is best achieved. Marketing communications can take a variety of forms, but they are usually described in terms of a promotional mix, namely advertising, (promotion using mass media), sales promotion (incentives such as a holiday competition or cash-back vouchers), public relations (including the generation of editorial coverage, known as press relations) and personal selling (one-to-one communications, either face-to-face or over the phone). This list is not exhaustive though. Exhibitions, corporate hospitality and direct marketing, for example, are all other forms of promotional activity which don't sit comfortably in any one of the above categories. Depending on the promotional strategy it may be necessary to use a range of methods. (Promotion is fully considered in Chapters 10 and 11.)

DID YOU KNOW?

Lawyers and accountants are finding their clients' loyalty being sorely tested by pressures from competitors offering low fees and are no longer able to rely on personal contacts and word-of-mouth for generating new business. But rather than advertise themselves, they are tending to adopted Public Relations techniques, and many now hold small seminars to which potential clients are personally invited - a forum for them to demonstrate their professionalism as well as their personalities (Fennell, 1995).

Place is the term used to represent the task of making products and services available to customers – also known as distribution. An important distribution decision is whether to use intermediaries to reach end-users (intermediaries being independent organisations whose primary function is distribution), or whether to attempt to reach customers direct. Take financial services, for example. Traditionally most insurance companies sold their products through agents and brokers who were paid commission for arranging sales. In recent years, though, there has been a growth in direct distribution, particularly over the telephone, with customers arranging their policies with the insurance companies themselves and benefiting from the reduced prices offered as a consequence of avoiding payments to middle-men. Decisions relating to the use of intermediaries are known as marketing channel decisions. Organisations have to determine not only whether to use intermediaries, but if so, how many of what sort in which locations? Another set of distribution decisions relate to what is known as physical distribution, including order processing, transportation, warehousing and stock-holding. Marketers have to face an inevitable trade-off here. These are the activities that ensure widespread and consistent availability of products and services for customers, but they are expensive. Investment in improving service through better physical distribution may not always lead to proportionately greater levels of sales. (There is more discussion of this in Chapter 9.)

Management

The management of the marketing function involves the planning, control and organisation of marketing activity so that it can be effectively integrated across the whole organisation.

Planning is the process of assessing market opportunities and matching them with the resources and capabilities of the organisation in order to achieve the objectives of the firm. By encouraging a systematic approach to marketing decision-making, planning should lead to the more effective identification of customer needs and the more efficient use of resources in meeting those needs. It also ensures that organisations are constantly forced to address emerging issues in their uncertain environments, thereby improving the chances of success and reducing the risk of failure. The forecasts that are made during the planning process have a major influence on production, financial decisions, research and development and human resource planning. (The process of marketing planning is fully explored in Chapter 12.)

Control of marketing activity is an important process for ensuring that things are going according to plan. It involves monitoring the progress of the marketing strategies being implemented and measuring their relative success or failure against the objectives they were designed to achieve. Control mechanisms enable corrective action to be taken where necessary before it's too late. If failure occurs, the cause can be investigated; it may be that the objectives set were too ambitious, or that the tactics chosen to implement the strategy were inappropriate or badly executed. Both can be changed if necessary, when it becomes clear that plans will not be fulfilled.

Organising the marketing function requires the allocation of responsibility for different tasks to different individuals. This is not always as straightforward as it may seem. Should managers be responsible for groups of products (and known as 'product' managers)? or should they be responsible for groups of customers (known as 'market' managers) to reflect the different segments in their markets? or should they be responsible for specific geographical regions, and be called 'territory' managers, particularly if their markets are international? Should a manager be responsible for all the market research, or all the advertising, or should these tasks reside with those who look after the product or customer groups? Such questions arise with regularity in many organisations, and the decisions made will affect levels of customer service – not just people's job descriptions. (There is more discussion of marketing organisation and control in Chapter 12.)

The scope of marketing

The origins of marketing lie in the post-war US consumer boom, when firms such as Proctor and Gamble, General Motors and Whirlpool pioneered attempts to introduce a consumer orientation to the supply of their manufactured goods. But the universal significance of a marketing approach has, in recent years, encouraged a wide range of very different types of organisation to adopt the marketing concept and introduce marketing techniques and practices in an attempt to 'create and keep profitable customers'. (Chapters 13 and 14 look at a range of applications of marketing in more detail.)

Product suppliers and service deliverers

A product is normally seen as being tangible, while a service is more intangible, consisting of human activity directed at satisfying customer needs. However, the distinction between the two is somewhat blurred. Most product suppliers add elements of service to their products to enhance the benefits they offer to potential customers. Few people buy carpets, for example, without the opportunity of having them fitted. 'White' goods such as washing machines are normally offered with service and repair contracts. Similarly, many services are accompanied by tangible features. Theatre audiences may experience the performance (a service) but may wish to consume drinks in the interval and purchase a programme to take home. Restaurants will be judged on the quality of their food (products) but their reputation is equally established on the basis of their speed of service and courtesy of waiting staff. Clearly, the concept of customer orientation is equally valid whether a business considers itself to be primarily a product supplier or service deliverer. In both situations, an understanding of customer needs should underpin decisions about what to supply and how to do it.

ACTIVITY **1.3**

University challenge!

Traditionally, universities haven't had to take marketing very seriously. Demand for places from students outstripped the supply of places on university courses, so many institutions limited their efforts to the production of a prospectus and would fill any spare places through the clearing system. Times have changed. A large increase in the numbers of degree courses available has made it more difficult for universities to recruit students for some of their courses, and a more pro-active approach is required if they are to attract good students to fill their places.

1   Make a list of all the sources of information you consulted in deciding which course to take. Do the same for four other members of your course.
2   Make a list of the key factors that determined your, and their, ultimate choice of Institution and course.
3   Using this marketing research, recommend the most effective ways for your institution to attract future students to your course.

Consumer goods and industrial products

Some organisations sell to consumers, who purchase for their own use or that of their immediate household. Some supply other businesses with the goods and services they need, ranging from capital equipment to raw materials and business services such as accountancy. Organisational or industrial markets can be quite different from consumer markets: buyers are motivated by different factors, display different patterns of demand, tend to want long-term relationships with their suppliers and often involve a number of people in the buying decision. Nonetheless, the principles of marketing can be equally well applied, even if the marketing tactics used are slightly different. Customer needs must be identified (perhaps involving collaborative research) and efforts made to supply them with products and services that offer greater benefits than the competition. These benefits should then be communicated to target markets, often one-to-one using selling rather than advertising as the main promotional tool. Distribution may have to be managed to accommodate a customer's just-in-time production plan (discussed in Chapter 9).

For profit and not-for-profit

The marketing concept emphasises that an organisation should only concentrate on performing 'exchanges' that will help it to achieve its own objectives. In the commercial world, the long-term objective for firms is likely to be profitability and marketing is well established as a doctrine that can help organisations improve their profitability. Not-for-profit organisations have non-financial goals, but marketing can be equally effective in helping them achieve these. Churches, political parties, universities, hospitals, museums and charities have all adopted marketing approaches in recent years, recognising that if they want to attract donations, votes, students, worshippers or visitors, they must first find out about their potential customers and set about matching what they offer with their customer needs. They too can benefit from studying 'buyer' behaviour, conducting marketing research and applying the tools of the marketing mix.

CASE STUDY **1.5**

The charity business

More and more charities are becoming sophisticated users of many marketing techniques, and in particular are adept at using target marketing. Charities are the third largest users of the mail after the financial services and mail order sectors, and find this a highly effective medium for fund-raising campaigns, as it enables them to identify key donors by name and approach them again.

The concept of 'donor-base' segmentation is widely practised, with databases being built up and divided according to the recency, value and frequency of gifts. The history of giving of each donor is monitored and up to 30 different categories of donor may be identified so that appropriate and different messages can be sent to each group. The profile of those who have already given can also be used to identify other groups who are likely to give. Response rates of up to 65 per cent are not unknown in this sector.

The messages sent to different groups are carefully thought out and can be very hard hitting and direct. A mailing from an asthma charity enclosed a drinking straw and suggested that recipients should breathe through it for 30 seconds to find out how it feels to suffer from asthma. Charities were among the first to recognise that men and women respond differently to promotional messages. Men tend to respond better if given information, while women prefer approaches that address problems and suggest ways of overcoming them.

Affinity cards are among the more recent techniques employed by charities to attract funds. By distributing credit cards for organisations such as Visa and Mastercard, charities either receive a donation for each successful new card application, or a percentage from each transaction in the region of 25p per £100 spent. The National Trust, one of over 400 non-profit organisations involved in this type of scheme, earned nearly £1 million in its first four years of operation.

Questions

1 What is being exchanged in a transaction between a charity and a donor?

2 What charities have you contributed to recently? What techniques were used to ask for your money and what do you think persuaded you to give?

3 What do you think are the main reasons why more charities have started to become 'marketing orientated'?

Sources Massey, 1995; Cole, 1994.

Domestic, international and global markets

As international transport and communications become ever more feasible, organisations frequently look beyond their domestic markets for business opportunities. The more involvement with foreign markets, the more important the marketing concept. Understanding the needs of customers who speak the same language and have similar cultural predispositions is difficult enough, but there are high risks involved in determining needs and the best ways of supplying them to markets that are culturally, economically and politically diverse and are thousands of miles away. Organisations have to determine whether foreign markets are similar enough to each other and to the domestic market to accept standardised products with minor adaptations to suit their local environment, or whether their needs are quite different from other countries, in which case products will have to be designed specifically to suit their needs, and promotion, distribution and pricing will have to be considered country by country (these and other international marketing issues are considered in Chapter 13).

Large businesses and small businesses

Small businesses often complain that they can't afford to 'do marketing' properly, as if marketing is a set of activities with a price tag attached. It isn't, of course, and there is no reason why a small business, any less than a multinational corporation, cannot attempt to identify the needs of its customers before deciding what to supply, and then to attract those customers with an appropriate marketing mix. The only real difference is likely to be the level of resources that can feasibly be committed to marketing strategies, and this is likely to mean that markets will have to be carefully targeted and that marketing tactics will have to be low cost and innovative – this doesn't mean that they will be any less effective.

External markets and internal markets

Most people working in organisations are aware of marketing as a function that encourages mutually beneficial relationships with its external customers: those with whom the organisation trades its output. The term internal marketing has arisen to describe the application of marketing *within* the firm, as opposed to *between* the firm and its external customers. It suggests that all employees should treat each other as if they are each other's customers, dependent on them to perform their own jobs. Thus a sales-person's external customer will be the buyer in another organisation, but his or her internal customers may include the order-processing team, which needs accurate information to ensure that the right goods are dispatched at the right time to the right destination, and the boss, who may need feedback on reactions to new products or details of competitive activity to be able to plan future sales strategies. At the same time the order processing team and the boss may be the sales-person's suppliers, per-haps providing up-to-date information about orders placed or negotiating the purchase of appropriate technology to enable the sales-person to work as effec-tively and efficiently as possible. In practice, formalised internal marketing is seldom a recognised function in organisations, but its application is evident in businesses whose human resource management strategies place considerable emphasis on internal communications, responsiveness, personal responsibility and common purpose.

Key concepts

Customer orientation: finding out what customers want before deciding what to produce and sell.

Economies of scale: when the cost of producing each product falls as the total volume of products being produced increases.

Effectiveness: producing products that satisfy customers (also known as 'doing the right things').

Efficiency: producing output at the minimum cost (also known as 'doing things right').

Goal focus: aiming to achieve an organisation's objectives.

Integrated effort: co-ordinating the efforts of different departments to satisfy the needs of customers.

Internal markets: customers within an organisation, such as colleagues in other departments.

Marketing concept: an approach to business that places customer needs at the heart of an organisation.

Marketing mix: the marketing tools that an organisation can use to influence demand (product, price, promotion and place).

Maslow's hierarchy of needs: a framework that describes the different types of needs that motivate people.

Product orientation: an overriding preoccupation with producing the products a firm would like to make rather than satisfying customer needs.

Production orientation: an overriding preoccupation with sustaining efficient production rather than satisfying customer needs.

Sales orientation: an overriding preoccupation with persuading people to buy rather than satisfying their needs.

Societal marketing concept: an approach to business that considers the interests of society as a whole as well as trying to satisfy individual customers' needs.

1 Marketing-led firms are driven by the needs of:
   a The product.
   b The organisation.
   c The employees.
   d The sales-force.
   e The customer.

2 Marketing is:
   (i) A business philosophy that emphasises the importance of meeting customer needs.
   (ii) A set of business activities designed to promote a firm to its potential customers.
   a Both (i) and (ii).
   b (i) but not (ii).
   c (ii) but not (i).
   d Neither (i) nor (ii).

3 What are the three elements of the marketing concept?
   a Customer orientation, product focus and employee motivation.
   b Product development, profitability and productivity.
   c Sales, advertising and market research.
   d Customer orientation, integrated effort and goal focus.
   e Analysis, strategy and tactics.

4 A sales orientation emphasises:
   a The need for economies of scale.
   b The importance of after-sales services.
   c Generating repeat business from satisfied customers.
   d Persuading customers to buy products or services.
   e Improving product quality and performance.

5 Environmental scanning is:
   a A process for identifying changes in markets.
   b A promotional technique.
   c An attempt to respond to the Green movement.
   d A system of reading bar-codes on packages.
   e A part of the marketing mix.

Which of the following are true and which are false?
   6 Income and age are likely to influence consumers' decisions when buying furniture.
   7 Grocery manufacturers usually distribute their products using intermediaries.
   8 You should never change a marketing plan once it is in place.
   9 The principles of marketing cannot be applied in public sector organisations.
   10 Many people have customers within their organisations as well as those outside.

Discuss the following

11 Under what circumstances might a firm adopt a sales, rather than marketing orientation? Do you think such an approach is ever excusable, or even desirable?

12 Some authors suggest that the marketing mix has more than just '4 Ps'. Suggest some other types of business activity that can affect demand for an organisation's products.

13 To what extent is the marketing concept relevant to the public utilities?

14 Do you think your university or college has adopted the marketing concept? If not, what alternative approach do you feel it is pursuing?

15 Explain the similarities and differences between the marketing of toothpaste and the marketing of a political party.

Further study
· · · · · · · · · · · · · · · · ·

Books

Baker, Michael (1995) 3rd edn, *The Marketing Book*, Butterworth-Heinemann.
An in-depth look at the key issues of marketing.
Kotler, Philip and Armstrong, Gary (1996) 7th edition, *Principles of Marketing*, Prentice Hall.
A comprehensive coverage of the fundamental principles of marketing.

Journals

A number of key articles that give a good insight into the nature of marketing and the reasons for its growth and development:
Abell, Derek (1978) 'Strategic Windows', in *Journal of Marketing*, vol. 42, July 1978.
Borden, Neil H. (1964) 'The concept of the Marketing Mix', in *Journal of Advertising Research*, June.
Bower, Marvin and Garda, Robert A. (1985) 'The role of marketing in management', in *The McKinsey Quarterly*, autumn.
Brown, Rick (1987) 'Marketing: a function and a philosophy', in *The Quarterly Review of Marketing*, spring/summer.
Levitt, Theodore (1960) 'Marketing Myopia', in *Harvard Business Review*, July/August.

References
· · · · · · · · · · · · · ·

'A missed opportunity' (1995), in *The Economist*, 11 March , p. 25.
American Marketing Association (1985) 'AMA Board approves new marketing definition', in *Marketing Educator*, spring, p. 1.
'An image eroded' (1994), in *Drug and Cosmetic Industry*, vol. 155, October.
Ashton, C. (1994) 'Morgan faces the future', in *Organisational Excellence*, April.
Beale, C. (1993) 'Virgin turns the dial', in *Marketing*, April 29, p. 22
Bernoth, A. (1994) 'Roddick's green halo wobbles', in *The Sunday Times*, 28 August, p. 3/4.

Brown, R. (1987) 'Marketing – a function and a philosophy', in *The Quarterly Review of Marketing*, spring/summer, pp. 25–30.

Buck, S. (1995) 'Fighting a war on two fronts', in *The Times*, April 19, p. 38.

Cole, N. (1994) 'Affinity cards take the credit', in *The Times*, 12 February, p. 26.

'CopyCotting catches on' (1994), in *Marketing*, October 20.

Cowe, R. (1995) 'Flat Coke', in *Marketing Business*, May, p. 24.

'Crazy ways for crazy days' (1993) in *Business Matters*, BBC2.

'Family Values' (1994/5) in *The Economist*, December 25–January 7.

Fennell, E. (1995) 'Hidden costs of price cuts', in *The Times*, 14 March, p. 35.

Garfield, C.A. (1992) 'Do profits and social responsibility mix?', in *Executive Excellence*, vol. 9, March.

Jacob, R. (1992) 'What selling will be like in the 90s', in *Fortune*, vol. 125, Jan. 13.

Kotler, P. and Armstrong, G. (1994) *Principles of Marketing*, 6th ed, Prentice Hall.

Langley, W. (1993) 'Euro-Dismal', in *Sunday Times*, 22 August, p. 9.

Levitt, T. (1960) 'Marketing Myopia', in *Harvard Business Review*, July–August. Reprinted in *Marketing Classics* (B. Enis and K. Cox, (1980) Allyn and Bacon, Inc, pp.3–21).

Maslow, A.H. (1970) *Motivation and Personality*, Harper and Row, pp. 80–106.

Marcouse, I. and Lines, D. (1990) *Business Case Studies*, Longman.

Massey, A. (1995) 'Information Exchange', in *Marketing Business*, March.

Mitchell, A. (1995) 'The winner takes the can', in *The Times*, April 19, p. 38.

Rhys, G. (1992) 'Short-term, Long-term', in *Autocar and Motor*, 30 September.

Smith, A. (1993) *The Wealth of Nations*, Oxford University Press.

Sylvester, R. (1994) 'Firms help themselves by helping charities', in *The Sunday Telegraph*, 16 October, p. 13.

'Troubleshooter in Eastern Europe', (1992) BBC1.

CHAPTER 2

The marketing environment

Objectives
....

When you have read this chapter you will be able to:
▶ List the key forces in the marketing environment.
▶ Give examples to illustrate the potential impact of forces in the macro-environment.
▶ Discuss the means by which firms can exert control over different elements of their micro-environment.
▶ Suggest appropriate strategies and tactics for responding to changes in the marketing environment.
▶ Understand the key features of an environmental appraisal system.

Introduction
....

An assessment of the environment should be the starting point for all marketing activity, because changes in the environment outside the firm will be continually affecting that firm's ability to 'create and keep profitable customers'. This chapter examines the nature of the marketing environment, distinguishing between those forces over which firms have very little control and those they can influence through their own marketing decisions. By using examples, it explains how changes in the environment can require marketers to adopt new strategies and tactics to assure continued relationships with their customers and the long-term survival and prosperity of their organisations. Finally, this chapter provides a framework for organisations to use for the appraisal of their marketing environment, and suggests a process for prioritising action to meet the new demands and challenges posed by those factors beyond their immediate control.

What do we mean by 'the environment'?
....

The marketing environment consists of those factors outside the immediate control of the firm which influence its relationships with its target customers. Some environmental factors affect many firms and many industries, and cannot be preempted or forestalled by the activities of any one organisation: such factors comprise the *macro-environment*. There is little, if anything, that a firm can do to influence its macro-environment. It must simply monitor developments and prepare for the inevitability of changes. This involves forecasting the nature and extent of potential changes and putting plans in place for responding positively to them when the time comes. An interesting example of this relates to the structure of populations. It is possible to predict population trends many years ahead with reasonable certainty, based on birth rates and life expectancy. If there is a dip in the birth rate, manufacturers of children's toys, through no fault of their own, may soon be faced with a gradual decline in the size of their target markets. As this group grows up, there will be a corresponding decline in demand for products that appeal to teenagers (such as music systems and CDs), to young adults (household items for their first homes, for example), to families (food and transport, perhaps) and to retired groups (though this market may not contract as much as life expectancy continues to be extended). There is nothing that any one firm can do to change this pattern, but by recognising its inevitability, all firms can prepare to meet these changes by extending their target markets and reconsidering their marketing activities.

Other environmental factors are more specific to particular industries and individual firms, and will affect certain organisations more than others. Such factors comprise a firm's *micro-environment*. Competitors are a good example of this. Changes in the strategies or capabilities of one firm in an industry are likely to have fairly swift repercussions on their competitors as customers are persuaded to change their allegiances. But retaliatory strategies can then be implemented by the other firms in the industry to minimise the impact of competitive attack. In other words, firms can do more than simply anticipate and respond to changes in their micro-environment; they can influence the changes and control the extent to which they interfere with the relationship between themselves and their target markets.

The rest of this chapter examines the nature of the macro- and micro-environments in more detail, and looks at the marketing task of monitoring and evaluating environmental changes and their impact.

The macro-environment

This comprises a complex set of uncontrollable variables which collectively form a framework within which organisations conduct business. There are four categories of variable that will influence the way in which organisations approach their marketing activities. They are commonly known as the STEP factors:

▶ *Socio-cultural* factors are concerned with patterns of behaviour among populations.
▶ *Technological* factors are concerned with the development of the physical potential of the world through its industries and its people.
▶ *Economic* factors are concerned with the systems for allocating scarce resources in society.
▶ *Politico-legal* factors are concerned with the controls put in place to protect the interests of the society.

Socio-cultural factors

For those responsible for marketing, there are two important aspects of the socio-cultural environment. Population structures (known as demographics) and patterns of beliefs and behaviour (known as culture).

Demographics

By looking at patterns and trends in population structure it is possible to predict likely consumer behaviour and demand in different markets, as a large number of the needs and wants that people express are firmly related to demographic features such as age, gender, marital status, race and occupation. Look at some of the changes in the UK's demographic profile over the past 20 years, such as

▶ *Population age distribution*: The slow-down in the birth rate that followed the baby boom after the Second World War is responsible for the current decline in youth markets. With the 15–24 year old group falling from 7.9 million in 1992 to 7.3 million in 1996 in the UK, record companies are acutely aware of the contraction of their key markets by eight per cent in just four years.

▶ *Ethnic minority populations*: These have risen consistently since the early 1950s, and have more than doubled between 1971 and 1991, from 2.3 per cent to 5.5 per cent of the UK population. Targeting these sub-cultural segments has become increasingly viable where ethnic differences affect buyer needs. Producers of make-up and hair care, for example, have launched products specially tailored to meet the needs of this growing segment and have created well-established and profitable brands.

▶ *Average household size*: Higher divorce rates, later marriage and a lower birth rate have brought about a reduction in the average number of people living in each household (from 2.91 in 1971 to 2.55 in 1987) and an increase in the total number of households (from 18.2 million in 1971 to 21.8 million in 1989). Of particular interest to marketers are those households with high incomes and relatively low financial commitments, such as 'dual-income, no-kids' couples (Dinkies), who are likely to spend disproportionate amounts on luxury durable goods and quality services, and are a good target for manufacturers of hi-fi systems, fashion retailers, holiday tour operators and restaurants.

DID YOU KNOW?

Life expectancy is rising, with boys born in 1996 being expected to live to 74 years old and girls to nearly 80. By the year 2051 it is forecast that nine per cent of the population will be aged 80 or over (Social Trends 25, 1995).

Culture

By examining the cultural background of a society, it is possible to identify the prevailing beliefs, values, perceptions and behavioural norms that underpin that society, and this will give a strong indication of the likely preferences for products and services. Core beliefs are passed on from parents to children and will be reinforced by a society's educational, legal and social institutions. Some beliefs are enduring, and will not change much from generation to generation. Moral views, for example, on the importance of honesty and the value of human life have prevailed in most societies for centuries. But other cultural norms have changed quite dramatically. Marriage is no longer considered to be a prerequisite for family formation; divorce and remarriage are creating a new version of the extended family; religious observance has declined.

Some cultural changes have had a major impact on marketing activity. For example, the role of women in society has changed dramatically in most Western countries. Labour-saving products such as the deep-freeze and the washing machine released time from shopping, cooking and washing to enable women to work. Household income rose and more couples and families could afford cars and second cars. Limited opening hours and poor parking facilities made high street shopping a problem, so supermarkets moved out of town, built bigger car parks, stayed open after normal working hours and offered a wider range of products to enable a one-stop weekly shop: and for those too tired for this after a hard week at work, a booming take-away restaurant and fast-food sector has grown up to obviate the task of food preparation entirely! It is clear that cultural change and marketing opportunities have gone hand-in-hand. The businesses that have lost out are those that failed to respond to the changing social environment, such as the thousands of small retailers who went out of business when the supermarket chains started to dominate the grocery market.

ACTIVITY **2.1**

Population predictions

In 1987 the Government Actuaries department predicted the population of Great Britain to change as follows:

		Year		
		1987	*1996*	*2006*
Population size		*55.4m*	*56.9m*	*58.0m*
Age distribution	0–4	6.4%	7.0%	6.1%
	5–14	12.3%	12.9%	13.6%
	15–29	23.7%	19.9%	18.6%
	30–44	20.5%	21.6%	21.3%
	45–64	21.5%	22.8%	24.8%
	65+	15.6%	15.8%	15.6%

Adapted from: The Marketing Pocket Book, 1990

1 How many more consumers will there be in the age group 45–64 in the year 2006 compared with 1996?
2 How many more consumers will there be in the age group 5–14 over the same period?
3 What should the following firms be doing now to prepare themselves for these changes?
   a Nike.
   b Levi Strauss.

c   Body Shop.

d   MacDonalds.

Technological factors

Technology is a driving force for change in society and can be significant to the marketer for a number of reasons:

▶   It can create better ways of satisfying existing needs. Many products offer only partial solutions to customer needs – record players provided an opportunity to listen to music at home, but records were easily scratched and sound quality was poor; slide-rules enabled complex calculations to be performed but their operation was difficult to master; soap powders removed everyday dirt from laundry but couldn't shift marks or stains. It is hardly surprising that CDs, calculators and biological washing powders have become so popular. Each of these has been developed from new technologies that have enabled customer needs to be met in more convenient and more effective ways.

▶   It can identify latent needs. Occasionally, new technologies even allow needs to be met that consumers haven't recognised themselves. The concept of a non-stick saucepan was an off-shoot of the US space programme, the material Teflon having been developed for space-craft, not kitchen pans. And before the days of bin-liners, who would have thought of using plastic film to reduce the number of times that kitchen bins needed washing out?

▶   It can enable new customers to be reached. Sometimes new technology makes it possible for firms to serve new groups of customers who previously offered insufficient potential for profitable transactions, or with whom it was physically impossible to trade. The multimillion-pound market for frozen confectionery, such as the Mars Bar ice-cream, has only been able to grow as a result of technological developments that have enabled chocolate (and not just 'chocolate-flavoured coating') to be successfully adhered to ice-cream.

▶   It can alter the patterns of demand. We have seen earlier how cultural trends such as the rising number of working women have created demand for new home technologies and retail formats. It is also possible that the reverse can occur, with changes in technologies affecting lifestyles and their associated patterns of demand. Much speculation goes on about the impact of information technology in the home. Toffler (1980) predicted that new technologies will herald a return to a cottage-industry-style economy, with many more individuals working from home as freelance producers, not of manufactured goods, but of information. What then of the markets for transportation if commuting is replaced by 'tele-commuting', and what will happen to the army of catering companies, cleaning companies and office furniture suppliers that rely on the existence of office buildings and groups of employees to create demand for their products and services?

▶   It can change the nature of competition in an industry. There was some discussion of this in Chapter 1. Consumers are not interested in the man-made boundaries between industries. They simply want better products and services to meet their needs, and it is quite possible that new technological developments will come from industries other than the ones whose products are being surpassed. The electronics industry, for example, is providing better solutions to a wide range of needs that were previously considered to be the domain of the service industries. Cash-point machines are more convenient for customers than queuing in banks and building societies; the Internet could reduce demand for postal delivery services; and perhaps it won't be long before students learn from multimedia software packages instead of teachers.

▶ It can increase the efficiency of marketing activities. By using new technologies, businesses are able to improve the efficiency with which they serve their customers, not only saving themselves costs but also gaining customers by offering better service than competitors. Direct marketing (as explained in Chapter 10) uses computer and printing technology to enable organisations to send their marketing communications direct to those people most likely to respond to them. Electronic point of sale (EPOS) systems enable retailers to keep a close eye on stock levels without needing staff to audit the shelves.

DID YOU KNOW?

The Post-it note came about because a scientist at 3M accidentally developed a non-permanent adhesive and couldn't think what it might be used for. A colleague who sang in the church choir and was fed up with dropping his page-markers on the floor every time he stood up, suddenly wondered if the adhesive would keep his papers in place, and it gradually dawned on everyone that the potential for sticking paper to paper non-permanently offered a number of potential applications – not just a 'better bookmark' (Nayak, P.R. and Ketteringham, J.M., 1986).

DID YOU KNOW?

Theatres that have installed box-office systems that enable them to record details of all those who buy tickets from them report significant benefits. By sending out direct mail specifically to those who have attended a particular type of performance before, they can reach individuals who are most likely to enjoy a certain type of programme, and also save the costs of press advertising.

Economic factors

The economy influences the total amount of money available to consumers and businesses to make purchases. It affects the levels of income consumers retain to spend on themselves and has an impact on the amount of profit and cash that businesses generate, thereby influencing the ability and willingness of individuals and organisations to perform transactions to acquire the goods and services they want. There are a number of key economic variables that marketers should follow closely if they are to make relevant and timely decisions about their products and services and the markets that they should serve:

▶ *Income distribution* is important to marketers, as the rich tend to display quite different purchasing patterns from the poor. Perhaps unsurprisingly, as family income rises as the percentage spent on food declines and the proportion of expenditure on luxury goods increases; this becomes particularly significant in economies where income distribution is fairly uneven, and there are sizeable groups of both 'haves' and 'have-nots' so that the economy is characterised by two quite separate groups of consumers. One (usually the larger of the two) is likely to be very price sensitive, looking for low prices to enable them to afford to make purchases at all, and the other is likely to be willing to pay much higher prices in return for superior quality and features.

▶ *Recession* reduces the total income and expenditure levels in an economy. Potential buyers tend to reduce their expenditure and focus on essential items only, either due to the fact or the fear of unemployment. Demand for consumer durables, such as cars, household goods, clothes and leisure products, usually suffers most. To overcome both the financial and psychological resistance that potential customers exhibit during a recession, marketers may need to emphasise the basic functionality and value for money of their products and services, rather than superior quality and performance.

▶ *Taxation* is a process by which governments divert money from the private sector of the economy to the public sector. Governments that impose high tax rates are effectively taking away purchasing power from individuals and spending money centrally on behalf of the whole community that they serve. High-tax economies tend to favour those businesses whose target markets consist of other organisations, rather than consumers. Educational suppliers, civil engineering contractors and manufacturers of defence equipment have traditionally thrived under centrally-driven economies, while a free-market philosophy is more conducive to profitable trading with individuals and households. Direct taxes, such as income tax, determine the amount of disposable income available to households to spend on goods and services of their own choosing, while indirect taxes, such as value added tax, increase the price of goods to the consumer. Products whose supply the government wishes to control for social reasons, such as tobacco, gambling and fuel, may be taxed more aggressively than others, and marketers are then left with relatively little influence over their own pricing strategies.

▶ *Interest rates* can have a major impact on consumer willingness to make non-essential purchases. There are two main reasons for this. First, credit of any kind gives people an ability to purchase now in anticipation of future income, and they tend to take advantage of this by using bank loans, mortgages and credit cards for major purchases such as cars, houses and holidays. But this facility has a price-tag attached in the form of interest payments and when interest rates rise, those with high levels of debt are faced with a rise in the cost of this borrowing. Consequently they will have less money available to spend on other things, and discretionary expenditure on items such as entertainment, holidays, clothes and leisure may have to be curtailed to make ends meet. High interest rates don't only reduce current discretionary expenditure, though, they also deter people from taking out new loans for the purchase of major items, which means that total expenditure on luxury and non-essential purchases is curtailed even further. Consequently, for marketers in some industries, interest rate fluctuations can pose a serious problem. Demand for their goods may increase disproportionately under low interest rates, only to fall away rapidly when rates start to rise. When rates are high, attracting new customers becomes difficult and marketing emphasis may have to be refocused, concentrating predominantly on beating the competition to make sure of attracting a sufficient proportion of the lower level of demand that remains.

▶ *Inflation* can start if high levels of demand in the economy enable firms to start raising prices without losing sales. Expectations of further price rises fuel people's willingness to spend now in anticipation of price rises in the future. Businesses may do well in the short term, and sell large quantities of their products at high prices, but in the long term this is likely to lead to higher wage claims as people see the value of their income being diminished. This in turn raises the costs of production, and businesses may try to raise prices again to prevent their profit margins stabilising at or even below the level they were before the price rises. The most immediate problem that inflation poses from a marketing perspective is that it may endanger international trade. If products become more expensive, sales are likely to fall in foreign countries which haven't experienced similar inflationary pressures as foreign buyers look for cheaper sources of supply. This is one of the reasons why governments are keen to keep inflation as low as possible and may raise interest rates in an attempt to dampen down demand that threatens to become inflationary.

▶ *Exchange rates* are another economic variable that affects international trade. If a country's currency increases in value against foreign currencies, products become more expensive in overseas markets, but if exchange rates fall, the prices paid by foreign buyers will also fall and demand is therefore likely to increase. One of the best defences a marketer can build against the fluctuations of the currency markets is to build market share in a number of countries, so that if the exchange rate becomes disadvantageous and undermines the marketing efforts in one, there are other markets that are not threatened and that may be sustained and grown.

▶ *The 'feel-good factor'*, as described by the British press after the recession of the early 1990s, refers to consumer confidence in the state of the economy and may or may not reflect the realities of the economic indicators. It is, perhaps, more a reflection of confidence in the government, people's hopes and fears for the future, their perceived wealth and expectations of future income and employment. The UK housing market has remained particularly depressed as a consequence of UK consumers having lost the 'feel-good factor' in the recession. When house prices fell, a significant proportion of home-owners were left with properties worth less than the value of their mortgages. When the depths of the recession were clearly over and the economic indicators pointed to growth, people were unable to move house, as they were unable to repay their mortgage debts. Those considering buying their first home were deterred by tales of the financial ruin of so many home-owners, and fear of unemployment persuaded others that large mortgages were a risk that they shouldn't take. While other sectors of the market were starting to take off, suppliers associated with the housing market, especially manufacturers of household goods, continued to suffer from very low levels of demand and constant pressure on prices.

Politico-legal factors

The economic factors discussed above often stem from political initiatives designed to improve the well-being of society, but the influence of governments is also felt through the legislation they introduce. Most legislation is created to protect people, though self-regulation by professional bodies with strict codes of practice is another means through which this protection is assured.

The laws affecting businesses tend to have one of three objectives: to protect consumers from businesses, to protect society from businesses and to protect businesses from each other.

Protecting consumers

To prevent firms from taking advantage of consumers, laws have been introduced to ensure that products meet specific safety and quality standards, as well as controlling the way in which they are sold and the type and extent of information that must be given to the consumer in conducting a transaction (see Figure 2.1). Some of these laws relate specifically to marketing activities, for example, to prevent misleading pricing claims and stamp out dishonest selling practices. Others simply attempt to redress the balance between powerful organisations and relatively defenceless consumers, giving consumers the right to honest information about the goods and services they buy and an expectation that these will be fit for the purpose for which they were intended. Of course, a genuinely marketing-orientated business should have no need to fear such legislation as it will pre-empt the requirements of consumer legislation in trying to meet its customers' needs, recognising that dissatisfied customers who have to resort to the law because of deficiencies in the products they have bought or the way they have been treated are unlikely to remain customers for long!

Another type of legislation exists to encourage and protect competition. Competition between businesses is usually in the interest of consumers as it encourages businesses to focus on customers' needs. A monopoly is said to exist when a single organisation or related group of organisations supplies such a high

figure 2.1
**Legislation to
protect consumers**

The following are just some of the Acts of Parliament designed to give consumers protection from undesirable business practices:

Consumer Credit Act (1974)
Consumer Protection Act (1987)
Data Protection Act (1984)
Fair Trading Act (1973)
Financial Services Act (1986)
Food Act (1984)
Medicines Act (1968)
Misrepresentations Act (1967)
Prices Act (1974)
Sale of Goods Act (1979)
Sunday Trading Act (1994)
Supply of Goods and Services Act (1982)
Trade Descriptions Act (1968)
Unfair Contract Terms Act (1977)
Weights and Measures Act (1985)

proportion of the output of an industry that it is able to prevent, restrict or distort competition. When this occurs, the Monopolies and Mergers Commission will review the situation and judge whether or not it is acting against the public interest and if it is, recommend action that should be taken to restore competitive market activity. Similarly, the Restrictive Practices Court will review any trading agreement between two or more businesses that concerns issues such as setting price levels or terms and conditions of sale. Those agreements found to be acting against the public interest will be terminated by the court.

CASE STUDY **2.1**
· · · · · · · · · · · · · · · · ·

Laker's litigation

In the 1970s, Freddie Laker became a household name as he battled to open up the North Atlantic airways. At this time, no passenger airline was allowed to operate on any route without government approval. Two carriers from each country at either end of major routes were licensed; this was thought to be enough to ensure competition in the interest of the consumer, but not so many that competitive pressures would force companies to skimp on safety. British Airways, British Caledonian, TWA and Pan Am were the chosen four.

Laker instigated costly court actions to prove that the arrangements constituted a cartel and were working against the public interest, ultimately winning the case and initially being allowed to run his 'Skytrains' between London and New York. From the beginning, in 1977, he offered a very different service from his competitors; passengers could not book in advance, but had to queue for tickets on the day of travel and were encouraged to bring their own sandwiches for the flight. Ticket prices, however, were only half those of the 'big four', and within three years Laker Airways had gained a 17 per cent market share on the London–New York route, 23 per cent on the London–Miami route and 30 per cent on the London–Los Angeles route.

But the environment was changing, and by 1980 there were four factors causing problems for Laker:

▶ The US government lifted all restrictions on air travel in 1978, which had encouraged a number of new operators to launch low fare services on the London–New York route.

▶ The cost of fuel oil doubled between 1978 and 1980 in the wake of the crisis in the Middle East.

▶ Economic recession in 1980 was depressing the market growth rate.

▶ No European governments would allow Laker a route to their capitals, thus limiting his potential for expansion.

The first three of these were also creating difficulties for the original four operators, all of whom were trading unprofitably. Pan Am was the first to retaliate and in the summer of 1981 offered a stand-by ticket at just £1 above the Skytrain price, shortly to be followed by other carriers. Laker fought back by reducing its prices still further, but soon started to make serious losses. As a relatively small business with a narrow portfolio of routes, the company was unable to sit out a price war for as long as its rivals and the business collapsed in 1982 with debts of £280 million.

Some while later, Freddie Laker returned to the courts in an attempt to prove that the original airlines had deliberately conspired to put his airline out of business by indulging in predatory pricing – cutting prices below cost to match or undercut new competitors, with a view to restoring prices when the new business had been forced out of the market. Although they never accepted Laker's charges, they did pay out £5.7 million in a joint out-of-court settlement.

Seemingly undaunted by this experience, in 1995 Sir Freddie announced his plans to compete once more against the transatlantic airlines. In 1996 he will be carrying up to 380 passengers at a time between Britain and Florida, in aircraft with his name written in eight-feet high letters on the side.

Questions

1   To what extent was Laker the victim of illegal trade practices: to what extent was he at the mercy of a changing environment?
2   What might Laker have done to protect himself from the consequences of hostile competition?
3   What changes are currently taking place in the aviation environment and how might they affect the fortunes of Laker's new airline?

Sources Harlow, 1994; Marcouse and Lines, 1990.

Protecting society

As discussed in Chapter 1 (in relation to the societal marketing concept), the decisions that firms may make in the best interests of their own customers may not necessarily be in the best interests of society as a whole. As a result, legislation is created in an attempt to ensure that people and their environment are protected from the adverse consequences of their own buying decisions. Children are particularly shielded from products that may cause them harm, such as tobacco and alcohol and they are prevented from driving cars until they are considered old enough to control them responsibly. Other legislation ensures that those who do drive cars are insured so that they can compensate others in the event of an accident. European law has been instrumental in the introduction of emissions control in cars and controlling the disposal of industrial pollutants, and in the US, plastic packaging has been banned in several cities. Such legislation creates both opportunities and threats in marketing. Although costs may be incurred in conforming to or pre-empting such legislation, those who respond soonest can potentially turn this to an advantage over their competitors.

Protecting businesses

Although competition is generally in the interest of consumers, there are certain circumstances under which businesses need protection from their competitors. In particular, if a new product or technology is to be brought to the market its innovators need to be assured that competitors are not able to by-pass what may be a lengthy and costly product development stage by simply copying the product when it is ultimately launched. Creativity and originality need to offer potential financial rewards if they are to flourish in profit-driven organisations. Legislation offers this protection in the form of patents, which are legal documents granting businesses that satisfy certain criteria the exclusive right to sell their own inventions. This type of exclusivity is very valuable in marketing terms. It enables firms to establish their products in their target markets without fear of competitive pressures, and usually this means that high price levels can be achieved and good profit margins sustained for the life of the patent.

The other form of protection offered against competitors is through the registration of trademarks. A trademark, which may include a logo, a word, a symbol, a design, or even distinctive colouring or lettering, cannot be copied within the geographical territory in which it is registered. Like a patent, it prevents imitators from by-passing a lengthy and costly process, but in this case the process is brand building rather than research and development.

Self-regulation

Businesses are usually keen to keep the legislation of their industries to a minimum, as it can prove restrictive, costly to conform to, and even more costly if court actions have to be defended. Self-regulation through voluntary codes of conduct is one of the ways in which businesses can forestall the legislation of their industries. In the UK, broadcast and print advertising and market research are two areas where strict codes of conduct are policed almost exclusively by self-regulation. In advertising, the very strict policing of the system has successfully circumvented government desire to impose blanket legislation against tobacco advertising, such as exists in some other countries. On the other hand, market research, which has an equally responsible set of guidelines, is beset by problems arising from 'cowboy' outfits who refuse to conform to the rules and become involved in 'sugging' (selling under the guise of market research) and 'frugging' (fund-raising under the guise of market research), both of which undermine the activities of organisations that are genuinely attempting to use market research to gauge consumer attitudes and behaviour.

ACTIVITY **2.2**

The retail revolution

When Napoleon sneeringly referred to Britain as a nation of shopkeepers, he was simply reinforcing the widely held belief that manufacturing is the mainstay of an economy and that running a shop requires little in the way of management skill or expertise. This attitude has prevailed until very recently, despite the fact that in most developed countries, retailing has long been the largest single industry and employs between seven per cent and 12 per cent of the workforce.

But over the past 15 years, retailers have proved that paying careful attention to a changing environment can also pay dividends to shareholders. British retailers are particularly successful and are among the most profitable retailers in Europe.

1   Make a list of the major socio-cultural, technological, economic and politico-legal changes that have affected UK retailers over the past 20 years.
2   Choose any one major supermarket and indicate how it has responded to these changes, and how successful its responses have been.

3   What changes are currently taking place and how should your chosen supermarket prepare to face them?

The micro-environment
....

This comprises those factors external to a business that directly affect the running of that business and over which it can exert some control. Changes in this sector of the business environment are of major significance to the marketing department, and are likely to influence marketing decisions at both the strategic and tactical levels. Five key factors can be identified:

▶ *Customers:* those whom an organisation wishes to engage in exchange processes (discussed in Chapter 1), usually by selling them something.
▶ *Competitors:* other organisations attempting to sell similar products to meet similar customer needs.
▶ *Suppliers:* those who provide the inputs to enable a business to produce its products and services.
▶ *Intermediaries:* those who make an organisation's products available to their end-users.
▶ *Stakeholders:* individuals or groups who have a vested interest in the activities of the business.

Customers

Those to whom an organisation supplies its products or services are described as *customers*. A *market* consists of all the customers of all the organisations supplying a particular product or service (groups of customers within a market who exhibit similar specific needs are called *market segments*, as discussed in Chapter 5). Markets express *demand* for products and services as customers acquire goods to satisfy their needs. The task of the marketing department in an organisation is to maximise demand for its own firm's products and services. To do this existing customers must be satisfied and not tempted to buy from another supplier, while competitors' customers must be persuaded to change their allegiances. Alternatively (or additionally), potential new customers can be attracted – those who have not previously been buyers of the product or service at all, and this will lead to an expansion of the market.

To enable them to perform any of these tasks, marketers need to understand as much as possible about the nature of their customers, their competitors' customers and their potential customers. They need to know:

▶ What are the characteristics of customers? Where do they live? how old are they? what lifestyles do they lead? what social class are they? how educated are they? what businesses are they in? etc. A profile of customers can be compared with a profile of the market to identify whether a particular organisation's products and services appeal more to some types of people than other. Such knowledge also enables organisations to decide whether new product features, price levels or different advertising messages are appropriate to their target markets.

▶ What needs are customers satisfying by using a particular product or service? In other words, what benefits are they seeking? People don't buy washing powders, they buy the promise of clean clothes. People don't buy theatre tickets, they buy an evening's entertainment. So if a better means of meeting their needs is made available, customers will switch to the product that offers them the most benefits.

▶ What criteria do customers use to choose between products? What makes one product or service better than another in the eyes of the customer? What features deliver most benefits to the customer? For example, when people decide which supermarket to shop in, some may choose on the basis of price levels, but others are more interested in the variety of goods available, the convenient location of the store, the perceived quality of the merchandise or the facilities they offer for parents with children.

▶ How valuable is the product or service to customers? If an organisation supplies an item that its customers find indispensable, those customers are likely to be relatively insensitive to price levels and the organisation has a good opportunity to trade very profitably. Undervaluing the benefits offered may mean that customers see themselves as getting a 'bargain' as opposed to good 'value for money'. While bargain offers have their role to play in promotional activity, consistently charging less than what the customer is willing to pay is a lost profit opportunity.

▶ Where do customers find information that influences their buying decisions? Some types of buying decisions are made spontaneously, and the sight of a TV advert can trigger a consumer's intention to try a new food product or buy an unfamiliar brand. Other buying decisions are more carefully considered, particularly more expensive items such as cars, home furnishings and insurance policies. Buyers who purchase products for their organisations as opposed to their personal use are the most likely to make strenuous efforts to gather information which will help them make a rational choice.

These issues and others are raised again in Chapter 3, where the nature of consumer and organisational buyer behaviour is examined in more detail, and Chapter 4 looks at the role of marketing research in helping to answer some of these questions.

CASE STUDY **2.2** **Virgin: from air fares to shares**

Financial services companies are big spenders when it comes to promotional activity. In 1994 they were the second largest users of direct mail (after mail order companies) and between them, building societies, banks and insurance companies spent over £300 million on advertising. Insurance company advertising alone accounted for £119 million, having trebled over the ten years to become the largest single category in the industry.

But how effective is advertising in persuading people to buy financial products and services? A 1994 study by BMRB for Mintel aimed to identify the key factors that influence choice of supplier in this market. Product price was the most commonly cited factor, mentioned by over 50 per cent of the sample of 971 adults, and being a well-known company was second, being mentioned by 37 per cent. Advertising came only tenth out of a list of 13 factors.

This type of research can partially explain why Richard Branson's Virgin Direct has confounded its critics and been successful in the already overcrowded market for Personal Equity Plans. PEPs are portfolios of shares that are tax-exempt, making them a particularly good investment for higher-rate tax payers looking for a medium-to long-term place to save relatively large sums of money. Traditionally they have been subject to high charges by their fund managers, but the Virgin Direct PEP offered very competitive fees to attract the price-sensitive investor. Richard Branson himself admits to having been worried that Virgin's youthful image would attract only young savers with little disposable income to invest, but a survey of Virgin Direct's clients just a few months after the launch of the PEP showed that the typical investor is married, middle-aged, earning a high income and already has other stock-market investments. This success seems to be positive proof that the Virgin brand has inspired confidence beyond its traditional youth markets.

Branson is now talking about buying part of British Rail when it is privatised next year.

Questions

1 What are the common factors that have led to Richard Branson's success in a range of industries?
2 What are the major influences in the macro-environment that affect the financial services industry?
3 Do you think the environment is sufficiently favourable for Virgin to purchase a part of British Rail?

Sources 'Advertising Financial Services', 1995; Virgin advertising material.

Competitors

Types of competitors

Competitors are organisations trying to satisfy similar customer needs and producing products that customers see as being alternatives for satisfying their needs. Having said this, it isn't always that easy for a business to identify its competitors, and it's probably best to consider them as being in one of four categories, as shown in Figure 2.2.

Direct competitors

These are usually the easiest to identify, and comprise organisations offering similar types of products or services to satisfy similar types of customer needs. Normally these products are also sold at similar price levels and possibly through similar distribution outlets. Coca-Cola and Pepsi, Persil and Ariel, Sainsbury and Tesco, and Ford and General Motors have all been direct competitors for many years. Because of the similarities of the physical characteristics of their products or product ranges, they have all made considerable efforts to differentiate themselves from their rivals in other ways. In particular, they spend large sums on advertising in an attempt to enhance the benefits that customers will gain from buying their product as opposed to their

figure 2.2
Competitor typologies

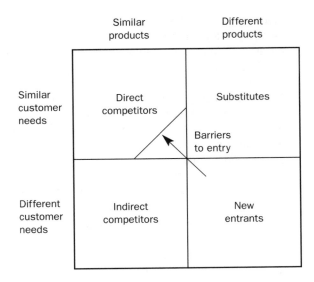

competitors'. But from time to time they use price as a persuader and undercut their competitors in an aggressive bid to gain market share. Direct competition can therefore be very costly. The strongest and the most soundly financed are likely to be the only ones to survive in the long term. Those contemplating entering into battle with their direct competitors should first consider whether it is necessary, as there may be some customers in the market who can be profitably served without being drawn into expensive head-on competition. If there is no opportunity for this, the potential reaction of competitors will be critical in determining whether it is a fight worth taking on, or whether it is a market best left alone.

CASE STUDY **2.3**

High performance at Avon Tyres

Avon is one of the smallest tyre producers in the world. It started life as a general tyre producer, but with the growth of multi-nationals such as Michelin, Goodyear and Pirelli, an over-capacity for the product in European markets and the increase in customer acceptance of remoulds and second-hand tyres, the company was facing financial difficulties in the early 1980s. Its initial response was to cut production by a third and make 800 employees redundant, but this was only part of a deliberate marketing strategy to reposition the company as a specialist manufacturer of high-performance tyres for motorcycles and cars. These are very small markets in comparison with the mass markets of standard domestic vehicles, but they provide an opportunity for Avon in a number of ways:

▶ Average motorists have very little brand loyalty and are therefore very price sensitive, but motorbike owners tend to be more selective and are willing to pay more for good quality.
▶ The major manufacturers rely on economies of scale to remain profitable, and are less interested in specialist markets where unit costs are quite high.
▶ The specialist biking press reaches target markets very cost-effectively and there is no need for heavy expenditure on mass media advertising.

▶ The high-performance sector is associated with quality, so the relatively small number of conventional tyres that Avon does supply can command a price premium due to their quality image.

Operating at the specialist end of the market can bring problems too, though. The company has to produce a wide range of products to suit a very discerning set of customers – 245 variations of motorcycle tyre and 200 sizes in the car range – and marketing activity has to be supported by flexible and responsive product development and manufacturing.

Avon is by no means the only producer competing on a small scale with very big competitors. The Tiptree brand of jam, produced by the family firm Wilkin and sons, is another example. With the market for jam in decline and supermarket own-brands dominating the shelves, the company is having to think of ways in which it can side-step some mighty opposition.

Questions

1 List the changes in the environment that led Avon to reconsider its marketing approach.

2 What are the difficulties faced by small firms who compete with multinational corporations?

3 What options are open to the Wilkin family for the future marketing of its Tiptree brand?

Sources Crainer, 1990; 'Family values', 1994.

Indirect competitors

These are organisations producing similar products but serving customers with different characteristics, preferences or needs. For example, Kwik Save and Marks and Spencer both sell food, but are trying to attract customers in different socio-economic groups. Molnlyke and Andrex are both brands of toilet paper, but the former is sold predominantly into businesses while Andrex is a household brand. Halfords sell car spares and accessories to DIY mechanics, while automotive parts distributors such as Partco and Brown Brothers sell to the motor trade. Although indirect competitors are less threatening than direct competitors, they have the potential to encroach on an established customer base if they try. This has been particularly apparent with the growth of international marketing. Businesses that used to confine their activities to their domestic markets have sought to increase demand for their products and services by moving into foreign geographical territories that were previously the domain of domestic suppliers. Some domestic suppliers, failing to recognise the severity of the threat from the new arrivals, simply buried their heads in the sand and refused to defend themselves from rivals whom they had difficulty taking seriously.

DID YOU KNOW?

When Honda first started to sell motorcycles in the UK in the early 1960s it was welcomed by the British Motorcycle industry on the grounds that if people enjoyed the fun and exhilaration of riding one of the small, low-priced Japanese models, they would soon trade-up to a more powerful and expensive British machine. It was less enthusiastic by 1965, when Honda launched a 444cc model to compete with the Triumph 500cc but at a lower price. By 1975, its business had been so badly affected by Japanese imports that the British government called in a group of management consultants to diagnose the problems of the British motorcycle industry and identify the factors responsible for its decline (Pascale, 1983).

It is worth noting here that competitors producing similar products, whether they are direct or indirect competitors, are described as being in the same *industry*. Marketers must be aware, however, that competitive threats can also come from outside their own industry, from firms producing substitutes, or from potential new entrants to the industry.

ACTIVITY **2.3**
• • • • • • • • • • • • •

Complements or competitors?

Do you think the following are competitors?

▶ Apple juice and orange juice.
▶ Cider and apple juice.
▶ Lager and cider.
▶ Canned lager and draught lager.
▶ Export lager and standard strength lager.

Compare your answers with other students. Why might you disagree?

Substitutes

Competitors offering substitute products may be selling very different product forms but are satisfying very similar customer needs. Hand-drills are mechanical tools and electric drills are power-driven, but they both enable a customer to make a hole in a wall. A paint manufacturer is in competition with a wall-paper manufacturer, even though the two products are produced by quite different industries, if the customer need is for home decoration. Substitutes often take organisations unawares. As discussed in Chapter 1 and earlier in this chapter, changing technology can create substitute products that improve the ways in which customer needs can be satisfied.

> **DID YOU KNOW?**
> *The multiplex has contributed to recent growth in cinema attendance, from a low point of 54 million in 1984 to 124 million in 1994. But 1995 figures are giving cause for concern; the new competitor is the National Lottery. It is thought that money that would otherwise be spent on cinema tickets is being used for lottery tickets, and that the punters are staying in for the 8pm draw on TV (Teather, 1995).*

New entrants

There are two main types of potential new competitor in a market:

▶ Firms who already sell to a particular group of customers sometimes decide to extend the range of products that they offer them. The launch of the Marks and Spencer Unit Trust was an example of this. Its entry into the market for financial services was carefully calculated to take advantage of the confidence its customers have in the dependability and consistency of its retailing performance. Its good reputation acted to reassure potential customers that their investments would be in safe hands.

▶ The other type of new entrant into a market usually comes from within the industry, by firms in 'upstream' or 'downstream' businesses trying to secure themselves either a source of supply or a tied distribution route. Paper mills, for example, have acquired paper merchants to ensure that they can influence the end-user markets for their products.

The likelihood of new entrants emerging to compete in a market depends on the extent to which existing competitors are able to create 'barriers to entry' to keep them out. Some of the strategies for doing this are beyond the scope of this book, but are covered extensively by Michael Porter (1980) in his book *Competitive Strategy*, in which he gives a comprehensive explanation of the dynamics of competition. Marketers are in a good position to raise two barriers to entry to deter new entrants, namely those of product differentiation and customer loyalty. First, the more efforts they make to design products that meet the variety of different needs within the overall market, the less chance that a new entrant has of finding a foothold for themselves, and second, the more satisfied their customers are with the products and services they buy, the less likely they are to change, even if a new supplier does enter the market

DID YOU KNOW?

The launch of the National Lottery Scratchcard has dented the fortunes of Coral, Ladbrokes, William Hill and other traditional operators in the bookmaking industry. The introduction of the weekly draw had only a limited impact on business, but the scratchcards are thought to have reduced turnover by up to eight per cent. This is attributed to the similarities between the instant gratification gained from the cards and the excitement of placing a bet with a bookmaker (Marketing Week, 9 June 1995)

Number of competitors

The number of competitors in an industry is of relevance to marketers, as it will partially determine the most appropriate type of competitive strategies.

A firm holds a *monopoly* when it faces no competitors in its markets. In this situation, any potential customers who need a firm's product have no option but to buy it from that company; they cannot shop around for lower prices, better product features or superior service levels as they might do normally. This could enable organisations to exert a lot of power over their customers, and particularly to charge and maintain very high prices levels. Clearly this is against the interest of the consumer, which is why the government goes to so much trouble to abolish monopoly power in markets.

The few monopolies that still survive tend to be the public utilities, and these are heavily regulated to prevent them abusing their power.

An *oligopoly* exists when an industry comprises only a few competitors. This situation has often arisen because between them, the firms in the industry have successfully deterred new entrants. Industries characterised by high capital costs, such as petro-chemical production, and those that are highly differentiated and spend a lot of money on promotional activity, such as cigarettes, confectionery and cars, are the most common oligopolies, as the costs of entering these markets are too high for most would-be competitors. Marketing in an oligopoly requires all firms to be sensitive to the activities of the others, particularly those of their direct competitors. Pricing is the most difficult issue. If one firm reduces its prices, the others are obliged to follow suit, else they are likely to lose customers. On the other hand, if one firm in the industry raises its prices, its competitors may not follow as they may hope to take advantage of their position as a lower-priced supplier to gain market share. The firm that increases its prices may be forced to retract this or risk losing customers to its competitors. The net result of this situation is that oligopolies are often at risk of a downwards price spiral which will undermine the profitability of them all. The obvious solution would be for the few firms in the industry to agree not to engage in such pricing tactics and to compete instead using other weapons such as service levels or promotion. But as explained earlier, such agreements are forbidden by governments who wish to maintain the highest levels of competition in the interest of consumers.

Perfect competition occurs when there are many competitors in an industry offering very similar products to customers with very similar needs and preferences. This is a very difficult situation for marketers, as the only criterion on which their customers are likely to base their buying decisions is price. A firm that is not the cheapest supplier will theoretically attract no customers, as buyers will shop around until they find the cheapest prices. In practice, there are very few, if any, perfectly competitive markets, as most consumers are unaware of the full range of suppliers for any particular product or service, unwilling to go to the trouble of seeking them all out and have some non-price based criteria for their buying decisions.

To avoid perfect competition, sellers attempt to differentiate their products from the other suppliers in their markets by creating unique features for their own products to give them an element of monopoly power. This is known as *monopolistic competition*. Some firms might specialise in a particular type of distribution outlet while others might offer a unique product feature or perhaps a higher (or more basic) level of quality. Different price levels can then be set according to the value that the consumer places on the particular benefits offered. An excellent understanding of customers is important for survival under this type of competition, and market research is usually fundamental to identifying the product benefits that are of value to the consumer and for which they will be willing to pay.

Suppliers

An organisation's suppliers are those firms and individuals that provide it with the resources it needs to produce its own goods and services. They may supply capital equipment or machinery that enable it to produce its own products. They may be suppliers of raw materials or components that will ultimately form a part of its own products. They may supply packaging materials or labels that enable its products to be safely and efficiently delivered to their end-users. Or they may provide services, such as photocopier repair and bookkeeping, which help with the running of the business. Because their suppliers provide them with the items they need to conduct their own businesses, under certain circumstances firms can be vulnerable to the power of suppliers. For example:

▶ if a supplier holds a patent on a product essential to their own production. For many years, Appleton Paper held a patent on 'NCR' paper (meaning 'no carbon required') and any printer wanting to produce carbonless business forms for their clients had no option but to buy from them. When the patent eventually expired, printers were free to buy from other suppliers who quickly entered the market and produced lower-priced versions of the paper.
▶ if an essential product has no effective substitute. Manufacturers of leather shoes would be ill-advised to make shoes out of synthetic material just because their suppliers increase the price of leather. They have little option but to pay the suppliers' prices, and may have to try to pass this increase on to their own customers to retain their profit margins.

▶ if customers specify (or even just prefer) products from certain suppliers. Builders may be required to conform to the specification laid down by an architect, involving a particular construction material from a particular supplier. Supermarkets' customers may prefer to buy the manufacturer brands that they see advertised on TV and expect to find them at their local retailer. This gives the retailer little option but to buy from those preferred manufacturers, though they may try to copy their products with an own-brand product to minimise the potential threat of this power.

▶ if it is expensive to change to a new supplier. This can happen if long-term commitments have been made to certain suppliers. If a business takes out a bank loan which then subsequently fails to offer interest rates as low as another finance house, it may face high penalty costs if it wishes to repay the loan and move to another provider.

▶ if suppliers are more powerful than buyers. A small company buying from a big supplier is at a disadvantage. If the supplier loses one of its customers, its business will hardly be affected, so a big company may offer disadvantageous prices and lower service levels to those who place relatively small orders, as the cost of supplying them is proportionately high in comparison with the value of those orders.

Marketing managers must monitor supplier activities carefully. Supply shortages that interrupt production, or cost increases that have to be passed on to consumers can both damage customer goodwill irreparably. Shortages will force customers to look to a company's competitors, and cost increases may require price increases that will be unacceptable to consumers. The potential seriousness of these problems has led many organisations to work much harder at establishing better relationships with their suppliers, based on the recognition of their mutual interdependence.

CASE STUDY **2.4**

Benetton

Although perhaps more familiar for retail stores and controversial advertising campaigns, Benetton is an organisation that owes much of its success to the way in which it manages its relationships with its suppliers. It is primarily a manufacturer, (its retail operations are nearly all franchise businesses, owned and managed by independent entrepreneurs) but produces very few of its garments itself, and can be described as a vertically deintegrated business, with 80 per cent of its manufacturing done outside the company by 350 sub-contractors who employ about 10,000 people.

The production cycle starts with the design of around 600 new styles and the preparation of a few samples of each. Based on these samples, shop owners start to place orders about seven months in advance of their selling season, and this is the point at which Benetton's planning department produces an outline production schedule for that season, identifying fabrics and styles. Raw materials are then ordered and appropriate sub-contractors identified to make up the garments. The centralised purchasing activity creates vast economies of scale. Benetton is the single largest purchaser of wool thread in the world and buys fabrics from 80 to 90 different suppliers every year. External contractors are given the exact quantities of yarn or fabrics they need and are advised as to the most appropriate machinery to buy. Much of the raw material supplied is in 'grey' (or undyed) form. Assembled garments are then dyed by Benetton itself when the season starts and it becomes evident what the fashion trends for colour will be. By retaining control of the dying process, the company is able to keep stocks very low and can respond quickly to public demand – an approach that is both efficient and effective. Because of its order quantities, Benetton is in a powerful position *vis-à-vis* both its raw material suppliers and sub-contractors.

Questions

1 Is it possible that Benetton could be threatened by changes in its micro-environment?

2 What do you consider to be Benetton's main competitive advantage?

3 To what extent can Benetton's strong position in the market be attributed to its controversial advertising campaigns?

Sources Jarillo and Martinez, 1987; 'The unravelling of Benetton', 1992.

Intermediaries

These are independent organisations involved in the promotion, selling and distribution of a firm's goods to the end-users of its products and services. There are three types of intermediary that can support an organisation's marketing efforts:

▶ *Resellers* are organisations whose role is to make products more easily available to their end-users. They include retailers, wholesalers, merchants, agents and any other form of business whose purpose is to make money by distributing the goods of other organisations. Marketers must attempt to engage the most appropriate resellers to help them maximise the availability of their products and services in their target markets. A danger is that, due to their close relationships with the end-users, resellers become more powerful than the manufacturers whose products they are distributing, and start to use this power to dictate terms of trade that are highly unfavourable to manufacturers, and in some cases can prevent them reaching their markets at all.

▶ *Physical distribution intermediaries*, usually warehouse operators and transport firms, are organisations involved in moving goods from manufacturers to their destinations. If goods are out of stock because a warehouse has failed to control stocks properly, customers may be lost to the competition, and if customers are disappointed and delayed because the goods they have ordered arrive damaged, they are unlikely to place more orders.

▶ *Marketing services agencies* include advertising agencies, marketing research firms, marketing consultants and any other businesses supplying the advice or facilities to help their clients target and communicate with their customers. Their strengths usually lie in their expertise in certain marketing functions and their objectivity when addressing the market, and their weaknesses are most likely to lie in the extent of their understanding of customers, markets and the competitive environment.

Stakeholders

This is a diverse group consisting of all those with an interest in or impact on the way in which an organisation goes about its business. Some of these people are of only indirect relevance to the marketing function. Shareholders and banks, for example, are financial stakeholders who are particularly interested in the profitability of a business, but will have only indirect influence over marketing decisions. Local authorities and pressure groups are community stakeholders who may attempt to influence the environmental or employment practices of an organisation, but not necessarily its commercial activities. Having said this, there are two important stakeholder groups that marketers should monitor closely as a part of their micro-environment:

▶ The *media*, including TV, radio, local and national newspapers and magazines, can have a major influence over large proportions of an organisation's target markets. Readers tend to have greater trust in the accuracy and reliability of editorial comment than in the messages they receive from advertising and promotional materials, so by publishing favourable or unfavourable comments on products and services, the media can influence the purchasing habits of consumers. This can be very useful for marketers who persuade the press to give them positive coverage, but devastating if reviews are poor and the press are highly critical. The impact of the press is always highly visible on Broadway, where theatre critics can effectively close a show if they publish a damning indictment of the quality of a performance. Marketers who continually maintain good relations with the media are in a position to maximise the opportunities of gaining useful coverage and minimise the possibility of damaging criticism.

▶ The *consumer movement* consists of groups whose objectives are to identify good and bad marketing practices and to draw them to the attention of consumers. Organisations such as the Consumers' Association test wide ranges of competing products and publish league tables of product quality and utility. They also put pressure on the government to legislate against unsafe products and misleading marketing practices.

CASE STUDY **2.5**   **Nestlé Infant Formula**

The sale of breast-milk substitutes to less developed countries has long been an issue that has concerned the consumer movement throughout the world. Attention has been particularly focused on the marketing activities of Nestlé, who by 1981 (the year in which the World Health Organisation voted to establish a code of practice specifically on this issue) had around 25 per cent of the world-wide market for infant formula. Over half of this market was in developing countries, where sales were growing annually by as much as 20 per cent – at least twice the rate of advanced countries.

Consumer protests centred on a number of issues:

▶ The product itself was unsafe in some circumstances if a population had only limited access to clean water and sterilising equipment.
▶ The price of infant formula was so high it would make a severe dent in a family budget and may mean that other members of the family have to go hungry: it also meant that the product was commonly over-diluted which could lead to infant malnutrition.
▶ Unethical promotional practices were being used to persuade mothers that infant formula was the best way of feeding a baby, the most controversial of which was the use of 'mothercraft nurses' who were company representatives dressed in nurses' uniforms who visited mothers after they left hospital, demonstrated how to bottle feed and left samples of the product or vouchers to be redeemed at retailers.
▶ Packaging and instructions were only given in English, even in countries where English was not the national language.
▶ The medical profession was sponsored in various ways and provided with educational materials, as well as free samples of infant formula for both professional and personal use.

Public opposition to Nestlé's activities first surfaced in 1973 with the publication of a series of critical articles suggesting that the aggressive promotional tactics being used were ultimately contributing to infant mortality in less developed countries. Initially Nestlé ignored the problem, but subsequently started to engage in lawsuits against the activists, a move that only served to bring the issue to wider public attention. In a further effort to quell public criticism, Nestlé and other manufacturers established a voluntary code of practice with a view to improving their image, but the code was not enforced and the attempt to self-regulate had clearly failed when a pressure group called the Infant Formula Action Coalition (INFACT) announced a US boycott of all Nestlé products – a boycott that later spread to nine other countries and resulted in the largest non-industrial boycott in history. Attempts by Nestlé to discredit the activists only led to further public relations difficulties.

When the WHO announced its intention to institute a Code of Marketing of Breast Milk Substitutes in 1981, Nestlé joined others in the industry to resist the move, but subsequently agreed to comply at a cost estimated around $10 to $20 million.

Questions
1 Why might organisations fail to adhere to their industry's code of practice?
2 What do you think was the true cost to Nestlé of the consumer backlash against its sale of Infant Formula in less developed countries?
3 Can you name any other companies who have generated controversy by defending themselves against allegations of improper marketing practices?

Source Akhter, J. (1987)

Assessing the marketing environment
· ·

As we have seen, changes in both the micro- and macro-environments of firms can have both positive and negative effects. They can create opportunities for generating more business from existing customers or the possibility of doing business with new ones. On the other hand, they can seriously damage an organisation's capability of serving its customers and create a mismatch between its products and the needs of its customers. For this reason, it is important that marketers adopt a systematic process of identifying the significant changes in their environment, analysing the relevance of those changes and forecasting their potential impact for the firm.

▶ Stage 1: *Scanning*. This requires the marketing department to review continually all aspects of its environment, so that any change can be identified at an early stage. Appropriate action can then be taken before the change becomes a threat to the way in which the business is meeting the needs of its customers, or so that the initiative can be snatched from competitors.

▶ Stage 2: *Monitoring*. When environmental change has been detected, evidence must be collected as to the nature of the emerging trends and patterns, so that a more precise picture of current changes can be drawn. Some changes may prove to be temporary and insignificant, while others will start to grow and clear implications of potential opportunity or threat will start to emerge.

▶ Stage 3: *Forecasting*. When monitoring has identified issues of relevance, forecasting is used to project the likely scope, speed and intensity of the environmental change. Projective techniques may be used to draw up future scenarios that the business may have to face.

▶ Stage 4: *Assessment*. Finally, the potential effect of the change on the organisation's ability to serve its customers in the future has to be assessed. Four categories of impact can be identified, according to the probability of a particular change taking place and the likely impact of this change for the business (see Figure 2.3).

Pro-active marketers will start to prepare for new trading conditions when it becomes clear that a change in the environment is likely to have a significant impact on their future ability to meet the needs of their customers. Contingency planning should begin if the probability of change is less certain, but the impact of the change is equally serious. Monitoring should continue if change appears likely, but the effects of the change appear to be less critical, and potential change that looks as if it will be slow to materialise and offer little in the way of opportunity or threat can be given the lowest priority.

Key concepts
· · · · · · · · · · · · · · · · · · · ·

Competitors: organisations producing products and services that satisfy similar customer needs.

Culture: the set of beliefs, values and attitudes that underpin society.

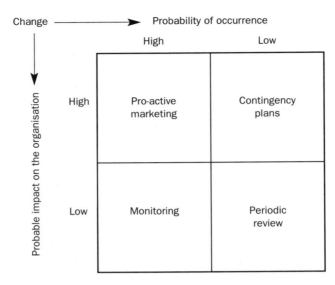

figure 2.3
Categories of response to environmental change

Customers: individuals or organisations who buy a firm's products and services.
Demographics: the patterns and trends of population and social structures.
Industry: a group of organisations producing similar products or services.
Intermediaries: organisations who help products and services to be transferred
     from producer to consumer.
Macro-environment: events that influence more than one industry and over
     which firms have very little control.
Micro-environment: forces that directly affect the running of a business and over
     which that business has *some* control.
Market: a group of people who wish to buy a certain type of product or service.
Market segment: a group of people with similar needs who wish to buy a
     certain type of product or service.
New entrants: organisations who start to trade in a market after existing
     competitors have established their presence in it.
Stakeholders: organisations or individuals who have an interest in or influence
     over the fortunes of a business.
Substitutes: products or services that satisfy similar needs but have a different
     physical form.
Suppliers: organisations who provide the resources needed by other firms to
     produce their own goods and services.

SELF-CHECK QUESTIONS

1   A competitor selling a similar type of product to satisfy different customer needs
     is described as being:
     a A substitute.
     b A new entrant.
     c A direct competitor.
     d An intermediary.
     e An indirect competitor.

2 Suppliers can become more powerful than the firms that buy from them if:
  (i) They sell an essential product that has no effective substitute.
  (ii) They are large organisations supplying a wide range of businesses.

  a (i) only.
  b (ii) only.
  c (i) and (ii).
  d Neither (i) nor (ii).

3 What does patent legislation do?
  a Prevents firms from communicating false information about their goods and services.
  b Protects consumers from monopolists charging high prices.
  c Ensures that firms use environmentally-friendly business practices.
  d Prevents competitors from imitating a firm's corporate logo.
  e Enables a business to enjoy monopoly power for a period of time after it has invented a new product.

4 What action should an organisation take if it forecasts a likely change in its environment that will increase the market strength of its competitors?
  a Leave the market.
  b Launch a new product.
  c Prepare plans to minimise the competitive threat.
  d Run a promotional campaign.
  e Reduce its prices.

5 If the inflation rate increases in the UK, British firms:
  a Will become more competitive in overseas markets.
  b Are likely to suffer from weak domestic demand.
  c Should reduce their prices.
  d Should reduce their marketing budgets.
  e Are likely to be subject to rising interest rates.

Which of the following are true and which are false?
  6 Cars and holidays both represent major purchases for consumers, who will use the same criteria in making purchasing decisions for both types of product.
  7 Marketers have no reason to be involved in decisions about the warehousing and transportation of their products.
  8 The market for breakfast cereal is characterised by monopolistic competition.
  9 Businesses can influence demographic trends in their macro-environment.
  10 Cultural trends can create demand for new technologies and new technologies can influence cultural trends.

Discuss the following:
  11 To which industries does the development of the internet offer marketing opportunities and to which does it pose threats?
  12 What are the advantages and disadvantages of competing in an oligopoly?

13 What initiatives have tobacco companies taken to avoid the threat of further legislation to restrict the consumption of cigarettes?

14 How have the big supermarket retailers, such as Sainsbury and Tesco, become so powerful over the manufacturers who supply them? To what extent have Marks and Spencer used a similar strategy?

15 Why are universities and colleges vulnerable to demographic changes? What actions could they take to minimise the threats posed by this?

Further study

Various sources can provide useful information for the assessment of the marketing environment including:

▶ Government publications such as 'The General Household' survey, 'Regional Trends', 'Social Trends', the 'Employment Gazette' and 'Business Monitor'.

▶ Market reports by research agencies such as Mintel, Euromonitor, A.C. Nielsen and NOP.

▶ Reports by professional associations, such as the Institute of Grocery Distribution, the Society of Motor Manufacturers and Traders and the Association for Business Sponsorship of the Arts.

▶ Report and accounts of organisations with a legal obligation to publish their figures.

▶ Trade magazines and publications such as the *Monthly Review of Packaging Material Prices, Petroleum Review, Campaign, Off Licence News,* and literally hundreds of others.

▶ A summary of useful statistics relating to a wide range of markets is published each year in the form of a *Marketing Pocket Book* (NTC Publications).

Books
Books on the subject tend to be written from the perspective of corporate strategy rather than marketing, but are nonetheless relevant.
Fahey, L. and Narayanan, V.K. (1986) *Macroenvironmental Analysis for Strategic Management,* West Publishing Co.
Highlights the notion of the macro-environment and the inter-relatedness of the STEP factors.
Palmer, Adrian and Worthington, Ian (1992) *The Business and Marketing Environment,* McGraw Hill.
An excellent and comprehensive text.
Porter, Michael (1980) *Competitive Strategy,* The Free Press.
A particularly good explanation of the impact of competitive forces in an industry.

Journals
Interesting articles on the marketing environment include:

Kotler, Philip (1986) 'Megamarketing', in *Harvard Business Review,* March/April.
Zeithaml, Carl P. (1984) 'Environmental Management: revising the marketing perspective', in *Journal of Marketing,* Spring.

References

'Advertising Financial Services' (1995), in *Marketing Business*, April, p. 47.

Akhter, J. (1987) 'Nestlé's Infant Formula' in *Principles of Marketing*, Lusch and Lusch, Kent Publishing Co., pp. 702–704.

Crainer, S. (1990) 'A niche for high performance', in *Marketing Business*, October, pp. 14–15.

'Deregulation no comfort to bookmakers, report claims' (1995), in *Marketing Week*, 9 June, p. 7.

'Europe keeps producers up to the mark' (1995), in *The Times*, 1 November, p. 23.

'Family Values' (1994), in *The Economist*, December 25–January 7, pp. 33–5.

Harlow, J. (1994) 'Freddie Laker stages a cut price comeback', in *The Sunday Times*, 18 December, p. 1.

Jarillo, J.C. and Martinez, J. (1987) *Benetton SpA (A)*, Harvard Business School.

Kotler, P. and Armstrong, G. (1994) *Principles of Marketing*, Prentice Hall.

Lee, J. (1994) 'Coke shows its bottle', in *Marketing*, 14 September, p. 6.

Marcouse, I. and Lines, D. (1990) 'The rise and fall of Laker Airways', in *Business Case Studies*, Longman, pp. 233–6.

Nayak, P.R. and Ketteringham, J.M. (1986) '3M's little yellow note pads: never mind. I'll do it myself', in *Breakthroughs*, pp. 53–69.

Henry, J. and Walker, D. (1991) *Managing Innovation*, Sage.

Pascale, Dr. R.T. (1983) *Honda*, Harvard Business School.

'The unravelling of Benetton' (1992), in *High Interest*, Channel 4 Productions.

Simmonds, K. (1987) 'Ciba Geigy', in *Short Marketing Cases*, Philip Allan Publishers.

Social Trends 25 (1995) The Central Statistical Office.

Teather, D. (1995) 'Virgin to cinema's rescue', in *Marketing*, July 13, p. 10.

Teather, D. (1995) 'Bold designs gain listing for Seltzer', in *Marketing*, March 9.

'The Family: home sweet home' (1995), in *The Economist*, Sept 9–15, pp. 25–7.

Toffler, A. (1980) *The Third Wave*, Pan.

Buyer behaviour

When you have read this chapter you will be able to:
- ▶ Distinguish between consumers and organisational buyers.
- ▶ Identify the factors that influence buyer behaviour.
- ▶ Understand the stages people go through when making decisions about what to buy.
- ▶ Indicate how and why these stages may differ according to the nature of the product being sought.
- ▶ Explain the different roles that people take in buying decisions.
- ▶ Recognise the implications of buyer behaviour for the marketing of products and services to both consumers and organisational buyers.

Introduction
. . . .

While it is relatively simple for a business to work out who is buying what, from where, and when or how much they buy, the reasons *why* people buy are usually far less clear. It is not always obvious why people respond in the ways they do to the products that are available to them, or how they make the choices they are confronted with. *By studying buyer behaviour marketers aim to find out how people make their buying decisions and identify the factors that influence those decisions.* This chapter looks at two types of buyer behaviour – that of consumers and of organisational buyers – and considers the implications of both of these for the marketing of products and services. *Consumers* are individuals who buy products and services for themselves or on behalf of their households. They are invariably either the users of these products or services, or responsible for the welfare and well-being of those who are. They buy things that enable them to survive the physical demands of life, but they also use these purchases to indicate their roles in society, to express their personalities, to reveal their attitudes and opinions, to emphasise the values they hold and to demonstrate their wealth. In other words, the products and services they buy are selected not only to satisfy their physiological needs, but also their sociological and psychological needs.

Organisational buyers buy products and services on behalf of the organisations they work for. The needs they are trying to satisfy are the needs of the organisation. They buy components for the products that their organisations assemble; they buy accountancy services to enable their organisations to audit their finances; they buy capital equipment so that their organisations can produce goods and services for sale. As organisational buyers are human beings, unable to step out of their personal attitudes and preferences when they walk into their offices, their behaviour as buyers bears some fundamental similarities to consumers. However, their own personal needs are expected to be secondary to the objectives of their organisations and consequently, the factors that influence their decisions and the way they go about making those decisions can be quite different from consumers.

This first part of the chapter will consider the nature of consumer buyer behaviour, which will then be compared with the behaviour of organisational buyers.

Consumer behaviour
. . . .

Influences on decision-making

People are thought to develop their individuality through both nature and nurture. Consequently, their behaviour will partly reflect their intrinsic likes, dislikes, beliefs, attitudes and values, but their position in society and the influence of those with whom they live will also play a part. This is as true of buying behaviour as of any other type of behaviour. A consumer's social environment, individual circumstances and personal psychology combine to influence the decisions they make about what to buy. (See Figure 3.1.)

Social environment

Culture

This refers to the prevailing beliefs, values, perceptions and behavioural norms that underpin a society. (Some explanation of these is given in Chapter 2.) They are usually reinforced by educational systems and legal and social institutions, and passed on from generation to generation, changing only slowly over time. Cultural differences may be apparent between nations or even groups of nations: the Western world strives to stay young and slim (hence the buoyant markets for hair colourants and low-calorie meals), while some Eastern cultures have more respect for age and associate slimness with poverty and starvation. Sub-cultural differences emerge between different religions, different regions and those of different social status. Food products are particularly sensitive to sub-cultural influences. The German bread market, for example, is characterised

figure 3.1

**Influences on
consumer behaviour**

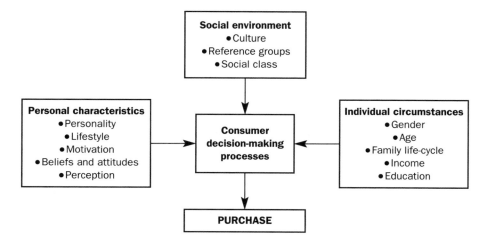

by hundreds of independent regional bakers producing local specialities for relatively small catchment areas. Mass production by national bakeries has failed to make any serious inroads into the market due to the strong and traditionally held regional consumer preferences. As global communications have improved, so cultural divisions have been eroded and consumers have learned to tolerate a more diverse range of products, (further discussion of this in Chapter 13), but nonetheless, cultural norms and practices remain a significant influence on consumer decision making.

CASE STUDY **3.1**

Pasta promotions

Despite ingrained cultural differences in food preferences between European countries, the arrival of the single European market and the increasing domination of the food market by multi-nationals such as Nestlé, Unilever and Grand Metropolitan is leading to an increase in the number of pan-European grocery brands.

It would be natural to assume that a pan-European pasta brand would be difficult to sustain. Not only is the market for pasta characterised by very different levels of development in different countries, the role it plays in a normal diet varies dramatically between countries. The Italians eat around 25 kg per year, compared with an average of 1.5 kg in the UK, and see pasta as a staple product. In the UK, however, the market is still developing rapidly. It is growing at around nine to ten per cent a year and the consumer is becoming more sophisticated. Pasta shapes and fresh pasta have both become popular: spaghetti consumption accounted for 80 per cent of the market in the early 1980s, a figure that had dropped to 35 per cent by 1993.

Italian-based Buitoni was founded in 1827, and gradually expanded throughout Europe and into the US. The company was bought by Nestlé in 1988, who have encouraged a uniform brand image across all markets, supported by a common visual identity and packaging, and carrying the basic advertising tag-line 'Share the Italian love of food'. At the same time, individual countries are allowed to select an appropriate product range to meet local tastes and create specific promotional strategies for different markets. The promotional strategy in the Italian market was quite straightforward: reinforce the brand to sustain and increase market share. The UK market was very different though. Exports to the UK at the time consisted mainly of dry pasta, tinned ravioli and some sauces. To expand the market, Nestlé identified a need to educate British households into trying new recipes. It has done so by showing advertisements with interesting and easy recipe ideas and is building up a database through direct response advertising as a foundation for a 'Buitoni Club', in an effort to retain consumer loyalty for life.

Questions

1   List five other food products whose consumption follows quite different patterns in the UK from other European countries. How do you account for this?
2   List five advertisements currently on TV that would not have any impact outside the UK. Why is this?
3   What criteria would you suggest a marketer should use when deciding whether to adapt a product or its promotion for use in a foreign country?

Source Mazur, 1993.

Reference groups

These are the groups in society with which a person interacts. They are known as reference groups to indicate that they are a point of reference for consumers in making their decisions. Reference groups influence buying behaviour in several ways:

▶ *Informational influence* is exerted when a group is a credible source of knowledge, perhaps being expert or having experience in a particular field. This type of influence explains the power of word-of-mouth communications in some markets, particularly markets for services where it is not possible for consumers to try the product before actually committing themselves to a purchase (more about this in Chapter 14). People rely on the recommendations of friends and neighbours, regarding this as more reliable that the supplier's advertising claims.

▶ *Comparative influence* occurs when consumers attempt to make buying decisions that will associate them with groups they wish to be a part of, and dissociate themselves from others. Teenagers, for example, are keenly aware of the brands and labels that are acceptable to their peer groups, and the ones that would exclude them. Marketers have been quick to take advantage of this, charging high prices for strong brand images created for products such as trainers, through powerful advertising campaigns directed at youth markets.

▶ *Normative influence* over consumer behaviour occurs when an individual experiences pressure to comply with the norms of a particular group. The reward for compliance is acceptance by the group, and sanctions may be taken against those who fail to conform. This type of influence is strongest with products that are highly visible, particularly clothing. In many organisations, executives will be under pressure to wear suits to work, regardless of the weather; members of a golf club may be forbidden from wearing denims; formal dress will often be expected of guests at a wedding.

Different types of reference groups exert different types of influence:

▶ *Primary groups* are those groups with whom a person has regular, but informal interaction. They include friends, neighbours, colleagues, and the family. Their influence can be felt in all of the above ways, though in

▶ particular through informational and comparative influence.
The *family* is one of the most important primary groups to influence buying behaviour, being the one with which most people will have maximum interaction over a lifetime.

▶ The family of orientation is the family a person is born into, consisting of parents, brothers and sisters, and in some countries more distant relatives too. This family grouping establishes purchasing patterns which a person learns during childhood. These can lead to entrenched attitudes towards favoured brands and suppliers. Selection of products and services as diverse as washing powders, instant coffee, banking services and holidays may all be influenced by family norms. To generate new customers, marketing activities may have to be designed to overcome the reluctance of consumers to break these norms.

A family of procreation consists of a buyer's partner and children. This family has a more direct influence on everyday buying decisions. In particular, different members of the family tend to influence different buying decisions. Putnam and Davidson (1987) found that the male tends to dominate the purchase of sport equipment, lawn mowers, and other domestic hardware, but kitchenware and food is mainly influenced by the female. Joint decisions are made on holidays, financial services and cars, but autonomous decisions may be made by either partner in the purchase of cameras, luggage and even the man's clothing! Where decisions may be made by either partner, marketers must recognise that they may have two distinct audiences, and two advertising campaigns may be needed to get messages across; using one campaign to appeal to both may be inadequate. Children's influence also varies by product category, predictably being strongest over toys and their own clothes, but also being significant in the purchase of breakfast cereals, fast foods and soft drinks.

▶ *Secondary groups* are those with whom people have more formal and less regular interaction. They may include religious groups, social or sports clubs and trade or professional bodies. Normative influence can be felt most strongly from these groups and the pressure to comply with their norms may even be enshrined in the constitution of the group – hence the threat of expulsion from some golf clubs for inappropriate dress.

DID YOU KNOW?

Joint decisions by children and parents are made for many food products. Research by Mintel has found that supermarket trolleys are much more likely to be filled up with well-known branded goods when children accompany their parents on a shopping trip, reinforcing the view that heavy advertising is more effective at influencing children than adults (Mintel, 1995).

Social class

Social classes (also known as socio-economic groupings) are groups consisting of individuals with similar social and economic circumstances who are considered to have similar status in society. The basis for defining this status will vary between societies, but is generally related to occupation, income, education and wealth. (See Figure 3.2.)

figure 3.2
Categories of social class

A	Higher managerial, administrative or professional
B	Intermediate managerial, administrative or professional
C1	Supervisory or clerical, and junior managerial, administrative or professional
C2	Skilled manual workers
D	Semi- and un-skilled manual workers
E	State pensioners or widows, casual or lowest grade workers, or long-term unemployed

Students living away from home are usually classified as C1.
Retired people with personal pensions retain their former social grade

People tend to have far more interaction with their own social class than with others, and consequently, social classes usually display similar values and similar purchasing patterns. For example, some sections of society watch more TV than others; others have a greater likelihood of attending live arts performances; brand loyalty for grocery products is lower among the upper middle class than others. It is therefore very important for marketers to respond to different groups in different ways, however tempting it is to think of ourselves as being in a classless society.

DID YOU KNOW?

Mail order catalogues have traditionally been aimed at C2D social groups, who tended to value their facility for payment by instalments. But, due to changes in employment patterns and the demographic structure of the UK, by 1997 there will be more ABC1 consumers than C2Ds. If they are to retain their share of the retail sector, the large catalogue mail order houses are faced with the choice of either taking their catalogues up-market or launching separate versions aimed at the ABC1s (Mintel, 1994/5).

Individual circumstances

Personal circumstances tend to stem from demographic characteristics. In Chapter 2, an explanation is given of the impact of changes in the demographic profile of a market, and the ways in which this can affect patterns of demand. At the individual level, a person's gender, age, family situation, income and education are likely to have a major influence on their buying decisions.

Gender

The influence of gender on consumer behaviour is highly visible. Mainly due to social norms, many of which can be traced back for centuries, men and women tend to buy different types of product and use different criteria when choosing what to buy. By identifying the behavioural differences between the sexes, marketers can reach huge untapped markets whose needs have never been fully satisfied. Car manufacturers, for example, have responded to the increase in demand from female drivers by focusing their attention on safety features, which are frequently at the very top of the list of characteristics sought by women drivers. This is quite a radical departure from the emphasis on power and speed that has dominated car design for many years in response to the characteristics thought most desirable by male drivers.

DID YOU KNOW?

Despite the rumours that 'new man' is prowling the aisles of UK supermarkets, there is no evidence to suggest that men are any more likely to do the weekly shop than their fathers or grandfathers. However, when they do visit the supermarket, male shoppers are more likely to buy well-known brands than experiment with new products, and spend an average of five per cent more than women per visit (CIA Medianetwork, 1994).

Age

Age determines some of the buying decisions people make. The type of leisure activities they participate in, the likelihood of their being in education or at work, their need for health care and their preference for styles and fashions will all change through their lives and the products they purchase will change with them. Certain products and services emphasise these differences in their brand names and promotional campaigns. The tour operator Club 18–30 is quite evidently aiming at young people who see their holiday needs as being different from other age groups. Saga takes a similar view, but concentrates on a different age group, the over 50s.

Family life-cycle

This is another important marketing concept that influences behaviour, and is related to age.

figure 3.3

The family life-cycle

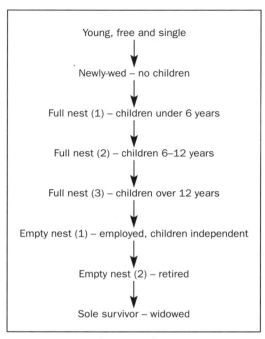

Adapted from Wells and Gubar (1966)

In 1966, Wells and Gubar described the stages of formation and progression of a typical family, and indicated the types of consumer expenditure most likely to be associated with those stages (see Figure 3.3). Much of this still applies over 30 years later. Young singles, for example, are likely to spend proportionately more on clothing, entertainment, fast food and leisure activities than other groups. They may have relatively low incomes, being at the start of their careers, but they have few financial responsibilities and are in a position to spend what they earn on their own pleasures. Compare this with the likely expenditure patterns of full nest couples, who may have considerably higher income levels but will be spending much of this on maintaining their families, paying for food, education, insurance and household items. The stage a person is at in the family life-cycle is thus more significant in determining purchasing patterns than age alone.

Developments in society since the mid-1960s have led to the formation of new life-cycle categories which were relatively insignificant at that time. DINKIES (dual income, no kids) are childless couples who may or may not be married to each other. They have high levels of income and are willing to spend money to save time and to acquire quality and style. Single parents may be on severely restricted incomes as well as being under time pressure, trying to juggle the demands of work and children. Low-cost convenience is likely to be an important influence over purchasing decisions in this situation. This may also be the case in second families, when an estranged partner is financially responsible for a former family, perhaps teenagers, as well as a new family of young children. Purchasing patterns in these situations are unlikely to conform to traditional norms either.

Income

Income is often linked to demographic characteristics, but not exclusively so. An individual's disposable income can vary for many reasons, in particular due to higher interest rates, unemployment or inflation (as discussed in Chapter 2). Certain products and services are more income sensitive than others. A person whose economic circumstances are suddenly reduced is likely to cut out discretionary expenditure, with consumer durables and leisure activities being hit the hardest. The criteria used in making buying decisions are likely to move away from style, towards functionality and price.

Education

Levels of education are usually related to income and social class but have other interesting influences over consumer behaviour too. People who left full-time education aged 16 display different purchasing behaviour from other groups. When choosing between products they are less likely to evaluate unfamiliar brands or compare prices, but tend to make their decisions on the basis of tradition, brand image and personal experience. This has implications for the way marketers address this segment of their markets. Rather than providing detailed explanations and justifications of their products and services, they may be better off reinforcing reliability and corporate image.

DID YOU KNOW?

Predicting the impact of educational background on purchasing behaviour is never straightforward. About half the visitors to the Victoria and Albert Museum have been in full-time education until at least the age of 20, but six out of ten visitors to the National Railway Museum completed their full-time education by the age of 16 (Hill, O'Sullivan and O'Sullivan, 1995).

Personal characteristics

The decisions people make about the goods and services they buy are further influenced by a range of individual factors relating to their own psychology. It is quite normal for those of the same sex who are at similar stages in the family life-cycle and have the same levels of income to display quite different personalities and lifestyles, to be motivated by different goals, to hold different beliefs and attitudes and to see the same things in different ways.

Personality

Individuality is immediately obvious in a person's personality – character traits such as sociability, self-assuredness, shyness and aggression, are what make individuals react in consistent and predictable ways to the situations they face. If marketers understand the reactions of different personalities to different types of product they can design their brands to meet different needs. Painkillers are an interesting example. Sensitive, self-controlled, and compliant types tend to buy brands that promise to gently soothe away pain, while more competitive, aggressive, and dominant types want to actively fight the pain and look for brands that emphasise power, strength and speed.

Lifestyle

One of the ways in which consumers express their personalities is through the lifestyles they choose. Kotler and Armstrong (1994) describe lifestyle as 'a person's pattern of living as expressed in his or her activities, interests and opinions', activities such as work, entertainment, sports, hobbies, holidays and community involvement; interests such as family, food, recreation, media, fashion and music; opinions on education, politics, social welfare, personal relations and religion. The tangible evidence of lifestyle lies in the way people spend their time and money to interact with their environment. This can be measured, (a technique known as psychographic profiling) to enable groupings with similar lifestyles to be identified. Different groups are likely to choose different products and respond positively to different images, giving marketers the opportunity to tailor their market offerings to meet these needs. (This is discussed further in Chapter 5.)

CASE STUDY **3.2**
··················

MOSAIC: patterns of lifestyle

MOSAIC is one of a number of commercially available databases that predict the 'lifestyle' of every household in the country. The system works on the assumption that people living in similar neighbourhoods are likely to have similar incomes, interests and purchasing habits.

By using information gathered from a diverse range of sources, including the 1991 Census, the Electoral Roll, County Court Judgements and the Postal Address File, its compilers have classified every group of households with the same postcode (usually around ten addresses) into one of 12 'lifestyle' groups. Each group is then further divided into 52 types, each with its own highly descriptive title. For example, 'Clever Capitalists' and 'Ageing Professionals' are both types within group 1, the 'High Income Families'; the 'Bohemian Melting Pot', 'Sweatshop Sharers' and 'Rootless Renters' are all types within group 6, 'Victorian Low Status' housing.

A description of each group and type is given, along with an indication of the likely demographic profile and financial status of residents. Those of the 'Clever Capitalist' type, for example, are described as '...wealthy people involved in business, particularly in the setting up and financial management of companies and in commercial trading, importing and exporting. The areas are characterised by company directors living in large detached houses though not necessarily with extensive grounds, in well-established residential areas within reasonable reach of city centres...'. The demographic profiles indicate that people in these postcodes have a more than average likelihood of having children, though not very young children. They will probably be outright owners of their own homes and will be professionals or managers working in service industries.

For marketing purposes, this type of information can be invaluable. It can be used to investigate a customer database and identify the type of person currently buying a product or service; it can be used in direct marketing, for targeting specific types of households who are most likely to respond to a particular product offer. Retailers have used it to identify catchment areas with the best potential and help them to find the best sites for new stores, and theatres have used it to identify the best areas for leaflet drops.

Questions

1 How might the following use MOSAIC?
   – A car manufacturer.
   – A university.
   – A charity.

2 Consider your own address. Do you think you are typical of the residents with your postcode?

3 What do you envisage as being the main disadvantages of using MOSAIC?

Source   CCN Marketing, 1995.

Motivation

Consumers are motivated to buy products when they believe that those products will satisfy their most immediate needs. In Chapter 1 there is a discussion of Maslow's hierarchy of needs. This explains that people are first motivated to meet their own basic physiological needs such as food, warmth, sex and safety, but when these needs have been met, they are motivated to satisfy their social and psychological needs. This creates important opportunities in marketing. Affluent consumers start to look for more than just the basic function from their products, which enables marketers to differentiate themselves from the competition by adding features to their products, both tangible and intangible, to meet the higher level needs that motivate purchase.

CASE STUDY **3.3**
· · · · · · · · · · · · · · · ·

Sex sells

Maslow's hierarchy of needs (as described in Chapter 1) suggests that the human race is primarily motivated to satisfy its basic physiological needs, before attempting to satisfy higher-order needs for safety, friends, status and self-development. Sex is one of these fundamental physiological needs, so it is hardly surprising that marketers have long recognised its potential to sell products and services.

The approach used by advertisers to appeal to this basic level of motivation has changed with the times. In the early 1950s, the 'get-your-man' theme was a common one. Perfume promotions promised to lead their buyers to the men of their dreams, but the disappointment that followed when the bottles of scent failed to deliver such promises meant that brand loyalty was low. Research suggested that women's dressing tables were reminders of 'dead enthusiasm', which was hardly an incentive to make a repeat purchase. Perfume makers responded to this by continually launching new brands, raising new hopes. But the effects of these were short-lived and served to confuse the customer – so much so that rumour persisted about the existence of a girl who, having looked at the mass of brands and promises for sale at the cosmetics counter, asked bashfully if there was a product suitable for beginners.

As time went on, permissiveness in society allowed more overt forms of sexual promise in daring advertisements. In one notable promotion for underwear, an attractive blonde woman was shown being dragged across the floor by a modern cave-man, with the caption 'Come out of the bone age darling'. It is hardly surprising that more recent attempts at using sex to sell have required a more subtle approach, with sexism of this nature being firmly rejected. A 1980s poster campaign for the Fiat 127 Palio suggested 'if this car was a lady she'd get her bottom pinched', but the graffiti that soon joined it said 'if this car was a lady, she'd run you over'.

Questions

1 List some current advertising campaigns that use sex to sell. How successful do you think they are?

2 Do you think 'sex sells' better in some countries than others? If so, which and why?

3 Identify advertisements that appeal to human motivation for:
 – safety
 – esteem
 – self-development

to sell their products. Suggest why they have chosen these themes.

Source Packard, 1957.

Consumers are seldom aware of their own motivations, which is why motivation research, using techniques such as role play, word association and psycho-drawing, is an important tool in helping marketers to understand the nature of these subconscious sociological and psychological needs.

ACTIVITY **3.1**
···············

Who goes to the theatre?
Research into theatre attendance by NOP in 1991 suggested that people's motivations for attending or participating in a theatrical or musical performance are many and varied. It also found that many of these motivations have little, if anything, to do with the arts event itself.

1 Describe the sort of people who might attend the following types of event:
 a A rock concert at Wembly Arena featuring a well known band.
 b Opera at Covent Garden.
 c A student production of Shakespeare at your University or college.
 d A fringe performance at the Edinburgh Festival.
 e A contemporary dance performance at a local theatre.
2 In each case, identify the range of factors that might motivate attendance.
3 What implications does this have for the way in which the different events should promote themselves?

Beliefs and attitudes
Each person holds views and opinions that stem from what they have learned in their lives, through personal experience or the experience of others. These views and opinions can lead to consistently held beliefs. Based on the account of a friend or an article in a newspaper, a consumer may believe that a certain brand is more reliable than others, or that another is more stylish, or more durable, or more expensive. Even if none of these beliefs are true, they will influence that person's buying behaviour as their expectations will cause them to reject the brands whose attributes are thought to be inferior to others. Beliefs can then lead to positive or negative attitudes which can be difficult to change. In the 1980s, beliefs about the reliability of Japanese cars and the quality of German cars in comparison with British vehicles created entrenched negative attitudes towards the UK motor industry, which were undoubtedly a significant factor in its decline during this period. It is essential that marketers make every attempt to correct false beliefs. Even if false beliefs lead to positive attitudes,

they can still be dangerous if they raise customer expectations to a level that cannot then be met.

Perception

Perception refers to the way in which people make sense of the world. Consumers select, organise and interpret the marketing messages they are exposed to, protecting themselves from the barrage of information they are faced with every day by screening out those messages of no use to them (known as *selective perception*), and remembering only those deemed important (known as *selective retention*). These selections will depend on a wide range of factors, including their past experiences, their current needs, their beliefs and attitudes and the complexity of the messages they are faced with. This has a powerful impact on their buying behaviour. Marketers can only hope to persuade potential customers that a particular product will meet their needs if they can break through the perceptual barriers and reach them with a message that is understood, retained and acted upon.

The decision-making process

Consumers make buying decisions by responding to their own needs, taking a series of steps that enable them to select the right product from a series of alternatives (see Figure 3.4).

Perception of need

Consumers may become aware of needs due to an internal imbalance, either physical or psychological, which can be met by the acquisition of products or services. Hunger may trigger a need for food and stress may trigger a need for a holiday. Only by purchasing those items can a person resolve the feelings of discomfort that arise from such needs. Alternatively, needs can arise as a result of exposure to some form of external stimulus. These are needs that would not have arisen spontaneously, but occur in response to changes in the external environment. A wedding invitation may trigger a need for a new suit, and a walk past an advertising hoarding may trigger a desire for a can of Coke or a bar of chocolate. Product sales can be increased if appropriate stimuli are used in promotional messages.

figure 3.4
The consumer decision-making process

Information search

Having become aware of a need, a consumer starts to look for ways of meeting that need. This involves a search for information about potential products and services. Four sources may be used:

▶ *Internal sources*: Buyers search their own memories for previous experience of satisfying a particular need. This is probably the most convincing reason why firms must make every effort to continually satisfy the needs of their customers, rather than make one-off sales with no concern for customer satisfaction.

▶ *Word-of-mouth*: Trusted personal contacts are consulted as a source of unbiased advice. Their experience is used as a substitute for personal experience of the products or services in question.

▶ *Public information*: Independent reports of the comparative performance of similar products are published by consumer watchdogs, such as the Consumers' Association, newspapers and magazines. Consumers may consult these at the information search stage. Financial advice given in the broad-sheet newspapers is widely read by those managing investments, for example, and book lovers examine critical reviews in the press before deciding what to read and buy.

▶ *Promotional messages*: These consist of information generated by the producers and sellers of products and services, including advertising messages, sales presentations, labels on packaging and sales literature. Although they are easily available, these information sources may be seen as the least credible in the eyes of consumers. This is particularly so in the case of services, such as hairdressing or insurance, when the consumer has no opportunity to sample the service before it is delivered. The high risk of such purchases encourages potential buyers to look for unbiased advice from those who have sampled the service before, rather than rely on company-sponsored information.

The information search enables consumers to narrow down the list of possible ways of satisfying their needs. Those that remain on a short-list at the end of the process are known as the evoked set. A consumer with a need for a long-term financial investment may start off considering possibilities such as property, shares, government bonds, endowment policies or building society accounts, but the information search may lead to the conclusion that the limited risk and ease of access to a building society account make this the best option. At this point, the different building societies and different types of accounts form the evoked set and the consumer is ready to evaluate these alternatives.

Evaluation of alternatives

This process involves the establishment of criteria that will be used to choose between options in the evoked set. One buyer may view proximity to a building society branch as a key criterion, while another may prefer a postal account and place little value on a branch network. Others may feel secure only with a long-established society with a national reputation, or value high interest rates above all. Each buyer will have a hierarchy of criteria, ranging from the 'essential' to the 'would like' to the 'marginal benefit', and this hierarchy will enable the items in the evoked set to be ranked in order of preference, with the final purchase being made of the item that emerges at the top of the list.

There are two important issues here for marketers. First, if the process of evaluation of alternatives is fully understood, there is less temptation to go in for price-cutting in response to what consumers often *say* is their key criterion for purchase. If consumer behaviour is carefully observed, factors such as quality, service and reliability often emerge as being the 'essential' attributes of a product, with low price simply being in the 'would like' category. Second, the selection criteria may include both tangible and intangible attributes of the product, as well as attributes of the seller of the product. Credit facilities, installation and after-sales service, brand image and the location and reputation of retailers may all be critical; in other words, the total product, and not just the core benefit offered, will be considered by the consumer at the evaluation stage in the decision-making process. (The total product concept is discussed further in Chapter 6.)

Purchase

This is the point at which a consumer makes a decision to buy and performs a transaction for the chosen product or service with the chosen seller, usually exchanging money for goods. Marketers must be aware that consumers can withdraw from the purchase process without completing the transaction. Suppose a chosen product is unavailable at a chosen retailer. Consumers may choose to buy an alternative product rather than switch retailers, particularly if brand loyalty is weak. Suppose they discover that the information they were given was inaccurate, and a product's price is higher than they were expecting. They may choose to delay or refrain from purchase altogether. Such issues reinforce the importance of consistency of service, product availability and truth in advertising.

Post-purchase evaluation

After they have purchased a product, consumers assess the extent to which it has satisfied their needs and met their expectations. As explained earlier, this assessment will then become part of their internal information search the next time they have a similar need. They will also share this evaluation with others who consult them for advice.

Cognitive dissonance can occur at this stage, particularly after the purchase of expensive or unfamiliar items. This refers to the doubts people feel after making such a purchase. It is common for consumers to continue 'shopping around' even after they have made a purchase, looking for information to reassure them that they have made a good choice. How often, having just bought a new pair of shoes or piece of kitchen equipment, have we then walked into the shop next door to see whether we could have found anything better or cheaper? How often have we glanced at the small ads in the newspaper just after we've bought a second-hand car? Supportive information at this stage can reduce this dissonance. If consumers are subsequently assured by their friends that they made a good choice, or are exposed to reassuring advertising messages, they are more likely to consolidate their satisfaction and less likely to try to return the goods.

Purchase classes

The speed at which consumers pass through the various stages of the decision-making process varies widely according to the nature of the product and the perceived importance of the decision. Five distinct purchase classes can be observed, each of which is characterised by a different level of decision-making effort.

▶ *Impulse purchases* are made with no planning. The visual stimulus of seeing a product available on a shelf is what prompts a person to buy. The motivation is sudden and instant, and consequently such purchases can lead to feelings of guilt. After the purchase has been made, consumers may realise that they have little need for the product and may regret the failure to evaluate more carefully (though this may not deter them from making a similar purchase in the future). The powerful urge to buy seems to override conscious rationality. Marketers have long recognised the potential for impulse purchase of non-essential items such as confectionery and magazines at supermarket check-outs. Faced with a short wait in a queue, shoppers are ideally placed to pick up the visual stimuli from such items, which are unlikely to have been on their shopping lists and would otherwise have been passed by in the aisles.

▶ *Routine purchases* are made of low-value items that are purchased on a regular basis. This normally includes grocery and household items that are consumed and replaced automatically, such as toothpaste, milk, detergent and pasta. Although these types of purchases are planned, consumers do not want to spend much time and effort on product choice. They will often have a preferred brand, but if that brand is unavailable when and where they wish to buy it, they will buy an alternative rather than wait or shop elsewhere. Manufacturers of these types of products become market leaders by establishing and sustaining these routine behaviour patterns. They ensure that their products are constantly available in as wide a network of retailers as possible, and advertise to reinforce the habit of buying their products. This makes it difficult for their competitors to threaten their position. Consumers will only change their behaviour if something new and different can encourage them to change their comfortable routines.

▶ *Familiar* purchases occur when a person is a frequent consumer of a product type, but is willing to put some effort into choosing a version or brand of that product. This is know as limited decision-making. It occurs when consumers are on the look-out for something new and different, but also when consumers are price conscious and looking for a better deal, or when they have become dissatisfied with their routine brand and are looking for a brand that meets their needs better. Product information is essential in this type of decision-making to enable people to make informed choices about the alternatives they are considering, Advertising can also be effective in encouraging consumers to shift away from routine purchasing and try something different.

▶ *Unfamiliar* purchases are subject to more extensive decision-making . These are products that consumers buy infrequently. They may be technologically complex and they are usually of higher value than impulse, routine or familiar purchases, though this is not always the case. A person who buys a dog for the first time may initially go to some lengths to choose an appropriate dog-food, even though the cost of dog-food is relatively low.

More commonly, household appliances, sports equipment and holidays are all likely to be seen as unfamiliar purchases and be subject to extensive decision-making by most consumers. Buyers will use a wide range of criteria to evaluate them and will spend time weighing up the evidence and deciding what to buy.

▶ *Critical* purchases are usually high risk, because the consequence of bad decisions can have serious implications. Where products such as houses, financial services and education are concerned, consumers often go to great lengths to ensure that they are well informed of all the relevant facts about their potential purchase before they decide to buy. They are likely to seek information from public as well as personal sources, and will be cynical of commercial messages unless they offer factual statements that can be substantiated.

Most products fall into different purchase classes under different circumstances. A tennis racquet may be an unfamiliar purchase for most of us, but for a tennis professional it is likely to be a familiar or even routine purchase. A shopper may buy crisps on impulse at the cinema, but see them as a routine purchase in the supermarket. By studying the decision processes that most commonly relate to their own products, marketers can identify any significant patterns and consequently provide the most appropriate messages to help consumers make informed decisions, and the best sales and service approaches to help draw them through those decision processes.

Consumer buying roles

A lot of consumer buying decisions are not the sole responsibility of a single individual. Indeed, the whole decision-making process may be divided up between a group of people, collectively known as the decision-making unit (or DMU), which may be involved at different stages and play different roles in the final decision to purchase. There are five distinct consumer buying roles:

▶ *Initiator*: the one who first comes up with the idea to buy something and who may suggest it to others.
▶ *Influencer*: someone whose advice carries weight in evaluating the alternatives. Sometimes this is a person whose opinions are respected by the other members in the DMU due to expertise or experience in buying the type of product in question.
▶ *Decider*: the person who makes the final decision as to whether to buy, what to buy, when to buy, how to buy, or any combination of these.
▶ *Buyer*: someone who performs the transaction and exchanges money for products or services.
▶ *User*: the person who consumes, operates or experiences the product or service.

Sometimes a single buyer takes all of these roles him- or herself, particularly with products that are exclusively for personal use, such as shaving cream, make-up, hair-care products or hosiery. This is more likely to occur in single-person households than in families. As discussed earlier, family members are often jointly involved in purchasing decisions; even if a wife invariably does the household shopping, the influence of her husband and children may have been significant in shaping her behaviour as the buyer. Decisions may be made jointly between two partners for purchases such as holidays, with one deciding on the location and the other a particular hotel or apartment. Children are the users of many grocery products for which they are never the decider or buyer, and conversely parents are the buyers of many products for their children which they never use themselves. Marketers must identify the relevant buying roles for their products and services so that they can send appropriate messages to the different members of the DMU, according to their input into the purchasing decision.

> **DID YOU KNOW?**
> While 86 per cent of men claim to buy their own outer-clothes, only 72 per cent admit to buying their own underwear! (Mintel, 1994).

ACTIVITY **3.2**
• • • • • • • • • • • • • •

Making decisions

Think of the last time you bought the following products:

▶ Confectionery.
▶ Toothpaste.
▶ A pair of shoes.
▶ A music CD or tape.

1 List the social, personal and individual factors that influenced your decision to buy the item you finally chose.
2 Identify the sources of information you used to help you make your decision.
3 Who else was in the decision-making unit?
4 In which purchase class was your decision?
5 How could information such as this help the producers of these products improve their marketing?

Organisational buyer behaviour
• •

Influences on decision-making

Organisational buyers are subject to similar categories of influence over their buying decisions as consumers, but within these categories, different factors are significant (see Figure 3.5).

The business environment

It is the business environment rather than the social environment that influences organisational buyer behaviour. The external business environment, namely the macro- and micro-environmental factors discussed in Chapter 2, will have an over-arching influence on the nature and quantity of products and services that an organisation buys, while the internal environment of the organisation itself will be important in the decision-making process.

The macro-environment
Factors such as the strength of the economy, the opportunities and threats posed by new legislation, interest rate changes, technological developments and environmental concerns may all affect the needs of a business.

figure 3.5
**Influences on
organisational
buyer-behaviour**

Organisational buyers will respond by increasing or decreasing their levels of purchase, looking for new suppliers as old ones become unable to supply new technologies and identifying new sources to meet new requirements. Even socio-cultural factors can have an influence. The unwritten rules of buying and selling in Japan, for example, are very different from those in Europe and the US, and the nature of the buying process may change accordingly.

The micro-environment

The most significant issue in the micro-environment which influences organisational buyers is the nature of demand from their own customers. Organisational buyers only buy goods and services if consumers or other businesses ultimately demand *their* products. This is known as *derived demand*. As a result of derived demand, they are less likely to stop buying a product or service altogether if the price goes up, as they need it to satisfy their own customers. Therefore, organisational buyers are also likely to exhibit *inelastic demand* (discussed in Chapter 8).

It is important to understand the significance of this from a marketer's point of view. First, demand from organisational buyers is likely to fluctuate more widely than from consumers. In anticipation of future increases in demand, buyers may increase the quantities they purchase by far more than is warranted by current demand from their own customers. If this forecast demand fails to materialise, they may stop buying altogether while excess stocks are used up, leading to a stop-go effect in their purchasing patterns. Inelastic demand can also cause problems. In a boom economy, when levels of derived demand are high, sellers will raise prices, make high profits and increase capacity to cash in on the opportunity. When the economy turns and derived demand falls, excess capacity makes them desperate to sell their goods, prices will tumble and the less efficient firms will go out of business. Business cycles such as these are common and hard-hitting in business-to-business markets. Finally, derived demand can lead to a vulnerability to bad debt. If a firm fails to satisfy its customers it may go into liquidation and be unable to pay its suppliers, causing the suppliers, through no fault of their own, to go out of business themselves.

Organisational objectives

Organisational buyers are paid to purchase the products and services their organisations need to conduct their business and achieve their objectives. Consequently, the business objectives and strategies of an organisation usually give direction to its buyers' decision-making processes. Suppose an organisation aims to be a cost-leader, undercutting other firms in its industry to become a market leader. The primary role of the buyer is to source products and services of an acceptable quality at the lowest possible price, so that costs can be kept low and profits can be made even at low prices. On the other hand, if an organisation wishes to be seen as the quality leader, the buyer may be willing to use higher-priced suppliers who offer a more reliable product and service, with a view to recouping these costs from higher prices to their own customers.

ACTIVITY **3.3**
....

Economic value to the customer

Although businesses are influenced by price-tags, they are often more interested in the 'economic value' of the purchase. The concept of 'economic value to the customer' is one that refers to the difference in *total* cost between an existing and a new product. This is a feature of some consumer markets too. Suppose a family needs replacement windows in their house. Although the *price* of single-glazed windows with wooden frames is likely to be lower than double glazing and UPVC frames, the *cost* over the lifetime of the window is likely to be higher if the cost of heat loss from the window and a regular need for repainting is taken into account.

Suppose a company is choosing between two suppliers to buy a new machine product.

	Machine A	Machine B
Purchase price (£)	£20,000	?
Delivery (flat fee)	200	200
Installation and commissioning (flat fee)	600	1,000
Productivity (items per hour)	500	1,000
Annual maintenance (per annum)	1,000	2,000
Emergency call-out fee (per call)	200	200
Expected life (years)	10	8

If you were the manufacturer of Machine B, how much would you charge for it?

Organisational systems

Organisations use a variety of formalised systems in an attempt to maximise their buying efficiency and effectiveness. As discussed in Chapter 9, the just-in-time production systems used by some manufacturers mean they carry very little stock and are dependent on their suppliers to deliver the right goods at the right time for their production lines. Under these circumstances, one of the essential evaluative criteria to be used in the buyer's decision-making process will be the reliability of the supplier.

Long-term supply contracts are a feature of the buying process in some organisations. Buyers can use them to exert buying power, requiring sealed-bids from potential suppliers to ensure the lowest possible prices. More positively, though, long-term contracts can be used to develop better relationships between suppliers and buyers, recognising that the transactions between them must be in the interests of both parties. (Relationship marketing is discussed further in Chapter 14.)

CASE STUDY **3.4**

Distribution in the fast lane

Lane Group PLC operates a fleet of around 300 vehicles from distribution centres around the UK. Formed over 30 years ago, the company has long been committed to an environmental policy. The management believes that a responsible attitude towards the environment is not only socially desirable but also commercially sensible and its business practices emphasise the effective management of waste and the conservation of natural resources. Environmentally friendly vehicles help to reduce fuel bills by up to ten per cent. Staff are educated on the firm's environmental policy and related legislation and an environmental audit is conducted annually.

These green credentials endeared the Lane Group to the Body Shop and created opportunities for a lasting and mutually profitable trading relationship. The Body Shop was looking for a distribution company that would place customer service at the top of its agenda, and has come to an agreement with the Lane Group whereby the drivers of the delivery vehicles are based at the Body Shop's own warehouse. The two firms operate a system of open-book accounting which allows the Lane Group to make specified profit margins on their business with the Body Shop, who pays a bonus if agreed service levels are achieved – the bonus is only paid if no more than 40 deliveries out of 14,000 deliveries a year to over 200 UK stores are late.

This type of relationship between buyer and seller is beneficial to both parties. The Lane Group knows that it is guaranteed profitable trading if it addresses the Body Shop's primary need for consistency and reliability in its supplier, and the Body Shop is assured of a distributor who supports its commitment to the environment and can enhance the service it provides to its franchisees.

Questions

1   What decision criteria do you think the Body Shop might use in selecting a distribution service?
2   To what extent are the personal characteristics of the buyer likely to have influenced the decision to use the Lane Group?
3   What would you see as the disadvantages of operating an open-book accounting system? Why don't more buyers insist on it?

Sources Jenkins, 1993; 'Crazy ways for crazy days', 1993.

Organisational structure

The way in which an organisation structures its buying function will influence the buying process itself. The roles, authority and domain of organisational buyers will vary between organisations, and identifying the decision-making unit is an important task for anyone trying to sell to organisations. For example, centralised buying is a feature of some large organisations. Its aim is usually to reduce costs by negotiating discounts for large quantities. This may mean that some organisational buyers do not have the authority to purchase certain of the products and services their organisations use. It may also mean that some organisations have the buying power to insist on buying direct from manufacturers instead of through distributors or agents.

Individual circumstances

Although organisational buyers are not buying for their own personal consumption, their age, gender, income (and therefore seniority) and education are still likely to affect their decision-making processes. In addition to these, training and experience in the role of buyer are other individual factors likely to affect buyers' behaviour. They may influence the rigour of their information search, their ability to evaluate, the value they place on personal contact with their suppliers and their willingness to try new sources of supply.

Personal characteristics

Issues of personality, perception, motivation and beliefs apply just as firmly in organisational buying as in consumer buying, but may exhibit themselves in different ways. Buyer motivation, for example, will stem primarily from the functional needs of the business, but the social and esteem needs of buyers may encourage them to prefer suppliers with whom they can enjoy social functions, or whose names are familiar and carry some prestige.

> **DID YOU KNOW?**
>
> *Whitbread offered its company car drivers the opportunity to choose a bigger or smaller car than they were entitled to under company policy, on condition they made up the difference in cost if they chose a more expensive model. They were entitled to a rebate if they chose a less expensive model. Four out of ten drivers opted for a more expensive model than the one allocated by the company, with a high proportion trading up to the 'aspirational' marques of Mercedes and BMW (Hobson, 1995).*

Personality characteristics can lead to different buying styles, with some buyers enjoying confrontation and the exercise of power over their suppliers, some being analytical and formally rational, and others encouraging open honest discussion with suppliers, rather than win/lose negotiations. The extent to which risk will be tolerated is another personal characteristic of buyers, with some willing to experiment with new technologies and new suppliers, while others wait for them to be tested with a proven track record before they are willing to consider them.

The organisational buyer decision-making process

Because of the complexity of some organisational buying decisions, more stages may be evident in the buyer decision-making process than in consumer markets (see Figure 3.6). There are six key stages:

- ▶ *Problem recognition*: Similar to the consumer's 'perception of need', someone in an organisation recognises that a problem may be solved by the acquisition of goods or services. Internally, this may occur due to a new product development, under-capacity or problems with quality control; externally this may occur when a buyer sees a product report in the trade press or is offered a promotional price by a potential new supplier.
- ▶ *Product specification*: Often in conjunction with other members of the decision-making unit who have expertise and can give technical advice, the

figure 3.6
**The organisational
buyer
decision-making
process**

buyer will draw up first a general description, and then a precise specification of the nature and quantity of the product required.

▶ *Supplier search*: The buyer will identify potential suppliers of the specified products, and may ask them to submit proposals or give sales presentations to demonstrate their capabilities and indicate their prices. This will enable the organisation to draw up a short-list, similar to the consumer's 'evoked set'.

▶ *Supplier selection*: This is commonly done by ranking the desired attributes of potential suppliers in order of importance. The list is likely to include a number of purely functional attributes, such as price, delivery, quality and after-sales service, but may also include less tangible features such as corporate ethics and communication skills. Suppliers will be chosen who most closely meet the key criteria. In many cases, organisations will choose more then one supplier for products they require on a regular basis, to ensure continuity of supply in case of one supplier's default, and to allow the price and service comparison of different suppliers over a period of time.

▶ *Ordering*: The placing of an order with a supplier may be a one-off activity, or may take the form of a contract to purchase under agreed terms over a period of time. Invariably these terms will include payment terms; while consumers usually pay cash up-front before they receive their products or services, organisations invariably set up accounts with their suppliers, receiving goods first and subsequently paying for them within a stipulated time period (though suppliers often insist on a credit reference with new customers).

▶ *Performance evaluation*: Buyers collect information about the performance of their suppliers and use this as an important source of information when a similar product is required again. Sometimes this information is used as part of a system for motivating suppliers to maintain excellent performance levels. Financial incentives may be offered for reaching delivery, service or quality targets.

This decision-making process has a number of implications for marketers. First, the earlier in the process they can make contact with the buyer, the more likely they are to be included in the supplier short-list. Many buyers appreciate the expertise of suppliers at the product specification stage and if a collaborative relationship can be formed, a phenomenon known as 'creeping commit-ment' may follow; the buyer will start to feel more comfortable with that supplier than others who are considered later on. Second, because the supplier search process is likely to be more disciplined and formal than in consumer markets, it is important that potential buyers can easily find information about sources of supply. Marketers must ensure that they are well represented in trade directories and the trade press, and that sales staff are as committed to building relationships with potential new customers as they are to 'closing a sale'. Finally, the monitoring of after-sales satisfaction is just as important for the seller as it is for the buyer. Particularly in the case of long-term contracts or repeat purchases, marketers should be fully aware of the levels of satisfaction of their customers so that they can use this in the negotiation of new business. The more satisfied the customers, the less likely they are to switch supplier on the grounds of price alone.

Organisational purchase classes

Just as consumers extend or curtail the efforts they put into the decision-making process according to the nature of the product they are buying, organisational buyers will approach the different stages in the decision-making process according to the nature of their buying task. There are three categories of buying situation (Robinson, Faris and Wind, 1967):

▶ *Straight rebuy*: When the buying task is familiar and recurring, routine ordering procedures are used to place orders with acceptable suppliers. The supplier selection stage of the decision-making process is automatic, which makes it very difficult for new suppliers to break in. The buyer uses routine procedures to reduce the effort required for purchasing such products, and is likely to be reluctant to interrupt comfortable and established habits unless a problem occurs or a new supplier offers something with considerably more benefits. The buyer's selective perception may even mean that messages from alternative suppliers are screened out, including the avoidance of sales calls.

▶ *Modified rebuy*: If buyers become dissatisfied with their routine purchases for any reason, they may decide to consider new suppliers; their objectives may be to get better prices, to change the product specification, to improve the delivery times or simply to review the effectiveness of their routine pur-chases. This provides an opportunity for new firms to get onto the short-list and current suppliers must reassess what they offer and prepare for the like-lihood of further negotiation.

▶ *New task*: Many buying decisions are likely to be new tasks that a buyer meets for the first time. In this situation, all the stages of the decision-making process are likely to be in evidence, though the amount of detail included in the product specification and the lengths to which buyers will go to find the best supplier are still likely to vary according to the value of the product and its importance in the operations of the organisation; capital equipment and component parts are more likely to be thoroughly scrutinised than office consumables or support services.

Organisational buying roles

Organisational buying roles are very similar to consumer buying roles, and as a result, the person entitled 'buyer' in an organisation is seldom the only important person in the decision-making process. One of the key tasks for marketers, therefore, is to identify the nature of organisations' decision-making units. These are likely to vary according to the nature of the products they are buying: the decision-making unit for computer systems is likely to be different from the one for office cleaning services, and those involved in deciding on company cars may have very little, if any, involvement in the purchase of raw materials or components. The buyer may be the person who arranges the transaction in all of these cases, but the users may be consulted in coming to a final decision and influence may be exerted by those with technical expertise or seniority.

Even the final decision may not be the responsibility of the buyer, but perhaps a departmental manager whose budget may bear the cost.

The only members of organisational decision-making units who are seldom present in consumer buying are gatekeepers. These are people who control the flow of information in an organisation, normally with a view to preventing irrelevant information from reaching the decision-making unit. Secretaries often act as gatekeepers, turning away unwanted sales calls and diverting direct-mail. If this is the case, the task of actually reaching relevant buyers becomes all the more difficult, and the role of marketing may need to encompass a strategy for breaking through this type of resistance.

> **DID YOU KNOW?**
> *Pyrex manufacturers, Corning Glass Works, came across strong resistance from engineers and purchasing managers when it tried to sell them Pyrex pipes for chemical food processing equipment, despite the demonstrable technological advantages the strengthened glass offered over alternative materials. Psychologists concluded that their resistance to glass stemmed from bad childhood experiences – broken glass usually meant a spanking! (Packard, 1957).*

CASE STUDY **3.5**

Air traffic control systems

Air traffic control systems enable the safe passage of aircraft across national boundaries, and are therefore, by definition, a matter of international interest. Consequently, the market for air traffic control systems in Europe is interwoven with a diverse range of interested parties, including commercial and industrial institutions, financiers and governments from a wide geographical base.

There are four key players in the decision-making unit:

▶ The *European community* acts as a catalyst for dialogue between Member States and provides some funding for air traffic control research.

▶ The *European Civil Aviation Conference* (ECAC) comprises the Transport Ministers from 28 countries, whose remit is to promote the co-ordination and better utilisation of European civil aviation, with specific reference to economic, technical, security and safety issues.

▶ *Eurocontrol* comprises aviation experts from 12 countries. They are responsible for developing operational plans for co-ordinated air traffic systems.

▶ The *Eurocontrol Agency* is responsible for the actual provision of air traffic services in some of these countries, and also for air traffic flow management and the collection of route charges.

Such complexity has created serious problems for the sellers in the market. A system of competitive tendering was introduced to prevent political pressure influencing the purchasing decisions, but this too created problems as companies were required to do a lot of research work before they could submit their bids, which made it a very costly exercise if a contract was not subsequently secured. Joint ventures between suppliers are becoming more common in the industry, as no single firm is able to comply with complex product specifications that are required and development costs can be shared.

Questions

1   What difficulties arise as a result of a diverse decision-making unit?
2   To what extent can a large number of participants in a decision improve the quality of the decision made?
3   What sort of consumer decisions might involve a large and diverse decision-making unit?

Source Hill, Macdonald and Robins, 1993.

Key concepts
● ● ● ● ● ● ● ● ● ● ● ● ● ● ● ● ●

Buying role: the nature of input a person has into the decision to buy a product or service.

Cognitive dissonance: doubts that arise after making a purchase, which lead to a feeling of discomfort.

Consumers: individuals who buy products and services for themselves or on behalf of their households.

Decision-making process: series of steps a buyer takes in selecting a product or service from a set of alternatives.

Decision-making unit: a group of people who exert an influence over a decision to buy a product or service.

Derived demand: demand for business products that originates from demand for consumer products.

Evoked set: a short-list of potential purchases that results from a search for information about products and services.

Family life-cycle: the stages of formation and progression of a typical family.

Gatekeepers: those who control the flow of information in the decision-making process.

Inelastic demand: when levels of demand for a product or service remain fairly stable regardless of their prices.

Organisational buyers: those who buy products and services on behalf of the organisations they work for.

Primary group: groups of people with whom an individual has regular but informal interaction.

Purchase class: a product classification that indicates the level of effort a buyer will exert in deciding what to buy.

Reference group: any group that influences a person's buying behaviour.

Secondary groups: groups of people with whom an individual has formal and irregular interaction.

Social class: a group of people with similar levels of wealth and power who share similar values and attitudes.

SELF-CHECK QUESTIONS

1 Which of the following are the most useful indicators of social class?
   a Household size.
   b Car ownership.
   c Occupation.
   d Personality.
   e Life expectancy.

2 Derived demand is:
   a The motivation behind impulse purchases.
   b The motivation behind organisational purchases.
   c A feature of the family life-cycle.
   d A normative influence on consumer behaviour.
   e A stage in the organisational buyer decision-making process.

3 Which of the following is *not a* stage in the consumer decision-making process?
   a Post-purchase evaluation.
   b Straight rebuy.
   c Evaluation of alternatives.
   d Perception of need.
   e Purchase.

4 What roles is a child likely to play in its parents' decision to buy a new car?
   a Influencer and decider.
   b Decider and buyer.
   c Initiator and decider.
   d Buyer and user.
   e None of these.

5 Which of the following elements of the business environment are most likely to influence the volume of raw materials and components an organisational buyer purchases?
   a Inflation.
   b Unemployment.
   c Recession.
   d Legislation.
   e Interest rates.

Which of the following are true and which are false?
   6 Internal sources of information are sufficient for making modified rebuy decisions.
   7 As organisational buyers are constrained by the systems of their firms, their personal characteristics do not affect their decision-making processes.
   8 Peer groups can exert comparative influence on consumer buying decisions.
   9 Marketers are unable to influence unfamiliar purchases with promotional messages.
   10 Consumers' lifestyles are reflected in the residential neighbourhoods they live in.

Discuss the following:
   11 To what extent can consumer perceptions of a product be influenced by advertising messages?

12 What criteria would you use to decide which products should be centrally purchased in an organisation, and which should be purchased by individual departments?

13 Who are likely to be members of the decision-making unit for the purchase of a new house?

14 To what extent will the concept of social class be of use to marketers in the twenty-first century?

15 What information sources is an organisational buyer likely to consult in the search for a supplier of computers?

Further study
....

Books
The literature on the subject of consumer behaviour is extensive. Excellent text-books include:

Assael, Henry (1994) *Consumer Behaviour and Marketing Action*, International Thompson Publishing.
Engel, James (1995) *Consumer Behaviour*, Dryden.

Both are American, but include universally applicable examples of consumer behaviour and its implications for marketing. Theoretical frameworks are explored in some detail. Organisational buyer behaviour is less well covered, but is included in most general texts on business-to-business marketing.

Monk, Donald (1985) *Social Grading on the National Readership Survey*, JICNARS. *Social class categorisation is clearly explained in this publication, which also provides a useful list of the social grades normally attributed to a wide range of occupations.*
Packard, Vance (1957) *The Hidden Persuaders*, Pelican Books.
A seminal work on consumer motivation. Still in print 40 years after it was first published, it provides a fascinating perspective on a wide range of behavioural issues and also confronts the ethical dilemmas that they pose for marketers.

References
....

'Crazy ways for crazy days' (1993) *Business Matters*, BBC2.
CCN Marketing literature, Talbot House, Talbot Street, Nottingham, NG1 5HF.
CIA Medianetwork (1994) 'Shopping Trends', in *Marketing*, 24 November, p. 13.
Hill, E., Macdonald, J. and Robins, M. (1993) '*Marconi Radar Systems Ltd. / Nobeltech Systems AB: International collaboration in the market for air traffic control systems*', in *International Business*, Preston, J. (ed.), Pitman.
Hill, E., O'Sullivan, C. and O'Sullivan, T. (1995) *Creative Arts Marketing*, Butterworth Heinemann.
Hobson, R. (1995) 'Tax fails to cool the buyer's ardour', in *The Times*, April 25, p. 22.
Jenkins, R. (1993) 'A green light for the distribution industry', in *Logistics Focus*, vol.1, issue 3, October, pp. 16–17.
Kotler, P. and Armstrong, G. (1994) *Principles of Marketing*, Prentice Hall.

Mazur, L. (1993) 'Brands across borders', in *Marketing Business*, October, pp. 36–9.

Mintel (1995) 'Family Planning', in *Marketing Business*, September, p. 60.

Mintel (1994) 'Marketing to Men', in *Marketing Business*, p. 47

Mintel (1994/5) 'Shop around the clock', *Marketing Business*, Dec/Jan, p. 47.

Packard, V. (1957) *The Hidden Persuaders*, Pelican Books.

Putnam, M. and Davidson, W.R. (1987) *Family purchasing behaviour: Family roles by product category*, Management Horizons Inc. (a division of Price Waterhouse).

Robinson, P.J., Faris, C.W. and Wind, Y. (1967) *Industrial Buying Behaviour and Creative Marketing*, Allyn and Bacon.

Wells, W. and Gubar, G. (1966) 'Life cycle concept in marketing research', in *Journal of Marketing Research*, 3, November, pp. 355–63.

CHAPTER 4

Marketing research

Objectives

When you have read this chapter you will be able to:

► Understand what marketing research can be used for.
► Recognise those situations in which marketing research is necessary.
► Set appropriate objectives for marketing research.
► Distinguish between primary and secondary data.
► Identify sources of secondary data.
► Explain the methods available for conducting qualitative research.
► Describe the key stages of a marketing research survey.

Introduction

The quality of marketing decisions is usually dependent on the quality of information that underpins those decisions. Questions such as 'who are my customers?' and 'what are their needs?' must be answered before decisions are made about what to produce, what to charge, how to promote and where to distribute. Marketing research is a process that organisations can use to generate the information they need to answer questions such as these. The term 'marketing research' is often shortened to 'market' research, though strictly speaking this is incorrect. *Market* research focuses simply on trends in the market related specifically to customer activity, whereas *marketing* research encompasses a much wider range of issues relating to an organisation and its environment.

This chapter looks at both the purpose and process of marketing research, examining a wide range of techniques and practices that can be used to gather data in the most effective and efficient ways.

What is marketing research?

Marketing research is a systematic approach to gathering facts and figures related to the marketing of goods and services. Tull and Hawkins (1992) give a very simple, but useful definition of marketing research, which emphasises the fundamental *purpose* of this activity: 'a formalised means of obtaining information to be used in making marketing decisions'.

The American Marketing Association (1961) gave more emphasis to the *process* of marketing research: 'the systematic gathering, recording and analysing of data about problems relating to the marketing of goods and services'.

More recently, though, the AMA has adopted the definition given by Kotler and Armstrong (1994), which sees marketing research as a *function* that creates an information channel between organisations and their customers:

the function that links the consumer, customer, and public to the marketer through information – information used to identify and define marketing opportunities and problems; to generate, refine and evaluate marketing actions; to monitor marketing performance; and to improve understanding of the marketing process.

This definition recognises the wide range of decisions that marketing research can inform. Before, during and after the implementation of marketing activities, marketing research can be used to provide a basis for rational decision-making and help to avoid the problems that arise from acting on 'hunches'.

The scope of marketing research

Different types of research can be conducted according to the type of marketing information required:

▶ *Market research* is concerned with identifying the nature, composition and preferences of current and potential markets. This may be used to help organisations identify levels of potential sales in a particular market, or to identify regional differences (particularly important when considering exporting or overseas expansion, as discussed in Chapter 13). It can also be used to help firms identify differences between different sub-groups of their customers, known as market segments (further discussion of this in Chapter 5).

▶ *Behavioural research* attempts to establish the underlying factors that determine consumer behaviour in a market (as described in Chapter 3). It is used to develop an understanding of why people buy, and how they go about making their buying decisions.

▶ *Competitor research* is concerned with identifying the nature of current and potential competitors and their strengths and weaknesses. Changes in market share are of particular interest, as they indicate how well a business is performing relative to its competitors. Competitors' pricing and promotional policies may also need investigation, as may any new products that they launch.

▶ *Product research* is particularly important when new products are developed (discussed in Chapter 7), to ensure that their characteristics match those required by potential customers. It can also be used to help businesses improve existing products and to identify gaps in current provision.

DID YOU KNOW?

In research to investigate ways of improving the brand profile of Twiglets, consumers were asked to describe the product and liken it to famous people. The product itself was found to be 'fiery red-orange, masculine, extrovert, eccentric and outrageously unique', and was likened to Mr Bean, Lenny Henry and John Cleese, but the packaging was likened to a policeman, a Ford Escort and even John Major! Design specialists were quickly called in to bring the packaging into line with consumer perceptions of the product. ('The Twiglet Zone', 1995).

▶ *Pricing research* can be undertaken to help understand the price sensitivity of customers; what proportion of sales will I lose if I put my prices up by ten per cent? are my prices too high relative to the competition? what price should I set for a new product? Experiments can be conducted to see just what sort of effect price changes might have on demand.

▶ *Promotional research* can be used to pre-test promotional campaigns before full-scale media costs are incurred, to see whether the chosen message, format and media will be effective. This is most easily done with direct mail letters, different versions of which can be sent to different addresses and the response rates compared; it can also be effective for TV advertising and sales promotion campaigns (discussed further in Chapters 10 and 11). Post-testing of promotions involves the evaluation of a campaign after it has run, to identify its impact and cost effectiveness.

▶ *Distribution research* may be undertaken to identify the relative effectiveness of different retailers, distributors or agents. This could help businesses to identify any areas where their coverage is poor, and where they require a more significant presence. It might also help them use their own sales force more effectively. Supermarkets use this type of research extensively to identify the best sites for the location of out-of-town superstores.

▶ *Economic and social research* is concerned with identifying trends in the environment. As explained in Chapter 2, unemployment, interest rates, inflation and population trends can all affect the long-term well-being of an organisation, and such factors need to be monitored to enable firms to pre-empt any negative impacts of such changes.

Is marketing research really necessary?

Needless to say, a lot of marketing decisions are taken every day without any marketing research being conducted. This begs questions as to whether marketing research is always appropriate. An organisation should ask itself a number of searching questions before embarking on a research programme:

▶ *Do I have enough information already?* It is always possible to generate more information to help make a decision, but at some point a manager will have to make a judgement that there is enough relevant information available to take a decision, and this may be before any research has been undertaken, especially if the problem is a straightforward one.

▶ *What difference will the findings make to my decision-making?* Some organisations commit themselves to certain courses of action and then conduct research to support their views, but there's no point conducting the research if the findings will have no influence on the decision. This also leads to the next question:

▶ *What if my research tells me something I don't want to hear?* The temptation is to dismiss the research as being wrong rather than face up to the unpalatable implications of unwanted findings; again there is no point conducting the research if positive outcomes alone are to be heeded.

▶ *How quickly must I make a decision?* Some problems need to be resolved so urgently that there is no time for research; a good guess at the right time may be more advantageous than an informed decision that is made too late.

▶ *Can research give me accurate answers to my questions?* There are questions that research finds very difficult to answer. Consumer buying *intentions*, for example, may be measured but these intentions may never translate into purchasing. Conversely, consumers may reject new product ideas in research, but persuasive advertising campaigns may be very effective in breaking down negative attitudes if the product offers real benefits.

▶ *How much will research cost?* This is likely to determine the type of research to be undertaken, and may affect the process of research as well as the decision as to whether or not research should be conducted at all. An evaluation has to be made as to whether or not the research offers value for money.

▶ *What are the risks if I don't do any research?* Risk equals the potential cost of making the wrong decision. For example, suppose an organisation is considering adding a product to its line, but the cost of conducting appropriate research is high. If the costs of introducing the new line are low, it may be more cost-effective just to launch it and risk failure in the market than to incur the research costs. On the other hand, if a wrong decision could potentially undermine the reputation of the whole business, then the risks are too high to ignore research findings, whatever the cost.

> **DID YOU KNOW?**
>
> *Marks and Spencer doesn't market test any of its food products before launching new lines. It's the taste of the food selectors that determines what will appear on the shelves. Inevitably some mistakes are made. Vichyssoise soup was a poor seller until it was re-named 'Leek and Potato' ('Off your trolley with Loyd Grossman', 1995).*

CASE STUDY **4.1**

Sinclair C5

Inventor Sir Clive Sinclair, who had achieved world firsts and technological break-throughs with his executive pocket calculator and pocket TV, determined as far back as 1973 to produce an electric vehicle. When the Government abolished tax on electric vehicles in 1980, and later passed legislation permitting anyone over 14 years of age to drive an electrically assisted pedal cycle without a helmet or insurance, Sinclair took this as his cue to develop the one-seater, three-wheeler C5, which fell somewhere between the status of car and bicycle.

Sir Clive openly admitted that he did not believe in market research, claiming that it is impossible to assess demand for a new product accurately when there is nothing like it already on the market, but he confidently predicted sales of up to 100,000 vehicles per annum and reached an agreement with Hoover to start production in the autumn of 1984. The research he did undertake was mainly connected with product development and 63 families from urban and suburban areas were invited to try the prototype vehicle. They were also asked how much they thought such a vehicle might cost. The higher-income families thought about £1,000, while the lower-income families suggested around £2,500.

The product price was finally set at £399 and distribution was to be by mail order. Test marketing was eschewed in favour of a single official launch which took place in January 1985 at Alexandra Palace, where journalists were invited to go for a test-drive through the hilly and snow-covered grounds. The few who did so expressed concerns about the road-worthiness of the vehicle under such conditions. Further complaints were soon forthcoming , and tests by the Consumers' Association produced a number of major criticisms:

▶ The height of the C5 on the road was at bumper-height of other cars, making it difficult to see and increasing the chance of injury in an accident.
▶ Spray, exhaust and the head-light beam from other vehicles affected visibility.
▶ The horn was ineffective, the headlight beam was insufficient and mirrors and indicators were optional extras.

▶ There was no reverse gear, so moving backwards usually meant getting out of the vehicle.

▶ The vehicle would travel no more than 15 miles on a fully-charged battery, as opposed to manufacturer claims of 20 miles.

▶ In hilly areas, drivers had to pedal a lot due to the motor cutting out.

▶ A maximum speed of 15 mph caused a hazard in urban areas with a traffic flow progressing at 30 mph.

It was subsequently revealed that, although safety consultations had taken place, the vehicle had been mainly tested on a test-track and in simulated accidents, not in heavy traffic.

Within three months of the launch of the C5 it was clear that sales would not meet targets. The root of Sinclair's problem seemed to be that it was being marketed as a serious means of transport – as a competitor to the moped and second car. Consumers, on the other hand, saw it as an upmarket plaything. Production was cut back by 90 per cent and within a further six months was halted altogether. The receivers were called in when only 14,000 had been produced.

Questions

1   Could market research have changed this to a happy ending?
2   What else might you have wanted to know from the 63 families who tried the prototype?
3   What indicators might you look at to assess demand for a new product?

Sources Marks, 1990; Griffiths, 1985.

The marketing research process

The marketing research process should follow three key stages:

Planning
A clear purpose for marketing research needs to be identified before any action is taken. This purpose normally relates to a problem, issue or opportunity facing the organisation which is causing uncertainty as to which direction to take. When the purpose of the research is clear, it is possible to set specific objectives that will indicate what the research aims to find out and to identify the data (facts and figures) required to achieve those objectives.

Implementation
There is no single best way of collecting data. The way in which the research is implemented will depend on the research plan. Although a survey may be useful, it is by no means the only tool for implementing marketing research and may not be the most cost-effective way of achieving the objectives. Alternatives should always be considered.

Interpretation
'Information' is created when the data collected are interpreted in the context of the research objectives. The final stage of the process of marketing research is

therefore to make sense of the findings and ensure that they are used to influence decision-making.

The rest of this chapter looks at these stages in more detail.

Planning marketing research
. . . .

Identifying the problem

Organisations frequently meet business challenges that cause them uncertainty. They may be very positive challenges (sales are rising) or decidedly negative (market share is falling). There may be a hypothesis as to the reason the issue has arisen, and this hypothesis may need to be tested. Alternatively, there may be no apparent reason and the issue may need to be thoroughly explored. In both cases a manager may need information to help develop an appropriate response to the situation, and research will be required to provide some answers.

Setting objectives

Research objectives are statements that set out exactly what an organisation wants to know, explicitly establishing the information required to make a decision relating to the particular problem, issue or opportunity identified. They are important for three reasons:

▶   They are the starting point for the rest of the research process, and are used as a guide to the type of data required and the best way of collecting them.
▶   They are used to help researchers highlight the most important findings when interpreting data and reporting results.
▶   They provide a benchmark for evaluating whether the research process was effective and cost effective.

Objectives may be any one or a combination of three types:

Exploratory objectives

Exploratory research is conducted if the nature of a problem or issue is unclear, or if an organisation needs preliminary information to formulate a hypothesis that can subsequently be tested in further research. It is concerned with 'exploring' possibilities rather than finding specific answers. Exploratory objectives may be set if a firm has an idea that it wants to develop, but isn't sure which way to go next; or if it can find no apparent explanation for a fall (or increase) in sales, and wants to identify possible reasons. Examples of exploratory objectives might be 'to identify areas of weakness in customer care' or 'to evaluate the impact of a new competitor'.

Descriptive objectives

When an organisation is seeking specific information to support specific decisions it will set descriptive objectives. In other words, it will use research to 'describe' the factors that will influence its decisions, such as the market potential for a product, customer attitudes, competitor strategies, price sensitivity or economic conditions. Descriptive objectives are very common, as the information obtained can be very cost effective, helping to avoid the financial consequences of making bad decisions. Examples of descriptive objectives might be 'to determine the average frequency of purchase' of a product, or 'to identify the demographic profile of heavy users'.

Causal objectives

Causal objectives are set if an organisation wants to understand more about the relationship between two factors. For example, is TV advertising effective in generating charitable donations? to what extent are buying patterns influenced by store layout? by what percentage will sales volumes increase if prices are reduced by ten per cent? Answers to cause-and-effect questions such as these can mean that firms are better placed to influence consumer behaviour, to eliminate inappropriate marketing tactics and to forecast demand.

Identifying data needs

When research objectives have been set, it is possible to identify data needs. *Data* are facts and figures used to generate *information*. The analysis of data (in the light of the objectives set) creates information that can be used in decision-making.

Conducting marketing research
....

When research objectives have been set and data requirements identified, it is possible to make decisions about the style and duration of research activities.

Quantitative research

If the research objectives require data to be collected about *how many* people hold similar views or display particular characteristics, the research is described as being quantitative. Conducting quantitative research usually requires data to be collected from only a small proportion (known as a sample) of the group of people of interest to the researcher. As long as the sample chosen is representative, statistical techniques can be used to make assumptions about the views of the whole group based on the responses from the sample.

Qualitative research

If the research objectives require information to be generated about *how* people think and feel about issues, or *why* they take certain decisions and behave as they do, then the research is described as being qualitative. Qualitative research is particularly useful for exploring the subtleties of consumer behaviour, when categorising and quantifying responses would be an inadequate means of drawing out individual characteristics. It tends to be conducted among very few individuals, and no attempts are made to draw conclusions as to the views of other people. Instead, the findings from qualitative research tend to be used either to set an agenda for further quantitative research (to see whether the views expressed are indeed representative of the views of others) or to add detail to some general findings that have emerged from quantitative research that has already been conducted.

Continuous research

Sometimes marketing research is needed to monitor changes that are occurring, for example in purchasing habits, in population trends, in customer satisfaction, or simply in sales figures. In this situation, the research has to be repeatedly conducted on an intermittent basis over a period of time, so that comparisons can be made and trends identified. This is known as continuous research.

CASE STUDY **4.2**
· · · · · · · · · · · · · · · · · ·

The TGI

The Target Group Index (TGI), published by BMRB International, is a continuous survey that has been running in Great Britain every year since 1969. Its primary objective is 'to describe, as accurately as possible, the characteristics of target groups of consumers'. It does this by asking questions about the buying habits of a sample of 24,000 consumers every year. The survey takes place on a weekly basis, with data being collected through detailed self-completion questionnaires. The questions themselves cover over 4,000 brands in more than 500 product areas, but also ask about other consumer behaviour such as newspaper readership and TV viewing. Lifestyle and attitude questions are also included and a full set of demographic data are gathered for each respondent.

By comparing the responses from one question with another (a technique known as cross-tabulation), profiles can be drawn up of different target groups. If the response to a question on preferred brands of lager is compared with responses to questions on lifestyle and attitudes, the types of consumers who buy the different brands can be identified and compared. Carling Black Label drinkers, for example, are more likely than average to buy take-away meals, to prefer branded products to own-brands, to snack between meals and only want to eat, drink and sunbathe on holiday. They are less likely than average to eat wholemeal bread or for friends to ask their advice about gardening!

One UK advertising agency has used TGI data to create profiles of eight different types of housewives, for which it has created names such as 'Take-away Tracey', 'Muesli Mum' and 'TV Dinah'. When one of its clients, Hellman's Mayonnaise, was concerned about the inroads being made into its market by supermarket own-brands, it used TGI data about mayonnaise eaters to identify the types of housewife most likely to buy mayonnaise. It was found that 55 per cent of it is bought by just 38 per cent of housewives, namely the 'Muesli Mums', 'Career and Connoisseurs' and 'Short-cut Gourmets'. Subsequent advertising campaigns could then be targeted specifically at creating brand loyalty among these groups. Groups such as the 'Take-away Traceys' and 'Kids and Chips' could be safely ignored, as they are much more likely to buy salad cream than mayonnaise.

Questions
1   What information can continuous surveys provide that *ad hoc* surveys cannot?
2   Given the evidence above, how would you promote Carling Black Label? What else would you like to know?

3 Would a continuous survey such as this be of any use in business-to–business markets? Discuss its limitations.

Sources BMRB International, 1995; 'Horizon', 1993.

Ad hoc research

This is a term given to describe one-off investigations of specific issues that will arise only once and for which more information is needed to make a particular marketing decision.

Data collection
....

Having identified the type of research to be undertaken, the researcher must decide upon the most appropriate method or methods for collecting the data.

First of all, sources of *secondary data* should be identified. Secondary data are facts and figures already available 'off the shelf', having been collected for another purpose or another organisation The researcher is a secondary user of already existing data, so the research technique is known as *desk research*.

If, as is often the case, secondary data fail to provide sufficient evidence for a marketing decision to be made, then *primary data* will have to be collected. Primary data are facts and figures collected specifically to provide the information required to reach the research objectives. There are a wide variety of research techniques that can be used to collect primary data, and these are explored in the following sections.

Sources of secondary data

As explained above, secondary data already exist. If they exist within the organisation conducting the research, but were collected for a different purpose, they are described as *internal* sources of secondary data. On the other hand, if they were collected by another organisation, whether for the purpose of marketing research or any other purpose, they are known as *external* sources of primary data.

Both types have their advantages and disadvantages:

▶ They tend to be less expensive than primary data (available for free, internally, or at relatively low cost from libraries and research publishers).
▶ They can provide data that would otherwise be impossible to collect (historical trends, for example).
▶ They can be used as a source of ideas and a starting point for further primary research.

But:

▶ The data required to reach the research objectives may not be available (either because no one has collected them, or because the owner of the data refuses to release them).
▶ The data that *are* available may be irrelevant (perhaps being so general as to be of little use, or only of use to other industries or markets).

▶ There may be doubts as to the accuracy of the data (such as errors in the original research design or an inappropriate sample).

▶ The data may be out of date (particularly in fast-moving markets driven by rapid technological change).

Internal data

A wide variety of potentially useful marketing data tends to be spread throughout the different departments of an organisation. Useful sources might include:

The customer database

This is likely to hold information about everyone that an organisation sells to. In some organisations this will include consumers or industrial buyers, but at a minimum the customer database will give details of retailers and other distributor customers. It is likely to give the name, address and sales history of anyone who has ever set up an account with the organisation and can be very useful for investigations to identify groups of buyers with similar characteristics, known as market segments (as discussed in Chapter 5). It may also be useful for identifying trends in purchasing patterns and for forecasting future demand.

> **DID YOU KNOW?**
> *'Data distress' is a growing problem for retailers and packaged goods manufacturers as they struggle to manage the vast increase in continuous customer information that is flooding into their organisations as a result of scanning data and loyalty cards. The MD of Nielsen, one of the largest suppliers of scanning data, likens the use of this type of information to drinking from a fire hydrant: 'it is possible if you attach it to the right nozzle', and advocates the use of new technology to help take advantage of the vast increase in available information (Fletcher, 1995).*

Management accounts

These contain a lot of details about costs and revenues. They may be able to reveal the profitability of different product lines, and to provide direction for the allocation of marketing budgets.

Sales-force reports

As the sales force are usually the members of an organisation who are closest to the customer, their observations of customer reactions can be very valuable. They may be able to spot needs for new products, to supply information about competitor activity, to pinpoint quality problems and to identify service deficiencies.

Previous marketing research

Although probably out of date, the findings from previous market investigations may be used as a benchmark for comparison with new findings, and trends may be plotted if the research has been continuous.

External data

Other forms of useful marketing data may come from a range of sources, some of which are available for consultation free of charge through public libraries and others of which are owned by private organisations who will make a charge for them.

Government statistics

In many countries throughout the world, governments publish statistics that have normally been collated to help them identify social and economic trends for the purpose of managing the economy and maintaining social welfare. UK statistics are considered to be some of the most accurate in the world and many of them are of direct relevance to businesses, the marketing function in particular (see Figure 4.1). The 'Business Monitor', for example, includes sales figures for different industries, and may enable a firm selling business to business to identify growing and declining market sectors. 'Social Trends' provides valuable information about consumer purchasing habits.

Trade associations and professional bodies
These usually represent the interests of the members of a particular industry or profession and may produce their own research on matters of common interest to those members. They may also provide (or sell) lists of members which may be of use as a sample population for conducting primary research in a specific industry sector. Other representative agencies produce research across a range of industrial sectors, including the Chambers of Commerce, the Confederation of British Industries and the British Institute of Management.

Universities
Because they are primarily research institutions, universities are excellent sources of objective data. They tend to keep good stocks of useful publications in their libraries, and their staff and students are continually engaged in undertaking new research, some of which is published in the form of theses and dissertations and not available elsewhere. Different universities tend to specialise in different subjects, so it is wise to start a secondary data search at an institution with strong links with the industry sector under investigation.

The trade press
The UK is well served by trade, technical, business, professional and academic journals, and many foreign journals are also published in the English language. These can be invaluable sources of information about competitor activities, new product launches, technological developments and customer trends. To take advantage of these, organisations should consider setting up well catalogued library systems to enable them to find the relevant material when it is needed.

figure 4.1
Government statistics

The bible for tracking down sources of government statistics is the *Guide to Official Statistics*, published every few years by HMSO.
This gives details of statistical information available, under the following headings:

1 General
2 Area, climate, environment
3 Population, vital statistics
4 Social statistics
5 Labour
6 Agriculture
7 Production industries
8 Transport
9 Distribution and other services
10 Public services
11 Prices
12 The Economy
13 General and public finance
14 Business and financial institutions
15 Overseas transactions
16 Isle of Man and the Channel Islands

Syndicated research and omnibus surveys

Commercial market research organisations regularly publish reports of their own investigations into particular markets or industries, which they sell either to subscribers or on the open market. This type of syndicated research tends to be available when the cost to any one organisation of generating the data would outweigh its benefits. By sharing the findings, everyone can benefit from information that would otherwise be unavailable. Continuous research is often syndicated due to the cost of collecting data over a long period of time. Media viewing, listening and readership profiles, for example, are useful to all advertisers to help them decide on the most cost-effective way of reaching their target audiences. Another means of cost sharing is by using omnibus surveys, which are regular interviews with large samples of consumers conducted by market research firms, who subcontract questions to anyone wishing to ask specific questions related to their own products

DID YOU KNOW?

Many European omnibus surveys sample only 1,000 people, and their classification of respondents is not always helpful. German research firms include 'civil servant' as a single occupation, but this may include everyone from government adviser to dustman. To purchase six questions on a face-to-face omnibus survey of 2,000 adults in the UK costs around £4,000, but the same questions would be 75 per cent more expensive in France and three times the price in Scandinavia. (Driving omnibuses, 1993).

Uses for secondary data

Internal and external data are commonly used for four purposes:

▶ To help clarify a problem, for example what exactly should we be investigating?

▶ To provide a background to a problem, for example a framework that puts the problem in context.

▶ To provide a benchmark for comparison with other research, for example to confirm or question the validity of new findings.

▶ To provide an answer to a problem, for example the problem has already been investigated by somebody else and the findings are available.

Whenever secondary data prove insufficient for reaching conclusions related to the research objectives, primary data must be generated.

Collecting primary data

Surveys are very useful and effective tools for collecting certain types of primary data and the final part of this chapter looks at the techniques associated specifically with this data collection method. However, a survey is but one of a range of methods available for generating primary data and is by no means the best in all circumstances. It is a very blunt instrument for conducting qualitative research, for example where the nuances of behaviour patterns, attitudes and motivations may be lost in the attempts to make respondents conform to a predetermined mechanism for answering questions. It is also dependent upon respondents telling a researcher what they do, or think, or feel, though they may be unwilling or unable to give truthful answers. The research will be misleading unless their responses reflect their actions.

CASE STUDY **4.3**
• • • • • • • • • • • • • • •

Focus groups meet in cyberspace

Market research among teenagers and children is invaluable in helping marketers to position their brands, but getting useful information from youngsters can require a different approach from adults. Family group discussions are useful, as they flush out some of the interaction between family members that can influence purchase decisions. Face-to-face depth interviews are a further means of revealing the subtle tactics used by this group to influence parents. Focus groups, however, normally produce poor results. Young members tend to be intimidated by the environment and produce monosyllabic answers rather than constructive discussion. 'Peer pairs' – two youths who know each other and sit with an interviewer – tend to work better up until the age of 14.

But all this is set to change. Researchers in the US are setting up panels of 8–12 year olds on the Network with a view to conducting on-line focus groups. Claims are being made that this approach is both faster and cheaper than traditional face-to-face research. It also has the advantage of visual anonymity which can encourage youngsters to put forward their views. Although they may be more succinct with their words, they are more likely to reveal their inner personalities. Critics of this approach argue that researchers lose one of the most useful sources of information in qualitative research – namely the body language, facial expressions and interaction between members of the group. The response to them is that the benefits outweigh the drawbacks.

One organisation that is unlikely to embrace the technique unreservedly is the Market Research Society, whose Code of Conduct requires special care being taken when interviewing children, and insists on permission to participate in research being granted by parents or teachers.

Questions
1 What types of information would be difficult to collect through the Internet?
2 Could the Internet be useful for issuing questionnaires? How useful would the responses be?
3 Draw up a code of practice for researchers wishing to use the Internet for focus groups.

Sources: Cramp 1995; Miller, 1994.

In fact there are many ways to collect primary data, and it is important that the most appropriate method is used for the type of research being conducted. Four commonly used techniques include the following.

Observation
This technique involves watching people, their behaviour and their actions, or observing the results of those actions. It is a particularly useful technique in situations where people find it difficult to give accurate verbal accounts of their behaviour. Suppose, for example, the research objectives were to identify the most common route taken by shoppers through a supermarket. Few people would be able to accurately report their movements after their visit, but watching their progress through the store on closed-circuit TV provides all the data a researcher needs. This is an example of *covert* observation, with the shopper being unaware that the observation is taking place.

DID YOU KNOW?
When Eurotunnel wanted information to help predict the volume of freight traffic that could potentially use the Channel Tunnel, it stationed a researcher with a clipboard on the cliffs overlooking Dover harbour to count and identify the trucks that were currently using the ferry services.

Overt observation can also be useful. One way of measuring the impact of press or TV advertising is to monitor a viewer's pulse and eye movement when exposed to the advert, to assess levels of interest and see how much attention is given to the brand name (though, of course, this gives no indication as to whether the person liked or disliked the advert, or had favourable or unfavourable attitudes towards the brand). Another example is the observation of users that may take place before the launch of a new product, such as a computer program, to find out how easy it is to use and identify aspects of the software that need to be improved. TV viewing figures are calculated by attaching monitors to TV sets in a sample range of households. The monitor indicates whether a set is on or off, and which channels it is tuned to at every second of the day. (More on this in Chapter 10.)

Indirect observation is concerned with observing the consequences of actions. Dustbin checks are an example of this. A selected sample of consumers (known as a panel) are paid to collect their domestic refuse in special sacks, which are taken away on a regular basis so that the consumption patterns of household products (as opposed to purchasing patterns) can be inferred from the discarded packaging.

DID YOU KNOW?

Secret filming in stores has revealed that shoppers do not acclimatise until they are about two-thirds of their way through a supermarket, so promotions by the door are relatively ineffectual. Hidden cameras on the shelves are used to reveal how packaging determines choice (Langton, 1995; Snowdon, 1995).

Experimentation

This technique is concerned with measuring the relationship between two marketing variables that are thought to be related in some way. Using a technique borrowed from the sciences, the researcher will set up an experiment by initiating some sort of marketing activity on a small scale and monitoring the results. Attempts are made to keep all other factors constant, so as to be certain that any divergence from the norm stems from the marketing activity undertaken.

Suppose, for example, a food retail chain wanted to assess the price sensitivity of its own-brand products. The objective of an experiment would be to identify the relationship between sales of own-brand items and prices. The hypothesis might be that a ten per cent increase in prices would lead only to a five per cent fall in sales volume (this information may encourage the retailer to increase prices, as it would lead to increase in sales revenue). The experiment could be conducted by recording normal sales levels for a range of own-brand items over a period of a week in all stores and raising the prices of those items by ten per cent in a sample of stores the following week. Electronic point-of-sale check-outs allow a rapid calculation of any differences in sales volume during the second week and statistical techniques can be used to decide whether there is sufficient evidence to accept the hypothesis. The extent to which 'extraneous' factors (perhaps the weather, or school holidays) would have affected results anyway can be assessed by comparing sales patterns for the second week in the non-experiment stores with the previous week. Provided there is no evidence to suggest that the sales trends observed have occurred everywhere, and not just in the stores with the higher prices, the retailer can be confident of the findings.

Unstructured interview

Qualitative data are often collected by means of unstructured interviews. Instead of using a formal response mechanism (such as a questionnaire) for recording respondents' views, the unstructured interview is used to probe beneath the surface of responses and encourages respondents to express their attitudes and motivations, rather than just their superficial views or observations. As a result, this technique is highly sensitive to the individual being questioned. The responses given cannot be quantified or assumed to be representative of others, but they are useful for giving the researcher deeper understanding of the issues under investigation. Two different approaches can be used to conduct unstructured interviews, namely the depth interview and the focus group.

Depth interviews

These are prolonged one-to-one interviews during which the interviewer asks questions on a series of topics, but is free to phrase the questions as seems most appropriate and to return to the most interesting points raised by respondents and probe them further. The interviewer has nothing more than a check-list of issues to explore and will use open-ended questions to encourage a full and explanatory response from the interviewee. Interviewers are a critical part of the research process in this type of investigation. The more skilled they are at leading respondents from topic to topic, and from the general to the specific, the more chance there is of getting to the bottom of hidden attitudes, motivations and opinions. Good interviewers are also aware of the non-verbal behaviour of their subjects, and will monitor and record the signals given out.

Focus group

This type of research (also known as group discussion) involves an interviewer, known as a moderator, chairing a discussion among a group of six to eight respondents. The moderator has a minimal role in the discussion and simply intervenes to keep the conversation on the right lines, preventing it from wandering away from relevant topics and acting as a catalyst for new ideas when a subject is exhausted. The whole discussion is recorded on tape, preferably video so that the non-verbal behaviour accompanying the decision can be monitored. The sound track should always be transcribed word-for-word before interpretation to retain as much objectivity as possible, and quotations can be selectively used to support any observations.

The greatest advantage of focus groups comes from the effects of group dynamics, which stimulate members to reveal beliefs and views that may not have been so freely expressed in one-to-to interviews. The group situation also reflects the fact that many of the buying decisions people make are in reality influenced by the views of others. Conversely, though, if the ambience of the location is thought to be intimidating or the group comprises some dominant individuals, less assertive individuals may be unwilling to participate fully, and one of the most important tasks for the moderator will be to encourage everyone to give personal views, rather than simply conform to the norms of the group.

DID YOU KNOW?
Focus groups are often conducted behind one-way mirrors to allow researchers to observe the non-verbal behaviour of the participants during the discussion. Although the group is told they are being watched, they soon forget this. One respondent is reported to have walked up to the mirror at the end of a session, checked her face and then pulled up her blouse to adjust her bra (Rooms with a view, 1994).

Survey

If research requires quantitative data to be generated, it is likely that a survey will be required. This is a data collection method based on a questionnaire. Identical questions are asked of a large number of individuals and a systematic record is made of their responses. The following section examines the whole issue of conducting a survey, from design and implementation through to analysis and interpretation.

Conducting a survey
....

The survey is a tool for generating quantitative data and the findings tend to be used for generalising about the behaviour, attitudes and opinions of whole populations. It is therefore important that the way in which the survey is conducted does not bias the responses and that the data collected are indeed a reflection of the views of the whole population and not just a few individuals.

The most effective way of conducting a survey is to progress methodically through a series of key activities (see Figure 4.2).

1 Set survey objectives and identify data required

It is essential that a survey starts with a clear set of objectives that indicate precisely what information needs to be generated. This in turn enables the researcher to draw up a list of data requirements, which will form the basis for

figure 4.2
Key stages in conducting a survey

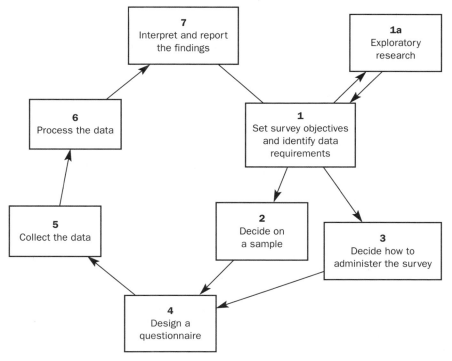

Source: Hill et al. (1995)

the questions to be asked. If it is difficult to state the objectives clearly at this stage, perhaps because the nature of the problem that prompted the survey in the first place is still unclear, it may be wise or even essential to conduct some exploratory research to refine the focus for the survey.

2 Decide on a sample

Surveys rely on the mathematical principle that the views expressed by a relatively small number of people (known as a *sample*) will be representative of a much wider group of people if the sample is of a certain size and composition. The researcher has to consider three parameters in deciding on the most appropriate sample for a particular survey.

The sampling frame

This is a term that describes the *type* of person to be questioned in the survey. The sex, age and other personal characteristics of potential respondents may be relevant, depending on the objectives of the survey. Should males, females or both be questioned? Should the sample contain all age groups or only certain age groups? Should the respondents have to fulfil certain criteria? The sampling frame for a survey of dog food preferences, for example, is likely to consist solely of dog owners. All the people who are members of a sample frame for a particular survey are known as the 'population', or sometimes the 'population of interest'.

The sampling procedure

The next decision concerns who, from within the sample frame, should be selected to answer the survey questions. This can be done in one of two ways:

▶ *Random sampling* (also known as 'probability sampling') is a process that first of all identifies by name every single member of the population of interest and approaches a proportion of them completely at random. As each member of the population has an equal chance of being selected and there is no bias in the selection process, this sampling procedure enables researchers to gain a very accurate reflection of the views of the population. In reality, the practical difficulties and costs involved in identifying every member of a population and getting responses from all of those who are randomly identified normally outweigh the benefits of high accuracy. Take the dog food example. Dog ownership is registered in the UK, so theoretically the population of interest should be easy to identify. But in reality, not all dog owners bother to buy a licence so the population of interest will be an incomplete list, and of those on the list, some may be unwilling to respond to the survey questions. Both of these factors will reduce the reliability and accuracy of the findings.

▶ Due to the high costs and logistical difficulties of finding a random sample, *non-probability sampling* is far more common. This is a term given to all sampling procedures that are not completely random. Normally they involve interviewers using their own judgement to select a sample, and this human intervention in the selection procedure introduces bias. With non-probability techniques, six times as many people need to be questioned to achieve the same levels of certainty given in a random sample. If large samples are not used, then sampling error creeps in, and the survey findings will be less trustworthy in terms of predicting the behaviour of the whole population and providing a firm basis for decision-making. There are three popular non-probability sampling methods.

▶ *Convenience sampling* occurs when an interviewer selects the most available members of the population of interest. Bias creeps in here as certain members of the population are more likely to be available and willing to respond than others, so the responses may be disproportionately taken from people with similar characteristics, attitudes and motivations.

▶ *Quota sampling* aims to cut down bias by requiring that the interviewer find a prescribed number of respondents in each of several categories. For example, a survey into holiday preferences may require interviewers to find equal proportions of male and female respondents, a target number of respondents from different age groups and a specific proportion who have children.

▶ *Self-selection sampling* is the least reliable form of sampling. Respondents are not chosen by an interviewer, but decide themselves whether or not to complete a questionnaire and participate in the survey. Consequently, the sample tends to consist of those who have strong views about the subject being researched and the findings tend to polarise and reveal extreme attitudes and behaviour patterns only. Nonetheless, this type of sampling can enable large volumes of data to be collected very cheaply, so the benefits from the findings may outweigh the disadvantage of inaccuracy in some situations.

DID YOU KNOW?

The National Readership Survey is one of the largest consumer surveys in the UK. Each year, 35,000 people are randomly selected to respond to a questionnaire about the newspapers and magazines they read. Addresses are taken from the Post Office Address File – a list of all homes in the country. When a researcher arrives at a house, a further random selection is made from all the adults in the household. If the chosen adult is not at home, the researcher must return at another time – another member of the household will not be acceptable ('Horizon', 1993).

The sample size

There is no hard-and-fast rule as to the best size for a sample. It will depend on the size of the population, on the sampling procedure used, on the desired accuracy of results, and on cost, time and logistical limitations. As a rule-of-thumb, though, except in the case of very large populations of interest, figures of over 500 fully completed questionnaires usually give the researcher some confidence that the responses given reflect the views of more than just those who answered the questions. Certainly if the sample is any smaller than 500 it is difficult to make reliable comparisons between sub-sections of the populations, such as the difference between the views of men and women, or different age groups.

CASE STUDY **4.4**

Unlucky seven?

1992 was the seventh time that opinion polls had been used to predict the outcome of a General Election in Britain, and the first to get the result quite dramatically wrong. On the day of the election, the pollsters were predicting a hung parliament or possibly a Labour victory. When the Conservatives swept home with a 21-seat majority, predictions were discovered to have been out by around 8.5 per cent. With a sample of 1,500 people having been surveyed from a population of 40 million adult voters, statistical theory suggests that the responses of a representative sample should have reflected the views of the whole population to within 2.5 per cent. So what went wrong?

A number of explanations were put forward. The researchers were quick to point out that polls are not barometers of human behaviour, but simply measures of current opinions and views. Some blamed the inaccuracy of the predictions on floating voters who made a late switch to supporting the Tories. Others were willing to recognise that their system of quota sampling may have let them down. Samples for the opinion polls were taken in 100 constituencies, selected at random. Interviewers were allocated to each area and required to ask questions of 15 people, who had to meet a number of criteria which would ensure that the sample was as representative as possible of the constituency as a whole. The criteria related to gender, age, social class and employment status.

Various hypotheses have since been put forward for the failure of this sample to represent the true intentions of the population. It may have been that those who refused to co-operate with the survey were more likely to be Conservative voters, perhaps disaffected by issues such as the poll tax and unwilling to admit their intentions. Age and sex is now thought to have little influence on voting behaviour. Social class is much more influential, but difficult to define, and many in the sample may have been wrongly classified.

A better predictor of voting intentions is past voting behaviour, but even this creates problems for the pollsters. People forget who they voted for in previous elections and tend to think they voted for the winning party. This is a particular problem in predicting support for minority parties. Half the people who voted Liberal in the 1975 election had either forgotten or were unwilling to own up to this by the time the 1979 election came around!

Questions

1   Why might voters deliberately or inadvertently mislead researchers in opinion polls? Could this also happen in consumer surveys?
2   Is it possible for researchers to improve their predictive performance at the next election? If so, how?
3   Does qualitative research have a role in predicting election results? Should it?

Source 'Horizon', 1993.

ACTIVITY **4.1**

Slicing the cake!

'You don't have to eat the whole cake to know what it tastes like!' Market researchers use this analogy to explain the use of samples to represent the views of a whole population. Statistical techniques enable us to predict just how similar to the population a sample will be. The size of the sample is critical to accuracy. An estimate of the population's response can be calculated from the sample's response by adding or subtracting the percentages given in the table below. So, from a random sample of 1,000, if the response rate from the sample is 30 per cent, the response for the whole population would fall somewhere between 27 per cent and 33 per cent.

Sample size	Response from sample				
	10%	20%	30%	40%	50%
100	6.0%	8.0%	9.0%	10.0%	10.0%
500	3.0%	4.0%	4.0%	4.0%	4.0%
1,000	2.0%	2.0%	3.0%	3.0%	3.0%
2,000	1.3%	1.8%	2.0%	2.1%	2.2%
4,000	0.9%	1.2%	1.4%	1.5%	1.5%

The table shows how the responses given by the sample more accurately reflect the views of the population as sample sizes increase. A sample of 500 can reflect the views of the whole population with at least twice the accuracy of a sample of 100.

Suppose an opinion poll is conducted among students to predict who is likely to be elected in the forthcoming Union elections. A random sample of 100 is taken from the enrolment list. When asked who they will vote for, the sample gives the following responses:

Frank Stein	31%
Jack Ripper	10%
Justin Time	36%
Daisy Roots	21%
no answer	2%

1   Do you think Justin Time will win the election?
2   Suppose 1,000 people had given these responses, not 100. How would this affect your prediction?
3   Suppose a quota sample of 1,000 were used instead of a random sample of the same size. How would this affect your prediction?
4   Suppose 20 per cent had refused to answer, rather than two per cent. How would this affect your prediction?

3 Decide how to administer the survey

There are four main types of survey, each with their own advantages and drawbacks.

Interview surveys

Face-to-face interviews, using the standardised framework of a questionnaire, are usually the most reliable way of obtaining accurate data from a large sample. The presence of an interviewer is shown to increase the likelihood of a respondent completing a questionnaire, and the response rate is found to be higher than for other data collection methods. This method also enables respondents to clarify any questions that are not understood and they can be shown visual aids such as advertising materials if required. However, as with depth interviews and focus groups, the skill of the interviewer will affect the quality of the results. 'The interviewer is, on the one hand trying to be "standard" in all his or her approaches to respondents, but, on the other hand, may need to react to individual circumstances for the successful completion of the interview – in short, the interviewer needs to act like a robot but retain the appearance of a human being' (Kent, 1993). Bias may arise simply from the process of social interaction, with misunderstandings between interviewer and respondent arising from differences in age, sex, social class, dress, accent or personality.

Telephone surveys

Telephone interviews can be conducted fairly quickly, with interviewers under close supervision if required. If the questionnaire is fairly short, the telephone survey can be a relatively inexpensive way of collecting data; the cost of making the calls is likely to be lower than the expenses incurred by face-to-face interviewers. However, this technique quite obviously depends on respondents being on the phone and this fact alone may mean that a telephone survey is inappropriate in certain circumstances due to the bias it would introduce into the sample. It has other limitations too. The questions must be very simple to enable respondents to understand them quickly and without the use of visual aids. Interviewers need to be particularly skilled, as visual communication is excluded.

Mail surveys

Mail surveys are usually very inexpensive, incurring neither interviewer nor telephone costs. They can reach scattered populations easily and, if anonymous, respondents may give more honest answers to sensitive questions than they would face to face or over the phone. Interviewer bias is eliminated and because respondents can complete them at a time to suit themselves, they are usually willing to fill in longer questionnaires. There are, however, a number of serious disadvantages to this method of data collection, and whether or not this type of survey is cost effective is less clear. Sampling is difficult to control, as response rates are likely to be low and the researcher has no control over who finally fills in the questionnaire. It may take a long time for responses to be received and some of these may be incomplete as there is no interviewer to clarify questions or encourage completion.

A lot of research has been undertaken to identify the factors that most encourage response to mail surveys. One of the most significant motivators is the inclusion of a covering letter that gives some background to the research, assures anonymity (or at least confidentiality) and gives clear instructions as to how to complete and return the questionnaire. A reply-paid envelope is essential in consumer surveys, and an incentive to respond, such as an entry in a prize draw or some discount vouchers, can also raise response rates. It can also help to send out reminders and a second copy of the questionnaire two or three weeks after the original one, making sure that accurate records are kept to enable those who have replied to be excluded from the follow-up.

Self-completion surveys

Probably the least expensive method of all, the self-completion survey, is a useful technique to use on a discrete and 'captive' population. It is commonly used to elicit views from those travelling on a train, boat or plane, or sitting in a cinema or theatre seat. Questionnaires are distributed to the whole population, though there is no interviewer; respondents are simply asked to fill them in themselves and return them before they leave. It is also a method used by magazines and regional newspapers conducting simple polls on social or local issues. Readers are invited to complete a questionnaire included in the publication and return it by a certain date. As explained earlier, sampling error is very likely to creep in as those most likely to bother to complete the questionnaires are those who hold the strongest views on the subject being investigated. Unless efforts are made by the researcher to encourage response from a representative sample, the findings may be worthless.

4 Design a questionnaire

Questionnaire design is critical to the findings of any survey. The style, length and layout of the questionnaire must be considered. Shorter questionnaires are generally better than longer ones, but there is no hard and fast rule as to how many questions should be asked. This will depend primarily on the objectives of the survey, but also the data collection method. Layout is important too. Respondents must be given enough space so as not to be forced to shorten their responses.

The wording of individual questions is equally important. Each question should be evaluated against a series of criteria before its inclusion in the questionnaire. Questions should be:

▶ *Relevant* – so that the questionnaire length can be kept to a minimum, only those questions that will provide data to help reach the objectives of the survey should be included.

▶ *Clear* – technical jargon, complex terminology, long words and ambiguous statements must all be avoided. Respondents who do not understand a question will either miss it out altogether or, worse still, guess at its meaning and give a response to the question that they *think* is being asked, which may be quite different from what was intended.

▶ *Inoffensive* – questions relating to sensitive issues such as salary, age, social class and ethnicity may be thought offensive unless worded carefully. These types of questions should be placed at the end of the questionnaire, to be answered after the respondent has built up a rapport with the interviewer (if any) and has already made a commitment to completing the questionnaire and is less likely to be put off.

▶ *Brief* – the meaning of questions of more than 20 words in length can be difficult for respondents to grasp quickly, particularly in an interview.

▶ *Precise* – each question should tackle only one issue at a time. If two issues are introduced, the respondent may have different views on the two issues but will be prevented from separating these if a single overall response is requested.

▶ *Impartial* – the wording or phrasing of questions can carry overtones that influence respondents to respond in a particular way. These are known as leading questions and should be avoided at all costs.

Before a questionnaire is administered, it should be tested on a very small number of people who are typical of the people to be included in the sample. This is know as the pilot stage, and is very important in ensuring that the questionnaire is adequate for collecting the data required. Questions that seem very straightforward to the researcher can be found confusing, incomprehensible or even offensive to the respondent!

ACTIVITY **4.2**
....

Asking the right questions

The manager of a small regional theatre is under pressure to generate more income from ticket sales. The problem is that people aren't coming to see 'good' plays, but are only interested in pantomimes and well-known musicals. The trustees believe that to generate more money, the theatre will have to put on a more popular programme. The manager has been resisting this idea and thinks that ticket prices should be raised instead, but he has agreed to conduct an audience survey to help him decide what to do next. This is the questionnaire he has designed.

1   Which age group are you in?
     1–16   ☐   40–50   ☐
     16–21   ☐   50–60   ☐
     21–30   ☐   60 +   ☐
     30–40   ☐

2   What is your occupation? ....

3   What is your income?
     Under £5,000   ☐   £25,000–£30,000   ☐
     £5,000–£10,000   ☐   £30,000–£35,000   ☐
     £10,000–£15,000   ☐   £35,000–£40,000   ☐
     £15,000–£20,000   ☐   over £40,000   ☐
     £20,000–£25,000   ☐

4   How often do you come to this theatre?
     Once a month   ☐
     Once every three months   ☐
     Once a year   ☐

5   What sort of theatrical performances have you been to in the past three years?
     a At this theatre

     ....

     ....

     b At other theatres

     ....

     ....

6   How much are you willing to pay for a theatre ticket?
     Up to £3   ☐   £10 to £15   ☐
     £3 to £5   ☐   Over £15   ☐
     £5 to £10   ☐

7   'The role of this theatre is to provide the local community with theatrical performances that have artistic merit.'
     Agree / Disagree

a What is wrong with each of these questions?
b What is wrong with the ordering of these questions?
c How would you select a sample for the survey?
d Design a questionnaire that would be more useful to the manager in deciding what to do next.

Question techniques

There are a wide range of tried and tested styles for survey questions.

Open-ended questions

These allow respondents to provide answers using their own words, collecting data with the minimum of direction to respondents. This can be useful if the range of possible responses is very wide. Also, as people use their own words, they have the scope to articulate their true feelings more accurately than if they are constrained to a limited range of options. The main disadvantage of open-ended questions arises when they have to be interpreted. To enable them to be processed using computer software, all the responses have to be read and categorised in a process known as *coding*. Inevitably some responses will be ambiguous and difficult to code, introducing bias at this stage. Examples of open-ended questions are:

How would you improve the service offered by your supermarket?

What is your opinion of German cars?

Closed questions

Also known as 'closed-ended', 'forced-choice' or 'fixed-response' questions, these provide a limited number of possible responses that the respondent must choose between. Respondents tend to find these easier to complete than open questions and they are easier to code, so most surveys use predominantly this type of question to maintain high response rates.

Closed questions tend to be of one of three types:

▶ *Multiple response questions* offer a range of possible answers for respondents to choose between. Sometimes they are required to choose just one, and sometimes they can identify as many as are relevant, for example:

What is your age? (tick one only)
Under 18 ☐   18–64 ☐   65 or over ☐

Have you ever been to the following countries? (tick as many as apply)
France ☐   Germany ☐   Belgium ☐   The Netherlands ☐

Sometimes a category has to be included for those who are unable to respond (the 'don't know' box), and if there is some doubt as to whether all possible responses have been identified in advance, space should be provided for respondents to write in their own answers (the 'other' box), so that the answers can be coded when the results are analysed, for example:

Where did you last buy eggs?
Supermarket ☐   Butcher ☐   Greengrocer ☐   Farm ☐
Have never bought eggs ☐   Don't know ☐
Other (please specify)..

Closed questions offering only two options such as 'yes/no' or 'true/false' tend to be of limited use, as it is usually possible to find a different question style that elicits more information. The only important exception to this is when dealing with mutually exclusive categories such as gender.

▶ *Scaled questions* enable respondents to express the strength of their attitudes and opinions. Bipolar questions put forward widely differing opinions on a subject and invite respondents to place their own view somewhere between the two extremes offered, for example:

How do you rate the new flavour (of a food product)?
Much too sweet ☐
A little too sweet ☐
About the right sweetness ☐
Not quite sweet enough ☐
Not nearly sweet enough ☐

Another technique is to ask people to indicate the extent to which they agree or disagree with a particular statement. This is useful for measuring attitudes, for example:

To what extent do you agree or disagree with the following statement:
'It is impolite for women to drink pints of beer.'
Agree strongly ☐
Agree slightly ☐
Neither agree nor disagree ☐
Disagree slightly ☐
Disagree strongly ☐

A numbered scale can also be used to identify perceptions, using a question format known as Semantic Differential. Words of opposite meaning are placed at either end of the scale and respondents are asked to indicate their position between the two extremes, for example:

Compared with my own car, this car is:

Very quiet	1	2	3	4	5	6	7	Very noisy
Very attractive	1	2	3	4	5	6	7	Very ugly
Very cheap	1	2	3	4	5	6	7	Very expensive

The main problem with scaled questions is that respondents are reluctant to express very strong opinions and tend to avoid the first and last categories in any list. This reduces the ability of these types of questions to capture true attitudes and opinions, which is why unstructured interviews are so useful for this task.

▶ *Ordering questions* enable respondents to express preferences and indicate priorities. Simple preference questions ask for one or more attributes or categories to be of more importance than others, but note that a box must be offered to accommodate those who are unwilling or unable to make a selection, for example:

Which three of the following reasons were most influential in your choice of University course?

Reputation of the institution ☐
Recommendation of friends / family ☐
Geographical location ☐
Nature of the course ☐
Accommodation provision ☐
Advice from careers officer ☐
Academic and social facilities ☐
Other (please specify)...
Can't say ☐

Ranking questions take respondents one step further by asking them to prioritise their preferences. In the example given above, respondents could have been asked to rank the influences in order, but this would have been a difficult task for such a long list. Ranking should be limited to short lists only, and even then it must be recognised that the intervals between ranked items may not be equal (the item ranked first may be seen as far more important than the rest of the list, with the others being seen as having almost equal importance).

5 Collect the data

The data collection method has already been identified by this stage (see stage 3) so the survey is ready to be administered. Interviewers must be briefed and trained for face-to-face and telephone data collection, and administrative systems must be set up for self-completion and mail surveys. If good preparation has been undertaken, this can be a very straightforward part of the research process.

DID YOU KNOW?
The Code of Conduct of the Market Research Society states that 'No activity shall be misrepresented as research'. It specifically outlaws 'sugging' (selling under the guise of market research), 'frugging' (fund-raising under the guise of market research), and a number of other practices that undermine public confidence in market research, and make it more difficult for genuine researchers to persuade the public to respond to their questions.

6 Process the data

Data processing converts 'raw data' (ie the responses given on the questionnaires) into a form that enables their underlying meaning to be identified. A range of computer software is available to make this task easier. A specialist data processing house may be required if sample sizes are large and the data are complex, but small businesses and those on low budgets can select from a number of relatively inexpensive packages to enable them to do the data processing themselves.

Data processing comprises three main stages:

▶ *Data input*: this involves the responses from each questionnaire being typed into the computer. It is a laborious process that requires no particular aptitude, though accurate keyboard skills are important for speeding up the process and avoiding the introduction of errors at this stage. Many interviewers now carry lap-top computers for instantaneous data entry, eliminating this time-consuming and expensive stage.

▶ *Data summary*: the computer will take the raw data and summarise how many people said what in response to each question. This is known as the *frequency* of the responses. As the sample has been designed to be representative of the whole population of interest, it can then be stated with some confidence that the frequency of response observed in the sample applies to the whole population. Visual displays of the data, in the form of pie-charts, histograms and tables, can then be produced to depict the frequencies more visually.

The computer is also able to calculate some summary statistics relating to the observed frequencies. The mean (arithmetic average), mode (most popular response) and median (mid-point of all the responses) can all help the researcher draw conclusions about the population. The dispersion (or standard deviation) of the findings is also important. The mean of a sample does not in itself imply that 'most people' hold a certain view. The dispersion of the views held must also be considered, as it indicates whether the mean was arrived at as a result of many people having similar views, or whether people have wide ranging views on a subject so that the average is simply a half-way position on a very long scale. The larger the standard deviation, the wider the range of opinions on a subject.

ACTIVITY **4.3**

What does the mean mean?
Suppose 20 people were asked the extent to which they agreed or disagreed with the following statements:

Statement 1
The government should allow alcohol to be sold to anyone aged 16 or over.

Statement 2
The blood alcohol limit for drivers should be zero.

1 = strongly agree
2 = agree slightly
3 = neither agree nor disagree
4 = disagree slightly
5 = strongly disagree

Twenty people's responses to the two statements might be as follows:

Statement 1
5, 5, 3, 3, 1, 1, 4, 4, 1, 2, 4, 5, 2, 1, 1, 5, 4, 5, 2, 2

Statement 2
3, 1, 5, 4, 2, 2, 3, 4, 2, 2, 4, 4, 3, 3, 4, 1, 2, 4, 4, 3

1   Calculate the mean for each of these sets of responses.
2   Calculate the standard deviation for each of these sets of responses (this can be done on a calculator or computer).
3   Explain what the differences between the two sets of figures imply in terms of respondent attitudes.
4   Why, in this example, would it be unwise to generalise about attitudes to teenage drinking and drink-driving?

▶ *Data analysis*: this involves the use of statistical techniques to identify interrelationships between the answers given, both within a single question and between different questions. Cross-tabulation, for example, is used to highlight any differences in the responses from different sectors of the sample. Do men and women hold similar views on a particular issue? Do young people have different attitudes from older people? These types of investigation can be undertaken with relative ease provided that the data have been input properly into appropriate computer software.

7 Interpreting and reporting findings

At this final stage, conclusions have to be drawn from the facts and figures in such a way as to create information that relates to the objectives set, and this information has to be communicated to marketing decision-makers. This is usually done in the form of a written report which is presented orally and followed by a discussion.

The interpretation of data and the reporting of findings should be approached cautiously. Surveys produce a wide range of facts and figures, some of which are of little or no help in achieving the objectives set. These should be omitted from the report. Sufficient detail should be given to enable the decision-maker to act with confidence, but too much information is confusing and some responses may not need to be explored in detail. For example, there is no need to list all the responses to open questions, and if a large number of small frequency responses are given to a closed question, some of the categories may be collapsed into one and reported under the heading 'other responses'. Graphical illustrations can be useful for highlighting trends or relationships, but key issues should be discussed in accompanying text as well.

CASE STUDY **4.5**
• • • • • • • • • • • • • • • • • •

Levi's ignores the signals

Keen to move away from its dependence on the market for jeans, Levi's US introduced a range of clothing including shirts, socks and shoes. But the customer base for these products was firmly among those who were already buying Levi's jeans, and the company wanted to move up-market into the market for higher-priced items. Menswear was seen as the most appropriate starting point, as that had always been the biggest selling range.

A market research firm was commissioned to conduct exploratory research into the menswear market. Five types of buyer were identified, including the two groups that contained current Levi's customers – namely the 'Utilitarians' who wear jeans for both work and leisure, and the 'Trendy Casuals', who tend to buy designer fashions, and might buy 501s but not standard cuts which are considered too mass-market. The group that interested Levi's, however, was the 'Classic Independents'. Comprising 21 per cent of the market, this group is described as a 'real clothes horse', has expensive tastes and an interest in quality. Further investigation revealed that these men like traditionally styled suits and buy through independent shops or tailors rather than chain stores. They also like to shop alone.

Armed with this research, Levi's started planning to introduce a range of high-quality wool suits called 'Tailored Classics' and set up distribution through department stores. A psychologist was subsequently engaged to conduct focus groups that would test out the acceptability of this concept on the target market. Members of the groups displayed serious misgivings about two key elements of the strategy. First they felt that off-the-peg suits would not give them the tailoring they required, and second, they found it difficult to accept that the name 'Levi's' could be associated with suits, rather than jeans. But Levi's director of consumer marketing chose to interpret only the positive feedback from the session, and expressed confidence that the brand name would be an asset to the range when people realised how good the clothes were. It was decided that by focusing more on jackets and trousers, resistance to the concept of a Levi's suit could be overcome.

The sales force soon started selling into the targeted retail outlets, but in less than four months it was clear that targets were not going to be met. Even after a price cut, 'Tailored Classics' only met 65 per cent of their sales targets and the range was discontinued shortly after.

Questions

1　Why do you think the company's marketing executives were unable to accept and act upon the concerns of the psychologist?
2　How might quantitative research have been used to probe the findings of the focus group more closely?
3　Could the same sort of misinterpretation be made even after quantitative research?

Source Marcouse and Lines, 1990.

Throughout the reporting of the findings, it should be made clear that it is impossible to make predictions with certainty based on a survey. No survey is absolutely definitive. Unless sample sizes are exceptionally large, sampling error alone makes it impossible to state categorically that the behaviour, attitudes and opinions of the sample are representative of the whole population of interest. To reflect this uncertainty, frequencies should usually be reported as integers rather than giving decimal places. The means, modes and medians observed in the data should be recognised as indicators of average views, and not as representing the opinions of Mr and Mrs Average.

Not every reader will want to look at the whole report, so it is advisable to write an Executive Summary which should appear at the front of the report. This is merely a brief summary of the findings, and main conclusions from the research, and recommendations if appropriate. More complex analysis, tables and graphical representations should be kept until later.

Key concepts
· · · · · · · · · · · · · · · · ·

Ad hoc research: an investigation to provide information about a specific issue.
Closed question: a question that provides a limited number of possible answers for the respondent to choose between.
Continuous research: an investigation that is repeated on an intermittent basis over a period of time.

Desk research: the collection of secondary data.

Depth interview: a prolonged one-to-one interview in which the interviewer probes the answers given by respondents.

Experimentation: an investigation that measures the relationship between two marketing variables.

Frequency: a summary of the different responses to a question.

Focus group: a group interview conducted by a moderator.

Omnibus survey: a set of interviews with large sample of consumers conducted by market research firms on a regular basis.

Open-ended question: a question that allows respondents to reply in their own words.

Population: the total group of people from whom information would be useful.

Primary data: facts and figures that are collected specifically to provide information that will help achieve the research objectives.

Questionnaire: a standardised set of questions designed to gather data that are relevant to the research objectives.

Quantitative research: an investigation to discover how many people hold similar views or display particular characteristics.

Qualitative research: an investigation to generate information about how people feel and why they behave as they do.

Sample: a small proportion of the population whose views are representative of the views of the whole population.

Secondary data: facts and figures that are already available having been collected for another purpose or another organisation.

Survey: a data collection method that makes a systematic record of the responses of a number of people to the same questions.

Syndicated research: market research data that is generated by a market research firm and sold to many organisations.

SELF-CHECK QUESTIONS

1   Which of the following may be an internal source of secondary data?
   a The Chambers of Commerce.
   b A customer database.
   c Government statistics.
   d The trade press.
   e Syndicated research.

2   Which of these descriptions fits the following question?
   a A multiple response question.
   b A semantic differential.
   c A scaled question.
   d An open question.
   e A coded question.

   To what extent do you agree or disagree with the following statement: 'Students should be required to complete their degrees in two years.'?
   Strongly agree ☐
   Agree slightly ☐

Neither agree nor disagree ☐
Disagree slightly ☐
Disagree strongly ☐

3 The *frequency* of responses to questions is a term referring to:
  a The number of respondents.
  b The profile of the whole sample's responses to each question.
  c The population of interest.
  d The central tendency of the sample.
  e The size of a sample quota.

4 Which of the following would be described as exploratory objectives?
  a To determine the relationship between price and sales volume.
  b To calculate the market potential for a new product.
  c To identify the relative spending power of different market segments.
  d To investigate the possible reasons for a decrease in sales.
  e To create a profile of competitors' customers.

5 Which of the following are *not* appropriate in a focus group?
  a Video recording of the discussion.
  b Audio tape recording of the discussion.
  c Transcription of the discussion after the discussion.
  d An interviewee leads the discussion.
  e Timid individuals are encouraged to speak.

Which of the following are true and which are false?
  6 Primary data should be collected before secondary data.
  7 More respondents are needed for statistical accuracy with a random sample than with a non-probability sample.
  8 Qualitative research requires a large sample if it is to be statistically reliable.
  9 Information can be generated from data.
  10 Direct observation is less reliable than indirect observation.

Discuss the following:
  11 What are the main advantages and disadvantages of using syndicated research instead of collecting your own primary data?
  12 How would you sample students from your university or college if you were conducting a survey to identify perceptions of catering provision?
  13 Under what circumstances might you choose to conduct a telephone survey rather than use face-to-face interviews?
  14 Why might it be useful to calculate the mean, the mode, the median and the standard deviation of responses in a survey to identify customer attitudes towards a new product?
  15 Is it possible to collect too much marketing information?

Further study
·················

Books

There are many excellent text books available which look at marketing research in far more detail than this chapter.

Baker, Michael (1991) *Research for Marketing*, Macmillan.
Chisnall, Peter (1992) *Marketing Research* (4th ed.), McGraw Hill.
Kent, Raymond (1993) *Marketing Research in Action*, Routledge.

These three titles give a good theoretical framework for further study. The American texts on this subject tend to be rather more exciting, though, giving examples of marketing research in practice. Take a look at:

McDaniel, Carl and Gates, Roger (1993) *Contemporary Marketing Research*, (2nd ed.) West Publishing.

To complete a study of marketing research, it is important to be aware of the nature of the software available for data processing and analysis. One of the most popular and easy-to-use systems is 'SPSS for Windows', a low-price student version of which is published by Prentice Hall. This includes most of the functions of the full version (but only permits relatively small surveys to be conducted) and is available, complete with simple instruction manual.

References
··············

American Marketing Association (1961) *Report of Definitions Committee of the American Marketing Association*, American Marketing Association, Chicago.
BMRB International (1995) *TGI: The Guide*, Hadley House, 79–81 Uxbridge Road, Ealing, London W5 5SU.
Cramp, B. (1995) 'Fountain of youth', in *Marketing*, September 14, pp. 39–40.
'Driving omnibuses' (1993) in *Marketing Week*, July 9, pp. 33–4.
Fletcher, K. (1995) 'The data invasion', in *Marketing*, February 23, p. 31.
Griffiths, J. (1985) 'C5's road to the receiver', in *The Financial Times*, 15 October.
Hill, E, O'Sullivan, C. and O'Sullivan, T. (1995) *Creative Arts Marketing*, Butterworth-Heinemann.
Horizon (1993) , 'Suggers, fruggers and data-muggers', BBC2.
Kent, R. (1993) *Marketing Research in Action*, Routledge.
Kotler, P. and Armstrong, G. (1994) *Principles of Marketing*, Prentice Hall.
Langton, J. (1995) 'The unseen eye keeping watch over shop flaws' , in *The Sunday Telegraph*, 22 January, p. 11.
Marcouse, I. and Lines, D. (1990) 'Even Levi's can make mistakes', in *Business Case Studies*, Longman, pp. 35–7.
Marks, A. P. (1990) 'The Sinclair C5 – why did it fail?' in *Management Decision* (UK), vol. 28, iss. 4, pp. 9–14.
Miller, C. (1994) 'Focus groups go where none has been before', in *Marketing News*, vol. 28, iss. 14, July 4, p. 2, 14.

'Off your trolley with Loyd Grossman' (1995) BBC2.

'Rooms with a view' (1994) in *Marketing*, 17 November, p. XI.

Snowdon, R. (1995) 'Why JWT is now asking the obvious', in *Marketing*, 14 September, p. 16.

'The Twiglet Zone' (1995) in *Marketing*, 9 February, p. 23.

Tull and Hawkins (1992) *Industrial Marketing Research*, Kogan Page.

Target marketing

Objectives
. . . .

When you have read this chapter you will be able to:

▶ Distinguish between undifferentiated, product differentiated and target marketing.

▶ Identify ways in which a range of different markets could be segmented.

▶ Apply key assessment criteria to identify viable market segments.

▶ Discuss the relative advantages and disadvantages of concentration strategies and multi-segment marketing strategies.

▶ Explain the process of market positioning.

▶ Draw a perceptual map and evaluate the relative merits of different competitive strategies.

Introduction
. . . .

As a result of studying consumer behaviour and conducting market research, organisations often come to the conclusion that it is not possible or desirable for them to attempt to sell their products and services to all the potential customers in their markets. This may be because the potential market is so large that the organisation has insufficient resources to supply it; it may be because customers are geographically very scattered; it may be because competitors have a strong foothold; or it may be because customer requirements from the product or service vary widely. Under these circumstances, firms have to decide which types of customer to aim for and then target their products and services only at selected parts of the market (known as segments). *The process of identifying market segments, selecting one or more of them and developing a marketing mix to meet their needs is known as target marketing* and is the subject of this chapter. (See Figure 5.1.)

The development of target marketing
. . . .

The concept of target marketing has grown in importance as markets have grown and become more complex.

New markets often develop when a producer recognises common needs among potential customers and tries to meet those needs by producing products

figure 5.1
The process of target marketing

119

or services that satisfy as many people as possible. At this early stage in the development of the market it is usually possible to sustain an *undifferentiated* marketing strategy and produce a single product to satisfy the whole market. The example of the Model T Ford given in Chapter 1 illustrates this. This mass-market approach is seldom sustainable though. As a market grows, and in particular if competitors emerge with alternatives to the single product offered, it is usually found that some variations in the preferences of different customers emerge. In response to this, organisations sometimes adopt a *differentiated* strategy, producing different versions of the product, all still offering the core benefit but using a range of alternative features to give customers choice. The range extensions that are often introduced to food products are an example of this, offering different flavours to cater for different tastes.

> **DID YOU KNOW?**
> *Product variants are seldom more popular than their original version, but the exception to prove this rule is peppermint Aero, which has consistently outsold the original chocolate bar.*

The whole philosophy behind both undifferentiated and product differentiated marketing is to find sufficient similarities between customers to be able to sell products that will appeal widely across the whole market. (See Figure 5.2.)

A *target marketing* strategy takes a different approach. It starts off by recognising that different groups of customers often have different needs and may even want different core benefits from the same products. Rather than trying to satisfy these sub-groups with the same products, or different versions of the same products, complete marketing programmes are designed to meet the specific needs of the members of these sub-groups. Target marketing is an approach that concentrates on identifying similarities between customers but also *differences* between similar *groups* of customers. Again the motor car provides a good example here. Although most people thinking of buying a car are fundamentally looking for a means of transport of some sort, the key criteria they take in to consideration when deciding which model to buy may vary tremendously. For some people, the car is a means for reflecting their status; for some it is a means of saving time; others want it to give them the thrill and excitement of

figure 5.2
The development of target marketing

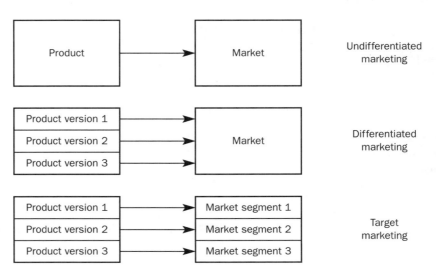

travelling at speed; and some may see it as no more than a business asset, perhaps for making deliveries. Each of these groups of customers is looking for something quite different when they decide to make a purchase. This enables the manufacturers to design a range of models and back them up with promotional campaigns to reinforce the ways in which these different models can satisfy different needs.

CASE STUDY **5.1**

Volvo stops playing it safe

Volvo has always been thought of as a safe bet. For year after year, advertising campaigns have reinforced the image of Volvo as a vehicle that will protect its drivers and passengers from misfortune. Images of dummies emerging unscathed from unspeakable accidents and advertising copy that talks about the 'crumple zone' have been used to target the safety conscious driver. It is no surprise, therefore, that Volvo consistently beats its rivals when customer perceptions of safety, durability and environmental friendliness are measured. But safety is not the only product attribute that interests drivers who could afford a Volvo, so other car manufacturers have emphasised the style, prestige and pleasure of driving their vehicles can offer, suggesting that safety is taken for granted. Recent research makes it clear that few customers perceive Volvo to be a stylish car that is exciting to drive – only seven per cent of their target market, as opposed to 60 per cent for BMW. The product's image has become one of a safe box on wheels, associated with worthy but dull family men – not one that is likely to lead to a sudden spurt in demand. The 44 per cent of drivers who reject the Volvo do so because it looks 'staid and boring'.

In an attempt to make the car attractive to a different (and larger) target market, Volvo has embarked on a major product update and programme of promotional activity. One of the TV adverts features a meteorologist using a Volvo to drive into the heart of a tornado to measure its force. It is an attempt to convince potential buyers that a Volvo is not only safe, but also exciting: risks can be taken safely. Press adverts boast that Volvos can accelerate faster than Porsches and Ferraris, and the emphasis on superior driveability is reinforced by involvement in the British Touring Car Championships.

Questions
1 Do you think it is likely that Volvo will lose its original customers by trying to attract new ones in this way?
2 Would it matter if it does?
3 Might Skoda be able to change its image using similar tactics?

Source Mitchell, 1995.

Market segmentation

This is the first stage in the process of target marketing, and is defined as '... dividing a market into distinct groups of buyers with different needs, characteristics, or behaviour who might require separate products or marketing mixes'

(Kotler and Armstrong, 1994). It involves an analysis of the nature and composition of a market to identify groups of potential buyers who have similar needs or characteristics, or display similar behaviour. These groups are known as market segments. The differences between segments may mean that different groups of buyers need to be offered slightly different products, or should be communicated with in different ways. They may find different price levels acceptable, or look for different levels of service from their retailers or distributors. Look at the market for shampoo, for example. There are different products for people with different hair types, for babies and children, for women and men, for those who have permed or coloured hair, for people with dandruff and hair loss, for those who wash their hair frequently, for those who are in a hurry and want to condition at the same time as washing, and for those who simply want a basic product as cheaply as possible. Shampoo manufacturers have responded to the different needs and preferences of different groups of consumers and produced a wide variety of products to match the demands of the different segments they have identified.

Segmenting consumer markets

There are four possible starting points when considering how best to segment a consumer market. These should all be explored before making a decision as to the most appropriate ways of dividing up the market.

Geographic segmentation

In some markets there are identifiable differences in buyer needs according to where people live. Different geographical areas, whether they be towns and cities, regions, countries or even continents, may have different needs. In international marketing, for example, it is common to have to adapt a product or promotional campaign to suit local tastes and needs (see Chapter 13). This may be due to characteristics which are related to geography, such as climate, but may equally reflect cultural differences. In northern Europe, for example, dental health and oral hygiene are the main benefits sought from toothpaste, so brands tend to be promoted by emphasising features such as fluoride and other properties that prevent tooth decay and gum disease. In southern Europe, however, the cosmetic properties of the product are promoted more heavily, as these are of more interest to buyers.

> **DID YOU KNOW?**
>
> *If you are fond of cod and chips or a Cheddar cheese roll, or if you buy green bacon from a butcher and look forward to Yorkshire pudding being served up alongside your roast beef, then chances are you come from the south of England. Northerners are much more partial to haddock, eat more Cheshire than Cheddar (which they think of as a cooking cheese) and use the term bun instead of roll. They describe unsmoked bacon as 'plain' and buy it from a pork butcher, and eat their Yorkshire Puddings as a starter with onion gravy, not as a main course (Parkin, 1995).*

Demographic segmentation

In other markets, geography is less relevant as a basis for segmentation but buyer behaviour is found to change according to the demographic characteristics of consumers. Depending on their age, their gender, the size of their families, their religion, their educational background, their income or their occupation, different people are found to want different features and benefits from the products and services they buy. They will choose different types of holidays at different ages, they require different types of cars according to the size of their families and they may celebrate marriage in different ways according to their religion (some of these issues are discussed in Chapter 2). There are many interesting examples of demographic segmentation. Pharmaceutical manufacturers produce reduced-strength drugs for children; low-cost retail formats are designed for low income brackets; and toiletries have traditionally been scented differently for men and women, though this may change if Calvin Klein proves successful with his unisex fragrance, cK One.

Multi-variable segmentation is also quite common. The retail chain Next, for example, targets 25–40 year olds in its main stores, but also ran a chain called 'Next to Nothing' in some cities which targeted those in that age bracket but on lower incomes than their normal customers. Some magazines aimed at women are also segmented on the basis of occupation, aimed at either housewives or working women.

> **DID YOU KNOW?**
>
> *Babycham was the first drink to be specifically aimed at women. It was launched nationally in 1952, a time when respectable British women were setting foot in public houses for the first time. TV advertising was used shortly afterwards making Babycham one of the very first drinks to realise the potential of this new mass medium. Since its launch more than four billion bottles have been sold and brand awareness stands at around 98 per cent among British drinkers (Frost, 1995).*

Psychographic segmentation

As discussed in Chapter 3, the decisions people make about the goods and services they buy are influenced by a range of factors relating to their own personal characteristics: the things that motivate them, their personalities, lifestyles and attitudes, etc. This provides opportunities for psychographic segmentation – to divide up markets based on the ways people think.

In the US, socio-economic grouping is usually identified by classifying people according to their occupation, a demographic variable, but in the UK *social class* tends to reflect the ways people think and the beliefs they hold, and so is considered to be an important basis for psychographic segmentation. Social class affects the ways in which people spend money and the value they place on different types of products and services. Leisure activities tend to be related to social class, as do preferences for reading matter, home furnishings, clothing and even food (as discussed in Chapter 3).

Personality can be used as a basis for segmentation if product preference is shown to be influenced by individuals' personality traits. Brands can then be designed with characteristics that reflect the personalities of their target markets. Certain brands of household products, for example, are designed to appeal to anxious or obsessive personality types. White-coated scientists are used to promote toilet cleaning products, to demonstrate their germ-killing properties and to satisfy housewives as to their power. The effectiveness of washing powders is assured in testimonials from smiling customers, comparing the whiteness of their laundry with their neighbours'.

CASE STUDY **5.2**
· · · · · · · · · · · · · · · · · ·

The Euro-personality

With the single European Market being a reality, and the prospect of a single currency on the horizon, marketers in Europe are less likely to think of their markets as comprising geographic segments, and are starting to consider alternative and possibly more relevant ways to identify clusters of people with similar needs. The two stumbling blocks that commonly arise for marketers who are attempting to appeal to consumers across national boundaries are cultural and language difficulties. Research by AGB Market Information suggests, however, that these may be of less significance than values and attitudes, many of which are shared by Europeans, regardless of their nationalities. This implies that psychographic segmentation of Europe may be a useful basis for targeting pan-European markets.

Six basic mentalities were observed right across Europe. The classifications were based on the extent to which Europeans value possessions as opposed to ideologies, or stability as opposed to new sensations:

▶ *The withdrawn*: socially disciplined and traditional in orientation, these are relatively passive people who feel the need to integrate closely into their local communities.

▶ *Dreamers*: these are young couples wishing to build a stable home environment for their children, who dislike conflict and seek only minimal interface with the outside world.

▶ *The ambitious*: also young, this group comprises urban dwellers who want to be seen as 'winners' in life. They are self-motivated and aim to improve their social position.

▶ *Militants*: these are the affluent, well-educated middle-aged, who want interesting jobs and enjoy cultural pursuits. They are socially conscious and tend to be involved in community projects.

▶ *Notables*: ultra-conservative in their attitudes, these wealthy and well-educated home-owners are staunch defenders of traditional morals and values, preferring family life to social involvement.

▶ *Contestors*: these are well-educated executives between the ages of 30 and 40, who are concerned with personal development and self-expression. They are open-minded, tolerant and keen to support issues related to ecology and social justice.

Questions

1 How might a manufacturer of consumer durables use these typologies to create a pan-European advertising strategy?
  Consider:
  – A car manufacturer.
  – A washing machine manufacturer.
  – A hi-fi manufacturer.
2 How can language difficulties be overcome in international advertising?
3 Which of the segments identified are most difficult to influence to buy products that do not originate in their own country?

Source Piper and Mead, 1990.

Lifestyle is another basis for psychographic segmentation, as discussed in Chapter 3. In recent years different lifestyles have been categorised by examining the geographic and demographic characteristics of the population. Households with similar demographic characteristics tend to live in similar types of houses and display similar lifestyles. These households tend to be grouped together in certain postcode areas, which can be identified from census data and other forms of market research. A number of firms have designed similar systems in which every residential postcode in the country has been classified according to the characteristics of people living at those addresses.

The first of these systems was ACORN, which stands for 'A Classification of Residential Neighbourhoods'. It is a system that uses information from the UK census on the characteristics of households, including age, family size, occupation and type and size of dwelling, to divide the UK population into primary categories, according to lifestyle. For example, category C consists of those described as 'rising', and comprises young professionals and executives in towns and cities who are either working or studying to make their way up in society. They tend to be relatively young, highly educated, live in high status neighbourhoods, and the level of mobility of this group is high. Each category is then broken down into groups, with category C, for example, being subdivided into three groups, namely the 'affluent urbanites in town and city areas', 'better-off executives in inner-city areas' and 'prosperous professionals in metropolitan areas'. Finally, each of these groups is broken down further into types, according to any distinctive differences within the group. Within Group 6, for example, are the 'well-off town and city areas', 'flats and mortgages, singles and young working couples' and 'furnished flats and bed-sits, younger single people'. In total there are six primary categories, 17 groups and a total of 54 types, all of which can be identified by postcode. (See Figure 5.3.)

Another system, MOSAIC, approaches things in a slightly different way. This classification system was compiled using data from a wider range of sources, which have resulted in the division of the population into 12 lifestyle groupings and 52 types (Case study 3.2 in Chapter 3 looks at the MOSAIC classification system in more detail). (See Figure 5.4.)

Both ACORN and MOSAIC can be very useful when trying to identify discrete lifestyle groupings for target marketing. Retailers use them to estimate the potential for the catchment areas of proposed new stores; sales territory planning can be done more efficiently; appropriate areas can be identified for direct mail and door-to-door leaflet campaigns; and organisations' own databases can be analysed and categorised to enable them to profile their 'typical' customer and look for others like them.

Behavioural segmentation

Markets can be divided into discrete sub-groups according to the way people react to and interact with the product itself. Although a more difficult concept to grasp, in markets where other forms of segmentation are found to have little relevance, behavioural segmentation probably holds the key to effective and innovative marketing. Behavioural segmentation can be based on:

Time of use
Different people consume the same products at different times. Although the conventional image of Corn Flakes is as a breakfast cereal, Kelloggs identified that a significant proportion of its customers ate Corn Flakes as a snack food later in the day. To sustain sales in the face of fierce competition, it decided to promote Corn Flakes to late-night snackers.

figure 5.3
ACORN categories and groups

Category A: 'Thriving'
▶ Group 1 Wealthy suburbs, large detached houses
▶ Group 2 Affluent greys, rural communities
▶ Group 3 Prosperous pensioners, retirement areas

Category B: 'Expanding'
▶ Group 4 Affluent executives, family areas
▶ Group 5 Well-off workers, family areas

Category C: 'Rising'
▶ Group 6 Affluent Urbanites, Town and City Areas
▶ Group 7 Prosperous professionals, metropolitan areas
▶ Group 8 Better-off executives, inner city areas

Category D: 'Settling'
▶ Group 9 Comfortable middle-agers, mature home owning areas
▶ Group 10 Skilled workers, home owning areas

Category E: 'Aspiring'
▶ Group 11 New home owners, mature communities
▶ Group 12 White collar workers, better-off multi-ethnic areas

Category F: 'Striving'
▶ Group 13 Older people, less prosperous areas
▶ Group 14 Council estate residents, better-off homes
▶ Group 15 Council estate residents, high unemployment
▶ Group 16 Council estate residents, greatest hardship
▶ Group 17 People in multi-ethnic low-income areas

Source: CACI Information Services, 1995

figure 5.4
MOSAIC groupings

1 High income families	7 Town houses and flats
2 Suburban semis	8 Stylish singles
3 Blue-collar owners	9 Independent elders
4 Low rise council	10 Mortgaged families
5 Council flats	11 Country dwellers
6 Victorian low status	12 Institutional areas

Source: CCN Marketing, 1995

ACTIVITY **5.1**

Timing it right

Segment the following markets according to the time that people use or consume the products or services, and indicate how this might affect the way you would promote and price them:

- Cereals.
- Coffee.
- Chocolate.
- Hotel rooms.
- Package holidays.
- Train journeys.
- Telephone services.

Benefits sought
Different people want products to benefit them in different ways. Consider the yellow fats market; butter is an ideal product for those who are most interested in taste; low-calorie spread is aimed at those who want to lose weight; polyunsaturated margarine will appeal to those who are health conscious; block margarine is preferred by those who want to make good pastry; and basic own label spreads will satisfy those for whom economy is paramount. Different brands have been created to provide the benefits sought by these and many other groups and combinations of groups in this heavily segmented market.

Applications
Different people want to use products for different purposes. Cotton wool, for example, has three primary applications; baby-care, child-care and cosmetic use. These three uses can then be subdivided into a number of further segments. In baby-care and cosmetic use, for example, cotton wool is used both to apply substances such as lotions and make-up, as well as for cleansing. Consequently, the market is characterised by product forms that are suited to these tasks. Flat cotton-wool pads are sold in polythene tubes for convenience for make-up removal, cotton-wool buds are an easy shape to use for make-up application, and cotton wool balls are ideal for general cleansing.

Related activities and products
Products are sometimes used because of, or in conjunction with, another product or activity. Car manufacturers, for example, have traditionally been very successful at selling spare parts to drivers of their cars. They assure their customers that only their own brands will give the quality and reliability they are looking for when their car is repaired, though generic alternatives are often much cheaper.

DID YOU KNOW?
Since the early 1970s, the frequent-wash sector of the shampoo market has grown from only one or two per cent of adults to 15 per cent of women and 25 per cent of men. The change has been associated with different attitudes to washing and bathing, as well as the boom in active sports and aerobics. The introduction of the Slazenger range of toiletries was specifically designed to appeal to this segment (TGI Services, 1994).

Expertise
Different people have different requirements from products because of their levels of expertise. The most obvious segmentation takes place between amateur and professional markets, with amateur musicians, for example, seldom demanding the same quality of instrument that professionals require for public performance. Differences in expertise also arise at the purely domestic level though. Enthusiasts of any description are likely to be more discerning in their purchasing habits. Keen gardeners, for example, are likely to be highly selective and

discerning in their choice of stock from a specialist garden centre, while others are more likely to be looking for simple selections of hardy plants that offer them a reasonable certainty of successful blooms.

Purchase patterns

Different people buy products at different time intervals. Some people are regular buyers of certain brands while others only buy them on special occasions. Theatre audiences tend to be characterised by a core of regular attenders, a proportion of irregular attenders who come from time to time and a large 'tail' of infrequent or one-off attenders who seldom or never return. These patterns can be scrutinised to ensure that appropriate promotional messages can be sent by direct mail to the right individuals – subscription offers for a series of performances, for example, are likely to be successful among the regular attenders but fall on deaf ears with the infrequent attenders.

Brand loyalty

Purchase patterns can also be examined in terms of brand loyalty. Some people, known as 'long loyals', always buy the same brand, regardless of price or competition and are difficult to persuade otherwise. 'Rotators' stick to two or three brands, moving only between their favourites. The 'deal sensitives' shift between brands easily in response to price and promotions, while the 'price sensitives' will purchase whatever product is cheapest, regardless of brand (*The Economist*, 1992). The proportion of shoppers in each of these segments varies widely from product to product. The key for marketers is to understand the composition of their markets so that the impact of pricing and promotional strategy can be maximised.

Segmenting industrial markets

Most of the bases for the segmentation of consumer markets are equally relevant in industrial or business-to-business markets. Organisational buyers can be divided up according to their geographical locations, their frequency of purchase, the benefits they are seeking from their products and the purposes for which they use them. There are, however, five other useful dimensions to consider:

▶ *Industry type*: different industries may have different requirements for, say, quality or design features, depending on the nature of their own products and target markets.
▶ *Technology base*: even within the same industry, different organisations using different technologies can be identified as being in separate market segments. Printing technology, for example, encompasses lithographic, flexographic and screen printing processes, each of which tends to print on different types of papers, as well as synthetic materials. Even among litho-printers there are both sheet-fed and reel-fed (known as web) machines. Paper suppliers may need to recognise where their own strengths lie as they may not be in a good position to supply the whole industry.

▶ *Company size*: large companies with factories, depots or warehouses in a wide range of locations are likely to have different requirements for service than small businesses. They may have specific delivery instructions; they may require different invoicing procedures due to a central buying function; or they may have less need for after-sales service due to in-house repair and installation facilities. They may also prefer to deal with other large businesses and perceive small businesses to be less reliable.

▶ *Urgency of demand*: some organisations are willing to hold stocks of products in anticipation of their own future needs, yet others wish to rely upon the speedy and efficient delivery of components, raw materials or services by their suppliers on a regular basis so that they can save themselves the costs of stock-holding. Another category here is the organisation that only ever needs a particular product in an emergency. A company may need to segment its market according to the urgency of demand if it is unable to meet the delivery service levels demanded by some customers in its markets.

▶ *Size of order*: the so-called 'Pareto effect' suggests that in many businesses approximately 80 per cent of turnover will be generated by only 20 per cent of customers. If a segment of the market can be identified as comprising consistently heavy users of a product, an organisation may choose to focus on this group to achieve economies of scale in distribution; they may allow competitors to occupy the rest of the market unchallenged, leaving them the task of selling and distributing small quantities to a large number of dispersed buyers. This sounds a very profitable strategy, but it should be remembered that turnover doesn't always equate with profit, and that small but growing businesses may be allowed to develop a loyalty to competitors in their early years, which will not be forgotten when they develop far greater buying requirements.

Criteria for assessing viable market segments

Having identified possible segments to target, it is important to assess their viability. There are four key criteria to bear in mind when assessing whether a segment has the potential to be commercially exploited:

▶ *Size*: Is the segment a worthwhile target? A segment should not be so large as to be indistinct from the mass market, but it should be large enough for it to be worthwhile treating its members as being different from others. Car manufacturers, for example, are sometimes approached by very tall drivers for whom there is insufficient headroom in their cars, and very short drivers who find visibility difficult. While some vehicles attempt to meet their needs with adjustable seats, there is currently insufficient demand from these groups to make it worthwhile launching a new range of vehicles to meet their specific needs.

▶ *Relevance*: Do differences between groups of consumers affect their buying behaviour? It may be possible to identify groups of people with similar characteristics, but they should only be recognised as a market segment if the characteristics or needs relate to the product or service being supplied. For example, the market for toothpaste may be segmented to appeal to children and adults, those with different dental conditions, and smokers and non-smokers, as buyers' dental needs and taste preferences may be affected by these. It is probably not very relevant, however, to segment the market for toothpaste according to gender as there is no obvious connection between gender and dental needs.

▶ *Identity*: Does this group of buyers have significantly different needs? The most promising segments, and the easiest to target, are those that are distinctly different from other segments, where the identity of the group of buyers is quite different from other groups. Buyers of business stationery, for example, demand different sizes and styles of paper and envelopes from domestic users and there is relatively little overlap between the two segments. But in the market for shampoo there is considerable overlap in what the different brands are offering to the market, and it is not so obvious why buyers should choose one brand over another. This makes it more difficult to attract buyers, who may be torn between two or more options.

▶ *Accessibility*: Is it possible to communicate with buyers in the segment? It must be possible for segments that are identified to be reached with marketing messages aimed specifically at them. This is not always easy. Young men are quite difficult to reach. As they tend to read relatively few newspapers or magazines and watch less TV than other groups, it is relatively expensive for organisations to target them. The media costs of reaching them to tell them of a new product or service designed with their needs in mind may outweigh the potential benefits of trying to satisfy those needs.

CASE STUDY **5.3**

Grey power

For many years, the over 50s were dismissed by marketers as offering little potential for profitable sales. Many consumers in this age bracket were on low incomes after retirement, and conservative in outlook, so the booming youth markets were the segments that drew most of the attention.

But times are changing. Demographically, this group is becoming more attractive by the day. About a quarter of the UK population is currently aged between 50 and 75, and this proportion is projected to peak in the year 2021 when half of the adult population will be over 50. Even by 2010 this segment will have more consumers than the 15–44 age group. They are also the wealthiest of age groups, owning about 80 per cent of the nation's private capital. Even though much of this is tied up in their houses, they tend to have low or negligible mortgages, which means that their disposable income is also relatively high compared with the cash-strapped youth of today. They out-spend younger consumers in many categories, including food, gardening and DIY products.

Psychographically, this group is also becoming more attractive to marketers. The over 50s are less convinced of the importance of saving than previous generations and are characterised by a mood of 'safe rebellion', and a belief that spending is justified as 'you can't take it with you'. Having sacrificed personal pleasure and time to provide for the family, the 'Greys' (as they are dubbed in the US) are wanting to break free from their roles as parents and home-makers and treat themselves to luxuries, including hi-tech gadgets such as video cameras and hi-fi systems, as well as holidays and cars.

Targeting this segment of the market must be undertaken with considerable sensitivity. Exhibiting Peter Pan-like tendencies, the last thing this group sees itself as is old and any direct reminders of ageing are likely to be rejected. Images of granddads and grandmas are scorned, and specialist holidays or products designed to meet the needs of this age group alienate many of them.

Questions

1 Suppose a car manufacturer wanted to increase its sales to the recently retired who have just given up their company cars. What imagery and media should it use?

2 To what extent are the 'over 50s' accessible to marketers? How might a financial services provider best reach this segment?

3 How should retailers respond to the growth of population in this age group?

Source Pryke, 1993.

ACTIVITY **5.2**
·············

Mix and match

1 Link each product group in column 1 with all the 'relevant' means of segmenting the market from column 2:

Product groups	*Possible market segments*
Cameras	Left- and right-handed people
Stationery	Blondes, brunettes and red-heads
Alcoholic drinks	Schools, colleges and universities
Kitchen appliances	Professionals and amateurs
Public transport	Business users and social users
Hair care	Heavy users and light users
Cars	Week-end users and week-day users
Theatre	Extroverts and introverts

2 Estimate the relative size of each of the relevant segments.

3 To what extent do these segments have different identities?

4 How accessible are these segments?

5 Are there any segments that you identified as relevant in question 1 that do not appear to be viable?

Market targeting
·····················

Having identified relevant and viable segments in a market, an organisation is faced with the decision as to which segment or segments to serve. There are two possible strategies: concentration strategies, whereby an organisation focuses all its attention on a single segment in the market (known as a *niche*); and multi-segment strategies where a series of separate marketing activities is designed for different market segments. (See Figure 5.5.)

Concentration strategies

Directing all the marketing effort of an organisation towards a single market segment is known as niche marketing. It can be very advantageous in certain

figure 5.5
Market targeting strategies

circumstances. When a concentration strategy is implemented, there is seldom any confusion in the eyes of potential customers as to whether or not that organisation is able to meet their needs, and the needs of the customers who are targeted are usually so closely scrutinised that even small organisations can realistically aim to be market leaders in their chosen market segment. The manufacturers of cereal-based health-foods, Jordans, clearly concentrate on health-conscious consumers and have succeeded in retaining a strong position in this segment even though other larger manufacturers dominate the market as a whole. Aiming at a small niche in the market can enable firms with limited resources to compete with better financed organisations. Case study 1.1 describes the family owned car manufacturer, Morgan cars. The company is well known for the production of traditionally-styled sports cars, yet is probably competing with some of the models in the ranges of much larger global manufacturers.

There are, however, two important disadvantages of niche marketing. First, an organisation can be vulnerable if powerful competitors turn their attention to that niche. Suppose, for example, a particular segment in a market starts to grow rapidly. The niche marketer will be faced by an increase in demand which may be difficult to satisfy in the short-term, and it is very likely that competitors, who may previously have ignored that segment as it was considered too small to be of interest, will suddenly invest heavily to attract new business in this area, and severely undermine the efforts of the niche marketer to take advantage of the market growth. This occurred to some extent in the 'Green' revolution of the late 1980s. Niche marketers had previously sold environmentally-friendly products quite profitably through outlets such as health-food stores and specialist mail order. An upturn in demand for ecologically-sound products was recognised by large manufacturers who put tremendous efforts into promotional campaigns and achieving mainstream distribution through large retail chains. Much of the growth in the market benefited them, rather than the smaller niche players who were unable to retaliate sufficiently to sustain their positions in the niches they had previously dominated. What to do under such circumstances is the second problem that faces niche marketers. Having established a strong reputation in serving a particular market segment, it is relatively difficult to change direction and persuade the market that a different segment can be served equally well.

DID YOU KNOW?

Lucozade is a classic example of a niche product that was revived by appealing to a new market segment. Known for decades as the drink for sick children, the product was suffering from increasing competition from cola and other fizzy drinks. By using the high-profile decathlon star Daly Thompson in its advertising, the drink soon became associated with sport, thereby maintaining the health platform for which it was famous, yet attracting a much larger and growing market segment.

Multi-segment strategies

Many organisations, particularly larger ones, implement multi-segment strategies, attempting to reach a number of different market segments by developing different marketing programmes for each segment. Kellogg's, for example, is one of the larger players in the market for breakfast cereals. It is particularly successful at targeting children, but also has a strong presence in the health segments, among weight-watchers and in mainstream adult markets, which are sub-segmented in various ways; recent advertising campaigns for Corn Flakes have addressed the 'lapsed user' segment using the slogan 'Have you forgotten how good they are?' and considerable efforts have been made to encourage non-breakfast-time eating by suggesting that Corn Flakes can be eaten as a snack at other times of day (as discussed earlier, in the section on segmentation by time of use).

Multi-segment strategies tend to offer greater scope for expansion and growth than concentration strategies. The combined size of the different segments aimed at tends to increase sales revenue and this can also lead to economies of scale in production. The main disadvantage of this approach is that it requires a high level of marketing expertise and will incur higher marketing costs than concentration strategies. Resources are spread more widely and without sound financial backing it may be that they are also spread too thinly to be effective in establishing a presence in the chosen segments. This can lead to a further disadvantage of mixed messages being received by consumers, with no segment really understanding that the product or service is aimed at satisfying its particular needs.

CASE STUDY **5.4**
. . . .

Hitting the target

Formerly the domain of direct-mail suppliers, financial services companies, book clubs and charities, direct marketing has struggled to shake off its associations with junk-mail, unwanted phone calls and promotional gimmicks. But database-driven direct marketing has recently experienced a boom as consumer goods companies have come to appreciate its potential for accurately targeting specific segments of their markets.

Efforts made by retailers to push their own-brands have hit manufacturer brands hard. Consumer loyalty now lies primarily with the retailer rather than with the well-known labels, and companies such as Heinz have had to recognise that consumer food markets can no longer be treated as homogeneous. A product differentiated marketing strategy using mass media to advertise an increasing array of brands is no longer sufficient to attract the more sophisticated shoppers of the 1990s. Heinz was one of the first consumer goods manufacturers to use direct marketing as a means for communicating directly with their own customers, by-passing the retailer network in an attempt to redress the balance of power.

Another convert to the technique is Helena Rubinstein, which was previously one of a number of cosmetic companies who used mainly free gifts to encourage sales and generate customer loyalty. It has generated a database of customers through detailed questionnaires asking for demographic, psychographic and behavioural details such as age, motivation and purchasing patterns. The database is linked to all Helena Rubinstein outlets which enables customer datafiles to be updated continually. Armed with this information, the company is in a position to classify its customers in many different ways and to build relationships with them by communicating personally with messages that are of direct relevance.

Questions

1   When is direct-mail junk mail? How can consumer goods manufacturers prevent their communications from being considered as such?

2   What are the advantages of direct marketing over using the media? Are there any disadvantages?

3   What were the last five pieces of personally addressed, unsolicited direct-mail communications that you received? Do you remember? If so, have they affected your buying behaviour in any way?

Sources   Teather, 1995; Denny, 1995; Mazur, 1995.

Market positioning

This final stage of the process of target marketing involves designing product features and creating a distinct image that appeals specifically to the chosen target market segment and sets the product apart from the competition. The term *positioning* refers to the way in which the product is positioned in the mind of the consumer – it is designed so that members of the target market segment will recognise that it is the best product for them. (See Figure 5.6.)

Product positioning involves a number of important stages.

DID YOU KNOW?

The slogan associated with the Tesco retail chain in the 1970s was 'Pile 'em High, Sell 'em Cheap'. The store offered a wide range of both branded and own-branded goods, home-wear and clothing as well as food, all at bargain prices. However, as consumer tastes changed and society became more affluent, the store started to reposition itself as a quality food retailer offering superior services at higher prices. The greater potential for profitability in this position enabled Tesco to achieve a ranking among the top five most profitable retailers in Europe.

Stage 1: Identify key product characteristics

The product features that members of the target market segment consider to be most important when considering which product to buy should be identified and given some sort of weighting. Note that these features may be tangible (such as colour, size, design), but also intangible (such as reputation or guarantees); this is discussed further in Chapter 6.

Stage 2: Draw up a perceptual map

This is a useful tool by which the current brands available to a market segment can be depicted visually. In its simplest form, the perceptual map consists of a grid that shows the two most important product attributes identified at Stage 1 placed on two axes of a grid (see Figure 5.7). Qualitative marketing research enables consumer perceptions about the current brands to be plotted, so that an organisation can see at a glance where competition is at its most intense and where there might be gaps in the market.

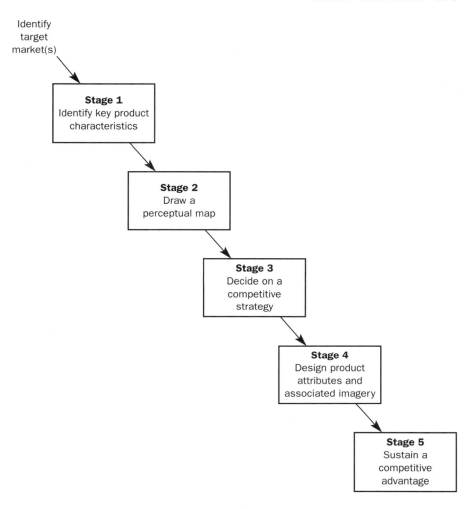

figure 5.6

The process of market positioning

Identify target market(s)

Stage 1
Identify key product characteristics

Stage 2
Draw a perceptual map

Stage 3
Decide on a competitive strategy

Stage 4
Design product attributes and associated imagery

Stage 5
Sustain a competitive advantage

Stage 3: Decide on a competitive strategy

The decision then needs to be made as to whether to compete head-on or to position away from the competition.

In Figure 5.7 it can be seen that different retail formats take different positions in food retailing. They tend to compete head-on with others in their quadrant on the grid but are less likely to see those in different areas of the map as holding any major attraction for consumers in their own particular target markets. A new organisation trying to enter this market will have to decide whether it should attempt to compete head-on with existing suppliers or to find a position on the map, such as the bottom right quadrant, where little competition exists. There are advantages and disadvantages to both strategies.

Avoiding the competition

At first glance it seems evident that a strategy to avoid the competition holds most potential. However, there is often a quadrant on a perceptual map that

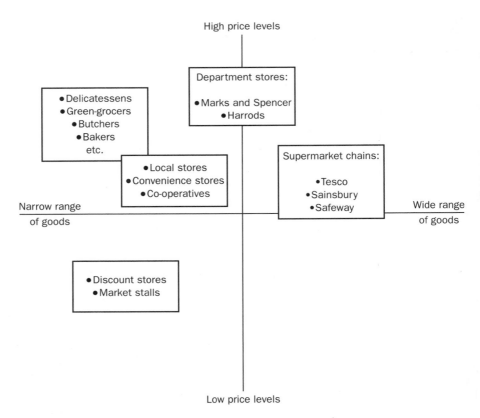

figure 5.7

A perceptual map of food retailing

looks promising from the point of view of satisfying a market need, but it may not be so easy to do this profitably. Sometimes, firms who launch into such segments may be successful to a point, but profitable growth may be difficult and they may be faced with the task of repositioning themselves if they wish to build their profit margins as well as their sales revenues. Note that costs involved in stocking a wide range of goods may be incompatible with sustaining a profitable low-price strategy in the example given.

DID YOU KNOW?

ASDA and Marks and Spencer opened adjacent branches in a new retail development on the outskirts of Leeds. Although the two stores compete head-on in some categories of food and clothing, the overall increase in consumer traffic generated by siting both stores together was anticipated to more than compensate for the increased competition.

Head-on competition

This may be equally, if not more, problematic. Unless the market is growing significantly there may be no room for extra supply without the profitability of all firms suffering badly. Nonetheless, large and well-financed firms are often reluctant to leave a segment unchallenged and are sometimes willing to challenge a leader head-on. Sales growth in Cadbury's Caramel, for example, spawned 'me-too' products in the form of Galaxy toffee bars and Rolo bars. Smaller firms with less financial backing may be squeezed out or will fail to find a foothold unless their product offering is demonstrably better that existing brands.

ACTIVITY **5.3**
•••••••••••••

On target with air freight

The role of an air freight forwarder is to pick up freight from a client, place it with the most suitable air carrier and collect it at the other end of the flight for delivery to its final destination.

Competition for air freight service operators comes from three sources:

▶ Other air freight service operators.
▶ Air freight divisions of the airlines themselves.
▶ Alternative transport systems, notably road, rail and sea.

Customers for air freight services are wide ranging, including:

▶ General industrial and commercial enterprises.
▶ Producers of medical supplies.
▶ Sellers of cut flowers.
▶ Dealers in precious stones.
▶ International organisations with overseas sales depots.

1   Why might organisations use air freight as opposed to other forms of transport – what benefits are sought by each of the customer types given above? Give a name to each of the market segments you identify.
2   Who is likely to perform the role of 'decider' in the decision to buy air freight services in each of these segments? How will this affect the way in which you use promotional activity to target the different segments?
3   For each segment, which two characteristics do you think are most critical in influencing the decision to purchase freight transport? Place these on the axes of perceptual maps and on each grid indicate where the different freight options lie.

Stage 4: Design product attributes and associated imagery

At this stage the features of the product should be designed, along with the type of imagery that will be used to help the targeted customer identify the benefits being offered to them. Features such as brand name, packaging, advertising themes, price levels and distribution outlets are all important in creating this position in the mind of the customer – in other words, the marketing mix is the tool box that enables that position to be established. (This is the subject of the following chapters.)

CASE STUDY **5.5**
•••••••••••••••••

Has it got to be Gordon's?

The market for gin is currently in decline in the UK. The product is firmly associated with formality and Englishness, and sales in recent years have fallen by a quarter as drinkers have switched away from the G & T to drinks that are perceived to be more relaxed and cosmopolitan, including white wine and vodka. Gordon's is the UK brand leader, accounting for nearly half the gin consumed in the UK. But the brand is losing market share to competitors, partly due to its market positioning.

Only 17 per cent of all gin drinkers account for about three quarters of the brand's total sales. These drinkers are typically both conservative and Conservatives, living mainly in the south of England – not an image that appeals particularly to young drinkers. In an attempt to woo them and compete with vodka, the company played down the distinctive taste of gin, portraying it as a simple clear spirit and reduced its alcohol content. This served only to undermine the core properties of the brand, to the delight of arch-rival Beefeater, who benefited from this error. The loss of sales to own-label products has continued to erode the Gordon's market share. Most of these cheaper competitors are produced by adding an essence to neutral spirit, whereas the manufacturer brands are made by redistilling ingredients such as juniper, coriander and cassia bark. But customers are generally unaware of any quality differences between the two. A recent Mintel report comments that 'the habit of drinking gin with a large measure of tonic and the lack of educational marketing by the producers have left consumers unaware of the difference'.

Such problems have called for some radical rethinking by Gordon's. Recent research shows that demand for stronger tastes is at last returning, following the upsurge of demand for low-strength drinks in the 1980s. The trick now is to attract the new and growing market segments without alienating existing drinkers. Among Gordon's solutions is an advertising campaign called 'Invigoration', which uses lavish imagery of bubbles and ice to depict the product as a refreshing experience. In an attempt to attract new drinkers, bar staff are being trained to improve the presentation and serving of the drink.

Questions

1   How would you go about repositioning the Gordon's brand?
2   Are there any segments that appear to hold particularly good potential for the brand? If so, which and why?
3   How would you research the market position of an alcoholic drink such as gin?

Source Mitchell, 1995.

Stage 5: Sustain a competitive advantage

The establishing of a market position that sets a product apart from competitors' products in the eyes of its target market is known as creating a *competitive advantage*. For an organisation to be successful, it needs to sustain that competitive advantage over a period of time and fight off those who would like to have a share of any profitable business that is established. The fundamental principles of marketing apply here. To sustain a competitive advantage requires the continual collection and use of marketing information to ensure that the needs of target markets are being met more effectively and efficiently than by the competition and that adjustments to the marketing mix – or even to the positioning strategy – are made if changes in the environment threaten the business.

Key concepts
. . . .

ACORN: a system that classifies residential neighbourhoods into groups of households who are likely to display similar lifestyles.

Behavioural segmentation: dividing markets into clusters of people who react to and interact with a product in similar ways.

Competitive advantage: the reason why a customer might choose a certain product rather than its competitors.

Concentration strategy: directing all the marketing efforts of an organisation towards a single market segment.

Demographic segmentation: dividing markets into clusters of people who share a demographic characteristic, such as age, gender, income bracket.

Geographic segmentation: dividing markets into clusters of people who live in the same area.

Market segmentation: dividing markets into clusters of people who are looking for similar benefits from the products and services they buy.

Market targeting: attempting to attract a specific market segment or segments.

MOSAIC: a system that classifies residential neighbourhoods into groups of households who are likely to display similar lifestyles.

Multi-segment marketing: attempting to attract a number of different market segments.

Niche marketing: attempting to attract a single market segment.

Perceptual map: a grid that depicts consumer perceptions of the attributes of competing products in a market.

Positioning: using the marketing mix to distinguish a product from its competitors and appeal to a target market.

Product differentiated marketing: supplying different versions of a product to give customers choice.

Psychographic segmentation: dividing markets into clusters of people who have a similar approach to life.

Target marketing: designing complete marketing programmes to meet the needs of different segments in a market.

Undifferentiated marketing: attempting to meet the needs of as many people as possible with a single marketing programme.

SELF-CHECK QUESTIONS

1 Which of the following are *not* bases on which to segment markets?
   a Climate and income.
   b Price and urgency of demand.
   c Time of use and application.
   d Company size and technology base.
   e Lifestyle and occupation.

2 ACORN and MOSAIC are most useful for segmenting markets on which of the following bases?
   a Geography.
   b Demographic features.
   c Lifestyle.
   d Purchase patterns.
   e Income.

3 Perceptual mapping is used to:
   a Enable different market segments to be visualised.
   b Indicate the relative market position of different competitors.
   c Determine the viability of different market segments.
   d Identify the psychographic segments of a market.
   e Distinguish between product differentiation and target marketing.

4 Which of the following are *not* useful as criteria for assessing the viability of targeting a new market segment?
   a The number of potential customers in the segment.
   b The number of competitors targeting other segments of the market.
   c The availability of media through which to communicate with the segment.
   d The extent to which the needs of a segment are significantly different from other segments.
   e The extent to which the proposed basis for segmentation is of relevance to potential customers.

5 Head-on competition may be the best positioning strategy for an organisation if:
   a Its competitors are strong and powerful.
   b Its competitors are concentrated in one quadrant of a perceptual map.
   c Customer needs in the market are highly differentiated.
   d Alternative positioning strategies hold insufficient volume potential to sustain the cost base of the organisation.
   e It does not currently hold a sustainable competitive advantage in any market position.

Which of the following are true and which are false?
6 Product differentiated marketing and multi-segment marketing strategies are both likely to involve creating a range of different products.
7 Behavioural segmentation is based on the way people interact with the product.
8 A concentration strategy is also known as a niche marketing strategy.
9 The marketing mix should be determined after the market has been segmented but before decisions have been made about market targets or positioning.
10 Customers who are consistently loyal to one brand may need to be treated as a separate segment from those who continually shop around to find the lowest prices.

Discuss the following
11 To what extent is demographic segmentation used by soap manufacturers to segment the UK market?
12 In what ways might pricing, promotion and distribution activity need to be changed if an organisation chooses to target 'deal sensitives' as opposed to 'rotators'?
13 How might store loyalty cards help make students a more desirable target market for supermarkets?

14 For what type of organisation might niche marketing be preferable to a multi-segment marketing strategy?

15 What do you think are the key product characteristics that suppliers of home computer software might place on the axes of a positioning map?

Further study
. . . .

Books
Every text book of marketing principles will contain some explanations of target marketing, but a more extensive discussion is given in:

Ries, Al and Trout, Jack (1981) *Positioning: the battle for your mind*, McGraw Hill.

Journals
Some of the early articles on the subject are still of interest today.

Haley, Russell (1968) 'Benefit segmentation: a decision-oriented research tool', in *Journal of Marketing*, July.
Looks at aspects of behavioural segmentation and gives an interesting example of benefit segmentation in the market for toothpaste.

Johnson, Richard M. (1971) 'Market segmentation: a strategic management tool', in *Journal of Marketing Research*, February.
A more difficult read but provides useful material linking marketing research to target marketing, and the ways in which positioning maps can be constructed.

Smith, Wendell R. (1956) 'Product differentiation and market segmentation as alternative marketing strategies', in *Journal of Marketing*, July.
Compares and contrasts these two approaches.

References
. . . .

CACI Information Services (1995) *ACORN Users Guide*, CACI House, Kensington Village, Avonmore Road, London, W14 8TS.

CCN Marketing (1995) *MOSAIC : a clearer view of your customers*, Talbot House, Talbot Street, Nottingham, NG1 5HF.

Denny, N. (1995) 'Has the DM medium finally come of age?', in *Marketing*, 1 June, p. 8.

Economist (1992), 26 September, pp. 82–7.

Frost, B. (1995) 'Babycham's pioneer purveyor dies at 83', in *The Times*, 7 September, p. 2.

Maddox, B. (1995) 'A classic duet of British success', in *The Times*, 8 March, p. 23.

Mazur, L. (1995) 'The personal touch', in *Marketing Business*, July/August, pp. 38–40.

Mitchell, A. (1995) 'Own-label and tonic please', in *The Times*, 15 March.

Mitchell, A. (1995) 'Volvo puts its foot down', in *The Times*, 10 May, p. 30.

Kotler, P. and Armstrong, G. (1994) *Principles of Marketing*, 6th ed., Prentice Hall.

Parkin, J. (1995) 'What goes in your North and South?', in *The Telegraph*, 9 September.

Piper, R. and Mead, J. (1990) *Classifying people: the European dimension*, Admap.

Pryke, S. (1993) 'Generation Gain', in *Marketing Week*, 2 July, p. 46.

Teather, D. (1995) 'Cosmetics industry gets DM makeover', in *Marketing*, 23 March.

TGI Services (1994) 'Brand Watch: Shampoo', in *Marketing*, 22 September, p. 11.

CHAPTER 6

Product

Objectives

When you have read this chapter you will be able to:

▶ Define the concept of a product.

▶ Distinguish between the core, actual and extended product.

▶ Classify a variety of consumer and organisational products.

▶ Evaluate the alternative ways of building a product range.

▶ Draw a diagram of the product life-cycle and discuss its key features.

▶ Recommend appropriate marketing activity at different stages of the product life-cycle.

▶ Use the Boston matrix to assess a portfolio of products.

▶ Explain the benefits of branding.

Introduction

This chapter focuses on the nature of a product and its role as part of the marketing mix. The different ways of classifying products are examined, and as most products have a limited life before they are replaced by something new and better, the concept of the product life-cycle and its implications are considered. The key factors that influence decisions as to which products to sell are discussed, and the importance of branding in helping an organisation to create a unique identity for its products is highlighted.

What is a product?

Fundamentally, a product comprises everything that a seller offers to a buyer in an exchange process. Lusch and Lusch (1987) expand on this, defining a product as *'a bundle of tangible and intangible attributes that a seller offers to a potential buyer and that satisfies the buyer's needs or wants.'* Consequently, a product may be a physical good, or a service, but more often is a blend of both. (See Figure 6.1.)

CASE STUDY **6.1**

The retail battlefield

In an attempt to create customer loyalty, retailers are following the example of the Americans in trying to beat their competitors on service rather than simply trying to undercut them on price. Different stores are engaging different tactics, but all of them are trying to make the shopping experience a desirable one rather than simply a domestic chore.

Asda is trying Singles Nights, at which it highlights those areas of the store – known as 'erogenous zones' – in which single shoppers are likely to linger, such as the ready-made meals and the wine sections. Unattached shoppers are invited to wear a name badge and a carnation in their buttonholes, and are offered free tea

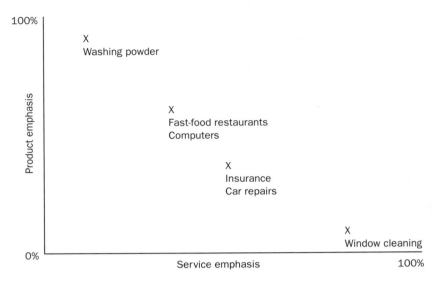

figure 6.1
**Product and service
components of
domestic items**

and coffee by candlelight. A 'lurve board' is available for 'Brunette in breakfast cereals' to communicate with 'Check-shirt in fruit juices', and for those too shy to make the first move, store staff in dinner jackets will make introductions.

Safeway is targeting the full-nesters, having launched subsidised crèches at a number of its stores. Children can be looked after by professional nursery nurses while their parents, who are linked to them by an electronic tagging system, can shop in peace – and hopefully spend more money. Other services offered include a dry-cleaner, parent and child parking spaces near the entrance to the store and a range of eight different types of shopping trolley. This whole parent-friendly approach is supported by a high-profile TV advertising campaign featuring TV toddler Harry and his family making various shopping trips to Safeway. Designed to reposition the store, the campaign reinforces both the features and benefits of the new services.

WH Smith has taken a different approach, restructuring its organisation to remove layers of store managers and increase the number of shop-floor sales staff. Deputy and departmental managers have been replaced by customer service managers, all of whom are trained to answer customer queries rather than simply to smile and be friendly. The introduction of a 'Bookfinder' computer system that lists every book in print has enabled staff to locate titles for customers, and those held at its central warehouse are guaranteed for delivery within 48 hours.

Both Tesco and Sainsbury have launched initiatives promising customers shorter queues. Schemes such as these are difficult to manage, as shopper traffic peaks at certain times during the day and across the week. Full-time staff may be under-occupied for most of the day and go to lunch just as the need for cashiers starts to rise. Part-time staff can be engaged to cover peak periods only, but they are often less motivated, less trained and have less product knowledge than full-timers, so customer service may improve in one way but suffer in another. Logistical difficulties such as these eventually put paid to the Tesco 'One in Front' campaign which promised that no more than one person would be kept waiting at a checkout queue at any one time. The scheme was finally abandoned following complaints to the Advertising Standards Authority.

Questions

1 To what extent is it possible for retailers to sustain a competitive advantage by increasing their range of services to customers?

2 What other factors influence consumer choice of retailer? List these and rank them in order of importance.

3 What else could supermarkets do to reduce the problems incurred due to peaks and troughs in demand?

Sources Gilchrist, 1995; Sylvester, 1995; Drummond, 1995.

A good has physical form and can be seen and touched. It is tangible, and when it is purchased the buyer becomes its owner. A service, on the other hand, is a deed performed for the buyer to experience rather than own (this is discussed further in Chapter 14). Thus a train ride is a service, as the customer can experience the journey but does not own the train. However, the quality of the journey will be partly determined by the tangible features of the carriage, so the tangible and intangible elements of the service are closely related and will both contribute to the buyer's satisfaction or otherwise with their journey. Similarly, when people buy food in supermarkets, although they are buying tangible goods they will own, store and ultimately consume, the quality of service provided by the supermarket will also affect their levels of satisfaction and influence their purchasing decisions. Thus the concept of a product encompasses all the physical, aesthetic, emotional, and psychological elements that people buy when they engage in a transaction with a supplier.

ACTIVITY **6.1**
....

Who needs what?

Listed below are a number of customer needs.

▶ To travel from London to Aberdeen.
▶ To improve my game of tennis.
▶ To be informed about current affairs.
▶ To keep my dog healthy.
▶ To eat hot food at home.

1 Identify all the products that could help satisfy these needs.
2 List the criteria that potential customers will use in deciding which product to choose.
3 How many of these criteria are tangible and how many are intangible?
4 How might this influence a) the price you charge for these products and b) the messages that you use to promote them?

The total product concept

Rather than try to distinguish between goods and services, it is perhaps easier to envisage all products as combining three distinct elements, as shown in Figure 6.2 and described below.

The core product

As the definition suggests, every product provides a basic function that solves a customer problem and satisfies a human need. This is the *core* product, without which the product would have no purpose. It is the core product that offers benefits to potential customers. Suppose, for example, a person is concerned about the increasing level of burglary in their neighbourhood. This problem could be resolved in a number of ways; a burglar alarm, a set of window locks and a large dog all offer the same core product, namely a feeling of security, and any of these could potentially supply the desired benefit of relieving the person's anxiety. The decision as to which of these items to buy will therefore depend upon more than just the core product.

The actual product

This consists of the *tangible* features associated with the core product, which are designed to deliver the desired benefits as effectively as possible. These features are an important vehicle for differentiating a product from its competitors. In the case of the security product, the window locks may deter casual thieves and offer the advantage of minimum disruption and DIY installation; the alarm will be better for alerting neighbours in the event of a break-in; and the dog may be the best for deterring would-be burglars from even attempting to enter a property. Different solutions are likely to appeal to different segments of the market, according to their perceived needs.

Within each product form there is also potential for differentiating the tangible features so as to distinguish a product from competitors and more closely meet the needs of a target market segment. Window locks are produced of different materials to give greater or lesser strength; alarms may be activated by pressure pads under carpets or by infra-red movement detectors; dogs may be trained to attack or simply to bark! All of these features may influence the customer's final selection of a solution to the security problem.

figure 6.2
**The total product
concept**

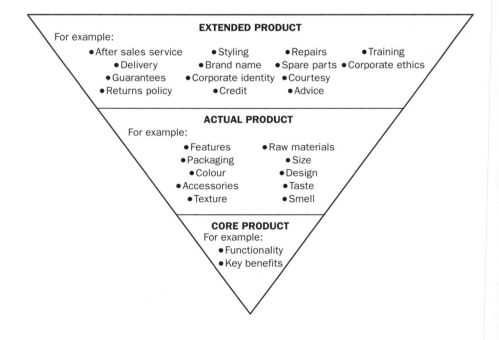

The extended product

This consists of the intangible features of a product that influence buyer choice. These intangible features tend to offer psychological benefits that enhance the value of the core and actual product in the consumer's mind. For example, the existence of guarantees, exchange policies or free service agreements imply product reliability; the availability of credit may enable customers to buy now rather than postpone a purchase; a delivery service can relieve customers of a logistical difficulty; a polite and helpful shop assistant can create store loyalty; and a strong brand image suggests a trustworthy company and quality product. Despite their intangibility, all of these features and many others can be the key deciding factor in consumer choices between different suppliers. This is particularly true in a world that, due to the standardised technologies of mass production, is increasingly characterised by uniformity of core and actual products. Intangible features have become the focus of competitive activity between suppliers, just as Levitt suggested they would back in 1969:

> In the future, competition will occur not between what firms produce in the factory, but between what they add to their factory output in the form of packaging, services, advertising, consumer advice, financing, delivery, warehousing and other things that people value.

Product classifications
....

As we have defined a product as embracing everything that a seller offers to a buyer in an exchange process, we can include a very wide range of items when we start to classify different types of product. Product classifications are useful when planning marketing strategies as they focus on the similarities between groups of products, and similar products usually respond well to similar marketing activities.

The most important distinction to make is between consumer and business products.

Consumer products

These are products purchased by consumers for their own consumption or that of their households. They can be classified further according to the levels of the decision-making effort that consumers are willing to expend in making their product selections (this is also discussed in Chapter 3).

Convenience products
These are products purchased frequently and with minimum effort on the part of buyers. Also known as 'low-involvement' products, they include:

▶ *Staples* (also known as fast-moving consumer goods, or FMCGs) such as bread, shampoo, coffee and all other food or household products bought on a regular basis, often by habit. With this type of product a well-established brand name gives consumers confidence to repeat their purchasing habits on a regular basis without reconsidering their choice, but maximum retail distribution is also important as consumers may not shop around if their preferred brand is unavailable in their normal store.

▶ *Impulse products* are unplanned purchases, usually triggered by some form of visual signal, particularly packaging. This category includes confectionery and magazines at the supermarket check-out, but also travel insurance at airports and ice-creams and hot-dogs at cinemas. Availability at the right time and in the right place is critical in the marketing of these types of product.

▶ *Emergency products* are purchased not because of sudden desire (as impulse purchases), but rather due to sudden need. This is an important distinction. The customer doesn't have time to shop around for bargains when a crisis occurs, so is unlikely to be very sensitive to high prices: the value of an umbrella to those faced with a long walk in the rain is far higher than to those who have no such immediate and pressing need.

DID YOU KNOW?

Supermarket chains in the US offer a home shopping and delivery service, which enables busy people to order goods from home and have them delivered. Customers claim that this saves them a lot of money, as they are not in a position to make impulse purchases. This supports other research that suggests that a person with a handful of items on the shopping list will have as many as three times that number of items in the trolley by the time they get to the checkout ('Off your Trolley with Loyd Grossman', 1995).

Shopping products

These are products that the consumer feels are worth comparing with other products before making a final selection – the term being derived from the expression 'shopping around'.

▶ *Homogeneous products* are those seen as being basically the same as each other, so the consumer is willing to look around for the lowest prices. Car insurance has moved into this category in recent years. However much insurance companies try to emphasise the quality, reliability and other features of the services they offer, many consumers are willing to phone around for comparable quotations and will normally choose the lowest.

This has created an opportunity for low-cost direct operators such as Direct Line to gain considerable business at the expense of large companies with high overheads, and in particular at the expense of insurance brokers.

▶ *Heterogeneous products* are compared on the basis of more than just price. Many consumer durables, which are products designed for use over a period of time, fall into this category. Clothing, 'white' goods (such as washing machines and fridges), household linens, cars and sports goods are all examples of heterogeneous products. Consumers will consider the tangible features of these products and if appropriate the associated services on offer, before making their decisions to buy. Within limits, customers are not especially sensitive to prices provided that the product they are considering has some demonstrable advantage over its competitors, so promotional activity should focus on pointing out unique attributes rather than low prices.

Speciality products

These possess unique characteristics that consumers are willing to seek out and alternatives are not considered to be satisfactory. This uniqueness usually stems from undisputed quality superiority or design exclusivity. Steinway pianos are an example of the former, actively sought by professional musicians and concert venues for their quality and reliability of tone. Design exclusivity is a hallmark of Laura Ashley fabrics and Jaguar cars, both of which are considered to be quite different from other products with similar functions.

Speciality brands can be created even in the absence of unique functional or tangible attributes of a product. Barbour coats, Levi Strauss jeans and Doc Marten boots are always likely to be treated as speciality products by a segment of the population, even if their competitors produce garments that are indistinguishable in all but name. The status of these products is unparalleled, even if their physical uniqueness cannot be sustained.

Unsought products

These are products that consumers have no particular desire to buy, but can be persuaded to buy through active selling and promotion.

- ▶ *New products* fall into this category if they are introducing a completely new concept to the market. Few consumers felt the need for bin-liners until the product was launched and people began to recognise the inconvenience of having to wash out their kitchen bins on a regular basis. The microwave oven was another example of a product for which consumers had to be persuaded of their need. Conventional cooking times had never been considered a particular problem until the benefits of quick defrosting and cooking were demonstrated.
- ▶ *Peripheral products* are unsought, not because they are new and untried, but because consumers' need for them is marginal. Prepaid funeral plans, encyclopaedias and double glazing are all products that many consumers feel they can live happily without, but can be persuaded of their importance by heavy promotional influence, particularly in the form of personal selling.

Business products

These include all products that enable a business to function; this in turn enables businesses to produce and supply products to consumers. As explained in Chapter 3, demand for business products is known as derived demand. If consumer demand for a company's products falls, whether this be due to seasonal factors, a down-turn in the economy, or competitor activity, that firm will subsequently cut back on its own purchases of raw materials, components, operating supplies and even business services. Consequently, organisations that sell business products need to be aware not only of current trends among their own customers, but also of trends among end-user consumers so that they can anticipate any future changes in levels of demand. Business products fall into three main categories.

Process products
These ultimately become part of a producer's own product.

▶ *Raw materials* are unprocessed items that are converted into more useful forms during a further manufacturing process. They may take the form of *farm products*, which are commercially grown or reared with the express purpose of supplying other businesses. Wheat and hops are key supplies in the baking and brewing industries, cotton and flax are converted in textile manufacture, and farm animals are reared for use in the food processing industry. *Natural products*, on the other hand, are not produced but extracted. They exist naturally, and the task of the producer is to extract them from the environment, as in the case of oil, minerals, and even fish. The market for raw materials is often characterised by perfect competition (as explained in Chapter 2), as it is virtually impossible for producers to differentiate their products from those of other producers. Consequently, the key marketing tasks for these businesses are to ensure consistent quality, and if possible to get their customers to commit themselves to long-term contracts.

▶ *Components* are processed parts or materials that ultimately become part of a finished product. *Component materials* are raw materials that have been through the first stage of processing. Businesses convert iron ore into iron, wool into yarn and timber into wood pulp, and then sell these manufactured materials on to other manufacturers for further processing. *Component parts* are one step further down the conversion process, consisting of manufactured products, such as wire, motors, batteries, and switches. Both component materials and parts may have two key markets through which sales can be made: OEMs (or *original equipment manufacturers*) and the *aftermarket*, where spares are sold for repairs to the original equipment. Motor vehicle parts, such as tyres and batteries, are extensively sold through both markets, but the more profitable of the two is the aftermarket. OEMs are generally large companies who buy such large quantities they are able to secure big discounts, whereas the aftermarket consists of a much greater number of smaller buyers including many local garages and shops. They have far less, and in many cases no bargaining power over their suppliers and consequently must pay higher prices.

CASE STUDY **6.2**
· · · · · · · · · · · · · · · · ·

Hopping out of decline
English hops are a primary ingredient in the brewing of beer and, in particular, traditional English bitter. Lager uses less hops, many of which are grown abroad and imported for the production of continental lagers under licence from overseas brewers.

There has been a gradual decline in the market for bitter, amounting to approximately 12 per cent over the last 15 years with a prediction of a further decline of one to two per cent volume per year until the end of the century. This decline can be attributed to a number of factors: demographic changes have resulted in fewer people in the heavy-drinking age groups, an increase in the number of lager brands reflecting changes in consumer tastes, a move towards wine consumption and greater awareness of health issues.

As a consequence of this, hop growers have been faced with serious problems. They need to be able to predict demand with some certainty, as hops are perennial plants that require growers to commit themselves to up to ten years' production in advance, some of which will be sold up to five years in advance of harvest. Farmers also have to select a strain of hop for planting. Alpha-type hops are used to give a bitter flavour. They are the easiest to grow, but English produce is barely distinguishable from foreign produce so brewers tend to buy the cheapest. Aroma-type hops such as 'Fuggles' and 'Goldings' are used in the only buoyant segment of the market, for brewing real ale. In this segment there is still support by brewers for the distinctive characteristics of English hops, but producers are beset with problems of disease which upset planning cycles, and brewers complain of broken contracts and high prices; demand is thought to be three times higher than supply.

Potential solutions to the problems facing hop producers include the production of hardier varieties of Aroma-type hops, in particular those that are suitable for mechanical harvesting. The export market also holds potential, with the North American micro-breweries being particularly keen to use English hops.

Questions

1   Can you think of any other farm products that are having to respond to declining demand? How are they responding?

2   Is there anything that hop suppliers could have done to prevent the decline in demand? If so, what?

3   What sort of market information would be useful for hop suppliers trying to predict future levels of demand?

Source Derrick, 1995.

Plant and equipment

These are purchased by businesses to enable them to produce their finished products. They are generally long-lasting products, which are considered to be assets of the business and may be depreciated over many years.

▶   *Capital goods* are installations such as buildings and fixed equipment at which the production process is located. This includes paper machines in the paper industry, radar systems and aeroplanes in the aviation industry and even shops in the retailing industry. Businesses that supply such products are usually faced with the task of high-level negotiations with potential buyers over considerable periods of time. Their customers' decision-making processes and decision-making units are likely to be highly complex, and the product will often have to be specially designed or customised to meet their needs. This type of product is also vulnerable to a down-turn in the economy. Firms cut back or even cancel investments such as these during recession, and suppliers are forced to reduce their prices as a result of their industry's over-supply relative to demand.

▶   *Accessory equipment* consists of shorter-lived durable items used in production or office activities, such as fork-lift trucks, hand tools, filing cabinets and computers. Standardised products are usually acceptable, and markets often span more than one industry. Fewer people tend to be involved in the buying process, and they are likely to be less senior in their organisations than the buyers for capital equipment. While price is important to customers for these products, it may be of less importance than the facility to rent or lease, which may help them to manage cash flow better.

Supplies and services

These are products consumed during the running of a business:

▶ *Maintenance, repair and operating supplies* (known as MROs) are items used in the running of a business or the production of a product but never become part of the product itself. These are the equivalent of consumer convenience products, ordered when required on a routine basis, and tend to be purchased across a range of industries. Maintenance items include paint, light bulbs and cleaning fluids; operating supplies include ink cartridges for computer printers, lubricating oil for machinery and paper for photocopiers; repair supplies are used to mend broken or damaged equipment, including adhesives, bearings and electrical fuses. Buyers are generally reluctant to spend much energy on product selection for any MROs, so contracts for supply over a period of time are often negotiated. Many suppliers of these products choose to distribute through industrial distributors (the equivalent of retailers for business products) rather than deal direct with the end-user business, as distributors can enhance the benefits to the buyer by offering an assortment of products, which can save time and effort in the purchasing process.

▶ *Business services* are purchased if a business needs to enhance its expertise in a particular area. Suppliers of skills to businesses include advertising agencies and accountants, but also data processing houses, recruitment consultants, cleaning services and even landscape gardeners! Service supply is a growing sector in the British economy in the 1990s. Handy (1991) describes the down-sizing that is taking place in many industries in the US as well as the UK, as many organisations reduce their own employed staff to a bare minimum by contracting out all the non-core services they require. Describing suppliers of these services as 'the contractual fringe', Handy explains how cost effective it can be for businesses to pay other businesses to undertake this type of work, particularly now that information technology makes communications so much easier: 'Londoners can now get their typing done more cheaply and as quickly in Taiwan as in London using the new communications technology' (Handy, 1991).

Creating a product range

It is very unusual for a firm to offer only a single product item. This may be the case for a new firm setting up in business for the first time, but in order to grow and protect themselves from competition businesses usually expand the range of products that they sell.

The *Product Mix* refers to the total set of all product items sold by an organisation. It can be expanded in three ways; firstly by creating a product line, and then by increasing the number of product items within each product line, or by increasing the number of product lines in the mix.

The *Product Line* is a group of closely related product items. The range of aerobics footwear produced by Reebok, for example, would be considered as a single product line as they are all intended for the same end use. Other product lines are defined on the basis of being aimed at the same type of customer, such as a range of toiletries designed for baby-care, or low-calorie foods aimed at dieters. Even price levels can define a product range, such as the budget range of own-label groceries sold by some supermarkets under logos such as 'plain and simple' or 'back to basics'. Design is another factor that can distinguish a product line. Most car manufacturers have relatively few product lines consisting of certain basic models, but they create a range of versions of each model and extend these from time to time by bringing out new editions that have the same basic design but include slightly different features and accessories.

The *depth of the product mix* refers to the number of items within each product line. If there are insufficient items in a product line to satisfy customer demands fully, a gap can be left open for a competitor to enter the market, so product lines tend to deepen over time as firms attempt to grow, to expand their market share and to deter competitors. However, careful consideration should always be given to the extra costs involved in extending a product line. New production capacity may be needed and additional promotional and distribution costs will almost always be incurred, so firms should plan the growth of their product lines with concern for marginal costs as well as potential future revenues.

DID YOU KNOW?

UK supermarket retailers carry anything up to 15,000 different product lines in their larger stores. When Aldi, the German supermarket chain, entered the UK market in 1990, it carried only 600 lines, all of which are heavily discounted. Product lines with high carrying costs, such as chilled foods and fresh fruit and vegetables, are kept to a minimum to help keep prices down.

The *breadth of the product mix* refers to the number of different product lines a firm sells. Some manufacturers specialise in one product line only, while others offer a range of product lines, sometimes aimed at completely different target markets. Large multi-national companies such as ICI provide good examples of this. ICI supplies product lines that range from paints to synthetic fibres, to chemicals and petro-chemicals, with different product lines being aimed at consumer markets and industrial markets and different marketing activities and structures being used to support the different product lines. The breadth of the product mix is a key consideration in retailing too. Department stores usually carry a very wide product mix, but may stock only a limited number of items in each product line. Speciality stores, however, have the opposite policy. They may carry just one or only a few product lines, but attempt to carry a wide range of items within each product line. The Tie Rack is a good example of this, specialising in a comprehensive selection of ties and scarves but offering little else.

Even if an organisation has a broad product mix, it may be involved in common marketing activities across the product lines, which can lead to economies of scale. Convenience products, for example, may all be sold through supermarkets, regardless of their product lines, and distribution costs may be reduced as a result. Any planned broadening of the product mix should take into account this type of *consistency*, which can improve the viability of a new product line.

The product life-cycle

After a product is launched there will be times when its sales levels will grow, times when they will be relatively static, and ultimately it is likely that its sales will start to fall, particularly if a new product comes along that satisfies consumer needs better (think, for example, of the gradual disappearance of vinyl records as consumers favour the superior quality and convenience of CD recordings, and how launderettes have become rare sightings in town centres, abandoned by many in favour of domestic washing machines). The concept of the product life-cycle is a useful model for describing these common patterns of sales growth and decline that can be observed over the lifetime of a product. Although not all products will follow this pattern precisely, and different products will move through their life-cycles at different speeds (some seeming to go on for ever, and others disappearing after only a fleeting period of success), the concept is still very useful for helping marketers to identify likely sales trends and plan appropriate marketing activities. (See Figure 6.3.)

Characteristics of the product life-cycle

The product life-cycle depicts four key stages that a product is likely to pass through between its launch onto the market and its disappearance from it.

Introduction
The introduction stage is the period just after the launch of a product during which sales growth is likely to be slow. The product is new and untested, so

figure 6.3
Characteristics of the Product Life-cycle

potential customers are likely to be wary of it and resistant to buying something new. Only the most innovative buyers will experiment and try out the new product (there is more discussion about the rate at which customers adopt new products in Chapter 7). Consequently, sales revenue from the new product is likely to be low. However, product costs are likely to be high. Not only will the firm be incurring heavy expenses for promoting the new product, but in addition it is unlikely to be fully utilising its production capacity and there will be few economies of scale to be enjoyed with such a low level of output. As a result, many products make a loss at the introductory stage, and firms should identify in advance how they are going to find the cash to see them through this difficult period.

Many products make it no further than the introduction stage of the product life-cycle. If customers try the product but find that it doesn't satisfy their needs, then there will be no repeat purchases, no recommendations made to friends and colleagues, and sales will gradually fall away. The take-off point is the point at which the products offering customers genuine benefits will survive and move into much more rapid growth, while those tried and found to be unsatisfactory will start to move into decline.

Growth

Provided a new product satisfies customer needs it will be fuelled by repeat purchases and word-of-mouth publicity, and sales will start to climb rapidly as a large number of new customers are attracted to the product for the first time. Profits start to be made as sales revenues increase faster than costs. Confident that the product is likely to be a success, competitors start to enter the market, copying much of the pioneer's basic idea but perhaps introducing new product features too. As the total size of the market is growing the new competitors can increase their sales by attracting new customers rather than undercutting each other on price, so they too are likely to be able to trade profitably. Only when the market starts to move towards maturity and fewer new customers are buying the product for the first time is price competition likely to increase, undermining levels of profitability.

Maturity

The stage at which a product's sales growth slows down is known as maturity. This slow-down is likely to lead to over-capacity in the industry as a whole, so at this stage there is a tendency for firms to start trying to attract customers away from their competitors by offering cheaper prices and increasing their promotional efforts. As this type of competitive activity intensifies, the least effective competitors are forced out of the market (known as the shake-out point), leaving just the strongest players to dominate a more stable market.

Saturation occurs during the maturity stage, at the point when sales growth slows down to zero. From this point on there will be no further net increase in the size of the market. Any new customers entering the market are simply replacing customers who have stopped buying the product, and all other sales are simply replacement sales or repeat purchases by the same customers.

High profits can be made at the maturity stage as sales revenues are high but costs can be kept quite low, with firms benefiting from economies of scale in both production and promotional activity.

Decline

The decline stage is the period when sales of a product start to fall. This usually occurs because a substitute product has been launched that offers the consumer superior benefits, so buyers are switching their allegiance to the new product. Competitive activity starts to intensify further at this stage, as the existing firms are chasing fewer customers to make their sales. Consequently, profitability is usually weakened and competitors have to consider whether it is worthwhile remaining in the market. Some choose to leave the market altogether, while others choose to curtail some of their promotional expenses, reduce their number of distribution outlets and focus solely on any remaining buoyant segments of the market.

Responses to the product life-cycle

Because the characteristics of the market change at the different stages of the product life-cycle, different marketing emphases are also appropriate. (See Figure 6.4.)

At the *introduction* stage, the firm that has pioneered the new product should be attempting to create wide product awareness and encourage product trial, so that the more profitable growth stage can be entered as soon as possible. The marketing mix should be managed to help achieve this objective. It is normally adequate to start off with a fairly basic product form, which satisfies a core customer need but offers a minimum of additional features. These can be added later as customer tastes and preferences start to develop and distinct market segments start to emerge. Prices charged are unlikely to cover costs, but one of two pricing strategies may be appropriate depending on the nature of the product and the likely competition: price skimming involves charging a high initial price, with a view to reducing it as the market grows and price penetration involves setting a lower price than is likely to be maintained over the long term, so as to expand the market as quickly as possible. (Both of these strategies are discussed in some detail in Chapter 8.) It is sometimes difficult to encourage distributors to sell new products; they are concerned that the product will not reach the growth stage and that they will invest time and money in a product that will not bring them any long-term revenues. Therefore, concentrating on securing distribution through just a few key outlets is likely to be a more successful strategy than attempting to gain wide-scale distribution from the word go. Promotional activity also needs to be fairly selective, and may be aimed at both distributors (to encourage them to stock the product) and end-user markets. Some sales promotion techniques can be particularly effective at this stage, to give potential customers an incentive to try the product.

At the *growth* stage it is important for the pioneer to try to maximise its own market share in the face of new competitors now entering the growing market. This normally involves sacrificing some short-term profitability, as high costs are incurred in improving product features and distribution intensity, and in extending promotional activity to reach mass markets. Advertising often replaces sales promotion as the most important promotional technique as efforts are made to establish a strong brand image that will become a valuable asset during maturity (the importance of the brand is discussed further at the end of this chapter).

	Introduction	Growth	Maturity	Decline
Marketing emphasis	Create product awareness Encourage product trial	Establish high market share	Fight off competition Generate profits	Minimize marketing expenditure
Product strategy	Introduce basic products	Improve features of basic products	Design product versions for different segments	Rationalise the product range
Pricing strategy	Price skimming or price penetration	Reduce prices enough to expand the market and establish market share	Match or beat the competition	Reduce prices further
Promotional strategy	Advertising and sales promotion to end-users and dealers	Mass media advertising to establish brand image	Emphasise brand strengths to different segments	Minimal level to retain loyal customers
Distribution strategy	Build selective distribution outlets	Increase the number of outlets	Maintain intensive distribution	Rationalise outlets to minimise distribution costs

figure 6.4 **Marketing responses to the product life-cycle**

Prices may have to be reduced slightly to reach the more price sensitive potential customers, but only as the market moves towards maturity should it become necessary to use pricing strategies to fight off the competition.

At *maturity* there is sufficient opportunity for some competitors to operate profitably, though the brand leader can hope to be more profitable than the rest. It is important for firms to focus on maximising profits as there is little, if any, prospect of further growth. Product lines may be modified or extended to include versions that appeal to the specific needs of segments within the total market. Prices in general should match or beat the competition in an attempt to prevent customers switching their allegiance, but this should not be taken to such extremes as to damage profitability.

> **DID YOU KNOW?**
>
> Research has found that, on average, brands with a market share of 40 per cent generate three times the return on investment as brands with a market share of ten per cent. In FMCG markets the ratio is even more striking: leading brands typically make 18 per cent return on sales, followers make three per cent and the rest are often unprofitable (Buzzell and Gale, 1987; 'The year of the brand', 1988).

Promotion is an alternative technique that can achieve the same aim as price cutting, but without undermining the generation of sales revenue. Advertising is effective for reinforcing brand benefits, while sales promotion can encourage buyers to switch across from competitors.

There is little long-term potential left for products at the *decline* stage so it is important for firms to minimise their marketing expenditure on these and instead use their resources, especially cash, to support new, cash-hungry products at the introduction or growth stages in their life-cycles. Competition intensifies at the decline stage so prices will normally have to be cut and it may be necessary to rationalise the product range and retain only those items that appeal to the larger and more profitable remaining segments in the market. Distribution can be phased out among the least effective distributors, as all but the most loyal customers will ultimately be abandoning the product in favour of something new and those who do remain are usually willing to make some efforts to track the product down. Promotional expenditure can be reduced to a minimal level, aiming specifically at the remaining segments, but towards the end may be withdrawn altogether. This type of activity at the decline stage is known as a harvest strategy. The speed at which such a strategy should be implemented will depend first on the speed at which product demand is declining and second on the reactions of competitors. If competitors leave the market quickly there will be more scope for a firm to remain profitable in a declining market for a much longer period of time.

CASE STUDY **6.3**
··················

Life at the launderette

The launderette has followed a text-book product life-cycle. The concept was introduced in response to consumer demand for the new invention of the washing machine, the purchase of which was beyond the pocket of most households. Despite the obvious drawbacks of having to carry laundry down the road to be washed, launderettes proliferated as housewives who were formerly tied to the kitchen sink on wash-days were suddenly released from the drudgery of hand-washing.

But the success of the concept was short-lived. Business reached a peak in the 1960s, by which time an estimated 12,000 outlets graced the streets of towns and cities throughout the country. As living standards rose, customers started to buy their own machines and the market went into decline. Currently only 4,500 launderettes remain, and turnover is in the region of £2 billion a year. They are mainly located in less well-off districts and areas with high levels of rented accommodation, such as university towns.

However, this may be set to change if 'Duds and Suds' have their way. An American-style laundromat of this name has opened in West London, aiming to make the experience both interesting and fun. A TV screen, easy chairs, snack bar, pool table and pinball machine sit alongside the washers and dryers, and uniformed staff can be commissioned to do the ironing while customers are waiting for their second wash to finish. Two similar outlets are already running successfully in Ulster and their owners are aiming to open branches in every major city in the UK.

Questions

1 Do you think the British are going to change the way they do their washing?
2 List the relative benefits of the launderette service described, compared with a domestic washing machine. Describe the best target markets for each.
3 Who or what would you consider to be 'Duds and Suds'' main competitors?

Source Sylvester, 1995 (2).

Variations of the product life-cycle

The product life-cycle is an important tool which gives guidance to managers as to the likely developments in its markets and the types of marketing activities that should be considered at each stage. It is not, however, a definitive description of the development of all products. Some products survive no longer than the introduction stage; some appear to have a never-ending maturity stage; some start to go into decline but are revitalised after a successful repositioning campaign.

Product classes are generic names for groups of products that satisfy similar customer needs, such as cars, soap, or margarine. Product classes tend to have the longest life-cycles, characterised by maturity periods that seem to go on indefinitely. Sales of product classes tend only to go into decline if changes occur in the macro-environment. Cars, for example, offer such unique benefits to customers over other forms of transport that they may never go into decline unless there is a change in legislation, perhaps to control their use or make them more expensive to buy or run. (See Figure 6.5.)

figure 6.5
**The product
life-cycle for product
classes**

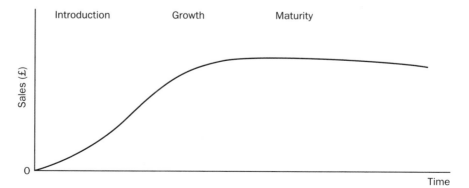

figure 6.6

**The product
life-cycle for product
forms**

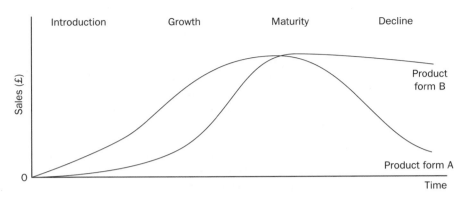

Product forms are sub-sectors of product classes that deliver the benefits offered within a product class in different ways. Cars, for example, might be diesel or petrol driven; deodorants might be aerosols or roll-ons; computer printers might be laser or ink-jet. Even if a product class has an extended maturity period, the different product forms may not survive for that length of time, or may experience growth at different rates and at different times. Environmental concerns about the Greenhouse gases emitted by petrol engines have led to a resurgence in demand for diesel-powered cars, though this could be reversed if recent concerns about other types of diesel emissions prove to be serious. (See Figure 6.6). Video cassettes are now common household products at the mature stage of the product life-cycle, but only the VHS product form has survived into maturity, with the Sony Betamax form having failed to survive the shake-out

Brands are products that belong uniquely to one producer. (There is more detail about the nature and purpose of brands at the end of this chapter.) The life-cycle of a brand is the most unpredictable of all, as firms attempt to create growth for their own brands by tempting customers away from competitors, thus causing their brands to move into decline. Successful brands may survive for many years if they can sustain some form of competitive advantage, but their life-cycles are often scalloped in appearance as firms start to lose market share in the face of competitive attack but then regain it when they retaliate with their own marketing campaigns. The big confectionery brands are typical examples of this. While new product launches can temporarily threaten the market leadership of the top brands, their success is seldom long lived. (See Figure 6.7.)

Fads may be product classes, forms or brands that are characterised by very short life-cycles. They are usually products that offer little in the way of benefits other than being unusual or exciting, and therefore lose popularity quickly when their novelty has worn off. Toys offered to children at Christmas often fall into this category; their producers need to be aware that, unless they have something new to offer the market, the following year they are unlikely to make any sales at all. (See Figure 6.8.)

DID YOU KNOW?

Cadbury's Dairy Milk was the best-selling confectionery brand in 1969, 1989 and 1994, and Cadbury's Dairy Milk, Cadbury's Fruit and Nut, Cadbury's Whole Nut and Aero were the top five brands in all of these years. Bourneville, Yorkie and Galaxy had more fleeting success, each taking a top-five position in one of these years only (Laitner, 1995).

figure 6.7
**The scalloped
product life-cycle for
brands**

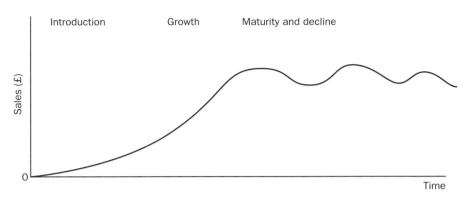

figure 6.8
**The product
life-cycle for fads**

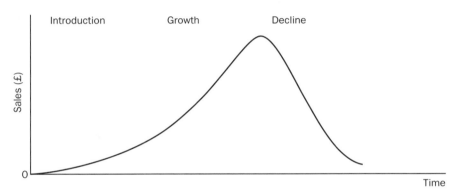

The product portfolio
. . . .

The product life-cycle has important implications for the overall portfolio of products that firms sell. If they have a lot of products moving towards the decline stage but few at the introduction or growth stages they will have little opportunity for success in the future. On the other hand, if they have a lot of products at the introduction or growth stage, but very few generating profits at the maturity stage, they are likely to experience financial difficulties as they need to invest heavily in promotional activity to increase the brand awareness and loyalty towards their new products.

The Boston Matrix is a useful tool for exploring these issues. It was developed by the Boston Consulting Group with a view to helping companies chart their product portfolios and recognise the financial and marketing implications of these. (See Figure 6.9.)

Stars are products that are achieving success at the growth stage of the product life-cycle. If a firm is gaining a dominant market share at this stage it is likely to continue to be successful at the maturity stage, so stars are important members of an organisation's product portfolio. However, heavy investment is required to sustain this success in the face of a growing competition (which is a characteristic of the growth stage), so although a star is likely to generate a lot of sales revenue, it will also incur heavy marketing costs. Hopefully the revenues will cover the costs, but if competition is particularly heavy they may not, and other sources of finance may be necessary.

figure 6.9
The Boston Matrix

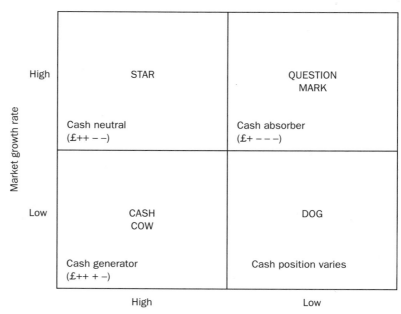

Question marks are products that are failing to achieve success at the early stages of the product life-cycle. Competitors are dominating the market, and as a result question marks incur high marketing costs in trying to get established but at the same time generate little revenue to sustain themselves. If question marks are thought to have long-term potential for success, it may be worth-while supporting them through this difficult time with cash from other sources, but if the competition is thought to be too strong and aggressive for the situation to improve measurably, then they should be harvested even at this early stage before too many resources are wasted.

Cash cows may be one source of finance for supporting stars and question marks. These are products that are achieving success when the market is no longer growing, usually at the maturity stage in the product life-cycle. Sales revenues are at their highest levels, but the marketing expenditure required to maintain a high market share is relatively low compared with the costs incurred when trying to build share in a growing market. Consequently, cash cows tend to generate more cash than they need to sustain themselves, thereby making funds available for use by other products in a portfolio.

Dogs are products that have failed to achieve the success being experienced by cash cows. In a market that is mature or in decline, these products have not succeeded in establishing a significant share of the market. At the decline stage competitors are likely to be aggressive, which may mean that a lot of money has to be spent merely in an attempt to survive in the market. However, if competitors are passive, it may be possible for a dog to thrive, particularly if the market is still at maturity, perhaps by concentrating on a single segment of the market of little interest to the market leaders. As a result it is not always clear whether a dog is a net cash generator or a net cash drain. This needs to be monitored closely, and a harvest strategy implemented if it becomes apparent that the effort of supporting the product is not being repaid.

ACTIVITY **6.2**
· · · · · · · · · · · · · ·

A product mix for chocoholics

Although we are often familiar with a brand name, we are not always familiar with the entire product mix. Cadbury's, for example, is well known for its Dairy Milk Chocolate, but what else does it sell?

1 Go to your nearest grocery superstore and try to identify every product item produced under the Cadbury's name.

2 Classify these products into product lines.

3 Identify Cadbury's key competitors for each product line and suggest who you think is the brand leader.

3 Indicate where you think each product line lies on the product life-cycle.

4 Estimate where each product line falls on the Boston matrix.

5 Suppose you have a promotional budget of £10 million to spend on the Cadbury's product portfolio next year. What proportions would you allocate to which product line, and why?

Branding
· · · · · · · · · · · ·

A brand is an element or combination of elements that uniquely identify a product as being produced by one particular supplier and thereby distinguish it from competitors' products. These elements usually include a particular name, logo, symbol and/or design that the customer then associates with a particular supplier and that the supplier, thanks to trademark law, has the exclusive rights to use for an unlimited period of time.

The importance of branding

Branding is an exceptionally important part of product strategy which offers important benefits to both customers and suppliers alike.

For customers, the brand:

▶ saves time and effort, as customers know what to expect and do not have to go through an extended decision-making process every time they buy the product.

▶ provides security and reduces the risk of purchase as the brand offers a consistency of quality: no one expects to fault Marks and Spencer on quality, whether it be in food, fashion or home furnishing products.

▶ can offer psychological rewards by association with a sought-after image that can convey status on the buyer: the value of the perfume Chanel No. 5 was immediately enhanced by the announcement by Marilyn Monroe that it was all she wore in bed!

For suppliers, the brand:

▶ can generate a loyal base of repeat customers who perceive it to be superior to competitor products in certain ways. This can then be used in promotional messages; for example, BMW emphasises good engineering; Volvo emphasises safety; Rolls Royce emphasises luxury.

▶ can command higher prices because of the value placed by customers on the security offered by the brand, which is why well-known manufacturer brands of products are almost always more expensive than their supermarket own-label equivalents.

▶ provides a platform from which to launch new products; although a product may be new and uncertain, customers will be reassured if there are links with a well-established brand. The Windows 95 launch by Microsoft has built on the success of the original versions of Windows software; although it incorporates many new and more sophisticated functions, the name carries with it the connotations of simplicity of operation and ease of use.

▶ can offer economies of scale in promotion if the brand is applied across a range of products; whenever any Ford motor vehicle is advertised the image of Ford is reinforced in the eyes of the customer. This is a benefit to Ford, but also to its dealerships who rely on positive customer perceptions to attract their customers.

▶ has value as an asset of the organisation. *Brand equity* can be valued, so a brand name can be sold if it is no longer required.

Who creates brands?

Branding can be used by either manufacturers or resellers to establish their positions in the market. If they wish, they can then license others to use these brands for their products.

Manufacturer brands are the most common types of brand. These are created and owned by the producers of products, who are responsible for designing their marketing mix in a way that is consistent with the qualities of their brands. Product features such as quality, service levels and packaging must reflect the brand identity. Pricing must be at a level that reflects the value offered by the brand. Promotional activity must emphasise the key attributes of the brand and the personality and status associated with it. Distribution should be through channels that are attractive to the types of customers who will favour the brand, by reflecting its quality and image. Channel members should be able to provide an appropriate ambience and supply any services that form an integral part of the brand.

CASE STUDY **6.4**

A brand leader's dilemma

In August 1995, Heinz shocked the market by announcing that it was to start producing own-label baked beans for major retailers. The company had been producing the market leading brand of beans for over 100 years and was known for its staunch opposition to such a move. Any brand leader considering own-label production has to consider the risks of undermining their branded goods and devaluing the market as a whole.

But market pressures had intensified, leading to under-capacity at the Heinz factories. In 1995 alone the market for baked beans had grown by 1.1 per cent in volume, but Heinz's share had fallen by 4.8 per cent to 41.2 per cent. In terms of value, Heinz had lost 2.3 per cent of its market but the market value as a whole had fallen by 7.3 per cent, serving to underline the deleterious impact of cheaper retailer brands.

The product Heinz offered to supermarkets was not the one contained in the branded can, however. Heinz went to great lengths to make it known that it had formulated a 'B' brand recipe, of inferior quality to the branded product, to be sold in the economy ranges. All retailers were offered the same recipe, all on short-term contracts of three months in case demand patterns should change and Heinz needed the capacity for its higher margin main brand. Tesco, Sainsbury and Kwik

Save were the first to take advantage of Heinz's change of policy, all of whom resell the product at about 16p, about half the price of the branded version. Another deal was struck with Nestlé to produce beans for the Healthy Balance and London Grill brands, under the Cross and Blackwell label – formerly an arch-rival of Heinz. The price war had forced Nestlé out of this market at the end of the previous year.

Questions

1 Is the own-label more likely to encourage customers to value the Heinz brand more highly? Or will it undermine the main brand?

2 How else could Heinz have responded to its declining market share?

3 Heinz has announced plans to expand its own-label operations across Europe. Do you think this is wise?

Sources Richards, 1995; Glemet and Mira, 1995; Cook, 1995.

Reseller brands are created and owned by retailers, wholesalers or distributors, who buy generic, unbranded products from manufacturers and take the responsibility for designing a marketing mix that will turn them into brands that are associated with themselves and not their manufacturers. Sometimes known as *own-label* products, these reseller brands have become more and more significant in recent years, particularly in the UK where the major supermarket chains, including Tesco, Sainsbury and Safeway, sell their own ranges very successfully in direct competition with the manufacturer brands on their shelves (own-label goods now account for more than 30 per cent of grocery expenditure in the UK). Other stores, including Marks and Spencer, have a policy of only selling own-labels, and the St. Michael brand has become synonymous in many countries across the world.

Licensing brands are brands that manufacturers or resellers permit others to use under certain conditions and on payment of a fee. Benetton, for example, have licensed a perfume manufacturer to sell a fragrance under its name. Character licensing is very popular too, with film and TV companies offering the manufacturer of clothing, household products, stationery and even food the opportunity to associate its products with a popular media icon.

> **DID YOU KNOW?**
> *Retailers have become adept at making their own-label brands look very similar to leading manufacturer brands, but usually manage to escape legal actions under the rather limited UK trademark laws.*
> *Twenty-five per cent of consumers claim to have purchased look-alikes by mistake, and almost 50 per cent believe (wrongly) that the look-alikes are produced by the brand leader anyway (Murphy, 1994).*

What's in a name?

Firms have a number of options to choose between in deciding how to brand their products.

Individual branding occurs when a firm gives each product in its product mix a separate and distinct name. Nestlé, for example, sell a range of confectionery products under the names KitKat, Yorkie, After Eight, Polo and Quality Street, but other than the appearance of the manufacturer's name on the packet, there is no attempt made to associate each brand with its producer. This strategy is popular if firms wish to actively target different segments of the market which may be alienated if they are associated with other segments.

Thus, although News International now owns both *The Times* and *The Sun*, it is unlikely that the company will ever make efforts to link the two as their readership profiles are almost mutually exclusive.

Family branding, on the other hand, is the practice of using a single brand name (often the name of the manufacturer) to link a range of products (and sometimes all products) in the product mix. Heinz uses its company name on its wide range of packaged foods, for example, to take advantage of its reputation as a quality supplier. Family branding can bring advantages by reducing the cost and risk of extending a product range, as customers will already be familiar with the organisation and are likely to be more prepared to experiment with something new. If, however, the new launch is unsuccessful, the negative impact can be very damaging to the core brand.

Other important decisions to make when selecting a brand name include the following:

▶ Might it be offensive or misunderstood (particularly in a foreign language)? Marketing text books are littered with examples of brands that would be very difficult to export, such as the French soft drink called Pschitt and the Chinese brand of men's underwear called Pansy.

▶ Should it be descriptive of the product? A brand such as 'I can't believe it's not butter' highlights the key benefit of the product, while others in the same market sector, such as Flora, Clover and Delight, offer few clues as to their superior features.

▶ Can it be remembered easily? Short, but meaningless words are easily remembered and quickly associated with a product; brands such as Jif and Kodak.

▶ Can it be registered? If a brand name has strong similarities with another in the market it may be refused registration on the grounds that consumers may inadvertently purchase a product by mistake.

ACTIVITY **6.3**
· · · · · · · · · · · · · · ·

What's in a name?

Famous examples of foreign product names that raise a smile in the UK include a washing powder called 'Colon', a toilet paper called 'Krapp', a toothpaste called 'Darkie' and a tin of tuna fish called 'grated Fanny'! But choosing a brand name that will work in international markets is more difficult than it sounds – Volkswagen launched the 'Sharan' in the knowledge that the name means 'Car of Kings', but in the UK it is associated more readily with Essex girl. Mitsubishi's successor to the Colt was the Starion, a combination of 'Star' and 'Orion', but rumours soon started to circulate that it resulted from the Japanese mispronunciation of the word 'Stallion'.

Suggest a new brand name for the following products and explain why you have chosen it:

▶ A tropical fruit juice.
▶ A roll-on deodorant.
▶ A domestic cleaning service.
▶ A low-calorie breakfast cereal.
▶ A satellite TV channel.

Source Hewitt, 1994.

The Scott-Ex puppy?

UK competitors were rubbing their hands in glee when American owners of the Andrex brand of toilet paper announced that the brand name was to be dropped in a global marketing push, and renamed Scott-Ex.

Andrex is Britain's seventh biggest selling brand, with an annual sales turnover of £3 million. It consistently sustains a premium price which has been as much as 40 per cent higher than the market average. It offers lower margins to retailers than competing brands. It has a relatively poor record for product innovation and a quality that has not consistently been established as the highest in blind tests. But despite all this, the brand has succeeded in remaining a powerful market leader. The most convincing explanation for this is the affection the public has for its 23-year-old advertising campaign featuring a Labrador puppy. The British are willing to pay far more than their European neighbours (an average of 12.8p per hundred sheets as opposed to 9p elsewhere), as they have been convinced that a toilet roll really ought to be soft, strong and very, very long.

American owner, Scott, believes that resistance to dropping local brands in favour of global brands is sheer sentimentality. It is committed to killing off the brand (though has conceded that the puppy could live on). Production of European toilet tissue has already been rationalised, with a single product quality being supplied across mainland Europe. The case for dropping the Andrex brand is strengthening as UK sales have been falling for over four years. Market share by volume has declined from a high of 31 per cent to a recent figure of 17 per cent, and by value the fall has been from 33 per cent to about 25 per cent. The decline has been blamed predominantly on supermarket own-label products, though some suggest that the quality dimensions on which Andrex can claim to be superior are no longer relevant to the customer.

Questions

1 Would you get rid of Andrex in favour of a global brand?
2 Name some other products that have abandoned their UK names in favour of a global brand name. Has this affected your perception of them?
3 Do you think the declining market share of Andrex is attributable more to a changing macro-environment or a changing micro-environment?

Sources Mitchell, 1995(1); Mitchell, 1995(2); Croft, 1995.

Key concepts
•••••••••••••••••••

Actual product: the tangible features of a product that deliver benefits to the customer.

Boston matrix: a portfolio planning chart used to classify products according to their market share and the growth rate of their markets.

Brand: a product that belongs uniquely to one producer.

Consumer durables: products designed for use over a period of time.

Core product: the basic function of a product that satisfies customer needs.

Extended product: intangible features of a product that provide additional psychological benefits to the customer.

Fast moving consumer goods (FMCGs): household products that are bought on a regular basis.

Product life-cycle: a model for describing the common patterns of sales growth and decline that can be observed over the lifetime of a product.
Product line: a group of closely related products sold by an organisation.
Product mix: the total set of all product items sold by an organisation.
Total product concept: the combination of tangible and intangible attributes of a product that combine to offer benefits to the customer.

1 A guarantee is:
   a A tangible element of the core product.
   b A tangible element of the actual product.
   c An intangible element of the extended product.
   d An emergency product.
   e An unsought product.

2 Which of the following are *not* true about 'stars' in a product portfolio?
   a They are likely to be cash neutral.
   b They only exist in growing markets.
   c They have a high market share relative to their competitors.
   d They need no further investment.
   e They have the potential to become cash cows.

3 OEM stands for:
   a Original Equipment Manufacturer.
   b Operating Equipment Maintenance.
   c Operating Equipment Merchant.
   d Organisational End-User Market.
   e Operating Equipment and Materials.

4 Which of the following may also be convenience products?
   a Consumer durables.
   b Impulse products.
   c Speciality products.
   d Heterogeneous products.
   e Business services.

5 Which of the following products is not an example of a family brand?
   a Nissan Primera
   b Johnson's Baby Lotion
   c Campari
   d Body Shop
   e Slazenger

Which of the following are true and which are false?
6 Saturation occurs at the growth stage of the product life-cycle when competitors start to leave the market.
7 Component parts are only sold through the aftermarket.

8 A 'dog' in the product portfolio should be harvested if competitive activity in the market is aggressive.

9 The actual product comprises the tangible features that distinguish a firm's core product from its competitors'.

10 A manufacturer brand may be sold by a retailer in competition with a reseller brand.

Discuss the following

11 Under what circumstances might household groceries be treated as shopping products or even speciality products?

12 What are the advantages and disadvantages of selling to the aftermarket as opposed to OEMs?

13 Describe the product life-cycle for recorded music. In what ways is this different from the life-cycle for tape cassettes?

14 Why might an organisation choose to invest further in its 'question marks'?

15 Family branding and product line extensions are becoming more and more popular. How do you account for this trend?

Further study

Journals

There are a range of important articles that develop some of the issues explored in this chapter. Some of them are classics, such as:

Day, George S. (1977) 'Diagnosing the Product Portfolio', in *Journal of Marketing*, April.

Doyle, Peter 'The realities of the Product Life Cycle', in *Quarterly Review of Marketing*, Summer.

Levitt, Theodore (1965) 'Exploit the Product Life Cycle', in *Harvard Business Review*, vol. 43, November/December.

Others are important for exploring new thinking in these areas, such as:

Chematony, L. De (1993) 'Categorising brands', in *Journal of Marketing Management*, April.

Lannon, Judie (1993) 'Branding essentials and the new environment', in *Admap*, June.

Mathur, S. (1992) 'Talking straight about competitive strategy', in *Journal of Marketing Management*, July.

Books

Most of the introductory texts on marketing principles and marketing strategy also cover this area quite comprehensively.

References

Baker, M. (1995) 'Homing in', in *Marketing Business*, June, p. 52.

Buzzell, R.D.A. and Gale, B.T. (1987) *The PIMS Principles: Linking strategy to performance*, Free Press.

Cook, L. (1995) 'Heinz breaks its taboo over own-label beans', in *The Times*, 23 August, p. 23.

Croft, M. (1995) Name Dropping, *Marketing Week*, 9 June, pp. 37–40.

Derrick, S. (1995) 'The Real thing', in *Marketing Business*, March, pp. 31–2.

Drummond, G. (1995) 'Food for Thought', in *Marketing Business*, March, pp. 6–8.

Gilchrist, S. (1995) 'Service takes over from price as the new retail battle ground', in *The Times*, 24 February, p. 27.

Glemet, F. and Mira, R. (1995) 'To brand or not to brand', in *Marketing Business*, September, pp. 20–1.

Handy, C. (1991) *The Age of Unreason*, Arrow Books.

Hewitt, M. (1994) 'A car by any other name', in *Marketing*, p. 15.

Laitner, C. (1995) 'You must remember this', BRMB Research, in *Marketing*, 5 January, pp. 12–15.

Levitt, T. (1969) *The Marketing Mode*, Mc Graw Hill.

Lusch, R.F. and Lusch, V. N. (1987) *Principles of Marketing*, Kent Publishing Co.

Mitchell, A. (1995(1)) 'Puppy on a roll takes on the world', in *The Times*, May.

Mitchell, A. (1995(2)) 'No value in image over innovation', in *Marketing Week*, June 16, pp. 30–1.

Murphy, J. (1994) 'Comment', in *Marketing Business*, July/August, p. 3.

'Off your trolley with Loyd Grossman' (1995) BBC2.

Richards, A. (1995) 'Heinz B brands turn to Europe', in *Marketing*, 28 September, p. 4.

Sylvester, R. (1995(1)) 'Supermarkets tempt lovers down the aisle', in *The Sunday Telegraph*, February 26, p. 6.

Sylvester, R. (1995(2)) 'Their beautiful launderette aims to clean up', in *The Sunday Telegraph*, February 26, p. 6.

'The year of the brand' (1988) in *The Economist*, 24 December, p. 93.

Woods, R. (1994) 'Sniffing out a trademark', in *The Sunday Times*, 10 July, p. 3.

CHAPTER 7

New product development

Objectives

When you have read this chapter you will be able to:

▶ Distinguish between different types of new product.

▶ Understand why organisations choose to become innovators.

▶ Identify sources of new product ideas and use structured techniques for idea generation.

▶ Develop relevant criteria for the evaluation of new product ideas.

▶ Design appropriate market research programmes at different stages of the new product development process.

▶ Explain how buyer behaviour influences the rate at which markets adopt new products.

Introduction

This chapter defines new products and examines the reasons why firms introduce new products. It discusses the processes they go through in attempting to ensure that their new products will gain acceptance by customers and be successful at reaching their target markets. Techniques for identifying new product ideas are explored and explanations given of the different research techniques and types of analysis that should be undertaken before a decision is made to launch a new product. Influences on the speed and patterns of new product adoption by customers are identified to help explain the process by which innovations gradually penetrate markets.

What is a new product?

A new product is quite simply a product that is perceived as new by the customer. It may be a brand new technology for which its inventor won a Nobel prize, or simply a reworking of an age old concept which, by virtue of its new design, offers new benefits to the customer. It may be tangible and have physical form, or intangible, such as a service or process. It may be unique and new-to-the-world, or simply a new brand that imitates a competitor's product or a new version of a product to extend a product line. The only important factor in defining a new product is that customers see it as being new and consequently change their normal buying behaviour patterns (more about this at the end of the chapter).

Having said this, it is possible to identify four broad categories of new product:

▶ *Major innovations* present radically new user benefits to customers, often through the development of new technologies. Compact discs, microwave ovens, the contraceptive pill and cellular telephones are all examples of new products that in their time have created new markets rather than entered old ones. These types of development are relatively rare as they

171

usually require high levels of investment during the development process and run the ultimate risk of either technical or market failure. However, this type of new product also offers the potential for very high returns if it is successful.

▶ *Product improvements* are innovations within existing markets that have the potential mainly for taking market share from competitors rather than building extensive new primary demand. Windows 95, for example, offers little that is new to the computer software market but is presented in such a way as to significantly improve the ease of use for customers.

▶ *Product additions* may offer new product features to a market, but offer limited new benefits to customers. This includes 'me-too' products, which are little more than copies of concepts that were developed by competitors. Alternatively they may take the form of a product line extension, which perhaps offers a new flavour for a food product or a new colour and accessories for a car.

▶ *Repositioned products* can be considered as new products under the definition given above, but are normally thought of as product adaptations rather than new products. They tend to offer little, if anything, of a tangible nature that is new. Instead they create new intangible features through a change of promotional emphasis. (See Chapter 5 for a more detailed discussion of product positioning.)

Why launch a new product?

New product development is only one of four strategic options available to firms when planning their product/market development strategies (in Chapter 12 there is a full explanation of the four strategic options outlined by Ansoff's Matrix), but it can be very important under certain circumstances, for example:

▶ if consumer tastes are changing so that existing products no longer satisfy their needs, as is the case with any product that is susceptible to fashion or style preferences.

▶ if the environment has changed so as to create new needs in the market; out-of-town shopping malls, for example, have grown in popularity as more and more people become car owners and traffic restrictions make the high street an increasingly difficult and expensive place to park.

▶ if competitors are actively developing new products or technologies that will accelerate the decline of existing products (this is discussed in more detail in Chapter 2).

▶ if growth potential in a market is limited by the total size of the market or the intensity of the competition.

▶ if a firm has a portfolio of products that are generating a lot of cash at the maturity stage of their life-cycles (it needs to prepare to use its cash cows to support stars and question marks if it is to survive in the long-term – see Chapter 6).

▶ if competition in a market is likely to intensify, for example if a patent is due to expire.

▶ if production capacity is under-utilised, perhaps due to seasonal variations in demand.

▶ if legislation threatens to curtail the marketing of existing products in the future, as is the case in the tobacco industry.

CASE STUDY **7.1**

The cream of Irish whiskey

In the late 1970s, with the product life-cycles of strong spirits maturing rapidly and further growth seeming unlikely, International Distillers and Vintners was keen to start looking for new product ideas for the distillers in its group. A range of factors encouraged it to consider the potential for a new liqueur:

▶ consumer tastes were moving towards lower alcohol products
▶ more women were buying alcohol
▶ the liqueur sector was diverse and relatively under-developed
▶ alcohol content is not an important factor in determining preference for liqueurs
▶ because most liqueurs are high proof and difficult to drink, they have a slow use-up rate.

This information led it to believe that there was a gap in the market for a pleasant-tasting light liqueur.

By coincidence, the company's Irish subsidiary, Gilbey's, was looking for new export opportunities at the same time as Express Dairies, a subsidiary of the Grand Metropolitan Group which owned IDV, was searching for new markets for its milk-based products. A consultant suggested the possibility of combining the Dairies' excess cream with whiskey from Gilbey's, and the concept of Bailey's Irish Cream was born. The development went through several stages. Problems arose as to how to keep the product stable without refrigeration, but when these were solved, a flavour was chosen (chocolate) and a name and brand image developed to exploit the product's Irish heritage. Focus group studies were carried out to test the new concept in London and New York, but results were inconclusive, even though people seemed to like the taste. It was decided that the risk of launching the product should be taken, and a pilot production line with a capacity of 25,000 cases a year was set up. Five years later, with sales of around one million cases a year and exports to more than a dozen countries, including the US, that decision seemed to be well justified. Consumers who disliked the strong taste of traditional liqueurs came to regard Bailey's as an acceptable alternative, and life-style advertising encouraged people to think of it as a safe but stylish option. Me-too products started to emerge with regularity, but many of them were rejected on the grounds of their artificial taste and few have survived. Although Bailey's can no longer be regarded as being at the forefront of this market, it has sustained a comfortable niche position for many years.

Questions

1 Bailey's succeeded, but many new products with such indifferent research findings fail. If you had been in charge of a new product, would you have risked a launch?
2 What sort of internal characteristics do you think characterised the company and encouraged the development of the product?
3 How might the Bailey's product line be extended? Do you think this would be desirable?

Source Espey, 1985.

Depending on their circumstances, firms will have a range of objectives for their new products. They may launch new products in an attempt to increase their market share or defend themselves from their competitors, but alternatively could be trying to improve their efficiency, exploit their strengths in areas such as research and development or distribution, or reduce their reliance on a single market.

Characteristics of successful new products

The most successful new products are those that supply new and better benefits which provide improved solutions to customer problems. Doyle (1994) has identified four benefit criteria that new products should meet if they are to thrive in the market. They should be:

▶ *Important*: the customer must find the new benefit valuable. Many products fail to find a market because their inventors have overestimated the value placed on the new benefits by potential customers. Market research in this area is crucial.

▶ *Unique*: the customer must believe that the benefits offered cannot be obtained from existing products. Lack of differential advantage is one of the most significant reasons for product failure, and is responsible for the particularly high failure rate of me-too products and product line extensions.

▶ *Sustainable*: competitors must find the new product difficult to copy. Patent protection can achieve this in industries such as pharmaceuticals, where the high costs of new product development can only be recouped if competitors are prevented from undercutting the innovating firm at the early stages of the product life-cycle.

▶ *Marketable*: the company must have the capability of producing, promoting and distributing the product at a price that is acceptable to customers.

> **DID YOU KNOW?**
> Bizarre offerings occasionally reach the market, whose benefits can at best be described as marginal. History alone will reveal whether Ohio Pasta (an American brand of pasta in the shape of the US state of Ohio, with a small circle in the middle denoting the capital city, Columbus) or Olympische Toorts (a Dutch snack consisting of filled puff-pastry rolls in the shape of the Olympic torch) can attract a loyal following! (Jones, 1993).

In other words 'to create successful new products, a company must understand its consumers, markets and competitors and develop products that deliver superior value to customers' (Kotler and Armstrong, 1994).

What is innovation?

When a firm decides to launch a new product it has a number of strategic options. It can:

▶ buy a branded product from another company and resell it as part of its own product mix.

▶ buy a generic product from another company, give it a brand name and resell as part of its own product line.

▶ negotiate a licence to produce and sell a product from the holder of patent or trademark.

▶ acquire a company and produce and sell its product mix in addition to its own.

▶ develop a new product for the market using its own efforts and resources.

Only the last new product strategy on this list can be classed as *innovation*, defined as 'all the activities of bringing a new product or process to the market' (Clipson, 1991). Innovation, also known as New Product Development (or NPD), is a systematic process that begins with the identification and analysis of new product opportunities that fit within the mission of the organisation. The potential of these is then evaluated using financial, market and technological criteria, and finally the option or options that appear to offer the greatest benefits to the customer and the best opportunities for the company are selected and developed.

Why innovate?

Innovation can bring significant advantages compared with the other new product strategies if it enables the innovator to get to the market first with a new product that can satisfy previously unmet needs. Evidence suggests that pioneers can earn an average return on investment that is 35 per cent higher than their followers, and that 70 per cent of market leaders describe themselves as having been the pioneers of their products (Buzzell and Gale, 1987). Other research shows that, on average, pioneers retain a market share of 29 per cent when their markets move into maturity, as compared with 17 per cent for followers and 12 per cent for late entrants (Robinson and Fornell 1985; Robinson 1988).

Having said this, poor management of innovation can be responsible for the failure of new products. Firms are sometimes too cautious, move too slowly and enable their competitors to launch first; they plan badly, resulting in ideas being poorly evaluated, markets being badly researched and insufficient budgets being allocated; and top managers may constrain their commitment to new products by refusing to sanction aggressive marketing activity if there are risks involved. Only when a new product that offers real benefits is coupled with an efficient process of innovation are the promised returns likely to be realised.

DID YOU KNOW?
3M (originally Minnesota Mining and Manufacturing) is recognised as one of the most innovative companies in the world. It spends six to seven per cent of its revenues on research and development – double the US average. Its 8,000 research staff are required to spend 15 per cent of their time working on projects of their own choosing, and it aims to generate 30 per cent of revenues from products that are less than four years old ('The mass production of ideas, and other impossibilities', 1995).

Key stages in the process of innovation

'Innovation is work rather than genius' (Drucker, 1985). Most successful new products result from a conscious search for opportunities and a systematic attempt to remove the uncertainty surrounding them. This process needs to pass through seven key stages if mistakes are to be avoided and new product failures minimised. (See Figure 7.1.)

Stage 1: Idea generation
This is the starting point for new product development. For every new product that is finally launched on the

figure 7.1

**The process of
innovation**

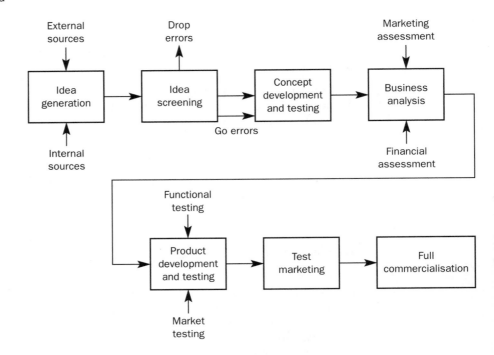

market, a firm typically investigates 57 other ideas that don't make it as far as full commercialisation (Booz, Allen and Hamilton, 1982). Consequently it is important that organisations make continuous efforts to identify sources of potential new products and develop an organisational climate that is receptive to new ideas and will encourage them to emerge.

Internal sources of new product ideas are those generated within an organisation itself. They may emerge from:

▶ a research and development department, motivated by technological possibilities.
▶ a production department, motivated by process possibilities, or attempts to fill capacity.
▶ a design department, motivated by aesthetic or ergonomic possibilities.
▶ a marketing department, motivated by a perception of customer needs.
▶ senior management, motivated by strategic opportunity.
▶ other employees, identifying opportunity in the course of their own work.

Formal techniques to encourage idea generation can be used both within and across these functional areas. One such technique is *brainstorming*. This involves a group of individuals meeting together with a view to freely suggesting possible new product ideas, based on both their personal and work experience. The ideas are recorded, but there is no discussion or criticism of them, and their evaluation takes place at different times, often by different people. The great advantage of brainstorming is that it maximises the number of ideas generated, and allows even wild ideas, which are likely to be the most original, to be systematically assessed.

ACTIVITY **7.1**
············

Spreading ideas

The purpose of brainstorming is to generate as many ideas as possible. By structuring a brainstorming session around a theme it is possible to find solutions to specific problems:

1   Get into groups of five or six, each of you with a small pad of Post-it notes. Designate one of the walls in the room your 'ideas' wall.
2   You are now each required to come up with ideas for 'things to spread on bread': every time you think of a new idea, write it on a Post-it note and go and stick it on the wall; take a look at the other ideas up there while you're there.
3   Continue doing this for 20 minutes – you should have at least 100 ideas between you.
4   Decide on the criteria that you will use for deciding which of your ideas may be worth pursuing and use them to put the Post-it notes into three piles of ideas: the good, the bad and the indifferent.
5   Take your pile of good ideas and attempt to rank them in order of merit.
6   Extract the best idea and write a letter to a company that might be interested in developing your product idea further, explaining why it should test the concept out on consumers.

Instead of things to spread on bread, you might like to work on the following:

▶   Alcoholic beverages.
▶   Hair care products.
▶   Kitchen appliances.
▶   Garden tools.

External sources of new product ideas are those that come from outside the organisation. They may emerge from:

▶   customers, in particular end-users, who make suggestions and complain if their needs are not being fully satisfied
▶   distributors or retailers, who recognise the need for new products that their customers would like
▶   suppliers, who have identified ways in which their raw materials or components could be used to produce new consumer or industrial products
▶   competitors, who produce products that could be copied or improved
▶   universities, who identify potential new product applications as a result of scientific research
▶   advertising and marketing agencies, who identify consumer or business needs in the process of researching markets.

DID YOU KNOW?

The red wine, Le Piat D'Or, was launched in 1979 as a result of wine tastings to identify the taste preferences of consumers. The consistent favourite was a standard Liebfraumilch to which a few drops of red dye had been added, so International Distillers and Vintners set about finding a red wine that tasted just like a German white (Joseph, 1994).

Stage 2: Idea screening

The purpose of this stage is to enable the organisation to eliminate any poor ideas before spending any money on investigating and developing them further. Two errors are commonly made at this stage:

▶   *Drop-errors* are made when organisations fail to spot the potential of an idea, which subsequently proves to be successful in the market. Decca made a classic drop-error when they refused to give a recording contract to the Beatles! This type of error is relatively rare in comparison with the next type.

▶ *Go-errors* are decisions to continue with the development of a product idea that subsequently fails in the market. Different studies quote different figures, but up to 80 per cent of consumer products are thought to fail shortly after their launch. Famous go-errors include the Sinclair C5, which failed to meet the needs of its target market, and Concorde, which will never pay back its investment.

The process of idea screening usually has two levels. The first requires the new idea to be assessed in terms of its market potential and the organisation's capability of producing and selling it. The completion of a standard proforma is often required to ensure that the idea is evaluated against a comprehensive, objective and consistent set of criteria. Ideas that survive this stage can be further evaluated on a numerical basis, which is particularly useful if the relative merits of different ideas are to be systematically assessed. (See Figure 7.2.)

The importance of the different evaluative criteria are weighted, and the extent to which each new idea fulfils the criteria is assessed. The combination of these two numerical scores enables an overall score for each new product idea to be generated; only those with the highest scores should be permitted to proceed to the next stage.

Stage 3: Concept development and testing

Ideas that make it past the screening stage need to be tested out on their potential market. This can only be done if the *product idea* is at this stage converted into a *product concept*; in other words, the idea needs to be developed so that its features and benefits can be explained to potential customers, who will be able to envisage a product and indicate how they might use it, whether they might buy it, how much they might be willing to pay for it and express any concerns or reservations they may have about it. For example, a company

figure 7.2
Idea screening grid

Criteria for selection	Importance of criterion (1 = low, 10 = high) (X)	Rating of new product proposal (1 = poor, 10 = good) (Y)	Weighted score of new product proposal (X x Y)
Consistency with corporate mission			
Use of existing distribution channels			
Production economies of scale			
Technological capability			
Financial risk			
Market familiarity			

might come up with the idea of producing a machine for peeling onions. A concept would have to be developed to describe the size of the machine, whether it would be manual or electric, how it would work and how it would be operated.

No saliva for 'Reviva'

When Anchor Foods (best known for its dairy products) wanted to test consumer reactions to its new juice drink called 'Reviva', it used a combination of a concept test, a product test and a test market to solicit opinions.

Selected consumers within the catchment areas of a range of Tesco and Kwik Save stores were sent coloured leaflets depicting a box of the new drink. The graphics made it clear that Reviva was a natural fruit juice blended with whey, and came in two flavours, orange and tropical. The text inside the leaflet explained that the effect was to produce a totally new drink, 'unique because for the first time it combines a full fruit taste with a distinctive smooth texture'. It also included a coupon for 20p off a one-litre pack of Reviva at either Tesco or Kwik Save.

Accompanying the leaflet was a letter with a questionnaire and reply-paid envelope. The letter explained that the questionnaire was designed to find out consumer opinions of Anchor Reviva based on the leaflet alone. Anyone who mailed it in would be sent a 50p voucher to redeem against any Anchor product. The purpose of this part of the research was to measure consumer acceptance of the product concept and to see what people thought of it in comparison with existing products. The letter went on to say that anyone who was going to use the coupon and try the product should indicate this on the questionnaire, and they would then be contacted by a telephone researcher who would ask a few more questions about their opinions of the drink itself. This part of the research not only tested out the strength of the offer in persuading people to sample the product, but also enabled the company to collect feedback about the qualities of the product itself – not just the concept.

The fact that the product was never launched nationally suggests that the research revealed a problem with the product and that the test-market was unsuccessful.

Questions

1   Why do you think consumers rejected 'Reviva'?
2   Do you think Anchor might have identified the problems without going to the expense of a test market?
3   Ribena has recently been joined by a product line extension called 'Juice and Fibre'. Do you think it will suffer the same fate as 'Reviva'?

Sources Anchor marketing research materials, 1989; Fox, 1995.

It is common for more than one concept to be developed from each product idea, so that potential customers can be asked to react to a number of different styles or versions of a product and the company can decide which concept has the strongest appeal. (This has been made much easier and cheaper by the availability of computer-aided design systems which make it relatively easy to generate drawings and models of different versions of proposed new products.) The onion peeler, for example, could be presented as either a stand-alone mechanical device, a stand-alone electrical appliance or simply an attachment for a food processor, and potential customers would be asked which version they would prefer to use.

ACTIVITY **7.2**
. . . .

No windfall in the Applewood

Taunton Cider has a good reputation for new product development, but recently had to withdraw a new low-alcohol cider called Applewood following an unsuccessful test market.

1 Create three different concepts for a low-alcohol cider.
2 Draw up a questionnaire to test these concepts on consumers.
3 Administer the questionnaire to a small sample of students and use your findings to conclude whether low-alcohol cider has any potential among this market segment.
4 Do you think any other market segments hold more potential than students?

Source Jones, 1993.

Stage 4: Business analysis

As a result of concept testing, businesses gain a better understanding of the nature and specifications of the products that will be acceptable in the market. This enables them to undertake a much more comprehensive assessment of the commercial viability of the new product.

A *marketing assessment* will be the starting point. This will include:

▶ a description of target markets
▶ a forecast of sales volume
▶ an indication of product positioning
▶ a judgement as to likely competitor reactions
▶ a calculation of potential sales losses from existing products as customers switch to the new product (known as cannibalisation)
▶ a specification of the new product features, including quality levels
▶ an assessment of achievable price levels
▶ a strategy for distribution
▶ a statement of promotional requirements.

A *financial assessment* will follow. Based on the marketing assessment, calculations can be made to project:

▶ sales value
▶ variable costs of production
▶ incremental fixed costs
   and these in turn will lead to an assessment of likely
▶ contribution and profitability of the new product.

Products that appear to offer the opportunity for profitable trading can continue to the next stage of the innovation process.

Stage 5: Product development and testing

Up until this stage the new products do not physically exist, except perhaps in the form of models or drawings. It is only at this point that a company must confront the task of determining whether it is technically feasible to produce them and whether they can be produced at a sufficiently low cost to enable a realistic price to be set. This may take many years, particularly if a product is scientifically complex. Pharmaceutical products, for example, have to pass through a lengthy period of pure research to identify the relevant chemical and physiological reactions before they can develop a basic formulation for laboratory and clinical trials.

A prototype or working model of a new product must be produced at this stage to enable further testing to take place. The testing may take two forms:

▶ *Functional testing* should be conducted to identify the best materials and components, to make sure that the product works, to assess its reliability and to ensure that it works safely. Much of this testing will take place on the prototype itself, but it is also possible for some testing to be done using computer simulations which can reduce the time and costs involved in this process.

▶ *Market testing* often takes places in parallel to functional testing. This is a form of market research, usually qualitative research, which aims to check out the acceptability of the product in the market by testing out prototypes on potential customers. Whereas the concept test might only indicate possible product attributes, a market test enables potential customers to assess both the tangible and intangible attributes of a proposed product. The feedback provided at this stage can help to finalise decisions on minor styling and design features such as colour and user controls, as well as marketing decisions such as packaging and brand name. In other cases, the feedback may be so negative as to suggest that the product should be abandoned. At this late stage there is likely to be some resistance to such a move by the staff responsible for the new product development, who will have developed a psychological attachment to it. However, to ignore such signals from the market can have very costly implications as the final stages of the new product development process normally require a heavy commitment to investment in both production and marketing. It's better to acknowledge failure sooner than later.

CASE STUDY **7.3**

Pulling the plug on Persil Power

Less than 12 months after the launch of Persil Power, manufacturer Lever Brothers was forced to concede that the product on which it had spent £200 million in development and promotion, and pinned its hopes for future market share would have to be withdrawn and reformulated.

The company had believed that, in introducing a constituent known as an 'accelerator' in its new laundry brand, it was creating a new and genuine product benefit, that of removing even the most stubborn of stains. Such was the belief in the new miracle ingredient that the accelerator was also added to Radion, Surf and Persil non-bio brands.

But industry scientists, including those at arch-rival Proctor and Gamble, had been aware for some time that the accelerator contained manganese, a chemical that had a tendency to damage coloured fabrics. Within weeks of the launch of Persil Power, P & G started to plant suspicion about its competitor's product, a suspicion that was soon publicised widely in the tabloid press, alongside photographs of holed and faded underwear. A Consumers' Association test supported the claims that the product did indeed damage delicate fabrics.

Lever's initial reaction was an attempt to reassure customers that such problems would only arise under extreme conditions. It spent £500,000 advertising a 'Care Line' which was set up to reassure customers and offer compensation for any clothes that they could prove had been damaged. The Advertising Standards Authority was not convinced though, and refused to criticise P & G for running advertisements that drew attention to Persil Power's defects. Lever hastily tried to reformulate the product, though simultaneously persisted in claiming that the whole problem had been blown up out of all proportion.

The final nail was hammered into Persil Power's coffin when Tesco announced that it was dropping the product from its shelves, a decision that was followed by Sainsbury and Waitrose shortly afterwards. In an attempt to salvage a declining market share, Lever announced that it was dropping the accelerator from all of its brands and that its marketing spend was to be put behind New Generation Persil, which had been launched as a replacement.

The cost of the Persil Power fiasco in terms of customer confidence and loss of brand image is inestimable, but in its next set of financial reports, parent company Unilever included a £57 million write-off element resulting from the debacle.

Questions

1   What lessons might Lever Brothers learn from this incident?

2   Was the aggressive P&G campaign ethical, justified?, both?, or neither?

3   What should be done with the Persil brand next? Can it ever fully recover?

Sources Gilchrist, 1995; Richards, 1995(1); Richards, 1995(2); 'ASA falls silent over P&G's ads knocking Lever', 1995; Brierley, 1995.

DID YOU KNOW?

Before launching the tortilla chip brand 'Doritos' in the UK, Walkers conducted 18 months of painstaking research. They found that British consumers like their tortilla chips to be four thousandths of an inch thinner than the American version (Mitchell, 1995).

Stage 6: Test marketing

This is the stage at which a new product is first made available to potential customers under real market conditions, but on a smaller scale than for the full-scale launch that will follow.

The purpose of test-marketing is to enable a firm to find out about potential problems with its new product and associated marketing activity before going to the expense of a wider introduction. A lot of information can be gathered about customer and retailer or distributor reactions to the product: precisely who are the buyers, and how often do they make a repeat purchase? This, in turn, enables more accurate forecasts to be made of future sales and profitability, and appropriate corrective action to be instigated in the event of limited customer enthusiasm. (See Figure 7.3.)

figure 7.3
Implications of test market results

Standard test-markets

A standard test market is commonly used for testing fast moving consumer goods. It should, as far as possible, be a scaled-down version of an intended national market, involving:

▶ a geographical area that is representative of the future total market area
▶ similar advertising media
▶ equivalent distribution outlets and sales effort
▶ intended price levels.

Sometimes this is not easy, and compromises have to be made. Reaching a set of communities that will represent the tastes and preferences from across the wide range of regional sub-cultures in a country is either difficult and costly, or sometimes impossible. TV regions and provincial cities tend to be used for pragmatic reasons. Local media availability and newspaper readership patterns may be different from the national scene, which makes it difficult to translate national promotional campaigns into local equivalents. Dealers and retailers may have different concentrations in different parts of a country, so replicating distribution intensity can also be a problem.

DID YOU KNOW?
According to US census data, Tulsa in Oklahoma is the most 'average' place in the US, with age distribution, housing prices and racial mix all approximating to the national ratios. Consequently it is a key centre for test marketing. The only products that aren't often tested there are 'sin' products, as Tulsa lies in the heart of the US bible belt – though researchers report that when they do test products such as alcohol, Tulsans drink it just as fast as anyone else in the country! (Kreitman, 1993).

Limited test-markets

If a firm cannot afford the time and expense of a standard test-market, or for some reason is keen to avoid alerting competitors to the potential of a new product, it may choose instead to conduct a mini test-market by making the product available through a selected store for a limited period of time only. Alternatively it may create a *simulated test-market* by showing consumers advertisements for a number of different products, including the new product, and then giving them a sum of money to spend in a store or 'shopping laboratory' operated by a market research firm. Both of these methods have drawbacks because they do not recreate the true market conditions that will be experienced when the product is ultimately launched, but they can indicate if a new product is fatally flawed and draw attention to changes that are required in marketing activity.

In industrial markets, specialist trade shows and exhibitions are sometimes used as simulated test-markets. New products can be presented alongside all the other products on a firm's stand, and in the same arena as competitors' products. Visitors to the show are likely to be members of the target market, and their interest and reaction to the new product can be gauged. The main problems that can arise are when potential buyers want to place orders for products which are not yet in full-scale production. Unless the product is unique and technologically difficult to copy, this could provide an opening for competitors.

Product-use tests
Because of the difficulties of test marketing industrial products, product-use tests are often conducted instead. A few potential customers are selected to borrow the product to use under normal conditions for a period of time. At the end of the trial they are allowed to keep the product in return for giving the company feedback on its performance.

Drawbacks of test marketing
Although test-marketing can reduce the risks inherent in launching new products, it is not appropriate in all circumstances and can even encourage false perceptions of the strength of the new product. For example:

▶ If the new product does not represent a major commercial risk, the costs of staging a test-market may outweigh the potential benefits of risk-reduction it may bring.

▶ The economic environment may change between test-market and full-commercialisation, changing customer willingness to pay for the product.

▶ Competitors may not retaliate at the test-market stage, but start gearing up for a me-too product if the new product seems to be damaging their market share in the test-market region.

▶ Innovative products may experience high trial, but prove to be fads with short product life-cycles.

▶ Competitors may attempt to undermine a test-market by price cutting their own ranges for the duration of the test, so that the new product is less successful than it would otherwise have been.

CASE STUDY **7.4**
········ ········

Only a Wispa of success?
Such was the demand for Cadbury's aerated chocolate countline bar, Wispa, when it was test-marketed in the Tyne Tees TV region in the autumn of 1981 that stories

started to circulate of brawls in the aisles of the local cash and carries and supplies to customers being rationed. Within three weeks of the launch it became clear that the pilot production line that had been brought into operation in the depths of the Cadbury's Bourneville factory would be totally inadequate to cope with the overwhelming customer enthusiasm for Wispa, so advertising was halted and the brand was withdrawn from the market to allow the company to gear up for full-scale production. In an attempt to convince competitors that the withdrawal was because the product was a flop, Cadbury's issued a statement that Wispa could not be produced consistently and profitably. The hope was that this would buy them time to install £12 million of computerised production plant to meet the anticipated levels of demand. The plans were kept a closely guarded secret, even to the extent of screening the operation off from other activities in the factory. Waste paper from the wrappers was burnt and the bars were packed in plain black bin-liner for trans-portation to the warehouse for storage ready for relaunch. Meanwhile, however, Rowntree Mackintosh, makers of the original aerated chocolate bar, Aero, had not been slow to recognise the signs from the test market and moved fast to install their own countline shaped Aero bars. Some 250 million were sold in 1983, before Wispa was relaunched. The move was designed to minimise the impending threat of the competitor product.

Wispa was finally relaunched in October 1983, starting in the North East of England again, but this time being rolled out across the whole country. It was supported by £6 million worth of high-profile TV advertising featuring the stars of 'Hi-di-Hi', 'Yes Minister' and 'It Ain't Half Hot Mum'. Cadbury's sales records were broken, reaching 70 million in 1984, and Rowntree Mackintosh had to admit that its 1984 sales of Aero, also at more than 50 million, were down on the previous year.

But competitors generally remained sceptical about the success of Wispa. Some believed that the biggest victim of the Wispa success was Cadbury's itself, whose other countline bars, including Flake, Double Decker and Star Bar, were all suffering as a result of the market being diverted to the new product. Other observers suggested that once the period of trial-tasting was over, the sales would fall; when people stopped consuming the hype, they would stop consuming the product. Within one year of its launch in the Tyne Tees region, sales had slumped by two thirds, and although Aero appeared in the top five confectionery brands every decade from the 1960s to the 1990s, Wispa appeared in the 1980s but by the '90s had disappeared again.

Questions

1 Why might Wispa's test market have given a false impression of the long-term potential of the brand?
2 Why do you think Cadbury's chose a roll-out strategy, and do you think it benefited the brand?
3 Is there still room in the confectionery market for new brands? Are there any potential market segments that are not targeted at all?

Sources Laitner, 1995; Huxley, 1985.

Stage 7 : Full-commercialisation

The final stage of the innovation process is the launch and full-scale commerciali-sation of a new product. Production capacity is geared up to produce the quantities indicated in the sales forecast and the full marketing plan is activated.

Because of the enormity of this task, some organisations use a *roll-out* strategy to launch their new products. This involves sequentially targeting only selected geographical areas within the total target market over a period of time until all sectors have been covered. It is a particularly useful strategy for firms with limited resources, which can spread the costs of the launch over a longer period of time, during which they also hope to start generating sales revenues. Larger firms can afford to launch to much wider markets and progress more quickly into international markets; some even choose to launch globally and gain a rapid penetration of world markets.

CASE STUDY **7.5**

Windows open on to the world

August 24 1995 was the day chosen by global software firm, Microsoft, to launch the latest version of its operating system, Windows 95. The product promised great improvements on its forerunner, Windows 3.1. Despite its success in the market (attributed mainly to the benefits it offered to PC users in comparison with the MS-DOS system), the old version was thought to be a clumsy wannabe in comparison with the slick, yet ten-year-old Apple Macintosh system. The new product incorporated features designed to match the Apple simplicity of operation and beat it in terms of sophistication, including an integral on-line service for accessing the Internet.

The program went on sale world-wide, accompanied by an explosion of promotional activity. Bill Gates of Microsoft allegedly paid the Rolling Stones £8 million to use their song 'Start Me Up' (though as author Douglas Adams pointed out, this song is better known for its refrain 'you make a grown man cry'!). In New York, the Empire State Building was illuminated in Windows' colours; in Australia the launch was hosted by Dame Edna Everage, wearing a coat made from hundreds of CD-ROMs and a box-shaped hoarding was towed around Sydney harbour; in South Africa, a team of sky-divers dropped in on Johannesburg wearing parachutes in Microsoft colours; and a submarine in the Baltic Sea was used to allow journalists to sample life without Windows. Retailers across the world opened their doors on the stroke of midnight to enable them to catch enthusiasts early. The action started in New Zealand, where computer boffins were fed with free coffee and muffins as they waited patiently to be the first customers in the world for the much-hyped product.

But within days of the launch, criticisms of the product were starting to emerge. Sales in North America reached the one million mark within four days of the product going on sale, but Microsoft's help-line was soon swamped with over 20,000 calls a day from users having difficulty setting up the software or finding that their computers were crashing. Microsoft admitted its problems in handling the calls, but said that the main causes were novices who had never installed an operating system before, and people who had bought the package without checking to see that their computers could run it. In the UK, however, the story has been rather different. Although Microsoft claims that sales have beaten forecasts, the help-line waiting times were very short and retailers have not sold out. A spokesman from Dixon's said that most buyers were computer fanatics who get every piece of new software.

One of the greatest problems is that too many users lack sufficient power in their existing computers. This creates problems, not only with the speed of the programme (or indeed, the lack of it) but also with the inability of corporate customers to install the new version on their older computers. They are concerned that the benefits of an up-grading do not yet justify the extra costs, including new software, hardware and training.

Questions

1   Has Microsoft launched Windows 95 too soon?

2   What advantages have been gained by a global launch and what are the risks?

3   What do you consider to be the critical success factors for a successful global launch? Name some other companies that could use this approach.

Sources Ward and Highfield, 1995; 'The defenestration of Bill', 1995; Ashworth, 1995.

Buyer behaviour and new products
···

The new product adoption process

Consumers and organisational buyers approach the decision to buy a new product using a process known as the *adoption process*. This is a sequential process consisting of five stages, each of which takes them closer to a decision to buy a new product and use it on a regular basis.

▶ *Awareness* is the first stage. The potential buyer knows of the existence of the new product but lacks information about it. Multi-media computers are currently at this stage in the adoption process for many households in the UK.

▶ *Knowledge* is the second stage. Potential buyers seek information about the product so that they have a basis on which to judge whether or not they have any need for it. Much knowledge about new products is acquired by word of mouth from those already using them, but informative advertising and PR activity are useful techniques for speeding up this stage. With regard to the multi-media computer, consumers will want to know what they can do, how easy they are to operate, and of course, how much they will cost.

▶ *Evaluation* is the third stage. The potential buyer weighs up the benefits and drawbacks of the new product and makes an assessment as to whether or not it could solve any problems.

▶ *Trial* is sometimes next. A trial is a process of acquiring or using a product on a limited basis before making a full (and usually financial) commitment to it. In the case of the multi-media computer, consumers may go along to their dealer showroom and ask to be allowed to use it in the shop. Fast moving consumer goods are sometimes given away in sales promotions, either attached to the packets of existing products or pushed through consumers' letter-boxes, and food products can sometimes be sampled in in-store promotions. Car showrooms allow potential buyers to go for a drive in a demonstration vehicle. In resale markets, distributors may ask their suppliers to let them buy on a sale or return basis.

DID YOU KNOW?
The Braun Supervolume hairdryer was designed to meet the needs of the 50 per cent of UK consumers who have straight hair. But the product's introductory period was a problem, as people didn't initially believe the advertising claims. It was only when word of mouth escalated that demand started to increase (Burnside, 1994).

▶ *Adoption* finally occurs if the trial stage has proved satisfactory. The customer is willing to purchase it outright and uses it whenever the need for this type of product arises.

New product adoption rates

The speed at which different individuals pass through the adoption process affects the speed at which products penetrate their markets and move through growth towards maturity in their life-cycles. Two factors have a significant influence on the new product adoption rate, product characteristics and individual characteristics.

Product characteristics

These can affect the readiness of potential buyers to adopt a new product, and the following are particularly influential in speeding up, or slowing down, the adoption process:

▶ *Relative advantage* is a term that describes customers' perceptions of the benefits of a new product in comparison with existing alternatives. The greater the perceived relative advantage, the faster the rate of adoption. The Apple Mackintosh, for example, was soon adopted in a market previously dominated by computer giants such as IBM as it offered product characteristics that were very valuable to the user, especially simplicity of operation.

▶ *Compatibility* refers to the extent a product meets customer needs and reinforces existing attitudes and past experiences. The more closely a product meets a pressing customer need, the quicker it will be adopted. Perhaps this is why machines that stamp initials on golf-balls have never really taken off in a big way.

▶ *Observability* refers to the ease with which product benefits can be demonstrated and communicated to potential customers. The financial services industry experiences some problems persuading people to adopt products such as pension plans. The benefits of such policies are only realisable much later in life, and it is difficult to encourage people to plan so far ahead. By the time they do get around to thinking about them, their costs have risen substantially.

▶ *Simplicity* concerns the ease with which new products are understood. This is another problem facing the financial services industry. Frequent changes in taxation and social policy make it difficult for consumers to evaluate which is the best place to save and invest their money for the future, and the uncertainty of future returns deters many.

▶ *Trialability* refers to the extent to which a product can be sampled before it is adopted. Examples given in the previous section show how it is possible to offer tangible products to customers on a trial basis, but services are often more difficult as the customer and service provider are linked in the delivery of the service (discussed further in Chapter 14). It would be too expensive for a package holiday company to allow its clients to sample a few days of a holiday before agreeing to stay the full fortnight, and a hairdresser is unable to offer just part of a new hair style.

Individual characteristics

These are also influential in the speed of adoption, though they are less easy to predict than product characteristics. Factors such as high educational levels, wealth and affiliation to both formal and informal groups tend to be characteristics shared by those who adopt new products first, but this will vary to some extent across product groups. Rogers (1983) identified five different levels of innovativeness in individuals.

▶ *Innovators* comprise no more than 2.5 per cent of the population. These are people who are willing to try out new ideas and products first. Venturesome by nature, they are prepared to run the risk of buying a product that ultimately proves disappointing rather than miss out on the chance of being first to experience something new.

▶ *Early adopters* represent the next 13.5 per cent of the population to adopt a new product. This group is less willing to experiment and more conscious of social pressures to conform than innovators, so they adopt new ideas more carefully. They tend to be respected members of the community and therefore likely to be *opinion leaders* for others, who will only buy the new product when the early adopters have given their seal of approval.

▶ *The early majority* consists of those who are more cautious of new products than the early adopters, but if they are exposed to sufficient information to help them make their own evaluations, they will follow the example of the opinion leaders. Described as 'deliberate' in their actions, this group comprises a significant 34 per cent of the population, and is therefore an important target for firms looking to take their products from the introduction to the growth stage of their life-cycles.

▶ *The late majority* are followers, only tending to adopt new products when their friends have done so. Heavily influenced by pressures to conform to social norms, they are unlikely to buy anything that would make them stand out from the crowd. For this reason they tend to rely on word-of-mouth rather than media as their primary source of product information. Another 34 per cent of the population falls into this category.

▶ *Laggards* are described as being oriented to the past. They resist new products for as long as possible, preferring to stick to tried and trusted products. Sometimes they adopt new products only when they have been superseded by something else, and then may be forced into it by the discontinuation of the items they usually buy. Sixteen per cent of people fall into this category, usually older people and those in the lower socio-economic groups.

figure 7.4
The diffusion of innovation

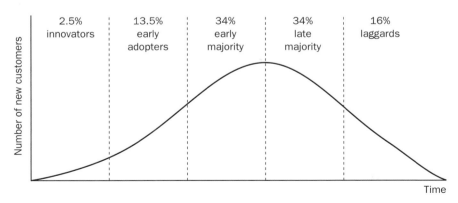

Source: Rogers (1983)

ACTIVITY **7.3**

Innovators or odd-balls?

Innovators are those within the first 2.5 per cent of all people to adopt a product. For marketers they are an important group of consumers as they are willing to take the risk of buying a new product before others have tried them and declared them satisfactory. But different people are likely to be innovators in different markets:

1 Create a pen-portrait of (and give a nick-name to) the sort of person that you think is likely to be an innovator in the markets for:
 - Computer software.
 - Gardening tools.
 - Soft drinks.
 - Ready-meals.
 - Men's toiletries.
2 What product benefits are most likely to tempt these people to try something different?
3 What sort of promotional message and which media are most likely to attract them?

Key concepts

Adoption process: the stages an individual goes through on the way to accepting (or rejecting) a new product.

Brainstorming: a technique that uses free thinking to generate a wide range of new product ideas.

Business analysis: a systematic assessment of the commercial viability of a new product.

Concept test: research that aims to find out whether or not a new product idea meets customer needs.

Drop-error: the failure of a firm to recognise the potential of a new product idea, which subsequently proves to be successful for another firm.

Functional test: research that aims to assess how well a new product will perform.

Go-error: a decision to continue with the development of a product idea that subsequently fails in the market.

Idea generation: efforts to identify sources of potential new products.

Idea screening: identifying and dropping poor new product ideas before money is invested in their development.

Innovation: the activities involved in bringing a new product or process to the market.

Market test: research that aims to assess the reaction of potential customers to new products.

Me-too products: imitations of products originally developed by competitors.

Pioneer: the firm which gets to the market first with a new product which can satisfy previously unmet needs.

Roll-out strategy: launching a new product in different target markets at different times.

Test market: introducing a product in a small sector of a target market to test its viability before incurring the expense of a full-scale launch.

1 Which of the following is not an external source of new product ideas?
  a Distributors.
  b Employees.
  c Customers.
  d Universities.
  e Competitors.

2 Under which of the following circumstances would you say that a 'drop-error' has occurred?
  a When a consumer rejects a product at the trial stage.
  b When an idea is rejected during brainstorming.
  c When a product is developed but ultimately fails in the market.
  d When a simulated test-market is used instead of a standard test-market.
  e When an idea that could have been commercially successful is rejected during screening.

3 A financial assessment of a new product's viability is made at which of the following stages of the process of innovation?
  a Idea screening.
  b Concept development and testing.
  c Business analysis.
  d Product development and testing.
  e Test marketing.

4 To which of the following categories of new product adopters are opinion leaders likely to belong?
  a Innovators.
  b Early adopters.
  c Early majority.
  d Late majority.
  e Laggards.

5 Which of the following sequences is the normal pattern for the adoption of new products?
  a Awareness, interest, desire, action.
  b Awareness, evaluation, desire, adoption.
  c Knowledge, evaluation, desire, adoption.
  d Awareness, interest, evaluation, desire, action.
  e Awareness, knowledge, evaluation, trial, adoption.

Which of the following are true and which are false?
  6 A new product that copies a concept that has already been developed and launched by a competitor is known as a 'mimic' product.
  7 The process of innovation always starts with a brainstorming session.
  8 Prototypes are made at the idea screening stage of the process of innovation.
  9 A product-use test is often used as an alternative to test-marketing in industrial markets.
  10 Laggards will never adopt a new product.

Discuss the following

11 What are the advantages and disadvantages of launching a product line extension rather than a genuine innovation?

12 Which are more acceptable – drop-errors or go-errors?

13 What criteria would you use to decide whether to use a roll-out strategy or a global launch for a new product?

14 Is there any point promoting to laggards?

15 Is it necessary to pass through all seven stages of the process of innovation if you are thinking of launching a me-too product?

Further study

Books

The subject of innovation is covered in a wide range of literature, beyond simply marketing texts. A good starting point for further reading is:

Henry, Jane and Walker, David (eds) (1991) *Managing Innovation*, Sage Publications. *This looks at a wide range of issues related to new product development and provides a number of cases to illustrate the points made.*

Rogers, E.M. (1983) *Diffusion of Innovations*, 3rd edition, Free Press. *A particularly interesting text.*

Journals

There are also a number of key articles, some of which are now thought to be classics:

Alford, C.L. and Mason, J.B. (1975) 'Generating new product ideas', in *Journal of Advertising Research*, December, pp. 27–32.

Drucker, P. (1985) 'The discipline of innovation', in *Harvard Business Review*, May–June, pp. 67–72.

Moore, W.L. (1982) 'Concept testing', in *Journal of Business Research*, vol. 10, pp. 279–94.

Star, S.H. and Urban, G.L. (1988) 'The case of the test-market toss-up', *Harvard Business Review*, September–October, pp. 10–27.

References

Anchor marketing research materials (1989) Anchor Foods Ltd, PO Box 82, Swindon, Wilts. SN5 8YZ.

'ASA falls silent over P & G's ads knocking Lever' (1995), in *Marketing*, 26 January, p. 1.

Ashworth, J. (1995) 'Tills ring at midnight as Windows 95 opens', in *The Times*, 24 August, p. 1.

Booz, Allen and Hamilton (1982) *New Products Management for the 1980s*, Booz Allen Hamilton.

Brierley, S. (1995) 'Unilever's NPD blues', in *Marketing Week*, 16 June, pp. 40–3.

Burnside, A. (1994) 'Braun goes straight', in *Marketing*, October 13, p. 25.

Buzzell, R.D. and Gale, B.T. (1987) *The PIMS Principles: linking strategy to performance*, Free Press.

Clipson, C. (1991) 'Innovation by Design', in *Managing Innovation*, Jane Henry and David Walker (eds.) pp. 96–105, Sage Publications.

'The defenestration of Bill' (1995) in *The Economist*, 8 July, pp. 73–4.

Doyle, P. (1994) *Marketing Management and Strategy*, Prentice Hall.

Drucker, P. (1985) 'The discipline of innovation', in *Harvard Business Review*, May–June, pp. 67–72.

Espey, J. (1985) 'A multi-national approach to new product development', in *European Journal of Marketing*, vol. 19, no. 3.

Fox, H. L. (1995) 'SKB adds fibre to Ribena juice', in *Marketing*, 19 January, p. 2.

Gilchrist, S. (1995) 'Persil Power tears £57m hole in Unilever profit', in *The Times*, 22 February, p. 1.

Huxley, J. (1985) 'Bar Wars', in *The Sunday Times*, 6 January, p. 57.

Jones, H. (1993) 'The test is yet to come', in *Marketing Week*, October 8, pp. 34–7.

Joseph, R. (1994) 'What! someone adores Le Piat d'Or', in *The Sunday Telegraph*, 2 October.

Kotler, P. and Armstrong, G. (1994) *Principles of Marketing*, 6th ed., Prentice Hall.

Kreitman, M. (1993) 'Letter from Tulsa', in *Marketing*, 7 October, p. 10.

Laitner, C. (1995) 'You must remember this', BMRB Research, in *Marketing*, 5 January, pp. 12–16.

'The mass production of ideas, and other impossibilities' (1995) in *The Economist*, 18 March, p. 100.

Mitchell, A. (1995) 'Fresh approach', in *Marketing Business*, April, pp. 6–8.

Morita, A. (1986) 'Selling to the world: the Sony Walkman story', in *Managing Innovation*, Jane Henry and David Walker (eds.) pp. 187–91.

Richards, A. (1995(1)) 'Tesco pulls the plug on Power', in *Marketing*, 19 January, p. 1.

Richards, A. (1995(2)) 'Persil's Power failure', in *Marketing*, 19 January, p. 10.

Robinson, W.T. and Fornell, C. (1985) 'Sources of market pioneering advantages in consumer goods industries', in *Journal of Marketing Research*, 22 August, pp. 305–17.

Robinson, W.T. (1988) 'Sources of market pioneer advantages: The case for industrial goods', in *Journal of Marketing Research*, 25, pp. 87–94.

Rogers, E.M. (1983) *Diffusion of Innovations*, 3rd ed., Free Press.

Ward, B. and Highfield, R. (1995) 'Computer users discover the catches with Windows', in *The Telegraph*, 2 September, p. 7.

Price

Objectives
. . . .

When you have read this chapter you will be able to:

► Identify the four main types of objective that organisations address through pricing goods and services.

► Recommend an appropriate pricing strategy and tactics to maximise performance in a variety of situations.

► Justify pricing decisions on the basis of external and internal factors, including simple financial analysis covering cost-plus pricing, marginal-cost pricing and target return-on-investment pricing.

► Calculate the price elasticity of demand for a given product or service and understand how this knowledge is used in pricing decisions.

► Appreciate the organisational and ethical context surrounding price as part of the marketing mix.

Introduction
. . . .

Price is one of the most important and far-reaching of the variables that marketing managers control. Pricing decisions affect profit, volume, share of market and social stance. In turn, pricing policy takes account of internal and external factors. Internal factors include costs and business objectives. However, the key to pricing success is the attractiveness of price to the consumer. External factors such as competition and customer expectation are paramount. Just as pricing carries image connotations for brands, so companies are increasingly being judged on the transparency and equity with which they treat price as a marketing variable.

Oscar Wilde once wrote that a cynic is 'a man who knows the price of everything and the value of nothing'. But the concepts of price and value are hard to separate. As consumers, price is what we are prepared to pay in exchange for goods and services. How much we are prepared to pay depends on how much we value what is on offer. At some times the purchase in question may be worth a great deal more than at others. A rose as a romantic gesture on 14 February, strawberries on the lawn at Wimbledon, last-minute Christmas shopping – these are all things for which people are prepared to pay 'over the odds'. Manufacturers propose prices to consumers, but at the end of the day what the consumer values is what counts. We can therefore define price as the expression, usually financial, of the value placed on a marketing exchange by the buyer. As well as money it can involve time, energy, attention, emotion and inconvenience.

Price in the marketing mix
. . . .

Price is the only marketing mix element that generates income. The other variables – making the product, telling customers about it, and making it available to them – all generate costs. So getting the price right is a decision of fundamental importance. This is true even in markets such as luxury goods where, at first sight, price might not seem to be as important as outright quality. Boxed confectionery or scent, for example, are surprisingly sensitive to price. This is because of competition, often involving discount retailers operating in spite of manufacturers' concerns about the up-market image of their products. Luxury goods customers, usually buying the product as a gift, will insist on quality. But in choosing between alternative possibilities, even small variations in price can make a lot of difference.

In response to this, much recent marketing thought has emphasised the connection between price and quality in order to defend the idea of profitable business. 'Adding value' allows a manufacturer to widen the margin of available profit by offering the consumer more benefits. Tom Peters (1988) claims that customers, both consumer and industrial, are prepared consistently to pay more for good quality – especially if they are convinced that what they are buying is the best available. The justification for a higher price can come from any or all of the marketing mix variables:

▶ *Product*: offering extra features, individual specification or innovatory design.
▶ *Promotion*: increasing the prestige and reputation of the goods or services in question through regular advertising and promotion.
▶ *Price*: providing credit terms that spread payment but justify a higher eventual price.
▶ *Place*: guaranteeing a specific delivery date, or operating hours of business that allow the customer greater convenience.

CASE STUDY **8.1**

'Added value'– being sold a pup?

Since 1972, which saw the introduction of the lovable labrador puppy into its advertising, Andrex toilet tissue has been the leading brand in its market. Its parent company Scott has supported the brand with a consistent level of advertising. Their investment in advertising continued even through the recessions of the early 1980s and 1990s when rival products cut back their promotional expenditure.

This kind of support for what is a very high quality product has made consumers fiercely loyal to Andrex. A third of its users never buy any other lavatory paper. Furthermore they are prepared to pay a premium over the average market price of all toilet rolls. The difference has been as much as 40 per cent at times, and never dropped below 20 per cent since the labrador puppy has been in the picture.

Questions

1 When consumers are reluctant to pay high prices (for example in a recession), how wise a business investment is advertising?
2 List some other brands of toilet tissue and comment on their pricing and appeal.
3 What advice might you give Andrex's rivals in the market in order to challenge its position?

Source Baker, 1993.

Just as each of the marketing mix variables can justify a higher price, so the price of a product will give the customer an impression of what to expect. In some markets, like champagne or theatre tickets, the lowest-priced choices are not always the fastest to sell because customers do not see them as having enough quality to make them good value. As we have seen, a sustained level of advertising may create a brand image that helps justify a higher price. Conversely, charging a higher price can help fund this kind of regular promotional activity. On the distribution front, it may be that low prices can justify high levels of inconvenience – such as those endured by bargain hunters in the traditional scrum of the January sales.

DID YOU KNOW?

Stella Artois, the premium lager brand, makes a virtue of its high price. Its advertising, in press, outdoor media and television, features the proposition 'Reassuringly expensive'.

Price is the easiest marketing mix variable to change in the short term. But it should not be seen as a tactical variable which can be altered without affecting the strategic balance of the rest of the mix. It has its tactical uses, as we shall see. But its profound importance to the success of any marketing plan forces us to recognise price as a strategic issue rather than a tactical detail. There are a large number of factors to take into account in making and reviewing pricing decisions. Decisions on pricing should not be taken lightly or with an exclusively short-term focus. Pricing mistakes can lead to disaster in a spectacular way. Towards the end of this chapter we will look at some of the research and calculations that can help minimise the risk of taking bad pricing decisions.

CASE STUDY **8.2**

It's not easy...

When Pepsico launched its cheese-flavoured snack Cheetos into the crowded UK savoury snacks market in 1990 it expected that the success of the brand elsewhere in the world would be replicated. In spite of launch advertising worth an estimated £5 million, British consumers found the product proposition 'It's not easy being cheesy' confusing. They were thus unwilling to pay the price demanded – which was in line with other products in the informal snacks sector. The brand was subsequently withdrawn and relaunched as a children's product, 'Chester Snacks' (after brand figurehead Chester Cheetah) at half the price.

Questions

1 Pricing that worked elsewhere in the world for this brand failed in the UK. How true is it to say that price is a cultural issue (ie has more to do with how we see the world than to do with the quality of a product)?
2 What kind of influences are active in pricing children's products?
3 What might Pepsico have done differently in deciding at what price to launch Cheetos?

Source Marketing, 1992.

Pricing objectives

There are four main types of objective that pricing decisions can help achieve. These are:

1 *Income related*: how much money can we make?
2 *Volume related*: how many units can we sell?
3 *Competition related*: what share of the available business do we want?
4 *Societal*: what are our responsibilities to our customers and society as a whole?

We will discuss these different kinds of objective and their accompanying strategies before moving on to illustrate relevant tactical support in each case. The techniques described are not necessarily exclusive to one objective. For example, selective discounting might be aimed at maximising income from a number of market segments, or at maximising volume through bringing in new business. Like any other aspect of marketing, pricing ought to combine creativity with flexibility.

Income-related objectives

Organisations need to make money to survive. Adjusting price is an obvious way of increasing the flow of money coming into an organisation.

The capacity to make more money in this way depends on the resilience of consumer demand to an increase in price. In other words, how many customers will go elsewhere or stop buying altogether if the price increases beyond a certain point? This question is what economists call price-elasticity of demand and later in the chapter we will be looking at how it is calculated.

It may be that an organisation can afford to lose some customers and still make more money so long as the remaining customers are paying enough. This process is often called moving 'up-market'. Decisions to move up-market to a more expensive product – like those taken by a number of Japanese automotive manufacturers in European markets in the late 1980s – can mean fewer customers overall, but higher income. In other words, the company chooses to target market segments that are modest in size but have high spending power.

Another reason for focusing on income rather than volume is when a company is first into the market with an innovation and wants to recoup its research and development investment while it still has the field to itself. Here the decision to maximise income from price is the beginning of a race against time before competitors enter the market. We have seen this process at work in the product life-cycle, which is covered in Chapter 6.

This kind of strategy is called 'skimming', taking its name from the image of 'skimming the cream' from a market. In other words it aims high, for a limited number of customers whose need for the product is great enough to justify a high price. It is a common approach on the part of high-tech and pharmaceutical companies keen to capitalise on an innovatory product. Colour televisions, pocket calculators and digital watches are all examples of products whose early availability was characterised by skimming prices.

A third reason to concentrate on the amount of money that can be made in the short term comes when a company is threatened by takeover. In order to convince shareholders of the financial health of the organisation, managers can take advantage of a number of measures to bolster profit figures. One of them is to impose price increases which may then be reconsidered once the shadow of takeover has receded.

Volume-related objectives

Particularly in manufacturing industries, production capacity needs to be fully utilised or machines stand idle and employment opportunities decline. There is thus a good reason for seeing the overall health of an enterprise reflected first and foremost in the volume of sales it generates.

Price obviously has a role to play in determining the quantity of goods sold. The laws of supply and demand hold that the cheaper something is, the more of it will be bought. This holds true up to a point. There is, for example, a limit to the number of shoes even the most helpless fashion victim can find a use for. This is what the economists call 'utility'. But most things we buy, we would buy more of if the price came down.

Volume objectives are approached by what is known as penetration pricing. As the name implies, this pricing policy aims at penetrating the market as extensively as possible with the aim of recruiting the maximum number of customers. This approach is usually contrasted with skimming. Instead of going for a limited but highly profitable sector of the market, penetration pricing sacrifices immediate profit for the long-term security of buying a large market share.

A similar approach is frequently seen in the office equipment market where hardware such as a photocopier is priced cheaply in order to generate volume sales for related consumables, such as toner cartridges, or peripherals. This is referred to as captive pricing – because it addresses a captive market of equipment users who cannot easily switch to alternative suppliers. This kind of pricing can be seen as a means of securing distribution for the firm's other products by sacrificing profits on the main item of hardware.

DID YOU KNOW?

Most white goods (consumer durables like washing machines and fridges) are sold at cost to American consumers? The retailers make their money instead on warranties and service agreements.

It will be clear that penetration as an option is limited to those organisations who have the resources to make it work. Unless the company has a large enough production capacity to cope with the demand it expects to create, and can pass on the benefits of its economies of scale (ie its ability to use mass production to reduce its costs) in the form of low prices, penetration is unlikely to succeed. Furthermore, only companies who are large enough to be able to plan in the long term will be able to wait for the returns penetration brings.

The choice of this option also depends on market conditions. If a market is already mature – that is to say its expansion has slowed down – there may be little point in buying market share. So while a penetration policy might yield dividends in a market like health drinks (which is seen to be growing), it would be less successful for a new entrant in a market like desktop personal computers (where the market has reached saturation point). Davidson (1987) advises that the best thing to do in a market with falling prices is to get out quick.

CASE STUDY **8.3**

Talk is cheap...

In the late 1980s the mobile phone-toting business yuppie had to go direct to either Cellnet or Vodaphone, the two companies who provide mobile-phone networks. Consumer choice was limited to their two tariffs (pricing structures combining a subscription fee with call charges at various levels). But in the 1990s companies like Peoples Phone have opened up the £3 billion market by acting as brokers between phone users and the mighty networks.

In effect they buy tariffs direct from the networks, and then sell them on, at prices that they decide, to users. This allows them to segment the market through price, making mobile phones available to previously untapped business and domestic users. In 1994 the Peoples Phone 'Emergency Tariff' offered subscribers access to the service for £9.99 a month – although individual calls on this method of charging were 99p a minute.

The target group of people for this tariff are customers who will only use the phone in an absolute emergency (for example, if their car breaks down). While the returns on such customers are minimal, Peoples Phone realises that as the market develops, existing customers can be encouraged to trade up to a different tariff – perhaps paying £15 a month basic subscription, but reducing call charges to 15p. At this point, Peoples Phone hopes, the subscriber's attitude to using the mobile phone might change to the point where there is more money to be made.

Questions

1 Pricing a service (like equipment rental or call charges) is different from pricing a product. How does Peoples Phone pricing demonstrate this?

2 Give an example of two other markets that can be segmented usefully by people's willingness to pay? What bases of segmentation would be relevant in such an exercise? (see Chapter 5).

3 How might a company like Peoples Phone decide the appropriate level of tariffs for its target market?

Source Bhoyrul, 1994.

Competition-based objectives

We have touched on the question of share of market when discussing the effect of price on volume. Obviously in a competitive market like confectionery that has been in existence for a long period of time (what is called a mature market) the overall growth in volume is likely to be slow. Organisations need either to create new customers or to steal customers from their competitors. Price can be a very useful tool in this war of attrition where success or failure is judged in terms of a few percentage points of market share, year on year.

Societal objectives

Competition between firms battling for market share has the effect of driving prices down. But in some markets competition is limited by the sheer size of the enterprises concerned. This can be seen to be against the public interest. Statutory controls are brought to bear to prevent such situations from developing – such as Anti-Trust Law in America or the activities of the Monopolies and Mergers Commission in the UK. Certain industries, such as broadcasting, transport and public utilities, are subject to watchdog bodies with advisory or regulatory powers. In the recently privatised UK power industry, for example, part of the undertaking given by the new companies is that they will abide by the decisions of an independent regulator in setting their prices.

This kind of pricing control stems from the widely-held conviction that for certain essential services, prices must be kept at a sufficiently low level to keep them within reach of all members of society. A similar kind of thinking applies to the pricing strategies of many non-profit organisations (particularly those in receipt of public funding). Such pricing decisions are a way of being seen to be accessible to a wide range of publics. But insofar as all organisations are subject to legislation, and particularly taxation, all organisations have an obligation to price in a way that is socially responsible. Potentially dangerous products such as cigarettes and alcohol attract high levels of duty which earn income for the public exchequer. This duty also helps to restrict their consumption to manageable levels by increasing their prices.

Putting pricing into practice

Tactics that focus on income

Differential pricing

Segmenting the market by ability (or willingness) to pay can maximise revenues by charging different groups different prices. A grocery manufacturer may segment the retail trade into major multiples (large supermarkets like ASDA), symbols (buying groups such as SPAR) and independents, and establish a pricing structure that offers the best terms to the largest customer. This can cause understandable aggravation for the smaller customer, but manufacturers defend the practice by arguing that the corner shop is competing on convenience rather than price.

Differential pricing is also common in service industries. Here the intangible nature of the offering means that income must be maximised at every opportunity (see Chapter 14 for more on service marketing). For example, airline seats cannot be stored – they are either occupied on a particular flight or they remain unsold for ever. As a result of this, travel operators aim pricing strategies at customer segments on the basis of when they are prepared to travel and when they are prepared to commit their money. Advance booking is encouraged by offering lower prices, as is travel at unpopular times. This policy can lead to disaffection among customers. It may be, for example, that two airline passengers in adjoining seats have paid radically different prices for no other reason than the times at which they made their bookings.

Bait pricing

This is a term given to a tactic that offers customers goods at a low price in order to attract them in the hope that they will buy other things. In the case of the supermarket loss leader, the low-priced goods may be offered at less than they cost the retailer. The loss is written off as a promotional expenditure. This can cause conflict between manufacturers and retailers (an example of vertical channel conflict is discussed in Chapter 9). Manufacturers oppose the practice on the grounds that such discounting devalues their brands. An additional reason for their opposition is their understandable reluctance to be pressured by other retailers into offering similar terms.

In some markets where personal selling is important (such as consumer durables like washing machines or cars) bait pricing can be used as a promotional device to lure customers into a sales room. This is often the case when an electrical retailer launches a new branch. Newspaper advertising announces that a product like a CD player is available at a crazy discount, to 'the first five customers'. Having attracted bargain hunters inside the shop, the sales staff can offer alternatives at a higher price – a tactic sometimes known as 'bait and switch'. It is also possible to suggest complementary products and warranties in order to enhance the profitability of the basic offer.

Bait pricing raises a number of ethical questions. Used insensitively such tactics run the risk of becoming counterproductive, but the excitement and consumer interest special offers can create is considerable.

Premium pricing

This aims at using price to maximise the image of quality in a product or service. Very often it will involve offering a range of goods or services at different price points. The relationship between price and quality can then be justified in the eyes of the customer by reference to the differences between each level when they can be displayed or demonstrated together.

This comparison can be used to legitimise a high price for the top range. But it can also make a middle-range offer look more attractive than it otherwise might by flattering it in comparison to a more expensive alternative. This kind of thinking is at the heart of the developing area of retail merchandising and catalogue design, where the relationship between items on offer is all important in guiding the consumer to make an appropriate purchase decision.

Another form of premium pricing attempts to avoid comparisons altogether. Common in professional services, this is a price that is quoted as an 'all-in' fee without specifying the details of what is being charged for. The implication is that to haggle over small details would be somehow beneath the dignity of the professional/client relationship. In the face of increasing competition in the services industries, however, this rather genteel approach to pricing is giving way to a cruder orientation towards value for money.

DID YOU KNOW?
British tailors and gentlemen's outfitters continued to charge in guineas long after the guinea coin (21 old shillings) was replaced by the sovereign (20 old shillings, or one pound) in the eighteenth century. Only the advent of decimalised currency in the early 1970s put a stop to this quaint (and highly profitable) image pricing policy. Customers perceived prices quoted in guineas as more or less the same as pounds. But over the average price of a suit of clothes the five per cent extra made a considerable difference to the profitability of the transaction. Pricing in guineas survives now only in the racehorse market, where shoppers are not known for their thrifty ways!

Tactics that focus on volume

Discounting

We have seen how differential pricing can maximise total income. Such a policy can work to protect and consolidate existing business. This is a very high priority in a competitive environment. But for firms wishing to recruit new customers and maximise volume, short-term discounts are a very important sales-generating tactic.

This is not only true of the kind of offer we might see on a supermarket shelf, tempting us to try a new product at a special price. It is also very popular in business-to-business market-ing, for example in the field of television advertising sales. In order to attract new advertisers to the medium, television sales executives have an armoury of special rates. The effect of this kind of dealing, however, is often to alienate existing advertisers. They object that their television advertising expenditure, at full rates, ought not to be used to subsidise the activities of new users of the medium (some of whom may even be their direct competitors). As we have seen with other kinds of pricing strategy, discounting needs to be carefully weighed up for its potential ethical fall-out.

CASE STUDY 8.4

Cruachan – the off-peak peak

A power station inside a Scottish hill would not exist if it wasn't for off-peak discounts on electricity. Off-peak electricity is available at bargain rates during the night when demand for power is low. Cruachan (which means 'the hollow mountain') was opened in 1965 at a cost of £24 million specifically to take advantage of this.

At night, turbines powered by off-peak electricity pump water from the loch at the base of the hill up tunnels hollowed out inside it to an artificial reservoir some 1,250 feet above. During the day, the turbines become generators driven by the water flowing back down through them to the Loch. In spite of an energy efficiency loss of between ten per cent and 15 per cent, this produces electricity that can be sold at peak rates.

Because of the way the respective prices of electricity and of large scale engineering projects have moved since the 1960s, Cruachan could never have been built in the 1990s. It remains, however, an ingenious feat of civil engineering that exploits a discount pricing opportunity. It also has a secondary function as a visitor attraction, complete with guided tours and an information centre.

Questions

1   To what extent can domestic consumers be encouraged to take advantage of off-peak electricity?
2   What alternatives are there to differential pricing (such as off-peak discounts) to spread demand for services such as electricity?
3   What changes in electricity pricing might threaten Cruachan's future viability?

Price bundling and multiple unit pricing

As shoppers we are familiar with the idea of the multipack, whereby we buy items like confectionery, soft drinks, batteries or stationery in packets of more than one. Usually there is a bargain element in the pricing – bought separately the items would cost more. We are being offered a volume discount in minia-ture. For the manufacturer the advantage is in the increased volume sold. For the retailer the advantage is in increasing the value of individual transactions and simplifying merchandising and display procedures.

In a multipack each item is identical in value. But another form of multiple-unit pricing combines a number of different products or services into one offered at a particular price. This practice, which is very common in services marketing, is known as price bundling. Common examples include a package holiday, or a visit to the theatre which also includes a meal, interval drink and programme. Again the incentive for the customer is an overall bargain (as well as simplicity and convenience). The advantage for the service provider is the volume of business generated. Bought separately the various elements of a holiday or theatre visit would generate more revenue. But it is unlikely that the individual consumer could be relied upon to buy each one, so the overall effect is to increase volume.

The practice is also used in business-to-business marketing, where it can yield further benefits for the seller. In the international television programme market, for example, programming is sold by producers to broadcasters in negotiated packages. The price depends on stations being prepared to buy not only what they actively want, but to include in their purchases programmes which they might not otherwise have considered. Often this may be of questionable quality (as viewers of late night television can verify!).

Clearance pricing

The ultimate gesture towards volume rather than profit is the clearance price. 'Everything must go' read the signs in the window of the shop about to close down. After all, it costs money to store goods – not only in overheads such as power and wages, but also in the cost of having their value tied up in stock rather than circulating in the organisation's cash flow. How much it costs to store goods depends on a number of factors (as discussed in Chapter 9 on physical distribution). Most estimates put the average cost of storage at about a quarter of the stock's sales value per year – which explains why businesses are keen on fast-selling lines. When stock becomes a liability, the idea of profit pales into insignificance beside the need to liquidate assets.

Clearance pricing is not just something that affects beleaguered chain stores in the high street. It also happens in international trade. Clearing stocks on an international level leads to the controversial practice of dumping. This involves selling goods at a price far below their normal domestic selling price in a foreign market. It has the advantage of getting rid of excess stock for the manufacturer with minimal impact on core business at home. Dumping is very unpopular with companies in the market where it takes place because of its destabilising effect. However, the practice of dumping can come home to roost when enterprising importers buy up large quantities of the dumped product in the export market and reimport them to sell in direct price competition with the domestic manufacturer.

Price promotion

Using price as the basis of promotional activity is a popular tactic within the overall strategy of going for volume. Certainly a reduced price offer (RPO) can bring business forward, even if its long-term effect is not to produce any net gains in volume. But RPOs do lead to the following identifiable advantages:

- ▶ increase positive cash flow for the manufacturer
- ▶ create incentive for display by the retailer
- ▶ provide an opportunity to make the pack stand out: '2p OFF'
- ▶ flood distribution channels to crowd out rival products
- ▶ keep the brand fresh in the mind of fickle customers
- ▶ encourage new customers at least to sample the product – thus rendering it more likely that they will return in future as occasional, if not regular, users.

> **DID YOU KNOW?**
>
> *Studies of consumer behaviour in Germany, Japan, the US and the UK by Professor AC Ehrenberg of London's South Bank University suggest that promotional price cuts hardly ever pay for themselves. His alternative recipe for success is a firmer emphasis on creativity rather than cost in promotional activity (Denny, 1995).*

Tactics that focus on competition

Parity pricing

The going rate is a vital concept in pricing decisions. If consumers can find broadly the same mixture of benefits elsewhere at a cheaper price there is little likelihood that they will remain loyal to your product in the long term. There are, as we have seen in the example of Andrex cited earlier, outstanding exceptions to this rule. But if a brand's price is out of line with what the competition is charging, there needs to be a good reason.

The effect of this approach to pricing is to allow manufacturers to concentrate on non-price factors in their competitive activities. But it can quickly lead to a kind of collusion on pricing. In some markets, because of the limited range of alternatives available to consumers, a few manufacturers can get together and inflate prices to their mutual advantage. A notorious example of this over the years has been the European air travel market, although a mixture of legislation and the efforts of individual entrepreneurs have gradually opened it up.

Undercutting

Professor Michael Porter, to whose thinking on competitive strategy we shall return in Chapter 13, sees 'cost leadership' as one of the prime strategic options open to successful companies. This involves reducing internal costs (often by massive investment in automation) in order to pass the savings on in the shape of permanently lower prices. An ability to undercut the opposition leads to a growth in market share for the cost leader. By the time the competition catches up (if it survives to do so) it may be too late. The wholesale rout of British motorcycle manufacturers by Japanese competition in the 1960s was an early example of how cheaper production practices leading to lower prices can successfully undercut an apparently impregnable industry.

Price leading

Prices in a number of markets are dominated by the decisions of a few well-established companies who have the weight and market share to set prices confident that their competitors will follow suit. Such confidence can come from the following sources of power:

- ▶ Control over distribution and availability (eg through owning their own network of outlets, as do many brewing companies).
- ▶ Dominant market share (often because of superior or improved quality, for which customers will pay).

▶ Strategic information systems (involving the collection and interpretation of sales/price/cost data which gives the organisation an advantage over its less well-informed rivals in forecasting and planning).

▶ A global perspective (taking the long view on how markets are developing, not only nationally but internationally, can lead to more accurate decisions).

Companies like this are known as price leaders. Smaller firms in the same market, or firms without the kind of strategic advantages listed above, find themselves adjusting their prices in reaction to the leaders. They are known as price followers as a result.

Spoiling

Much competitive activity is aimed at frustrating, on a tactical basis, the plans of rival organisations. Pricing tactics are important here because of the speed with which they can be implemented, and their direct appeal to consumers. For example, if a competitor is conducting a test-market exercise with a new product in a particular area (as discussed in Chapter 7) the first a company may hear of it is from its sales force. Or perhaps the news may come from the company's advertising agency who have picked up increased media activity on the part of the rival as part of its media tracking. Speed of reaction is therefore essential. A surefire way to distort the results of such test-marketing is to lower prices – perhaps by means of a special promotion limited to the area or to a specific group of retailers. The objective of such promotion would be to prevent the new product from gaining a foothold.

Survival pricing strategy

Because of the effects of competition, some organisations go to the wall – or face inevitable takeover. Pricing decisions can help them forestall closure for as long as possible, or survive as going concerns and offer a more attractive proposition to prospective purchasers. Pricing in these circumstances is aimed neither at income nor at volume so much as at mere organisational survival. It may be that a family firm, for example, is determined to see it out until the retirement of the owners. In this case, the long-term health of the company is irrelevant – what matters is the next three or four years. Alternatively, larger companies can afford to take losses in some markets just to retain a presence. Their more profitable activities elsewhere will help them over the lean times until market conditions are more favourable.

Tactics that focus on societal considerations

Differential discounts

As we have seen, differential pricing can be used to maximise income by charging a range of prices to match different segments of the market. Similarly, prices can be lowered on a long-term basis by differential discounts to encourage access to a product or service by certain target groups. Thus arts organisations or travel operators who are in receipt of public funding will often structure their prices to include discounts for retired people, students and children of school age. This is commonly known as 'concessionary' pricing (a rather grudging phrase).

Non-financial pricing

Pricing strategy is just as important to non-profit organisations as it is to commercial ones. Many non-profits charge for their services. For example, agencies like Age Concern are becoming increasingly involved in providing services like day-care for frail elderly people on a local basis on a contractual footing with local authorities. This involves the negotiation of a fee from the local authority as well as making a small charge to users for lunch and materials used.

We can also analyse their pricing activities on a non-financial basis. Volunteers, for example, will be involved in an exchange process with the organisation. In return for their time and commitment the organisation will offer opportunities for involvement and achievement. Because of the limited pool of volunteer labour available, organisations depending on volunteers need to compete with each other to offer the best value for this non-financial commitment. Flexibility such as offering morning or afternoon sessions rather than expecting a whole day, or providing transport and training, can increase an organisation's competitive success in this respect by making the non-financial price more attractive to the volunteer.

Barter

A development of non-financial pricing, barter involves the exchange of goods or services without recourse to financial currency. A simple example of such a system would be a baby-sitting circle, whereby parents exchange the duty of looking after each other's children in order to free them for other activities. On a more sophisticated level, local and regional networks exist where skills can be traded – car maintenance in exchange for gardening, for example. But some kind of objective agreement on the respective value of the services involved is necessary. The system is attractive to many participants because of the community-based nature of the activities, a human alternative to the impersonal transactions of big business.

On the other hand big business itself is no stranger to non-financial transactions. Countertrade, whereby physical goods are exchanged without money changing hands, has shown itself to be a popular form of international trade. It not only takes care of currency difficulties, but it can be a way of avoiding tax.

Public sector pricing

Although the major determinant of price is not so much what something costs to manufacture as what the market is prepared to pay for it, pricing in the public sector is a matter of public accountability. Taxation is a price we all have to pay, and its rationale needs to be clear. Initiatives such as the Citizen's Charter and developments in fiscal policy have led to calls for greater transparency on costs in relation to prices from organisations like the police and health services. Value for money for the taxpayer seems a simple enough objective. But as with all pricing issues, this raises a number of ethical problems. For example, if value for money is to be stressed in the health service, hard decisions need to be taken in the face of conflicting priorities.

How much is enough? Factors in setting prices

Our survey of pricing strategies, and the related tactics, has shown that price is a complex and flexible variable. But whether the objectives served by pricing strategy are predominantly related to income, volume, competition or social responsibility, the factors impacting on price setting are the same. They come from the three Cs: costs, competitive environment and corporate culture.

Costs

How costs are made up
Manufacturing a product or providing a service involves costs. These fall into two sorts:

▶ *Indirect costs* (also known as *fixed costs*): the overheads like lighting or heating which remain the same, whether you produce one thing or hundreds. Indirect costs are so called because they are not directly related to the amount made. But the organisation's accountants will establish a way to divide them up between the various product lines being made by a company so that each carries its share.
▶ *Direct costs* (also known as *variable costs*): costs such as ingredients which vary with the amount made. Thus the more loaves of bread a baker produces, the greater the variable costs represented by flour.

The distinction is a very simple one. Just remember that fixed costs don't change, but that variable costs vary with the amount produced. So, while permanent salaried employees will be a fixed cost – temporary labour bought in to cope with a large order will be a variable cost.

Added together the two sorts of cost become the total cost of production. It's easier to understand with a diagram (see Figure 8.1).

figure 8.1
Fixed and variable costs

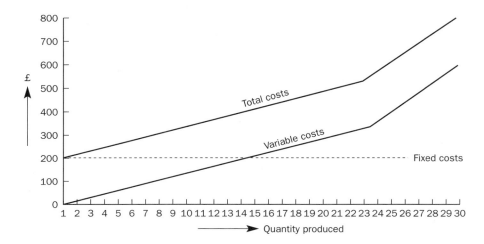

Let's stay with loaves of bread. As we would expect, the total variable cost goes up as each loaf is manufactured. But the fixed cost remains the same however many loaves are made. The average cost of each loaf, therefore, goes down as more are made – confirming our instinct as consumers that things ought to be cheaper by the dozen. In fact, as you can see towards the extreme right of the graph, the variable cost rises steeply after a certain point in this example. There might be a number of explanations for this. Perhaps the variable labour to achieve this level of output has involved expensive overtime working. Extra machines may have been hired to cope with the demand. Possibly ingredients have had to be bought short term. It is not always true to say that the more you make the cheaper each unit is.

Break-even analysis

In order to cover the costs, enough loaves need to be sold at a sufficient price. Calculating this requirement is known as a 'break-even analysis' and is a fundamental part of our understanding of the relationship between cost and price. It is particularly useful when weighing up a business proposition. If we price our bread at 70p a loaf, how many do we need to sell to break even? If that price looks unrealistic, how many more units would we need to sell at 60p to make the same amount of money?

The answer can be expressed by an equation:

$$\text{Break-even point} = \frac{\text{Fixed costs}}{\text{Price per unit} - \text{Variable costs per unit}}$$

Returning to our graph of fixed, variable and total costs, we can draw another line (Figure 8.2). This represents the cumulative sales value of a quantity of loaves at a chosen price point. Where this line meets the total cost curve is called the break-even point. All income beyond this point is profit. The graph shows the revenue for a single price P, but a number of alternative scenarios can be plotted to determine the optimum price.

figure 8.2

Break-even analysis

ACTIVITY **8.1**
· · · · · · · · · · · · ·

Break-even analysis

You run a direct marketing music company making and selling budget CDs (so you need not worry about margins to retailers in this example). Calculate the volumes necessary to break even at the following price points given the information in this example:

1   £3.50.
2   £4.10.
3   £5.30.

Your fixed costs (office overheads, recording and studio fees) are £18,000.

Your variable costs (manufacturing per CD, royalties and copyright) are as follows, because of the economics of the production plant:

▶ Up to 5,000 units: £1.25 per CD
▶ 5,001–7,500 units: £1.20 per CD
▶ 7,501 or more units: £1.10 per CD

The price point to the consumer includes VAT at 17.5%.

It all seems so simple. It *is* simple. But this beautifully simple idea is not as useful as it might seem when it comes to pricing in the real world. Costs are only part of the picture.

Cost-plus pricing

If we know our costs, the argument goes, then all we have to do is to pass them on in the price, plus a percentage for profit. This is known as cost-plus pricing, and it has a kind of transparency about it which appeals to our common sense. It lies at the heart of many consumers' expectations of price, particularly in the kind of public sector examples we have discussed earlier. Certainly unless a company were using a loss-leader pricing strategy in order to generate volume across a portfolio of products, or had reasons to liquidate stock in a hurry through clearance pricing, there would be little point in pricing at less than cost.

But the apparent simplicity of costs as the sole determinant of pricing is complicated by three considerations:

▶ It can be impossible to know your true costs until some time after you have manufactured your product, or provided your service. We have seen how the cost of individual units varies with the quantity produced. What happens if your estimated final costs are wrong in setting your price?
▶ A cost-plus price may be irrelevant to the market. It may either be more than the going rate (in which case you need to review your production procedures or find a different business to be in), or it may even be significantly less than you could get (in which case you are missing a valuable opportunity which is unlikely to last).
▶ It makes you a slave to your suppliers. Although price increases are invariably explained to consumers as the result of unavoidable fluctuations in the price of raw materials, successful organisations will have enough of a buffer in their pricing structures to be able to exercise some control over the timing of such increases with an eye to their possible effect on demand.

CASE STUDY **8.5**
••••••••••••••••••

Tring something simple

The manufacturing costs for most CDs average at 60p , but full price recordings retail at £14.99 or more. Budget-price CD company Tring International reveals the costs behind its £2.99 superbargain discs as follows:

60p manufacturing
5p packaging
10p copyright fees
15p music and royalties
5p overheads and administration

95p total cost

Tring sells on the discs to retailers at £1.30, representing a 37 per cent gross profit. After VAT the retailer is left with a profit of £1.25 on the final price to the customer of £2.99 (almost 100 per cent margin).

Part of Tring's success is from keeping costs, and therefore risks, down. The history of the highly successful £2.99 recording of *Les Miserables* is a case in point (it sells over 7,000 units a month). The original cast of the musical are all under contract to other companies. Rather than rehearsing a new cast from scratch Tring booked the stand-in cast (all free of any ties) from the West End for two hectic days in a studio with an experienced producer. By using multi-tracking, ten singers were made to sound like 20. Agreeing a fixed fee with the producer in advance lets the company know exactly what its costs ceiling will be.

An alternative source of product is licencing agreements with artists for existing recordings. The company has released nearly 200 tracks from original Sixties stars over the last three years. The terms of the deal usually mean that Tring will own the recording for a period of 20 years – but the company's 1993 stockmarket flotation was stymied by rumours of major copyright disputes. This is commonplace in the record industry, and most litigation is settled for four-figure sums. However, the rumours were strong enough to wipe something like £15 million off the company's anticipated stockmarket value.

Questions

1   Tring's pricing is both a strength and a weakness. Discuss.
2   Tring has been excluded from the BPI, the trade body of the British record industry, because of its disputes with other members. How might this exclusion affect Tring's pricing decisions in the future?
3   Half of Tring's business is in overseas markets. How might this affect its pricing decisions in the future?

Source: Rubython, 1994.

Target return-on-investment pricing

This has affinities with cost-plus pricing, insofar as it assumes that costs can be known (or estimated) with enough accuracy to feature in the calculation of price. But it represents a more pro-active stance on the part of the organisation to its objectives. It sees pricing as a means of obtaining a target level of financial return on the money invested in the business.

The calculation is as follows:

Price to achieve return on investment (ROI) =

$$\text{Unit cost} + \frac{\text{Target percentage return x investment value}}{\text{Number of units sold}}$$

This approach to pricing is prone to the same difficulties as any cost-based approach, but it has the advantage of forcing the consideration of whether a proposed price is feasible from a purely commercial point of view.

Marginal cost pricing

Like the previous two techniques this is cost-based, which rules it out as a stand-alone guide to the right price. But it helps to understand what is meant by marginal-cost pricing when weighing up certain kinds of marketing opportunity and examining the costs involved.

In a nutshell, the marginal cost of something is the cost of making one more unit. The related concept of marginal revenue is the income to the organisation of selling one more unit. As we have seen in our brief look at how costs behave as you produce more units (Figure 8.1) the marginal cost can start to accelerate after a while as the law of diminishing returns begins to set in. Marginal-cost pricing assumes we can draw a break-even analysis graph and put a marker on the spot where marginal cost equals marginal revenue, as shown in the graph in Figure 8.3.

Where the two lines intersect is the point of maximum profitability. Sell more than that quantity, and you begin to make less money – after a while you even begin to lose money. And having established the ideal quantity, all that remains is to establish the ideal price – a simple matter of checking up on the left-hand axis of the graph. But of course for the graph to work at all, you would have had to have made a pretty accurate stab at the right price in the first place.

Alas, marginal-cost analysis can only be savoured in retrospect. In common with much economic theory it helps to understand it when you are juggling with pricing concepts, but it is not a great deal of use on its own.

figure 8.3
Marginal cost and marginal revenue

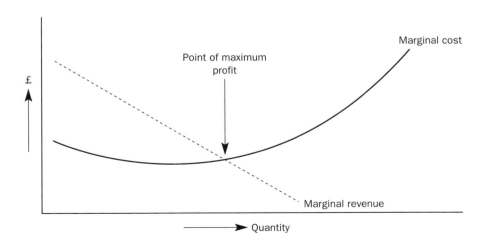

Competitive environment

As Figure 8.4 shows, all four of the environmental factors discussed in detail in Chapter 2 have a bearing on how pricing decisions are taken. Perhaps the most immediately important ones are economic and political. Changes in taxation, for example, can change the price of some goods and services overnight. Added to these general factors are industry-specific ones of competition (not only from existing rivals but from potential alternatives) and the ongoing struggle between suppliers and distributors. Monitoring and understanding the trends as they emerge can help organisations make better pricing decisions through planning.

Consumer expectations of what kind of price represents acceptable value will depend on two things – what they recognise as value themselves and what the competition is offering. This gives the marketing strategist the chance to sidestep the tyranny of cost as a factor in price setting, and explore the opportunities afforded by perceived value.

figure 8.4
Environmental forces acting on pricing decisions

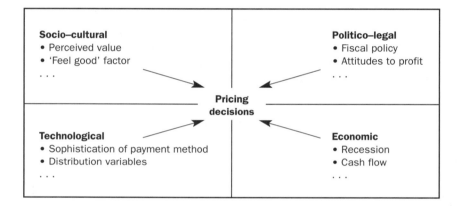

Elasticity of demand

The perceived value of a product varies from market to market and between brands in the same market. It is reflected in the propensity of customers to continue buying a product in the face of a price increase. One of the most important pieces of wisdom a brand manager can acquire is an understanding of the sensitivity of his or her brand to price increases. In the language of economics, this is known as its price elasticity of demand. It is difficult to generalise in any useful way about how brands respond to price increases. But on an individual level, especially looking at a number of years' back data, it can give an invaluable insight into the likely effect of future pricing decisions.

The concept of elasticity of demand is based on the idea that the cheaper a product is, the more of it will be sold – a principle acknowledged in our earlier discussion of volume-based pricing strategies. Another graph, shown in Figure 8.5, plots two lines showing a relationship between the price of a product and the quantity demanded. The first line (A) shows a product where, in spite of increases in price, demand remains at a relatively buoyant level. This is the pattern for products like cigarettes, or services like heating. Unless they become literally prohibitively expensive, our dependency on them means that we will continue buying them. They have what is known as inelastic demand.

figure 8.5
Elasticity of demand

The second line (B), however, shows a different story. Here, as the price goes up the quantity demanded falls steeply. In this kind of pattern we are looking at discretionary, non-essential purchases like foreign holidays or theatre tickets. Demand drops as soon as they become too expensive relative to the other purchases which consumers can use as substitutes (holidays at home or evenings in, respectively). This scenario is called elastic demand. It is as if the rising price is connected to the level of demand by an extremely stretchy piece of elastic which 'gives', rather than taking the quantity with it.

We can sharpen up this homely image of elasticity by putting some numbers on it. The formula is as follows:

$$\text{Price elasticity of demand} = \frac{\% \text{ change in quantity demanded}}{\% \text{ change in price}}$$

Where the answer to the formula is –1, the change in price is balanced out by the change in quantity demanded – in other words the company sells fewer units but the extra money compensates for this exactly. A two per cent increase in price resulting in a two per cent decline in demand is a case in point.

When the formula yields less than –1, the demand is deemed elastic: ie the brand is sensitive to changes in price. An example would be a five per cent increase in price leading to a ten per cent drop in quantity demanded. This would give an answer of –2. Unless an increase in sales could be expected for some other reason like a price increase from competitors or an improvement in value, this would mean that total income would fall as a result of the increase.

Where the answer is more than –1, demand is inelastic, and price does not have such an effect on the quantity demanded. Thus a price increase of ten per cent which yielded a sales decrease of five per cent would indicate a relatively inelastic elasticity of –0.5. This would suggest that the product actually sold better at the higher price – a marketer's vision of heaven.

Dreaming apart, the calculation based on historical information should yield a quantifiable insight into how much risk attaches to a price increase (or how much extra sales might result from a price cut).

Elasticity of demand

The most recent thriller by a best-selling author has been published in paperback at £5.99 in June. Its immediate predecessor in the same series (featuring the same detective) was published at £4.99 in paperback two months before Christmas. After three months, the new book has sold ten per cent fewer copies.

1 Calculate the price elasticity of demand for her books suggested by this evidence.
2 Comment on the accuracy and usefulness of elasticity of demand as a measure in these circumstances.

Corporate culture

Who is involved in the pricing decision?

One of the problems of too rational an account of the factors affecting pricing decisions is that it runs the risk of ignoring the human side of the process in many organisations. Depending on the culture and structure of the organisation, a number of people's views may be involved in the decision. Typically the views of marketing, sales and finance will be represented.

Of these three the finance department will see things in their most abstract terms. While marketing managers and accountants view each other with mutual suspicion (as spendthrifts and bean counters, respectively) they actually have a lot in common in terms of their interest in the long-term profitability of the brand. However, the duty marketing managers feel to act as the voice of the customer in decision making, tends to make them cautious about price increases.

The sales perspective, while having superficial similarities with the marketing position, will often be looking at a short-term orientation towards shifting volume rather than the long-term profitability of the brand. This can affect arguments about pricing for large customers, for example. The sales view will often argue that the volume to be gained is worth the sacrifice of some profit. The marketing view will counter that business on too generous terms with a large customer will destabilise the market in the short term and may even affect the brand's ability to sustain a higher price in the long term.

Successful organisations will seek to involve a range of inputs in determining their pricing strategy, but will have clear overall objectives and procedures to ensure that customer orientation is as important here as in any other marketing decisions.

Pricing and ethics
• •

Since the abolition of Retail Price Maintenance in the 1960s, British retailers have been free to charge what they like for products and services. There is still the concept of the Recommended Retail Price (RRP) which is often featured on packaging featuring details of Reduced Price Offers for purposes of comparison. Society relies on competition between sellers to keep prices at a reasonable level, with legal powers to enforce this. In the UK the Monopolies and Mergers Commission (MMC) investigates any possible collusion between sellers to fix the price of goods or services to the disadvantage of the consumer. In the USA the same process is fulfilled by Anti-Trust laws.

Legislation governing pricing can only hope to be effective within the bounds of national jurisdiction. The increase in international trade has opened up domestic industries to competition from economies with much lower labour costs. Textiles is one example of an industry where domestic producers have been unable to compete with cheap foreign imports. Protectionist legislation can help slow the collapse of such industries by making life more expensive for importers. But their main hope lies in diversification or concentrating on market segments as yet uncatered for by their foreign rivals.

Such examples raise questions about the ultimate compatibility of corporate social responsibility with the profit motive. British consumers may regret the 1990s demise of their domestic coal industry, for example, but few are prepared to consider anything but the most economical option in terms of heating their own homes or businesses. There are, however, signs that in certain market sectors, segments are developing whose sensitivity to ethical issues makes them prepared to pay a premium. Recent marketing responses to this include Shared Interest, an investment company that offers modest returns on venture capital applied by individual investors to development projects; Clipper Tea and Cafedirect which pay producers over the market rate for connoisseur teas and coffee; and a number of brands of detergent that guarantee a low environmental impact at a price. The green consumer, who became a force to be reckoned with in the 1980s, is maturing into a consumer who expects a great deal more, ethically, from suppliers than being environmentally friendly. Whether the majority of consumers will be prepared to pay the premium of more ethical pricing in the long term is another question.

Summary
•••••••••••

This chapter has argued the importance and far-reaching nature of pricing as a marketing variable. It can support a wide range of objectives, and is subject to a complex variety of influences itself.

Key concepts
•••••••••••••••••

Bait pricing: pricing a limited number of goods at rock bottom levels to entice shoppers who may then pay full price on other purchases.

Barter: exchanging goods and services directly for other goods and services.

Break-even analysis: calculating the point at which goods sold at a certain price will equal in value the cost of their manufacture.

Captive pricing: pricing aimed at a committed market (eg for hardware-specific software).

Clearance pricing: low pricing aimed at clearing uneconomical stocks.

Cost-plus pricing: setting prices with reference to the cost of manufacture, adding a margin for profit.

Differential pricing: charging different prices for the same goods or services to different market segments.

Dumping: clearing stocks of goods in foreign markets at extremely low prices.

Elasticity of demand: a measure of how well demand for goods or services stands up in the face of price changes.

Fixed costs: overheads that do not change with the quantity of something produced (also known as indirect costs).

Marginal cost: where a quantity of a good is being manufactured, the cost of making one more unit. In combination with the idea of marginal revenue (the benefit of selling one more unit) used as a guide to optimising the relationship between price, profit and volume.

Parity pricing: pricing at the going rate for a particular industry.

Penetration: pricing at a level that maximises volume rather than profit.

Premium pricing: using price to enhance perceptions of quality or luxury.

Skimming: pricing at a level that maximises profit rather than volume.

Tariff: a structure of prices that often includes fixed charges and variable charges to the consumer.

Variable costs: costs that increase with the quantity of something produced, eg ingredients. Also known as direct costs.

SELF-CHECK QUESTIONS

1   Which of the following can be used as a reason to concentrate pricing strategy on income rather than volume?
   a Moving upmarket.
   b Market penetration.
   c Recouping investment in an innovative product.
   d Cost leadership.
   e Countering the threat of takeover.

2   For which of the following might you expect penetration pricing to work best?
   a Organisations with substantial production capacity.
   b Small- to medium-sized enterprises.
   c Companies with strong financial reserves.
   d A competitor in a mature market.
   e A manufacturer in a growth market.

3   Demand is deemed relatively elastic when:
   a Any change in price is balanced by a change in quantity demanded with no overall effect on revenue.
   b Price changes have little effect on the overall demand for the good or service.
   c Putting the price up ten per cent leads to a drop in volume of two per cent.
   d Putting the price up ten per cent leads to a drop in volume of 15 per cent.
   e The answer to the price elasticity of demand formula is less than -1.

4   The break-even point is calculated by an equation involving which of the following groups of figures?
   a Elasticity of demand; fixed costs; marginal costs.
   b Selling price; fixed costs; variable costs.
   c Direct costs; overheads; indirect costs.
   d Variable costs; target return; marginal costs.
   e Selling price; variable costs; direct costs.

5 Variable costs are so called because:
   a They change with the time of year.
   b Exchange rates can send them up or down.
   c They change with the quantity of a product that is produced.
   d They cannot be added to fixed costs.
   e Services are variable in quality.

Which of the following are true and which are false?
   6 Price is an influence on consumer perceptions of quality.
   7 Societal pricing policies concentrate on satisfying the wants of the target market through low prices.
   8 Captive pricing is a technique that sometimes sacrifices profits on hardware to profits on supplies.
   9 RPOs rarely pay for themselves in generating net extra volume.
   10 Costs are the most important influence on pricing decisions.

Discuss the following
   11 How can companies in the 1990s assure their customers that their prices are fair and ethical?
   12 Discuss the role of non-financial factors in pricing decisions.
   13 Outline, with examples, the relationship of pricing decisions to the other parts of a marketing mix in the following areas: a consumer durable, a service and a fast moving consumer good.
   14 Reducing price as a promotional tactic is fraught with danger. Do you agree?
   15 Why is it important for marketers to know the price elasticity of demand for their brands? What methods can they use to determine it?

Further study
••••••••••••••••••

Books
Sizer, John (1969) *An Insight into Management Accounting*, Penguin.
The background to pricing decisions is ably recounted in this useful guide to an area that still manages to mystify many junior marketing managers.

Hirshleifer, Jack and Glazer, Amihai (1992) *Price Theory and Applications*, Prentice Hall.
Lots of detail, with some excellent examples.

Journals
Oxenfeldt, A. (1960) 'Multistage Approach to Pricing', in *Harvard Business Review*, July–August.
A classic paper proposing a six-step approach to setting prices which seeks to involve every relevant aspect of a business's policy.

The Economist and *Investors' Chronicle*.
Both useful regular sources of information on the wider financial context in which business pricing decisions are made.

The Financial Times.
Offers a daily perspective on the pricing environment, and is keen to target student readers.

References

Baker, C. (1993) *Advertising Works 7*, NTC/IPA.

Bhoyrul, A. (1994) 'Power to the People,' in *Business Age*, April, pp. 60–2.

Davidson, H. (1987) *Offensive Marketing*, Penguin.

Denny, N. (1995) 'What price customer loyalty?', in *Promotions and Incentives*, April, p. 22.

Lister, D. (1993) 'Opera House to launch cut-price performances', *Independent*, 5 May, p. 15.

Peters, T. (1988) *Thriving on Chaos*, Pan.

Rubython, T. (1994) 'The Truth about Tring', in *Business Age*, April, pp. 70–4.

CHAPTER 9

Distribution

Objectives
....

When you have read this chapter you will be able to:

▶ Isolate the contribution that distribution makes to a successful marketing mix.

▶ Name the major channel intermediaries and describe their functions.

▶ Recommend appropriate distribution channels in a number of marketing situations.

▶ Appreciate the environmental forces operating on retailing in the UK and their relevance to goods and services marketing.

▶ Evaluate alternative strategies in physical distribution and logistics management.

▶ Recognise the importance of interpersonal contacts in the distribution channel.

Introduction
....

This chapter introduces distribution, or place, the most mysterious of the four elements of the marketing mix. Traditional definitions tend to see it as moving goods or services from those who produce them to those who consume them. But all businesses are involved in purchasing as well as supply. Our examination of the topic will emphasise how businesses can sharpen their competitive edge by reviewing operations at both ends of the process, both as customers and suppliers.

Marketing involves a complex series of relationships between organisations. Distribution shows us how these relationships can be managed to increase the benefits available to the customer. An organisation's ability to satisfy consumer needs efficiently and effectively hangs on its relationships with its own suppliers. Even something as apparently technical as how a company organises its warehousing can give a business a competitive edge. The benefits can be passed on to the consumer as quality improvement or price reduction.

Distribution covers a range of operations and activities. We can define it as the choice and management of ways to optimise the availability of a product or service to the maximum number of relevant customers at minimum cost. It not only involves the co-ordination of supply to the final customer, but also the movement of goods and services into the organisation.

Some marketing writers relegate distribution to the status of an 'order filling' activity in contrast to the 'order getting' function of advertising, selling, sales promotion and PR (Wilson, et al 1992). But it is a very powerful element of the marketing mix, capable of a much more active role than this classification suggests. The fact that it is less immediately obvious than the promotional side of marketing should not blind us to its power. The booming telephone banking and insurance industry is an example of a whole new market sector created just by rethinking traditional forms of distribution.

The changing face of shopping

List three changes in the way that consumers shop in the 1990s compared to the way they shopped in the 1970s. You might want to think about the differences in the way that your generation shops in comparison to the way that your parents' generation used to.

What are the main STEP factors that have driven these changes in shopping behaviour in each case?

DID YOU KNOW?

Japan is truly a nation of shopkeepers. Its distribution chains are famous for their length and complexity, with products often travelling through more than a dozen different intermediaries before reaching the final consumer. The reason is to a large extent historical, because of the growth in trading companies in Japan during the eighteenth and nineteenth centuries. But it also reflects the Japanese passion for shopping. Frequent visits to the shop, buying goods in small quantities, and a taste for specialised products (especially in the area of food) have all led to the development of intricate distribution patterns. The mysteries of Japanese distribution are often cited as one of the main barriers to Western infiltration of the Japanese market.

Distribution channels

Distribution channels manage the series of exchanges that a product or service goes through as it is transferred from its producer to its final user. Channels can be constructed of a number of go-betweens or none at all, as direct marketing, which is discussed in Chapter 10. The intermediaries concerned can either be individuals or organisations, who may or may not take title to the product as it passes through their stage of the process. Taking title to something means owning it outright. This obviously involves more risk than merely acting on someone else's behalf. But it also gives the title-taker more control and a greater chance of profit. As is invariably the case in business, the greater the risk the greater the potential gain.

The idea of intermediaries is an uncomfortable one for many consumers. There is a distinct aroma of the Gravy Train about the succession of different people waiting in line for their cut of the profit margin before a product reaches the final user. The consumer, after all, pays for all of this. But intermediaries justify their existence by providing useful services. There are four main reasons why businesses use them.

Specialisation

The mix of skills and experience that marks out successful manufacturers is not necessarily compatible with running a distribution operation. Using intermediaries leaves businesses free to focus more single-mindedly on their core functions. Distribution systems involve heavy investment and costs, so it usually makes better sense to contract this service out. Even enormous manufacturing concerns who have their own fleets of vehicles and depot networks tend to top up with contractors.

Customer utility

The consumer normally requires that a number of different products be available together at one place and time. This may be for the purposes of comparison or simply because of the limited time available for shopping. This kind of variety cannot be offered by a company dealing direct. The sharp end of customer contact is the job of the retailer.

Complexity

The growth in size and complexity of the manufacturing industry has required a similarly complex system for exchanging goods and services between companies, and getting them to the end-user. Think of all the various materials, ingredients and processes that go into something as commonplace as a jar of instant coffee. Bringing all these elements together into the finished product, and then getting that product into your home, requires an extensive network of distribution.

Distance

The increased geographical separation of the end user from the producer of goods and services has ensured the growth of distribution systems. Traditionally, manufacturers have had strong markets in their immediate locality. We can still see concentrations of particular types of industry in specific areas – although this is becoming less and less the case as technology evolves. The greater geographical dispersion of customers means that distribution has become increasingly important as part of a successful marketing strategy.

ACTIVITY **9.2**
··············

What is the point of distribution channels?

Write notes for a short presentation explaining to a meeting of the local Women's Institute what a marketing channel is and what it does. Try and find examples of channels with four, three, two, one and no intermediaries with which to illustrate your explanation.

DID YOU KNOW?

Technology has made crisps a national institution. For a long time, inadequate packaging technology restricted potato crisps to being sold locally by the companies who made them (often as a sideline from their main activity). Now over 300,000 outlets in the UK stock crisps: pubs, newsagents, supermarkets, stations and cafes.

Having explained the growth of the distribution industry, let us now look at some typical distribution patterns, as shown in Figure 9.1.

There is no golden rule about what sort of pattern will suit what sort of business. The judgement needs to be taken on an individual basis. The more intermediaries there are, the longer the channel is deemed to be. For products like newspapers or perishable foodstuffs, this aspect of channel dimension is critical. Indeed, one of the historical reasons why England has a thriving national daily newspaper industry, is that road and rail communications were good enough. Compare this situation with France where practically all the high-circulation dailies are regional.

Companies frequently use more than one distribution system at the same time. A major food manufacturer will tend to have its own sales force directly servicing retail accounts above a particular size as well as a further tier of sales calls on wholesalers and cash and carries. Such companies are using at least two

figure 9.1
**Distribution channels
of various lengths**

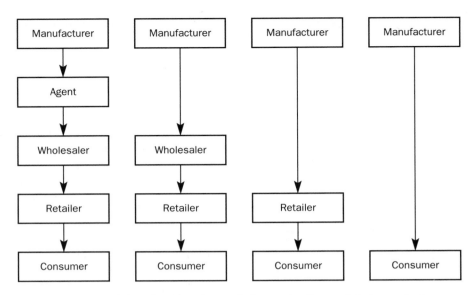

of the varieties of distribution channel shown in Figure 9.1 (manufacturer →
retailer → consumer, and manufacturer → wholesaler → retailer → consumer).
In this way the varying service requirements of each size and type of customer
can be met. Co-ordinating an exercise like this is a highly demanding management task.

CASE STUDY **9.1**

Avon calling

In spite of being the simplest route, the shortest path to the customer is not always
the best. Avon pioneered the direct selling of cosmetics in the consumer's home,
and achieved meteoric success in the 1960s and 1970s. The Avon Lady, usually a
housewife herself, would call on acquaintances bringing her stock with her – or
organise daytime gatherings in her own home or a friend's.

The sound of the doorbell even became the centrepiece of the organisation's
television advertising. But the mid-1980s saw the business in decline. Eighties
woman, with her new-found independence, was spending less time in the home. She
was beginning to think of shopping itself as a pleasurable experience rather than a
chore. Cosmetics are a key product area in the leisure shopping market. Avon found
itself left behind by this sudden environmental change – a mixture of socio-cultural,
economic and technological influences. What had, in the past, been a very effective
distribution system suddenly lost a lot of its relevance, in spite of the quality and
value for money of Avon's products.

Avon is fighting back in the 1990s by placing more emphasis on direct selling to
female colleagues in the workplace by its part-time representatives. It is also actively
seeking out new marketing opportunities on a global basis – there are 14,000 Avon
Ladies in the Guangdong province of China alone.

Questions

1   Cosmetics, clothes, books, costume jewellery, cookware and sex aids are all
      sold by in-home retailing. Name a product category that this distribution method
      would not suit, and explain why.

2 Comment on the challenges that might face Avon in its Chinese operation.
3 Can you think of any other distribution methods that have become outmoded because of environmental changes?

What happens in distribution?
....

All channel members are involved in sorting activities: they sort out and keep stocks of various individual producers' or manufacturers' products. They also provide a means of breaking down bulk goods into appropriate quantities for the next channel stage, or for the consumer. They provide assortments of goods together in one location so that buyers are offered choice and convenience – the utilities of place and time. (See Figure 9.2.)

Information flow

Channel members facilitate the flow of information between the market and the manufacturer. Regular contact with retailers and wholesalers is an important way for manufacturers to find out what is going on in the market. Often the first a company will hear about the launch of a rival product is on the distribution grapevine.

Promotion

Distribution channels are also an essential link for information travelling from the manufacturer to the consumer. They participate in sales promotion, a subject we shall cover in greater depth in Chapter 11. Advertising aims direct at the consumer in order to create demand which will pull the product through the distribution channel. Concentrating on the channel itself, perhaps by offering intermediaries financial bonuses, free stock, or other incentives, is known as a push strategy. Most manufacturers use a combination of both techniques.

Pre-sales services

Channel members reduce the number of contacts a manufacturer needs to make with customers. Depending on the type of intermediary, they can also get involved in pricing, packaging, grading or assembling products to suit the final customer's requirements.

figure 9.2
Distribution functions

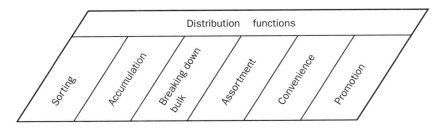

Post-sales services

Channel members consolidate exchanges by transporting goods to their new owners, channelling money in the other direction. Wholesalers share the manufacturer's financial risk in tying up capital in stock, and take on the direct risk of financing the distribution process itself.

In spite of their profit margins, channel intermediaries can actually reduce the price consumers pay by offering manufacturers the benefit of their economies of scale.

Who does what in distribution?

Channel intermediaries fall into two main types: merchants and functional intermediaries. Merchants actually take title to (ie become the legal owners of) the goods they then resell. The risks are substantial in such a commitment. If the goods do not sell, it becomes the merchants' problem. But, at the same time, the potential profit to be made is correspondingly higher than in being an agent or functional intermediary.

Functional intermediaries never actually own the goods that pass through their hands. They earn a commission or fee for the services they provide. These can include transport, storage, finance, or acting as the manufacturer's (or service provider's) agent in a particular market.

There follows an alphabetical guide to the main sorts of distribution intermediaries. It is not exhaustive (for example, the various sorts of retailers are dealt with in greater detail in a later section) but it gives the essential information about the main players in the distribution process.

Agent

A functional intermediary with a contractual agreement to work on behalf of a particular buyer or seller. Agents find customers and negotiate, but never actually take title to the goods in question, receiving a fee or commission for their work.

Broker

Similar to an agent, but with fewer functions. These are mainly limited to bringing together buyers and sellers. Brokerage is particularly common in the food industry. Buyers and sellers benefit from it in order to cope with fluctuating market conditions.

Cash and carry

A type of wholesaler (see below) whose customers are not offered credit, and have to collect their purchases themselves. Popular with smaller independent retailers, who will often use the cash and carry (eg Makro) in conjunction with traditional full-service wholesalers and company sales representatives in order to deal with their stock needs.

Direct marketer

Direct marketing is characterised by a direct relationship with the customer (including delivery of the goods) which circumvents all the traditional channel intermediaries. This kind of marketing approach is dealt with at greater length in Chapter 10.

Facilitator

Firms like hauliers, warehouses, banks and insurance companies help expedite exchanges without taking title to the goods concerned.

Franchisee

An individual or an organisation granted the exclusive right to exploit a successful business idea by its originator (franchisor) in return for a consideration. Examples include Tie Rack and Body Shop as well as services from fast food to rodent control.

Franchisor

The owner of a successful business idea who franchises it out to a number of franchisees (see above).

Industrial distributor

Similar to a wholesaler in consumer marketing terms, but offering industrial buyers the facility of inventory and location. Industrial distributors tend to specialise in particular product sectors.

In-home retailers

Companies, like Avon or Tupperware, who sell direct in people's homes rather than using traditional retail environments.

Licensee

Similar to franchisee (see above) but usually used in an international marketing context. The licensee (eg Coca Cola Export Corporation in the UK) pays royalties on sales or supplies used in manufacturing the product to the licensor (in this case Coca Cola in the US).

Merchandiser

A worker, sometimes freelance or part time, who supervises displays and stocks for particular manufacturers in retail outlets. Merchandisers are often used tactically to supplement the efforts of a traditional permanent sales force.

Retailer

The final link in the distribution channel with the consumer. Frequently specialises in a certain product area (eg electrical equipment) and offers advice, credit and after-sales service to customers. A high level of service input is made at this stage, especially in product fields like food and fresh produce.

Wholesaler

An intermediary that buys stock from a manufacturer and sells to another reseller. Like retailers, will sometimes specialise in a particular product area.

Usually offers credit, delivery and frequently has its own sales representatives servicing retail accounts direct.

Channel conflict

What is good for a manufacturer (outlets for all its brands) is not necessarily good for a retailer (who should only be interested in the fastest-selling products offered by each company). Even though both manufacturer and retailer are members of the same distribution channel, their priorities and interests are different. Distribution channels are made up of autonomous organisations with their own needs and agendas. This means that conflict can occur.

Let's look back at the diagram of typical distribution channels shown in Figure 9.1. Vertical conflict is the name given to conflict that travels 'down' the line of the distribution channel. It occurs between two or more members of the same channel, for example a wholesaler and a retailer.

Horizontal conflict is the name given to conflict that travels 'across' the line of the distribution channel. It occurs between two or more members of different channels who are at the same stage in each. Horizontal conflict might occur between two retailers, one of whom wanted to extend its opening hours in the face of opposition from the other.

CASE STUDY 9.2

Battle of the books

In 1991 Britain's biggest books retailer, WH Smith, found itself in conflict with several major suppliers of books because of differences about what credit terms were to be made available. This is an example of vertical conflict: ie tension down the line of distribution between intermediaries seeking to better their position at the expense of the interests or working practices of other members of the chain.

In the same year another bookshop chain, Dillons, cut the price of a number of best-selling books. This radical departure from the Net Book Agreement (the convention of selling new books at their face value as set by publishers) created tension not only between Dillons and publishers, but also with other book retailers. This is a conflict across organisations at the same level in a channel of distribution, and is therefore called a horizontal conflict. This was the beginning of the end for the Net Book Agreement which, having regulated book retail prices for 40 years, collapsed in 1995 amid a flurry of price-cutting.

Questions
1 What are the advantages of tensions between channel intermediaries for consumers?
2 What disadvantages might be involved?
3 What environmental factors could be said to have exacerbated the tensions between the intermediaries in this example?

Coping with channel conflict

Instead of having a collection of organisations working independently of each other in a distribution channel, there has been a growing trend towards integration by businesses keen to improve their profitability. The difference between autonomy (ie each channel member being independent) and integration is illustrated in Figure 9.3.

Integrated distribution channels are known as Vertical Marketing Systems. Vertical conflict between members of a channel is prevented by an approach that treats the channel itself as a system. A system is a complex organisation that behaves as one unit. There are three main ways of establishing a vertical marketing system (VMS), and each method has been responsible for profit breakthroughs in companies enterprising enough to change their relationship with other channel members.

Corporate VMS

The first is the Corporate VMS, where two or more stages in the channel come under common ownership. Examples include off-licence chains and grocery retailers who service their outlets with stock from their own national network of depots. This is equivalent to owning the wholesaler stage of their distribution channel. The advantages in terms of payment systems, information flow and promotional co-operation are obvious.

Administered VMS

This form of integration sees one part of the chain assume control by co-ordinating the activities of other members (often its suppliers). Although there is no ownership involved, the bargaining power of the controlling organisation is sufficient to ensure co-operation from the other members. An example is the way major retailers specify clearly what is acceptable in terms of delivery and timing from suppliers. Such details can even include packaging specifications and label contents.

Contractual VMS

This controls channel conflict by establishing formal agreements between channel intermediaries. Examples include franchising and dealerships, where the exclusive rights to retail a product or service are granted to particular organisations or individuals. This ensures them a level of support (promotion, merchandising and a

figure 9.3
**Conventional vs.
Vertical Marketing
Systems**

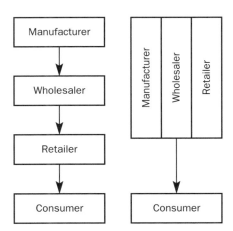

tried and tested business idea) as well as the absence of immediate competition. It also ensures the franchising organisation has a high degree of control. Contractual systems can also link organisations horizontally in distribution channels. For example, one way in which smaller independent retailers can challenge the buying might of their larger rivals is to form buying alliances themselves. This is the idea behind symbol grocers like SPAR, or chemists carrying the Numark brand.

Choosing the right channels

The factors that come into play in choosing the right distribution channels for a particular marketing purpose are illustrated in Figure 9.4. Some of these are internal considerations, others are external. Given that both types of circumstances change over time, it follows that successful companies keep their distribution arrangements under constant review. History is full of examples of companies who have come to grief by losing contact with their markets through inappropriate distribution channels. It makes sense to evaluate channel relevance every six months or so. It may be that a window of opportunity has opened through a change in only one of the six factors shown in Figure 9.4.

Consumers

Marketing organisations, by definition, put the consumer at the centre of every decision. This is nowhere more relevant than in decisions about distribution. Questions to be answered include the number of customers, their geographical distribution, how often they purchase, and where they expect to find the products or services in question.

A dispersed market will need to be serviced through a network of distributors. On the other hand, a geographically concentrated market of frequent users

figure 9.4
Factors in channel decisions

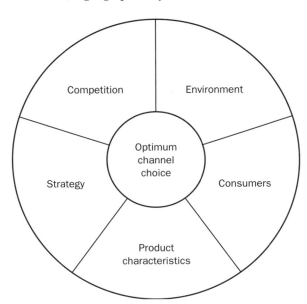

of a product or service (which is a typical consumption pattern in industrial markets) will lead to shorter links.

Product or service characteristics

Mention has already been made of the particular needs of perishable goods like newspapers or fresh fruit and vegetables. Here time and channel length are crucial to getting the goods to the customer in a way that preserves their benefits intact. The features of many industrial products (eg size, heaviness, expense) will require a high level of involvement by the seller in the physical distribution process itself. Dangerous substances, or those particularly prone to pilfering, will need systems that guarantee the maximum amount of security. This will cover aspects such as paperwork as well as the choice of warehousing and transport used.

Services need careful thought as to what patterns fit their characteristics best. Where the service is an expert one such as medicine or business consultancy, personal interaction is usually necessary. Choices here include the location of this activity and the time at which it should take place. On the other hand there are certain sorts of services which can take place more efficiently without direct human intervention. To a large extent telephone banking and cash dispensers are the result of a drive to reduce fixed costs by financial institutions. But they also reflect modern patterns of consumer behaviour.

DID YOU KNOW?
Midland Bank launched the telephone banking service First Direct in 1989. By 1994 it had amassed a customer base of 500,000 ABC1 adults, and spawned a series of imitations from high street competitors. First Direct's leading position in the market has come from the service side of its operation. TSB had actually been first in the field with phone-banking in the late 1980s with a system that depended on a central computer which customers activated by tone dialling. But people prefer to bank with a human voice at the other end of the line, even at two o' clock in the morning.

Organisation

Organisational culture and characteristics influence distribution choice. Different businesses have different strengths and weaknesses which need to be borne in mind. Financial strength, market position, and quality of marketing information are all relevant factors in deciding what to delegate to intermediaries and what might be best done oneself.

Smaller organisations can find their size an advantage here. Their scale of operations allows them to experiment in a way that national concerns would find daunting and counter-productive. Distribution relationships are frequently long term and difficult to change, especially for large and complex organisations.

Competition

It has already been stressed that channel intermediaries, unless they are part of a vertical marketing system, will each have their own business agenda. In spite of a perfectly good working relationship, there is no absolute claim on loyalty on either side. It is in the interests of channel intermediaries that competition for their services be maintained.

It is therefore prudent for firms to keep an eye on what the competition is doing. Channel intermediaries themselves may be a good source of information on this. Companies who have their own sales forces use them not only to sell their products, but also to gather information about what is going on in the market place. Business contacts are an invaluable source of data.

Finally, under the heading of competition, it needs to be remembered that any channel choice has cost and revenue implications. Finding a cheaper way of getting the product to the consumer, or of ensuring early payment through systems management, can establish a long-term competitive advantage that it is difficult to undermine.

> **DID YOU KNOW?**
>
> *Benetton's phenomenal success as a fashion retailer is due in no small measure to its physical distribution system. At the heart of the operation in Italy is a fully automated warehouse which can guarantee to replenish out of stock lines in Benetton stores in a matter of eight days anywhere in the world. This allows the company to make the most of the fast-changing fashion market, where product life-cycles are measured in months rather than years. Affectionately known as 'Big Charlie', the computerised warehouse was opened in 1985. It can send out 28,000 boxes of merchandise daily, using only eight workers per shift. Investment in high technology and physical distribution systems has given the company a major source of competitive advantage.*

Environment

The external environment (political, economic, socio-cultural and technological) is constantly changing. Advances in communications technology have suggested new ways of making many services available to users. Socio-cultural changes, such as the growth in single-person households, have helped drive the development of direct marketing.

Political change may make certain forms of channel irrelevant. The advent of the Single European Market, for example, has affected the way that new cars are sold in the UK. Traditionally in the UK there had been a jealously guarded network of manufacturer-specific dealerships. But since the single market, dealers have been able to offer a much wider selection of manufacturers to their customers. Procedures for importing and exporting models have simplified.

Strategy

As an element of the marketing mix, distribution needs to work with the other elements in a strategic combination. The shorter the chain of distribution, the more control a manufacturer has over the presentation of the final product. This is particularly the case in exclusive distribution situations, where part of the contract will stipulate how the product is to be merchandised.

Price-setting also affects distribution. Merchant intermediaries fix their own resale prices. Agents, on the other hand, adhere to their clients' wishes in setting a price to the customer. The cost of the distribution channel needs to be included in pricing decisions. Especially for smaller businesses this is a complex calculation where the actual cost of providing the goods or services to the consumer is frequently underestimated.

Another factor to bear in mind is that high-priced goods tend to be distributed differently from lower-priced goods. This reflects the different forms of buyer behaviour associated with different price levels. Higher priced goods tend to be the object of extensive search behaviour, where consumers will take trouble to find out about alternatives and compare the value available in the market. This will involve visits to specialist retailers. Lower-priced, more frequently purchased goods, on the other hand, tend to be more widely available. They are bought more often, with less effort.

Finally, promotion is an important influence on distribution. We have mentioned the role that channel intermediaries can play in push and pull promotional strategies. For any promotional strategy to work, the distribution system has to be effective in getting the product to the consumer in the first place. It is no use advertising to empty shelves. It is nevertheless surprising how much more effective some manufacturers are at stimulating demand than they are at supplying it.

Consideration of these six factors ought to result in a distribution pattern that provides adequate outlets for a product or service in a way that maximises exposure to the target market at minimum cost.

The general pattern of distribution that emerges will be one of three main types.

Intensive distribution

Involving a presence in every conceivable outlet. This is ideal for frequently-purchased, low-cost items that are easy to merchandise. Examples of products that follow this pattern include batteries, confectionery and condoms.

Selective distribution

Here the distribution pattern is less general, and customers will have a clear expectation of where to find what they are after. It is a typical pattern for what are known as shopping goods, where comparison on performance and price is common. Electrical equipment is a good example.

Exclusive distribution

In this pattern the goods or services are only available in contractually appointed outlets. Quality and service are reflected in premium prices. Luxury fashions and cars are typical of exclusive distribution, but so are other less expensive franchise operations such as fast-food chains and Body Shop.

Retailing
....

Retailing has been the growth industry of the last 15 years in Britain. Government figures show that in the five years from 1985 to 1989 alone the volume of retail sales has risen by over 20 per cent and the value of retail sales (including inflation) by 40 per cent.

Much of this boom has been accounted for by the major multiple grocers like Tesco, ASDA and Sainsbury. Even in the recession-hit 1990s, the food retailing sector is reckoned by many City analysts to be one of the most stable areas of the economy. On the other hand, the meteoric growth rate that many of these companies had become used to has slowed considerably.

CASE STUDY **9.3**
....

Value brands cause City shivers

The introduction in the mid-1990s by major retailers of special product lines offering exceptional value to consumers caused widespread concern to City investors. They saw the new ranges, including Tesco's Value brand, Sainsbury's Essentials and

Safeway's Savers, as likely to have a deleterious effect on profits. The firms in question countered criticism by pointing out that this third level of brands (known as 'tertiary' brands) alongside their existing roster of manufacturer's brands and own label equivalents was necessary to stimulate further growth in the sector. There is also a sense in which the bargain basement image of tertiary brands gives the own label offerings of stores like Sainsbury and Tesco a greater aura of quality – and thus the long-term potential for more profit. In the short term, annual financial results show that though value lines have driven volume growth, trading margins have been correspondingly slimmer. British retailing, however, remains among the most profitable business sectors in Europe.

Questions

1 Discuss the packaging imagery of some 'value' brands with which you are familiar. How does it contribute to (or limit) their success?

2 What are the influences a supermarket chain can bring to bear on its customers' perceptions of value for money?

3 How might 'value' brands affect a supermarket's relationship with its suppliers?

Place in retailing has a very literal meaning. The actual location of an outlet is of crucial importance. Pedestrian shopping malls in city centres are developed by property companies to exploit high foot traffic around business districts. There has been a parallel development of out-of-town shopping locations aimed at the motorised shopper. Proximity to motorway junctions is a crucial priority for locations like Gateshead's Metro Centre and Sheffield's Meadowhall. They attempt to create a relaxed atmosphere that shoppers will find intriguing and enjoyable. Given the popularity of both destinations for coach-party excursions, it would seem that this has been achieved.

DID YOU KNOW?
Shopping-loving Britain now has more square feet of retail space per citizen than any other country in Europe?

Selling by design

The traffic of shoppers is streamed in a way that helps them relate profitably to the merchandise available. The different assortments of merchandise on display as shoppers enter a store are meant to draw them through into other areas. In a fashion shop, outer clothing gives place to informal clothing, then to night-attire, underwear and lingerie. Relationships between groups of merchandise are emphasised so that the shopper can contemplate a cluster of complementary purchases rather than isolated items. Even the carpet can come into operation to help guide the consumer. Darker colours indicate routes, lighter colours browsing areas.

Outside in the mall this theme of harmonious relationships continues. Competing businesses are not placed in juxtaposition. There is a natural pattern of different sorts of shops both in terms of their proximity to one another and the kind of location they favour on an individual basis. The maximum window space, but minimum floor space, of a corner position would, for example, be worth far more to a jeweller than to a clothing retailer.

Malls are a relatively recent import from North America. They represent a retail response to environmental and customer changes over the last two decades. Their basic technique of selling by association is one that can be profitably transferred to many other businesses.

CASE STUDY **9.4**

The Victoria Gardens Shopping Centre

In the elegant Yorkshire Spa town of Harrogate, the Victoria Gardens Shopping Centre offers an example of a retail development that combines tradition and innovation in a friendly shopping environment. Opened in 1992, the centre is on four levels, joined to a car park by a footbridge and directly opposite the town's railway station.

On the lower ground floor a traditional market offers fresh fruit, vegetables and flowers as well as an assortment of miscellaneous merchandise of the sort you can find in any well-established urban market. The next two floors have a number of high-street names who benefit from the central position and the high levels of shoppers it attracts, and the fourth floor concentrates on more specialised shops selling a range of goods from perfumes to soft furnishings.

Clive Bayley, the centre manager, comments: 'In many ways the nearest comparison with running a shopping centre would be running an organisation like a radio station or a newspaper. You are in the business of delivering an audience of shoppers to your tenants in just the same way as a radio station delivers an audience of listeners to its advertisers. Another point of similarity is that we have to provide the equivalent of editorial matter. A newspaper needs to command its readers' continued attention by its features and news stories. Here the equivalent is special events and themed activities. Our shoppers have very high expectations and we have to match them by making the experience of visiting Victoria Gardens a relaxed and enjoyable excursion for them. Finally, just like a radio station or a newspaper, we rely on audience research to show us where we are going. We spend a great deal of time and expense on finding who our shoppers are, how often they visit us, and what they like doing when they are with us.'

Questions

1   What are the advantages and disadvantages of a town-centre shopping mall as opposed to:
– A department store.
– Mail order.
– An out of town development.
2   As a shopping centre manager, what kind of information would you look for from research to keep your tenants (ie the shops renting space from you) happy?
3   Suggest three promotional themes for a shopping centre over the course of a calendar year. How would you enlist the co-operation of your tenants and guarantee a good response from shoppers?

A–Z of retailing

The following is an alphabetical list of common sorts of retail outlets each of which has a particular place in the market.

Category killers

This is a name given to any retailer who seeks to corner the market in a particular product category. Taking advantage of economies of scale, products are offered at substantial discounts to customers. Trading margins are slim, but the idea is to see off competition unable to match prices within the category in question (hence the rather melodramatic name). Examples of this sort of operation in the UK are the American import Toys 'R' Us, and the office stationery and equipment retailer Staples.

Convenience stores

These fill a gap left by the rise of the major multiples. They cater for shoppers who need the convenience of location and opening hours that these general purpose grocers (frequently offering alcohol and video tape rental) offer. Located in residential areas, they are often operated as franchises (eg 7/Eleven) and provide an opportunity for symbol grocers (see below). Petrol stations are finding the convenience store a useful profit enhancer in the face of slim margins on fuel.

CTNs

CTN stands for Confectioner, Tobacconist and Newsagent. This type of store is characterised by early opening – which leads to opportunities to augment sales of the basic product line with morning goods such as milk and bread. Books, stationery and toys are another area offering growth, having clear connections with newspapers, magazines and confectionery. CTN owners tend to prize their interaction with their customers who are usually daily visitors.

Department stores

Having been a dominant force in retailing in the 1950s, these have declined in importance. Their role in bringing together an assortment of different retailing concessions (like shops within shops) has largely been assumed by malls. On the other hand, there are still a number of very successful department stores who have bucked this trend. Their secret lies in targeting their customers carefully and supplying a high level of service (at a price) which differentiates them from the competition. They are an example of niche distribution. An interesting straw in the wind for the future, however, is the remarkable popularity and social significance of department stores in Japan at the moment.

CASE STUDY **9.5**
....

Not so much a department store, more a way of life

The 'Depaato' is a cornerstone part of Japanese shopping, but there is nothing quite like it in the West, in spite of the Western origin of its name (abbreviated from 'department store'). Seibu, the biggest chain in Japan, gets between 200,000 and 300,000 shoppers a day in a typical outlet. Deferential customer service is built into the store's way of working. The Seibu training manual includes no fewer than three recommended ways of bowing (depending on the circumstances).

The Japanese word for department store literally means 'Hundred Goods Shop', and the emphasis is on profusion with a dizzying variety of new products. Every major Japanese newspaper has a department store correspondent to keep track of developments. Dazed customers, in danger of being overwhelmed by the choice, are guided through carefully themed arrangements of products and services.

The idea is to provide complete assortments of products and services. A special instore shopping environment called 'Loft' specifically targets younger consumers. Leisure is one of its specialities. In the store's own swimming pool you can learn how to scuba dive. Nearby is a travel agency desk where you can book a diving holiday, and there are tempting displays of diving equipment and swimwear.

Young Japanese consumers spend a great deal of money on swimwear, and Loft's managers had noticed that when young women came to make their purchases they usually bought their boyfriends with them for approval. The store decided to refit the swimwear floor with extra large changing rooms and admit couples to them. The innovation proved so popular that at weekends there were between 10 and 20 couples queuing at a time, and soon all Seibu's competitors followed with similarly enhanced facilities.

Questions

1 How might the Depaato concept be adapted for the UK?

2 Can a consumer have too much choice?

3 Theming merchandise helps a store reduce customer confusion. Comment on ways in which theming merchandise can be useful in other areas of retailing.

Hypermarkets

These are an even bigger version of superstores (see below). Precise definitions vary, but most analysts accord hypermarket status to stores with more than 100,000 square feet of selling space. They are more common in North America than the UK, and their location makes them the exclusive domain of the motorised shopper.

Multiple grocers

The Sainsburys of this world, these have spearheaded a revolution in size, location and technology since the first supermarket chains began to develop in the 1960s. Succeeding decades have seen a concentration of more and more retail power in the hands of this sector. By the early 1980s, for example, two-thirds of all UK food purchases were made through multiple grocers. This is an alarming prospect for any manufacturer, as a delisting from the stocking policy of a major multiple can bring dire consequences. As competition intensifies, manufacturers are finding their margins increasingly squeezed.

The success of the multiples has stemmed largely from the following factors:

▶ their realisation of their value as an intermediary to other parts of the chain.

▶ investment in technology to improve their efficiency and information flow. Data collected from Electronic Point of Sale (EPOS) scanners enable these sorts of outlets to know exactly which lines are moving and which are staying on the shelf too long.

▶ productivity. They have reduced the numbers of their outlets while increasing the size of each. They have exacted terms of business from manufacturers that have allowed them to establish own-label brands as high-volume sellers. They are employing fewer people, but those people are doing more for them.

▶ extended opening hours. The legalisation of Sunday trading for five hours opening (usually between 10am and 4pm). More extended trading hours are still the province of the smaller convenience store.

Speciality stores

These tend to be small, boutique-like enterprises dedicated to a single area of merchandise. They frequently offer subsets of a generic product (eg religious books, classical music, golf equipment, etc.) with well-informed personal service. Typically they occupy city-centre locations, near established high street names, in order to benefit from the consumer traffic attracted by the bigger stores.

Supermarkets

See multiple grocers (above).

Superstores

These are similar to self-service supermarkets, but with a lot more space. Criteria vary, but most superstores have at least 60,000 square feet of selling space, and 15 checkouts. Out-of-town locations are the norm, with adjacent parking and petrol availability. Analysts have varying views as to the number of large superstores a population can support, but the sector is a buoyant one in terms of new building projects. Grocery superstores have now been joined by others specialising in home improvement products and gardening.

Symbol grocer

This will form a network of independent grocers who share a common corporate identity, joint buying and promotion in order to muster more clout with manufacturers. A prime example of this is SPAR, whose accent on being local and convenient (with extended hours) brings together the two themes of the utility of time and place offered by the retailer.

Variety stores

These are similar to department stores (see above), but aim at the middle-market customer, and will tend to specialise in a particular assortment of merchandise. This category of store includes the doyen of British retailing, Marks and Spencer whose main strengths are in clothing and food. Other stores in this category include C&A (clothing), BHS (clothing and household goods) and Woolworth (houseware, children's clothing and home entertainment). Again, accurate positioning to appeal to distinct market segments has guaranteed these retailers their unique niche.

Voluntary groups

These are similar to symbol grocers (see above). This kind of shop includes outlets like Numark chemists, all of whom are independent businesses, but who combine to increase their buying power.

Warehouse clubs

These outlets are an American idea whose time may not yet have come in the UK. The first in Britain was CostCo, although its 1993 opening in Thurrock, Essex, was deemed to have been only a partial success. Customers (members) pay a subscription for the privilege of shopping. Their credit rating is scrupulously checked before admission to the select band of warehouse club shoppers. Once inside, shoppers have access to an amazing range of bargains – from power boats to toilet rolls. Discounts are very impressive. Several manufacturers have refused to supply warehouse clubs as a result. In spite of their slowness to take off in the UK, they represent an industry worth over $40 billion in the US.

All of these retail businesses are catering for carefully-defined segments of the market. There is some overlap, admittedly, but even though the same consumers may use a convenience store and an out-of-town hypermarket, the occasions on which they do so will be different as will their set of motivations when shopping. The retail trade is in a constant state of evolution to cope with this growing awareness of the segmented nature of its market.

The wheel of retailing

An attractive theory that goes some of the way to describing this evolution is the wheel of retailing, popular with American academics in the 1960s. It suggests that retailing is a cyclical industry. Grocery outlets start out by trying to compete with their rivals on price. As they become established, the effect of this policy on their profit margins becomes a problem. They then try to move up-market to a better quality (and more highly priced) range of merchandise and selling style. This creates a gap at the lower end of the market for a new player to take the field with a low-price strategy.

This certainly fits the life-cycle of some famous retailers. Debenhams, now one of the most successful upmarket department stores, began life in the 1920s as a cut-price retailer. Similarly, Tesco which started in the sixties as the original 'pile it high, sell it cheap' discount store, has moved up-market to a position not dissimilar from that of Marks and Spencer. This in turn has opened a gap in the market for the Scandinavian company, Netto, whose stores tend to be situated near less well-off council estates, and whose retailing atmosphere is very spartan. The choice available in Netto is limited, but all products are stocked on the basis of their cheapness.

DID YOU KNOW?
Consumer culture has even reached the heritage industry? The National Trust turned over £21 million in its 200 shops in 1993. The shops have a house style reminiscent of Laura Ashley, with a quiet, wood-based decor. Some 10.2 million people bought 250,000 notelets, 127,500 mugs and 127,000 teatowels. Gardening books, pot pourri, and other carefully chosen merchandise helped the Trust towards a total profit of £3 million on its retailing operations.

Category management

As retailing has become more competitive, the pressure is on to squeeze as much profit as possible from each inch of shelf space. This has led to the development of a new marketing discipline – category management. Category management treats an entire product area as a strategic business unit (SBU) in order to maximise returns from it.

Pre-sweetened breakfast cereals form such a category. This product area features a number of well-known brands (Frosties, Sugar Puffs and Corn Pops to name but three), and has seen much new-product activity in recent years. Several own-label offerings have also made an impact on the market. Customers for the product category constitute a well-defined group – housewives with children. The variety such customers demand leads them to be purchasers of portfolios of brands rather than exclusively loyal to just one or two. Added to the variety of products on offer is a wide range of pack sizes, and a high level of advertising and promotional activity. The in-pack free gift is a popular form of sales promotion in this category – and a frequent source of parental harassment by small children.

Such a product category presents the retailer with a series of choices. Quite apart from which product lines to stock, the optimum range of pack sizes needs to be determined. Furthermore, how ought the products be displayed relative to one another on the shelf? And what should their merchandising relationship be with other 'morning goods', or with the entire range of other merchandise carried?

The temptation would be to class such decisions as an art rather than a science. But the advocates of category management argue that there are hard scientific principles waiting here to be uncovered and applied. Retailers now have an unprecedented wealth of information at their disposal. Electronic data capture at point of sale has meant that they know to the minute what is selling where.

The advent of smart card customer loyalty schemes such as Tesco's Club Card means that retailers can even track the buying behaviour of individual consumers. The accumulation and manipulation of such information using computers means that retailers can gauge very closely the effects of minute variations in pricing, display and stocking policies. The nearest analogy for this is not so much the familiar techniques of fast-moving consumer goods as the exacting discipline of direct marketing. Like direct marketing, category management emphasises a results-led, quantifiable approach.

Physical distribution and logistics

Physical distribution deals with the actual movement of products from suppliers to users. It concentrates on tangible products, but service providers can gain valuable insights from considering the strategic choices involved, and drawing parallels with their own operations. From a customer perspective, speed of delivery is often as important as price.

High quality physical distribution can give a business an edge. The challenge is to balance the level of service with cost. It has been estimated that this part of the marketing mix accounts for something like one-third of all marketing expenditure, so it is an area offering rich rewards for companies who can successfully rationalise their operations.

The best way to examine the process of physical distribution is to look at it as a system. We have seen in our discussion of vertical marketing systems that this term implies a degree of control and interdependence. The relevance of the system concept here is that in order to improve the level of service offered in one aspect of the system, it may be necessary to compromise on another. The order of priorities each time will be dictated by considering the consumer's needs and attempting to satisfy them more accurately and profitably than the competition.

In fact this is the essential difference in meaning between the terms 'physical distribution' and 'logistics'. Logistics is the term favoured by marketing professionals. It starts with the consumer and works back through the system to ensure that each stage serves the needs and expectations of the end-user. Figure 9.5 illustrates the main functions carried out by a Physical Distribution/Logistics system. These are order processing, materials handling, warehousing, inventory management and transport. We will now examine each in turn.

Order processing

This first stage in a distribution system is a crucial one from the marketing point of view. It involves contact with the customer and offers an opportunity to introduce service advantages over the competition. The system design here should include speed, ease of use and efficiency.

Materials handling

Frequently the physical attributes of the product (eg perishability, weight, bulk) will be the decisive influence in how it is stored and transported. Balancing service levels and cost here means working out the most efficient use of warehouse space, which will affect the shape, size and nature of the packaging used.

For services, which by their nature cannot be stored, this aspect of distribution is less relevant. However, there is a parallel with choices about whether the service is provided by its originator, or is mediated through representatives or even reproduced through media of various sorts.

figure 9.5
Physical distribution activities

Warehousing

Again the focus here is on tangible products rather than services. The geographical location of warehouses relative to production and consumption locations is a key consideration for manufacturers. The functions that warehouses perform are several. They even out peaks and troughs in production by carrying a buffer of stock. Products are therefore immediately available to the next stage of the distributive process. A service analogy here can be drawn with information sources. Picture libraries, databases, information services and mailing list brokers are all service equivalents of warehousing.

Inventory management

Adequate stocks of working materials are vital. But too much money tied up in this way can spell cash-flow disaster. On average, stock will account for between a third and a half of the assets of most businesses. Careful thought must be given to how much to reorder, and at what intervals. Typically the cost of storage averages out at about 25 per cent of the stock's value per year. This figure includes the opportunity cost of having money tied up in it (which could at least be earning interest) and the overheads (insurance, maintenance, security) involved in the process of storing itself.

There are two main lines of approach to solving the problem of having sufficient stock without tying up an excessive amount of capital. The first is to order the same amount of stock at each reorder but vary the intervals between each reorder according to your need. The second is to have regular intervals, but vary the quantity each time according to need. The first approach is called the 'fixed order approach', the second the 'fixed interval' approach. Over a wide range of stock the calculations involved in either approach are complex and cumbersome. As a result this aspect of optimising distribution is usually handled by information technology, using computer models to gauge appropriate reorder quantities and intervals.

Just-in-time

What started as a stock control idea from Japan, has rapidly gained popularity with Western businesses. This technique, pioneered by car manufacturers Toyota in the 1960s, is called just-in-time manufacturing, or JIT for short. It aims at maximising the efficiency of the manufacturing process by carrying the minimum level of stock necessary. As a result there is increased attention to other aspects of manufacture (smaller manufacturing batches mean a greater emphasis on quality, more accountable use of time and resources, and finally a better product).

Advocates of just-in-time link its application to quality improvement. A favourite image is that of a flowing river. If you lower the amount of water that is in the river, hidden rocks and obstacles become apparent. By removing the rocks you can make the passage of a boat going down the river safer and more effective. Similarly, by lowering the level of stock flowing in a production system you can uncover snags and inefficiencies and eliminate them. This makes for a swifter and more effective production system, leading to fewer defects and an improvement in quality which the consumer will notice and appreciate.

Transport

This final aspect of physical distribution adds time and place utility to a product by moving it from where it is produced to where it is used. It is one of the most frequently contracted-out aspects of distribution, although many major manufacturers will maintain their own fleets of haulage vehicles. Typically, more than one form of transport will be used (eg road and rail, or canal and road) in the process of distributing any one product. As with other aspects of physical distribution, a balance needs to be struck between cost and service levels.

DID YOU KNOW?

A Carlisle-based haulier who specialises in the rapid despatch of fresh food around Europe has a fan club of 10,000 people? Eddie Stobart Jr runs a fleet of over 500 distinctively liveried trucks which top the lists of 'truck spotters' – bored motorway drivers and passengers who while away the time by looking out for the famous green, white and yellow Stobart vehicles. Stobart's nearest rival for spotularity is the equally enigmatically named Norbert Dentressangle, a French haulier.

Distributing a service

Services are distinguished from physical goods by their intangibility. You cannot store them or carry them – so many of the problems associated with physical distribution do not apply in the area of service marketing. However, some services rely on tangible products as part of their delivery (such as equipment or materials). Interpersonal contacts are usually essential to service delivery, a fact that influences their distribution patterns decisively.

Distributing a service through intermediaries has the advantage of encouraging clear thinking about the service itself. Just as agents and sales representatives need intimate knowledge of the product they are offering, so service agents and franchisees need to have an expert understanding of the service they are broking. Training, monitoring and systems aimed at consistency of presentation are essential prerequisites of reliable service delivery through intermediaries.

Location and time as elements in service distribution

A major distribution decision for any expert service (such as law or medicine) is quite literally to do with place. Where should the transaction happen? Either you visit your client, or your client comes to you. For many business services place decisions have a close bearing on the nature of what is being offered. It may be, for example, that a neutral location is the best choice: as in counselling and training.

Sometimes the service offered will depend very heavily on the personality and expertise of the individual at the centre of the company. This is frequently the case with design or PR consultancies, where the client is buying the insight or creativity of a particular director with whom they may have worked over a number of years. Using intermediaries such as other staff or agents in a situation like this needs to be done with care.

Time is as important as location in service delivery. By their very nature, emergency breakdown services have to be in distribution on a round the clock basis. Medical practitioners, on the other hand, have surgery hours for non-urgent cases which are handled on an appointment basis. These two examples illustrate how service distribution decisions are a matter of balancing cost (to the provider) and utility (to the consumer).

Physical environment in service distribution

Atmospherics is the name given to the distribution technique that seeks to create service delivery conditions that reinforce certain dispositions in customers (see Figure 9.6). The technique is particularly useful in a service environment such as health care (to reinforce feelings of safety or well being) or financial services (reassurance and reliability). Major refits of banks and building societies in the UK have emphasised the importance of extending the corporate identity of the company concerned into the retail environment itself. Thus colours and textures that consumers have learned to associate with companies like Lloyds, Midland or Barclays are now incorporated into the physical environment presented to their customers. The effect is not just a psychological one. Because of the intangible nature of services, it actually helps consumers to use them more easily if there is an element of consistency and familiarity in their presentation. So, a readily identifiable style of interior decor may be as important in financial services delivery as an easy to complete paying-in slip or a rational queuing arrangement.

DID YOU KNOW?

Some Japanese companies have explored the use of aromatic effects to put their customers in a more relaxed and, possibly, free-spending mood. Smell is certainly an important element of some retailing operations in the UK such as Body Shop and the scented candle specialist Wax Lyrical. More explicitly, experience museums, such as Tetley's Brewery Wharf in Leeds and York's Jorvik Centre, use smells as an overt element in their created environments.

figure 9.6
Atmospherics

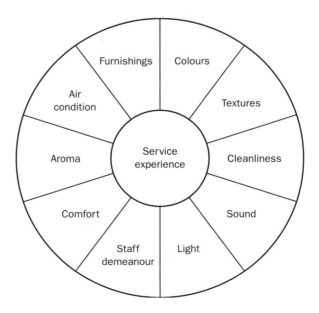

ACTIVITY **9.3**

Atmospherics audit

Using the atmospherics diagram (Figure 9.6) as the basis, compile a check-list of atmospheric attributes. Use the check-list to conduct an audit of part of your college or organisation used for important service delivery (eg lecture theatre, common room, canteen, library). Rate each attribute on a scale of 1–6. It may be interesting to do this individually and then compare your ratings with those of other people to determine how subjective or objective atmospherics are.

Summary

This chapter has examined distribution: the activities of various organisations that link manufacturers to their eventual customers. These intermediaries justify their margin on a product or service by reducing contact costs and facilitating the process of exchange. Their contribution to the process includes sorting products into categories, building up stocks, making appropriate quantities available to buyers, and transferring information and revenue between buyers and sellers. Well-managed distribution can be a decisive source of competitive advantage.

Key concepts

Category management: a retailing philosophy that focuses on groups of products rather than individual brands.

Channel conflict: clashes of interest between distribution intermediaries. Can be horizontal (between intermediaries at the same stage in two separate channels) or vertical (between successive intermediaries in the same channel).

Channels: groupings of individuals or institutions linking buyers and sellers.

Conventional distribution system: channel consisting of independent intermediaries (as opposed to a vertical marketing system where there is formal co-ordination).

EPOS: Electronic Point of Sale information system involving laser technology to read bar codes providing instant information on product movement.

Functional intermediaries: channel members whose activities do not involve ownership of the products with which they deal.

Inventory: the amount, and variety, of stock carried by a business.

Mall: architectural development combining an assortment of retail units in an indoor environment.

Merchandising: activity aimed at maximising the impact of display at point of sale.

Merchant intermediaries: channel members whose activities involve ownership of the products with which they deal.

Pull strategy: promotional activity that aims to stimulate demand in customers to 'pull' goods through the distribution system.

Push strategy: promotional activity that targets distribution intermediaries in order to 'push' goods through the system..

Vertical marketing system (VMS): a distribution system where two or more channel members are connected by ownership, administration or legal obligation.

1 Name six functions carried out by distribution intermediaries.

2 What is wrong with the following statements?
   a Distribution patterns are strictly industry specific.
   b Buyers and sellers only use one distribution pattern.
   c Push promotion aims to stimulate consumer demand.

3 Cash and carries are:
   a Discount retailers who do not accept credit cards.
   b Functional intermediaries who offer transport facilities to small- and medium-sized enterprises.
   c Wholesalers who offer credit facilities to club members.
   d Wholesalers who neither deliver nor offer credit facilities.
   e None of these.

4 Horizontal channel conflict occurs between:
   a Successive stages in a distribution chain.
   b Brokers in the UK and retailers in France.
   c Service providers and manufacturers.
   d Cable television operators and equipment manufacturers.
   e Two channel intermediaries at the same stage of parallel chains.

5 VMS means:
   a Vertical Management Scenario.
   b Virtual Management System.
   c Very Major Service.
   d Vertical Marketing System.
   e Vertical Matrix Section.

Which of the following statements are true and which are false?
   6 Competition, environment and strategy are some of the influences on choosing the right distribution channels.
   7 Exclusive distribution is always connected with high-priced goods.
   8 Category management treats groups of products as SBUs.
   9 Hypermarkets have at least 60,000 square feet of selling space.
   10 JIT leads to quality focus.

Discuss the following
   11 Giving two examples of each, differentiate between merchant intermediaries and functional intermediaries.
   12 What are the three main strategic options open to distribution patterns? Give examples of each type.
   13 Explain the following terms:
      a Category killer.
      b CTN.
      c Symbol grocer.
      d Broker.
      e Inventory.

14 Outline the 'wheel of retailing' theory. What do you think are its limitations?

15 What are the five main functions fulfilled by a physical distribution system?

Further study
••••••••••••••••••

Books

The area of distribution is surprisingly neglected when it comes to specific text books, perhaps because of the potential breadth of the subject.

However, Martin Christopher has developed interesting approaches in the following books:

Christopher, Martin (1986) *The Strategy of Distribution Management*, Butterworth Heinemann.

Christopher, Martin, Payne, Adrian and Ballantyne, David (1991) *Relationship Marketing*, Butterworth Heinemann.

Takes the argument to its logical conclusion in an account of long-term customer service.

References
••••••••••••••

Wilson, R., Gilligan, C., Pearson, D., (1992) *Strategic Marketing Management: planning, implementation and control*, Butterworth Heinemann.

CHAPTER 10

Promotion–introduction, advertising and direct marketing

Objectives

When you have read this chapter you will be able to:

▶ Relate basic theories of communication to the practicalities of promotional management.

▶ Draw on the main practitioner theories of how advertising works to increase profitability.

▶ Explain the organisation of a typical advertising agency.

▶ Understand the client/agency relationship, especially in terms of selection, briefing, management and evaluation.

▶ Appreciate the contribution of media planning to successful campaigns.

▶ Recognise the relevance of direct marketing as a promotional tool in a variety of marketing situations.

▶ Understand the self-regulatory framework of the UK advertising industry.

Introduction

Promotion is the part of the marketing process that communicates the benefits of the product. In a competitive market-place, you cannot expect goods and services to sell themselves. No matter how high a product's quality, unless customers know about it you are unlikely to make a sale. Much of the emphasis in promotional thinking has traditionally been about creating new customers, but it is equally (if not more) important to remind existing customers of the benefits of what you have to offer.

The two promotional techniques we will focus on in this chapter, advertising and direct marketing, tend to be associated with new customers and existing customers respectively – although they are both highly flexible techniques. Other promotional methods such as sales promotion, public relations and direct selling are dealt with in Chapter 11. It is important, however, to see them all as aspects of the same process of informing and persuading customers of the advantages of your offer over the competition. The more flexible and innovative a company's approach to its promotional strategy, the fresher its impact is likely to be on a market-place saturated with commercial messages.

Integration – the way forward in promotion

In the past, promotional services have been offered by specialist agencies. Each discipline (such as advertising or sales promotion) argued its case to the client in competition with the alternatives. Very often this resulted in a tactical approach to promotion, with the various strands operating in separate compartments. The 1990s, however, have seen the advent of an approach called integrated marketing. This emphasises the use of appropriate promotional disciplines in combination with each other. Integrated marketing recognises the fact that an organisation's total communication to its customers is more important than any single promotional technique. The move to break down traditional divisions between marketing disciplines has resulted in high levels of creativity and effectiveness, and squeezed maximum value out of budgets.

Integrated marketing has been driven by the following factors:

▶ *Social*: increasingly sophisticated customers.
▶ *Technological*: computer databases, 'smartcard' electronics, new advertising media.
▶ *Economic*: rising demands on marketing efficiencies.
▶ *Political*: deregulation of media, changing attitude to promotion.

CASE STUDY **10.1**

Dr Martens – famous without trying?

In 1945 Dr Klaus Maertens was recovering in Munich from a skiing accident. With an engineer friend, Dr Herbert Funck, he devised a special shoe (originally made out of old tyres) to help him hobble around more comfortably. A footwear legend was born!

The shoes spread across Europe. They were particularly popular with elderly people. The turning point came in 1959 when Maertens and Funck advertised in the trade journal *Shoe and Leather News* that they were looking for a British manufacturer to produce the shoes under licence in the UK. At that time the Tuf shoe brand, featuring a special process whereby a solid rubber sole was bonded to an upper, was leading the British footwear market. R. Griggs & Company, a traditional Midlands shoe and boot manufacturer was anxious to find a product to compete with the onward march of Tuf. It enthusiastically responded to Dr Maerten's advertisement, and on 1 April 1960 (a date commemorated in the famous number 1460 which gives the particular boot its brand name) the first pair of boots came off the production line in Northampton.

During the 1960s they achieved a steady popularity as functional workwear with the police, postmen and milkmen. Then, by a bizarre twist of fate, they became an essential item in the 1970s skinhead craze. This gave them an unenviable kind of fame. Docs have remained part of the uniform of many a style movement since – from 1980s punks to 1990s grunge. They are also a firm favourite with students.

Exports and fashion are becoming more important to the company. Worth £7 million in 1990, exports had increased more than five-fold to £38 million in 1992. In 1993 R. Griggs & Co invested £3 million in a joint venture with London fashion designers Red or Dead to create a line of apparel called DM Clothing. In 1994, just in time for Christmas, the Dr Martens Department Store opened its doors for business in London's ultra trendy Covent Garden. It offers Docs and accessories on five floors (including a cafeteria called the Doctor's Orders).

Dr Martens is probably the most famous brand in the footwear market today. Its acid, alkali, petrol and oil-resisting 'bouncing' soles are a legend. Yet, unlike other household names, it does little if any advertising.

Questions

1 In spite of not advertising to any significant extent, Dr Martens is a famous brand. Why?
2 If your company sold a product that became associated with a youth movement such as skinheads, how might you reduce negative publicity?
3 Docs still sell vast quantities of shoes and boots as workwear. What potential conflicts might its excursions into fashion create, and how might integrated promotion resolve them?

Source: Company Information; Caulkin 1993.

The promotional mix

To understand how the various techniques of promotion are integrated, we can think of them as a combination of elements. A popular way of doing this is to talk about the promotional mix, often seen as consisting (like the marketing mix itself) of four components:

▶ Advertising.
▶ Public relations.
▶ Sales promotion.
▶ Personal Selling.

Like any theoretical approach to a practical subject this is fine so long as it is useful. However, it does lead to problems of classification. Where, for example, might one place exhibitions or conferences in this scheme of things? It is also hard to pigeonhole direct marketing using these categories. These are each important areas of promotion, so we ignore them at our peril. The traditional concept of the promotional mix should not limit our imaginations in devising an appropriate strategy for a particular product. Promotional planning should consider all the options, every time, or it risks becoming routine and complacent.

ACTIVITY **10.1**

Technology and promotion

New promotional media are continually becoming available as electronic and printing technology develops. Scratchcards, holographs, interactive video, the Internet, even something as relatively banal as advertising on supermarket trolleys ('the last advertisement the consumer sees before making a purchase') all took a leap of the imagination to conceive.

This exercise asks you to think of a new promotional medium aimed at one of the following groups:

1 Women aged 18–25.
2 People doing a weekly shop at an out of town supermarket (and therefore using a car).
3 AB men interested in sport.

What kind of companies might be interested in taking advantage of your new idea, and how much might you be able to charge them for using it?

Understanding communication

The communication process at the heart of marketing promotion can be seen as the journey of a message from its source to its target, to elicit a response. This model might describe an advertiser sending a commercial message to a consumer who responds by purchase. Sometimes called the 'process' model, it is certainly popular with marketing writers and features in many text books. It corresponds to most people's common-sense expectation of how promotion works. They see advertising as a stimulus that can generate a predictable response in the market. (See Figure 10.1.)

The encoding and decoding involved in the model are similar to the way in which a marketing brief is turned into a creative promotional approach from which the consumer is expected to take the intended meaning. The channel can stand for the medium used. Noise is anything that interferes with the successful transmission of the intended meaning (eg smudged printing, or even unclear language).

figure 10.1
Process model of communication adapted to advertising

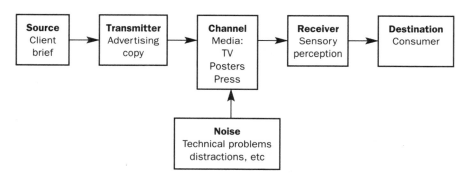

Adapted from: Shannon, C. and Weaver, W. (1949) *The Mathematical Theory of Communication* University of Illinois Press

Hierarchy of effects models

This basic model is similar to popular models of advertising which have been around since the early part of the century. These are often called hierarchy of effects models, because they suggest that customers have to pass through a number of stages to reach the desired outcome of a sales response. While each model has its own emphases, all of them move through three main stages: *cognitive* (making people aware of the product), *affective* (gaining approval of the product) and *behavioural* (prompting action about the product – buying it, with luck!).

Hierarchy of effects models are open to criticism on two counts: they do not seem to cover products that are bought habitually, and they imply that consumers are passive. But they help us think about planning and analysing our communications in a systematic way.

Three influential examples of such models are as follows:

Starch

Daniel Starch (1925) 'To be effective an advertisement must be seen, read, believed, remembered and acted upon.' An early, but still widely quoted, model emphasising the need to make advertising easy to understand, credible and interesting.

AIDA

E.K. Strong (1925): AIDA: Attention, Interest, Desire, Action. Another classic model. The idea of 'desire' is unique to AIDA. It means convincing the target group that this product is the one for them. Careful research into what they are looking for is therefore essential in order to stress the benefits that matter.

DAGMAR

Russell Colley in his book *Defining Advertising Goals for Measuring Advertising Results* (1961) (DAGMAR for short) claims that an advertisement must carry the customer along a continuum towards purchase. The four main stages are: awareness, comprehension, conviction, action. Colley's contribution was to focus attention on what exactly advertisers wished to achieve in particular campaigns in order to judge their success. So it might be that moving a target group from being aware of something to understanding it denoted a successful campaign, even if the act of purchase was still some way off.

In real life people are not as logical in their responses as sequential models assume. But this does not prevent the models from being useful. For example, AIDA can serve as a check-list for message structure, or as a guide to the layout and design of an advertisement or sales presentation. Practically any press advertisement you can find will demonstrate the principle. A headline grabs the attention. The reader's interest is then captivated by an illustration or a photographic image. The words of the ad ('body copy') demonstrate how the product or service on offer will provide a sought-after benefit (thus stimulating desire). A coupon, or telephone number, or list of stockists, will complete the structure – allowing the reader to become a customer by converting interest and desire into the action of purchase.

An alternative view

In spite of appealing to our common sense, hierarchy of effects models often seem a million miles away from what is actually going on in the real world of customer communication. No matter how ingeniously a message is transmitted, customers ruthlessly select only what they are interested in.

They screen out the vast majority of promotional messages before actively interpreting what is left. After all, they have been exposed from an early age to countless promotional gambits.

Far from being naive receivers for commercial messages, consumers are sophisticated and selective. They use advertising rather than being used by it. As we have seen, sequential models of communication have something to offer, but they are by no means the end of the story. It is all too easy to end up talking at rather than with our customers. At best this is a waste of money and effort, at worst it can have a permanently alienating effect.

An alternative way of looking at communication is to work backwards from the recipient. Because all effective marketing starts with the customer, the relevance of such an approach to promotional communication ought to be clear.

Instead of putting the onus on the effective transmission of intended meanings, this approach recognises that receivers create meanings themselves. As a result, the way in which the building blocks of meaning relate to each other becomes of crucial importance. These building blocks are called signs, the systems in which they operate are called codes, and their wider environment is called culture. The study of signs and their relationships is called semiology (or semiotics).

At its most basic level it is both a simple and a useful idea. It boils down to talking the right language to the customer. So, if you are targeting an 11–17 year old market with a soft-drinks promotion, the kind of imagery you choose ought to be on their terms. The success of irreverent brands like Tango and Irn Bru in this market suggests promotion more in tune with their youthful customers than the more sedate approaches of the cola giants. What this means in practice for communications management is an increased provision for qualitative research before campaigns are devised, and a willingness for clients to trust the more outlandish ideas of their promotional agencies (provided, of course, that they are backed by reasoned argument and evidence).

CASE STUDY **10.2**
. . . .

Jeans means signs...

In the late 1980s, Levi's had the UK jeans market buttoned up with the unprecedented success of its 501s. Its trend-setting television advertising featured vignettes of 50s America set to familiar songs. Apart from guaranteeing their soundtracks a new lease of life in the pop chart's top 40, the commercials established Levi's as the authentic American jean.

Any other jean using American imagery risked being just one more advertisement for Levi's. Yet blue denim and America are an unshakeable combination in customers' minds.

Wrangler decided that it needed to carve out a piece of America which was all its own. Its UK advertising agency at the time, Simons Palmer, began an extensive qualitative research exercise to discover what America meant to its customers. The research involved the arduous task of visiting nightclubs up and down the country to track down members of its youthful, free-spending target market. When discovered, the unsuspecting consumers were hustled into quiet rooms, and shown concept boards that depicted different kinds of America before being allowed back on to the dance floor.

The results of the survey looked promising. Cowboys, Levi's-style 'cherry pie', country and western, were all passed over in favour of a gritty, urban version of America. Contemporary, grainy, slightly dangerous – it was easily as authentic and stylish as Levi's territory, but occupied a very different area in consumers' minds. Having come to terms with the signs and the codes, the agency went back to the drawing board and came up with its commercial 'Cross Town Traffic', shot on location on the streets of New York and cut to the classic Jimi Hendrix track.

The commercial featured a taxi driver who opts out of the urban chaos of New York by abandoning his yellow cab in the middle of the street and disappearing down the nearest subway as a gridlock develops behind him. It ended with an appeal to individuality which was rather provocative in view of the success of 501s: 'Be more than a number'.

Apart from causing a genuine traffic jam of monster proportions during its filming, the advertisement also created a storm of controversy when aired in cinemas and on television in the UK. One of its sequences, filmed from a moving vehicle, featured what turned out to have been a real knife-fight over the bonnet of a parked car. The tabloid press, traditional 'guardians' of the nation's good taste, were swift to pick up on this unseemly fact and proceeded to castigate the company and its agency (generating tens of thousands of pounds' worth of free publicity for the brand in so doing).

In spite of the controversy, Wranglers' careful exploration of semiotics allowed it to establish a compelling and original positioning for its product. It was true to its customers' perceptions of jeans imagery, but offered something quite different from the mythology of Levi's. The idea has been built on in subsequent campaigns, emphasising the urban, slightly rebellious, but highly individual nature of the brand.

Questions

1   What factors might affect the choice of a piece of music for a jeans commercial?
2   What do you think of the line 'Be more than a number'?
3   The controversy that the ad generated acted as a valuable source of free publicity. What are the potential dangers of such spin-offs?

Theories of advertising

Advertising is any form of paid-for media communication designed to inform and influence existing or potential customers. It is a major marketing expense, but in spite of the amount of money that is invested in it, there is very little hard and fast scientific research about how advertising works. Clients and agencies invest plenty of time and money in trying to understand how their own advertising works, but this information is precious and confidential. It is unlikely to be shared, except in a highly sanitised and flattering form which may not give the full picture.

A further problem is that it is almost impossible to generalise from advertising research. Experiments and surveys can only be carried out with specific examples of advertising. So a company might learn more about how its own press advertising works from research. But whether this would hold true for anyone else's advertising, or for advertising in a different medium, is another question entirely.

So if you are looking for a science of advertising that is as rigorous as physics or mathematics, you are in for a disappointment. However, there is no shortage of advertising practitioners who are willing to share their philosophy of what constitutes effective advertising with you as a client.

The principles to which they subscribe are based not so much on scientific experimentation, as on common sense and experience. Each agency's distinctive approach to advertising will aim at differentiating it from its rivals in a highly competitive market-place. Yet there have always been two main schools of thought – those who believe in the hard sell, and those who favour gentler tactics.

Hard sell versus soft sell

Saatchi and Saatchi are famous for hard-hitting advertising, often on a grand scale. Saatchi's work for British Airways often grabs headlines for being extraordinarily expensive as well as impressive. The 'Manhattan' television commercial, for example, featured what appeared to be the entire landscape of New York being airlifted across the Atlantic. It was rumoured to have cost half a million pounds to create and produce, before a penny was spent on airtime (the cost of actually broadcasting the commercial on television). Of such stuff are advertising legends made.

The agency has a single-minded approach to advertising. It believes an ad should have a simple and direct message, hammered home in an unforgettable way. This approach is a newer version of a well-established practitioner theory of advertising – the Unique Selling Proposition, made famous in the early 1960s by Rosser Reeves, who worked for the American agency, Ted Bates. Reeves argued that advertising operated on a platform that was basically rational. To pull users across to your product you needed to argue a case for it. Your advertising needed to stress your product's unique features, driving home its advantages over the competition with a compelling sales message.

An alternative approach to how advertising works can be found at the J. Walter Thompson agency. The agency has produced famous campaigns for Guinness, Oxo and Persil over the years. JWT ads like these work by endowing the product with an attractive personality with which its users can identify – the Oxo family, for example, personifies the brand. This approach is in the tradition of brand image advertising, often identified with the name of David Ogilvy who made it a hallmark of the famous agency he founded in the 1950s.

Brand image advertising takes the benefits of the product for granted, and focuses instead on creating positive emotional and psychological associations with the product. It is a gentle but confident approach, soft sell as opposed to hard sell. Its advocates maintain that it works best with expensive, highly visible purchases which are themselves connected with status (such as luxury goods). But the breakthrough that agencies like JWT have made is that even frequently-purchased items like clothes washing detergent and lavatory paper can be given an aura that reflects their performance and quality if they are called Persil and Andrex.

Of course successful advertising campaigns contain elements of both approaches, varying the mixture according to the product and the market. Saatchi's work for a brand like Fairy Liquid, for example, hammers home the benefit of kindness to hands and value for money, but also surrounds the product with warm associations. After all, as consumers we are driven by a combination of the rational and the emotional. We are therefore more comfortable with advertising that reflects this.

ACTIVITY **10.2**
· · · · · · · · · · · · · · · ·

Hard sell and soft sell

Find one hard sell and one soft sell advertisement in a newspaper or magazine.

Come up with a list of changes that would make the hard sell softer and the soft sell harder.

How appropriate are the revised approaches? Might they appeal to a new market segment from the current one?

Advertising and sales

Not all advertising activity is meant to have a direct effect on sales. For example, a company like Shell will run general advertising campaigns in order to improve its image with investors and environmentalists. This kind of advertising, known as corporate advertising, is not tied to any particular product, so its effects would be impossible to gauge from measuring increased sales. Research into attitudes or stock market prices would be a better method of seeing if it was working.

Some advertising activity is actually meant to deter sales. For example, the horrific drink-driving campaigns that are unveiled each year before the Christmas season will be aimed at preventing the purchase of alcoholic drinks by their target group.

All advertising has one thing in common, however. It aims at affecting behaviour (and we can include what people think as well as what people do in this category). The behaviour most advertising is associated with is purchase behaviour – either to induce it in the first place, or (more commonly) to keep it stable in the face of intense competition. The widely accepted model of how this works is that advertising supports sales with a short-term impetus whose effect survives after the advertising activity has finished. After a while, if no further advertising takes place, the effect decays. This may also be due to the activities of rival firms, whose advertising is now supplanting your own in the minds of the consumers to whose needs it is relevant.

Most advertising researchers agree that advertising cannot make you buy something you are not already in the market for, but that it can have an effect on the actual choice you make between the alternatives. Another way of putting this is that advertising cannot itself expand a market, but can affect brandshare within a market. So car advertising is unlikely to make the UK car market bigger (that will happen for other reasons, connected with lifestyles, income and technological infrastructure). But it might make the difference between whether you buy a Volvo or a Volkswagen if you are looking for a family car of a certain size.

Opposed to this view is the argument that advertising (particularly television advertising with its power and wide distribution) can actually make people buy more of what they might not have wanted originally. The classic case here is tobacco advertising, whose opponents maintain that banning advertising and promotional activity would lead to a sharp decrease in the numbers of people who smoke. They point to research where this has been the case in other countries. The tobacco and advertising industries' reply is that the advertising is entirely aimed at existing smokers in a battle between the rival manufacturers to steal each other's customers. In fact, Gallahers, the manufacturer of Silk Cut cigarettes, argue that if tobacco advertising were banned it would be harder to persuade existing smokers to switch to a lower tar (and thus allegedly safer) brand.

Whether consumers are compelled by advertising to do things they would not otherwise or (as seems more likely) just use advertising to help them choose products that support their normal behaviour, its effects on sales need to be set in the context of the short and the long term. (See Figure 10.2.)

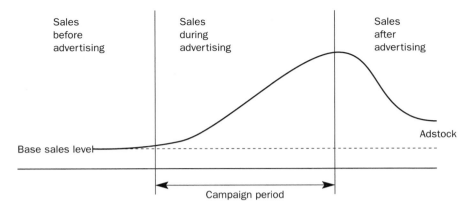

figure 10.2
Advertising and sales: short-term effect

The advertising campaign has had a discernible effect on sales. Perhaps it has led to people trying the product for the first time as an alternative to their usual purchase. Although the surge has died back shortly after the end of the campaign, the overall level of sales has risen. This residual effect of advertising is known as adstock. It may well be that the cost of the advertising campaign will not be covered by the short-term increase in sales. It thus becomes important to acknowledge the longer-term effects when justifying advertising budgets. Depending on the type of advertising and the kind of market in which it operates, this long-term effect may operate over a matter of years, with each successive burst of advertising refreshing and renewing the level of adstock in cumulative steps.

Because it is so expensive, advertising is often the target of cost-cutting measures. In a crisis, companies have been known to raid the advertising budget in order to bolster up their short-term profit figures. The problem is that turning off the advertising tap, while safe enough in the short term, starves the brand of much needed exposure. Sales will bump along, supported by goodwill, but sooner or later the competition will steal a march. Ironically, their advertising will be all the more effective if it is not challenged. (See Figure 10.3.)

Share of voice and share of market

Share of voice is the name advertising agencies give to this idea of how much advertising activity one company is conducting compared to its competition.

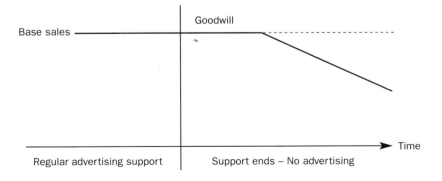

figure 10.3
Withdrawing advertising

There is an observable relationship between share of voice and share of market. So, for example, Ford's share of advertising in the UK car industry will have a relationship with its share of the number of cars sold in any year.

A long-standing American research project called PIMS (Profit Impact of Marketing Strategy) has collected information over the years about advertising and marketing activity from a large number of major companies. Participants are guaranteed anonymity in return for being able to share the benefits of the information. The findings suggest that in advertising, as in life, success breeds success. Increasing share of voice is most effective for brands that already have a very large share of the market. Similarly, a pound spent on advertising an already successful product in a growing market can be expected to yield more in benefit than a pound spent trying to resurrect the fortunes of an ailing brand.

ACTIVITY **10.3**

Advertising and profitability

Nobody spends advertising money unless they have to. Whatever the task of the campaign, be it to launch a new brand, or remind people of an existing one, the overall objective will be to increase profitability. Because there will be a limit on the amount of advertising money available, hard decisions need to be taken on how it is allocated. What decisions would you take in the following situations, and why? Where there is not enough information to make a decision, what more would you need to know and how would you use the knowledge?

1   Your company's biggest brand, a wholegrain breakfast cereal, is losing share to supermarket own-label products up and down the country. You last advertised it on television three years ago, but took a decision to withdraw support in order to concentrate on the launch of a promising new product – a chewy cereal bar. The new bar has not lived up to expectations, although its new brand manager has just presented an optimistic market forecast and your advertising agency has unveiled a new creative treatment for the bar.

2   Your company is facing a hostile takeover by a large multinational, whose main interest in it is to acquire the portfolio of successful detergent brands you have developed over the past 50 years. The board is leaning on you, as marketing director, to cut all advertising until the end of the year. It plans to bolster the half-yearly profit figures with the money. This will convince major institutions in the City that they are better off keeping their shares than selling them – and thus ensure the continued independence of the company.

3   You have ten per cent of the highly competitive UK office cleaning market. This puts you in third place, trailing competitors with 18 per cent and 25 per cent respectively. The rest of the market is highly fragmented on a regional basis, with no single company enjoying more than a five per cent share. Nobody does any extensive advertising in this sector, but an advertising agency has been in touch with you recently. Its presentation made the point that being the first in with advertising would give you an enormous advantage. Your finance director looks like she would take a lot of convincing, but as the managing director you feel there may be something in the agency's suggestion.

How much is enough?

Given the high cost of advertising, and the uncertainty surrounding its precise effects, the question of how much to spend is a vexed one for many businesses. Yet precisely because of the vulnerability of advertising budgets, marketing managers need to be able to defend them on rational grounds. The following factors are commonly applied in appropriating advertising spends to brands.

Competitive activity

What do competitors spend? It is impossible to establish a precise figure on this. However, monitoring the amount of advertising undertaken by competitors can lead to a pretty accurate estimate of the kind of spend involved. It is important to compare figures on a like with like basis, as well as taking into account the residual effect of past advertising. But any large discrepancies may signal the need to question the size of the budget.

History

Looking at what was spent last year and adding an element for inflation often features in budget preparation. Unfortunately the market may have changed, or the last few years may have represented an underinvestment which, if continued, will only make matters worse.

Percentage of sales

Advertising Association figures reveal different going rates for what is known as the 'advertising to sales' ratio in different industries. For example, in the 1990s, 13 per cent of the price of a typical bottle of shampoo goes on advertising, as compared with eight per cent for coffee and less than 0.5 per cent for petrol. The more important image is to the product, the higher the ratio is likely to be. However, if sales of a particular brand are going down due to too little advertising, this yardstick is not of much assistance.

Objective and task

This is the most rational method of budget setting, and the most popular with marketing theorists. It operates on the principle that you should first decide what you want to do (objective) and then cost the necessary action (task). The problem is that the ideal programme of activity soon becomes so extensive as to exceed the availability of funds. But as an exercise in prioritisation, this approach has much to recommend it. It forces planners not to take anything for granted.

For example, the actual number of times an advertisement needs to be seen before it registers with its audience is likely to vary with the nature of the product and the nature of the advertisement itself. A reminder-type advertisement for a familiar product might only need to be seen once or twice. But a ground-breaking new advertisement for an unfamiliar product might need three or four exposures before it sank in. Effective frequency as this is called, is a key factor in trying to extract the maximum value from the advertising pound. Too few exposures and the advertising budget will have been wasted in an ineffectual campaign. But too many exposures are just as wasteful of the money spent on the excess – perhaps with the additional effect of irritating consumers into the bargain.

None of these factors in isolation offers a watertight solution to the problem of establishing an infallible figure. But applied together they can provide the marketing manager with a degree of confidence about the size of her budget.

ACTIVITY **10.4**

Irritating advertisements

What advertisements do you find particularly irritating on television and radio?

Is your irritation due to their content or their frequency (how many times you see or hear them)?

Has their irritation factor got anything to do with being effective?

Agencies and clients

Advertising, like many other marketing services, is usually entrusted to a specialist company called an agency. Agents act on behalf of others – so the relationship with the client, the person who is actually footing the bill for the advertising at the end of the day, is crucial.

How agencies make money

In the beginning advertising agencies used to work for media owners rather than advertisers. In nineteenth-century America they acted as sales representatives for media owners, selling space to advertisers and taking a commission from the media owner for doing so. As time went on they also began writing ads to fill the space for their customers, and then added on more services until they emerged as fully-fledged agencies. From these roots the current system of agency remuneration developed.

Media owners pay recognised advertising agencies a standard commission of 15 per cent on the time or space bought. So, if the price of a TV spot is £1,000, the agency only pays £850 to the station (ie 85 per cent – the full price, minus the agency's 15 per cent commission). When the agency bills the client it adds 17.65 per cent to the figure to make it back up to £1,000. On activity that is non-commissionable, such as buying artwork or research, the agency bases the price to the client on the same kind of principle, grossing up the cost price of the purchase by 17.65 per cent. In all these transactions the agency is acting as the principal. In other words if the client goes bust, the agency is still responsible for paying the media owner – a further justification of its right to commission. If an agency goes bust, which sometimes happens, the media owner cannot get redress from the client for any outstanding debts. So media owners will only offer commission to recognised advertising agencies whose management and finances are regularly reviewed by a number of trade bodies.

There is, however, an increasing move towards charging for work on a fee basis. This makes sense for smaller clients and for special projects, like new product development, where advertising expenditure may be out of the question for several years.

Why use an agency at all?

There are a number of reasons why clients prefer to use agencies, as follows.

Reduced contact costs

Like the distribution intermediaries discussed in Chapter 9, they reduce costs and inconvenience. The countless transactions involved in creating, producing and placing advertising are consolidated into one relationship for the client.

Advertising expertise

Agencies are full of specialists who, between them, can offer many lifetimes' worth of experience in some pretty mysterious areas. Media research, campaign planning, buying advertising space and time, strategic advice: these are all things that it is worth sourcing from experts. The problem is that it is always easier to solve other people's problems than your own, and the readiness to give advice that characterises some agency personnel can cause friction.

Economy

Because of their buying power agencies can achieve prices for services like market research or printing which their clients would have difficulty matching.

Creativity

This is the single most important reason for using an agency. It's the one thing that clients cannot do for themselves. Agencies can view their clients' business dispassionately, providing insight and objectivity. But most of all they can come up with the Big Idea and have the skills to make it work.

Who's who?

The way that advertising agencies are structured reflects the kind of work they do. Some are very specialised, such as media buying shops. Others, known as full-service agencies, will be of a size that reflects their capacity to offer clients the full gamut of advertising services – from planning and devising advertising strategies to realising and carrying them out. Figure 10.4 shows the structure of a typical agency of this sort – offering account handling and planning, creative and production, and media planning and buying.

The main point of contact with the client will be the account director. It is a common joke about advertising agencies that everyone is a director (as it impresses clients to have senior-sounding personnel on their business). But the job title implies a real degree of autonomy and responsibility. In a fast-moving service environment, these are the team captains who need to organise the agency's top players to achieve the client's goals.

Although the precise job titles may differ from agency to agency, Figure 10.4 is a guide to the main roles in any advertising agency structure.

Senior account director

The team captain – maximising the service to the client, while watching profitability. Will have a number of account groups, rather like a senior marketing manager responsible for several groups of products.

figure 10.4
Agency structure

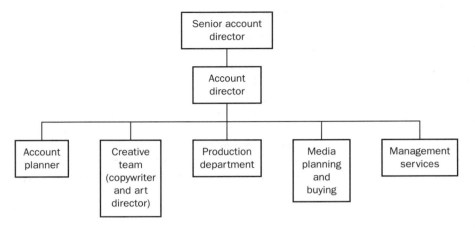

Account director
Dubbed 'the Suit' by the rest of the team. Needs a strategic and diplomatic approach in order to be able to deliver the impossible to impatient clients.

Account planner
The brains of the team – thinking long term, representing the customer, updating the creative brief, researching and evaluating. Wins arguments without shouting.

Creative team: copywriter and art director
Only as good, as they will remind you, as their last ad. Sensitive, observant, insecure. Under enormous pressure, which is why they need to be managed carefully and well.

Production department
Some agencies have in-house artwork studios, but much print production (and all radio or TV) will be placed externally. The production department co-ordinates, spots talent and negotiates to get the best deal.

Media planners and buyers
Often a dual role (particularly for press planning/buying). Plan where to spend the media money to best effect, and negotiate for the lowest price as they spend it.

General management services
A good financial controller (backed by reliable systems) is essential to a successful agency because of the need to maintain positive cash flow. Only the largest agencies will have a personnel function – usually recruitment and training is handled by staff active in other areas.

Account management requires a clear head and a tough skin. Acting as the point of contact with the client means that sales skills and diplomacy are at a premium. But insight and strategic skills are just as necessary. The account director will work closely with the client in order to understand the problem that the advertising will aim at solving to their mutual benefit. In most agencies the account planner will make a significant input at this stage, to create something called the creative brief. This is the first step in the process of managing the advertising process.

The creative brief

Creativity is the most important aspect of what clients demand from their agencies. But it is a very difficult commodity to manage. Ingenious advertising is all very well and good when it comes to winning awards. But truly creative advertising needs to be relevant and effective. In the words of Bill Bernbach, whose ads for Volkswagen in the 1960s made it into a cult car in America, 'If it doesn't sell, it isn't creative.'

The creative brief is a systematic technique to help clients clarify their problems so that appropriate solutions may be offered. The full brief will usually consist of a lengthy document, detailing market background and outlining the characteristics of the target audience.

It will be crystallised on to one side of A4 as a summary creative brief – usually cast into the form of a series of questions and answers. The precise format varies from agency to agency, but most are broadly similar in the areas covered. The three most important questions are as follows.

What is the problem/opportunity?

As we have observed, no one spends advertising money lightly. There has to be a problem to solve, and the more tightly defined the problem the more capable it will be of solution. In this sense a problem (like a declining brand) is an opportunity (to revitalise it). Smith Kline Beecham is expert at this kind of problem definition. It managed to change Lucozade from a rather tired proposition for peaky people in the early 1980s to an energy drink for 1990s sporting superstars. Advertising was an important tool in this process.

Whose behaviour are we trying to affect?

Advertising aims at changing behaviour, even if that behaviour is the way we think about something. Trying to define the audience for the campaign is crucial in order to set realistic objectives in this respect. Are we talking about encouraging existing users to consume more, or reminding lapsed users of the virtue of our brand, for example? And what kind of people are they? Talking your audience's language is the first step to getting through to them. You know when you've been Tango'd, if you are in the right age group. The careful segmentation that is an aspect of all successful media campaigns will be evident here in a precise definition, often using demographic terms.

What is the single most important message we want them to take from the advertising?

Thinking back to the section on communication theory at the beginning of this chapter, this is where common-sense semiotics comes in. The question as posed here recognises that the audience are active interpreters of the advertising rather than passive recipients of its message on the advertiser's terms. It's vital to envisage the advertising from their viewpoint as you articulate precisely what effect you are looking for. So, to pick a famous example of advertising, Rowntrees urges us not to have a delicious chocolate biscuit snack (which might be how a less enlightened advertiser would see the proposition) but to 'Have a Break – have a Kit Kat'. The core benefit of a Kit Kat is the excuse it gives us to relax, and that is what we recognise in the advertising.

The brief will also include any other information that can be pressed into creating the right kind of advertising results. This can include details of recent market research surveys, articles from magazines or journals, guidelines on media preferences expressed by the client, seasonal trends, news of competitive activity and so on. The essence of the brief, though, will be contained in the answers to the three main questions we have looked at – defining the problem, focusing on the market and articulating the benefit.

The creative brief is thrashed out and agreed by the client working in close co-operation with the account director and the account planner. The problem is now presented to the creative team. They need to respond with a compelling interpretation in words and images. Creative teams comprise an art director, providing pictures and visuals, and a copywriter responsible for the verbal side. The two people will frequently have worked as a pair elsewhere. Being able to turn out high-quality advertising ideas on a regular basis across a wide range of products is a very specialised skill. It helps if you can form a partnership with a kindred spirit: two heads are better than one. In an apparently non-visual medium like radio, an art director can help a copywriter by visualising the pictures being evoked. And in a poster or press ad that consists entirely of words, the art director can advise on the style of typography used.

Managing the relationship

The creative brief is just one technique for managing the relationship between client and agency. As in any partnership involving a service, at all times it must be clear what action is approved. There is plenty of room for confusion. Many students who spend time in advertising agencies are amazed by the complexity of the processes involved in getting something as apparently simple as a press ad into the paper. Another common observation is how last-minute everything seems to be – due to the time pressures involved in servicing a number of demanding clients. These conditions require robust systems to make them work without getting wires crossed. Some of the most useful ones in an A–Z of popular advertising jargon are as follows:

Brand reviews

A periodic, usually annual, assessment of the standing of each brand in the agency's care. The review involves substantial input from the client's marketing team as well as reports from the account planner and media personnel. This is an opportunity to stand back and take a strategic perspective, which will then feed in to a medium- and short-term action plan.

Call reports

Decisions taken in meetings, with action responsibilities, will be recorded in what is known as a Call Report (a business call rather than a social call). This is circulated immediately after the meeting – typed from dictation in order to save time. After all, if the issues involved are important enough to justify a meeting, they will be urgent enough to require immediate communication. Even something like a telephone call will be Call Reported in order to disseminate the results of any decisions taken or approvals given on the telephone.

Client meetings

On a regular basis to review progress on work, to approve creative work, to share information, effective meetings are a cornerstone of successful client/agency relations. They are expensive because of the amount of time they tie up, so need clear objectives and outcomes.

Media schedules

These are the written plans outlining advertising activity involving media expenditure. They need to be approved by the client before a penny is committed. Usually advertising will take place in a series of bursts through the year – and frequently clients will insist on approving each burst of advertising separately. Alternatively, advertising that goes on continuously but at a lower level (called 'drip' advertising) may be approved by calendar period. Media owners are as anxious as anyone else to ensure that their services are sold, and will offer discounts to encourage early commitment of funds. So client approvals need to be clear and well-timed.

Production estimates

Advertising involves the production as well as the creation and placing of advertisements. Production budgets can vary enormously, from £60 for a radio advertisement to half a million pounds for a TV extravaganza. The production estimate is a way for agencies, and their more enlightened clients, to keep tabs on exactly what is being spent through a detailed breakdown of costs: photography, actors and models, materials, sets and locations, typography, setting, reproduction...for any medium the list is extensive. Receiving quotes from different suppliers, and negotiating prices, can liberate a substantial sum of money to be used to increase exposure.

Evaluating advertising

Having made the right selection of advertising agency, and managed the relationship carefully, how does a client evaluate the results? Like any marketing activity, advertising needs clear objectives. Measuring success against precisely defined objectives means that valuable experience can be built up.

As we have seen, the sales effects that advertising should help produce are hard to trace immediately or exclusively to advertising activity. It is easier, and more useful, to trace the effects of advertising through the following shorter-term measures:

▶ *Recall*: asking people what they can remember seeing advertised in a particular period.

▶ *Attitude*: measuring consumer attitudes to a product or idea before and after a campaign.

▶ *Exposure*: calculating, from regularly published viewing, listening and readership figures, how many people in your target group will have had a chance to be exposed to your advertisement and how often.

Recall and attitude surveys can be conducted on an occasional or a regular basis. Spontaneous recall is when a respondent can remember an advertisement off the top of their head. Prompted recall is when respondents are given examples of products or advertisements, and agree that they have seen them recently. Such research provides many advertisers with a dispiriting reminder of how much work they still have to do to make any headway into people's attention or memory.

Media research

Measuring exposure keeps an entire industry busy. UK media research is a remarkably intricate network of regular surveys funded by media owners, advertisers and agencies, dedicated to establishing precisely what any kind of media exposure is worth. With TV expenditure alone exceeding £2 billion each year in the UK, this is far from an academic exercise.

Television advertising results are dominated by the computerised sophistication of the BARB (Broadcasters' Audience Research Board) survey. This reveals what the UK television audience are watching at any particular time, and is of keen interest not only to advertisers, but to programme makers from both commercial and public sector TV. It collates data from a sample of almost 4,500 homes spread across all the TV regions, carefully selected for being representative of the population. By indicating their presence in front of a programme with electronic handsets (dubbed 'people meters') Mr and Mrs Average claim to watch about three-and-a-half hours of television a day – less in summer and more in winter. It is possible to know how many viewers have seen your ad in certain areas overnight.

The nation's reading habits, on the other hand, are reported at six-monthly intervals through the National Readership Survey (NRS). This takes data from 35,000 interviews a year to assess what respondents have 'seen or looked at in the last 12 months' – a pretty rough measure of readership which nevertheless serves as the basis for audience calculations. Readership is always higher than circulation, of course, because a copy of a newspaper or magazine will tend to be read by more people than actually buy it. This varies from publication to publication – for a newspaper it can be as little as two or three readers per issue, for a trade magazine circulating in a company it could be six or seven. The number of times a publication is referred to (and thus offers a chance for an advertisement to be seen) varies from title to title, with programme listings magazines like the *Radio Times* heading the ranks.

Other media have their respective research sources, each with its catchy acronym. RAJAR (Radio Joint Audience Research) gives quarterly figures for radio listenership. And OSCAR is the outdoor industry's version of media research. Posters have been notoriously under-researched in the past, but the

Outdoor Site Classification And Research project launched in the mid-1980s has offered credible statistics on audiences for particular poster sites.

Media research terminology

All of these media research sources have a common terminology to describe what is being bought and at what price. Crude as comparisons between media inevitably are, these terms nevertheless give us a framework for evaluating the effect of advertising in any media:

▶ *Cost Per Thousand (CPT)*: The cost of reaching 1,000 members of your target audience in a particular medium.

Although it is a useful statistic when comparing like with like (for example two free newspapers in a specific circulation area), it is not very helpful in making comparisons between media. For example the cost per thousand for a poster is many times less than for a television spot, but the two forms of communication are very different.

▶ *Coverage*: The number of people reached at least once by an advertisement, or series of advertisements.

Within this number (usually expressed as a percentage of the target audience) many will have seen the ad more than once in the course of the campaign. A television campaign would have to run for a very long time in order to get 100 per cent coverage of the entire audience because of the recalcitrant 'light viewer', but coverage levels of 75 per cent to 80 per cent are common for most campaigns.

Television advertising has spawned its own terminology for coverage – the Television Rating Point (TVR) or 'ratings'. A TVR is equivalent to one per cent of your target audience viewing a particular spot. So if 30 per cent of London men are glued to the Bond movie on ITV, that means you have bought 30 London men TVRs. The problem is that this measurement does not take into account repetition of the same audience. The next spot you buy might score 20TVRs, making a total of 50TVRs in all. But the unit makes no distinction between those who have already seen your ad and those seeing it for the first time. So rather than having reached a total of 50 per cent of the target audience, your ad may still have reached only 30 per cent, but two-thirds of them will now have seen it twice. Only careful scheduling to include different sorts of programming will maximise the number of people who see your ad at least once.

▶ *Frequency*: The number of times an advertisement is seen.

Received advertising wisdom is that most ads need to be seen more than once in order to communicate effectively, although recent research has suggested that an interested buyer does not need much prompting. Effective frequency will differ from case to case, but exceeding it can be wasteful. The trick with clever media scheduling is to maximise the number of readers, listeners or viewers exposed to the advertisement the targeted number of times.

Which medium to use?

With nearly 1,500 newspapers, 2,400 magazines and almost twice that number of business publications from which to choose, the inexperienced advertiser faces a bewildering variety of media. Which of them is best suited to advertise a particular service or product? The best kind of media planning starts out from the idea that what you are buying is not so many inches in a newspaper or seconds on a television screen, but people. What kind of people are your customers? What sort of media do they pay attention to? Where do you need to reach them in the best frame of mind?

As we have seen, the kind of media research carried out through large surveys like the NRS can link age and social characteristics to media usage. And media owners themselves can be a useful source of information on what kind of audience they can deliver. They have a vested interest (as agencies do) in a client's advertising being successful, so they can be listened to with confidence (although they are always selling in competition with other media).

An important source of information in this decision is a large scale regular survey called the Target Group Index, or TGI. This looks at the consumption patterns of a representative sample of consumers. It asks questions about the products they buy and use, but it also covers what they watch, read and listen to. Subscribing to this survey (an example of the omnibus type of survey mentioned in Chapter 4) allows a marketing organisation to draw direct correlations between its customers and the audience of certain media.

Media characteristics

Thinking in more general terms about choosing the right place for a promotional message, it is clear that different media have different strengths and weaknesses. Their characteristics can be borne in mind not only when planning an advertising campaign, but also for making sure a public relations programme is being accurately targeted.

A short guide to the strengths and weaknesses of the major UK media is as follows.

Television (roughly a third of UK advertising expenditure)
On the positive side:

▶ High audiences, as many as 15 million people watch big films on ITV. But they are becoming increasingly spread over the viewing opportunities available from multi-channel television.
▶ TV is excellent for demonstrating product usage.

On the minus side:
▶ The short time span of most commercials (30 seconds) is a limiting factor.
▶ High wastage (ie viewers not in your target market).
▶ There are a number of restrictions on what can be shown on television.

Press (roughly 60 per cent of UK advertising expenditure)

On the positive side:

▶ Highly targetable.

▶ Can provide a very good environment for advertising matter.

▶ Handles detail well.

▶ Can be used to get direct response (eg from reply coupons).

On the minus side:

▶ There is a confusing profusion of titles available to the media buyer.

▶ Can be low impact.

▶ Can present the advertiser with timing difficulties in co-ordinating the appearance of a campaign.

Radio (two to three per cent of UK advertising expenditure)

On the positive side:

▶ Radio is a growing medium allowing accurate geographical targeting.

▶ Relatively low cost compared to other broadcast media.

▶ Speedy access to audiences.

▶ With the advent of national stations such as Classic FM it is moving on from its local image.

On the minus side:

▶ It is seen as a background medium – something you listen to when you are driving or doing housework.

▶ It cannot handle complex messages.

▶ In spite of its progress as a national advertising medium, it is still relatively fragmented.

▶ The absolute numbers of people it reaches can be low compared to other media.

Posters (4 per cent of UK advertising expenditure)

On the positive side:

▶ Possibly the oldest advertising medium.

▶ Impressive size and ubiquity. There are something in excess of 100,000 panels in the UK.

▶ Like radio, posters are relatively cheap.

On the minus side:

▶ Tend to be seen as low-impact and are complicated to buy.

▶ They have to compete with a lot of visual clutter and are subject to damage and defacement.

CASE STUDY 10.3

The ironing board test

In 1981, in partnership with Saatchi and Saatchi and Trinity and All Saints University College, Leeds, the research consultant Kay Brandon carried out a study into the advertising communication potential of radio which has since become an advertising classic. As radio is chiefly a secondary activity (accompanying some other primary activity such as housework) it was important that the research design should reflect this. Accordingly, respondents were invited to recruiters' houses to try a new ironing aid on their own laundry. As the recruiter left them to iron, she put on the "radio" as background entertainment.

The "radio" was actually a 15 minute tape interspersing music, a short story and commercial breaks featuring a variety of advertisements. At the end of the tape, respondents were asked questions about the ironing product (a genuine product test for a manufacturer who had agreed to take part in return for a brief report of findings) and also about what they had heard on the radio. The results showed that the commercials achieved a high level of detailed recall in spite of the radio being a secondary medium.

Source: Admap, June 1991.

1. How might you design a similar test to gauge the effectiveness of the communication of posters to groups of people travelling to work?
2. Discuss any ethical questions arising from the "hidden" research aspect of this study, and any precautions you might take to ensure that respondents did not feel uneasy or dissatisfied with having taken part in such an exercise.

Direct marketing

We have seen that traditional advertising activity is very difficult to link in isolation with sales effects. It evidently has a contribution to make, but for all their sophistication, current methods of evaluation still leave much to be desired in terms of linking promotional activity with sales effects. Direct marketing, on the other hand, is highly accountable as a promotional technique. Pressure on marketing budgets, the growth of information technology, and increased competition among companies in all markets has driven a revolution in direct marketing in the last 20 years.

Direct marketing is any form of promotion that adds value by establishing a direct relationship with the customer. It covers a wide range of activity. Sophisticated mailshots to a carefully targeted niche market, mass leaflet drops in the hope of establishing a list of customers who may respond to future offers, magazine advertisements with a reply coupon, even customer care telephone numbers on low-fat spread or soft-drinks cans: all are forms of direct marketing. They are all aiming to forge an unmediated relationship between buyer and seller which will lead to long-term mutual benefit.

Direct marketing is not just a promotional medium, although so much of it is done through the post that it is dangerously easy to confuse it with direct mail. In fact any advertising medium can be used to foster a direct relationship with the customer – even the fleeting television or radio commercial can contain a telephone number, as pioneering insurance company Direct Line has proved. And, while it eliminates the need for traditional intermediaries, direct marketing is not just a channel for getting goods or services to the customer. It is a whole philosophy of marketing – a way of doing business that creates and keeps a customer in a demonstrable relationship. This continuing relationship should contribute to the customers' greater benefit and the organisation's greater success.

Database marketing

Direct marketing is often referred to as database marketing. This is because of the central importance it ascribes to information on the customer. Knowledge is power, and in database marketing knowledge about your customers gives you the power to satisfy their needs more effectively than your competitors. A database is simply a list. But the enormous advantage of maintaining and manipulating databases on computers is that information on purchasing behaviour can be cross referenced with other characteristics of your customers. The result is that it becomes much easier to tailor your marketing activity to their situation. This ability to customise marketing activity offers a dual benefit. The customer is only targeted with goods that are appropriate (and thus begins to see such promotion as helpful rather than intrusive). The organisation cuts down on inefficiencies in the marketing budget.

> **DID YOU KNOW?.**
>
> *Timing is everything in a direct marketing campaign. BT's recent 'Keeping in touch with family and friends' campaign targeted students about to leave home for full-time education. They and their parents were seen as a likely market for phonecards, mobile phones and 'temporary student' line installations. Because of the difficulty of reaching them once they had entered student accommodation, the mailing was timed to hit them before they went to college – alongside the UCAS mailing confirming their places.*

Customer acquisition

This is the most expensive part of the process. The idea of acquiring a customer may sound a trifle manipulative, but the phrase reflects the way in which direct marketing regards the customer as an appreciating asset. Another way of putting it would be to see customers as a portfolio of investments which will increase their value over time. They involve a substantial outlay and not all of them will perform as well as hoped. But by careful review and maintenance they can yield substantial dividends.

Customers are acquired in the following ways:

Collecting information from existing customers

Theatres can convert single-ticket buyers to subscribers, mail order companies can convert chance shoppers to regular purchasers, by data capture at point of sale.

Fishing for prospective customers

Trade exhibition stands offering the prize of a bottle of champagne for the first business card drawn out of the hat, advertisements inviting further enquiries, even leaflet drops to particular areas targeted through geodemographics are all ways of trawling the market-place in search of a group of people who are sufficiently interested to respond with their personal details.

> **DID YOU KNOW?**
>
> *Even a well-maintained in-house database tends to go out of date by between 12 per cent and 16 per cent each year. Companies need to refresh their lists by searching continually for more people like their best customers, and target them accordingly. Knowing your customer has never been more important.*

Renting other people's customers

Sometimes this is done on a reciprocal basis. Some charities pool lists with complementary organisations in the hope that they may find new supporters (although other charities make a point on their literature of emphasising that they do not make their members' names and addresses available). And if lists are not available for love, they are more commonly available for money. There is a burgeoning industry of list brokers fuelling direct marketing. List brokers can provide direct marketers with selections of potential customers to fit specific briefs. Lists can be sourced direct from their owners (for example, specialist magazine publishers) or compiled fresh from existing sources. Because of the high cost, canny list renters or list purchasers will insist on testing a sample of the list first with a trial offer. In spite of the frequently high cost per thousand rentals and comparatively low response rates, commercially available lists can be a useful short-cut to establishing the best kind of list of all – a list of people who actually have bought from you.

Existing customers

Sociologists demonstrate that people tend to behave in similar ways within peer groups. It is likely that your existing customers know many other people who are highly likely to respond to your offers. As a result MGM (Member Get Member) or FGAF (Friend Get A Friend) are frequently-used tactics for customer acquisition. If they are sufficiently pleased with the service they receive, existing customers can even act as your advocates (see Chapter 3 on buyer behaviour). Often the promise of a free gift will spur them on to do what comes naturally.

> **DID YOU KNOW?**
> Direct marketing turns much conventional marketing wisdom on its head? For example, in traditional marketing the most important aspect of the marketing mix is the product. In direct marketing, by far the most important aspect of the mix is the list you use. Drayton Bird (1989) suggests that it is at least twice as important as the offer you are making. No matter how good your product, how compelling the promotional message, how reasonable the price...if the offer reaches the wrong people you are wasting your time.

The test mentality

In spite of the popular image of junk mail, direct marketing in all its forms is one of the most rationally-driven of all marketing communication techniques. Every aspect of a direct marketing package is capable of being tested. For mailings the colour and shape of the envelope, for press ads the size of the illustration or the arrangement of copy, for charity requests the size and order of the suggested donations... the permutations are endless. The next time you receive a piece of direct mail, examine each element carefully. Each part will be identifiable by a small code – a guarantee that its effectiveness in generating response is being measured. It may be that half the mailing has gone out in one kind of envelope, the other half in another. Similarly with press ads that seek a direct response, a publication may be printed so that half of its edition carries one version of an advertisement and the other half an alternative version. All else being equal it should be possible to measure their relative effectiveness at pulling response.

One thing that this kind of test approach seems to confirm is that gimmicks work well, even in direct marketing aimed at what one might expect to be rational customers. *Which?* Magazine, for example, avoids the newsagents stall and is distributed entirely by subscription. Its stern pages cut through marketing hype to test the true performance of products from family cars to blue jeans. Yet the Consumers Association has no qualms about using blatant promises of inclusion in free draws and the lure of mystery free gifts to entice likely subscribers to its magazine. As it explains in one of the many inserts in its mailings, such techniques have been proved by research to work.

Five secrets of direct-mail success

1   Start selling before they open the envelope. Thinking back to AIDA, this is the opportunity to grab the prospect's Attention. So a message on the

envelope itself (perhaps a teaser to arouse curiosity), or an intriguing device seen through a window in the envelope, can save your mailing from the wastepaper basket.

2 Being interesting is more important than being brief. Research shows that people are willing to read four-page letters quite happily, so long as they are interesting. The following layout devices can help:
– try to end a page with a sentence that runs into the next page
– indent paragraphs to keep the eye moving down
– keep paragraphs short
– keep it personal.

3 Include a response device. If this has the name and address of the respondent pre-printed this makes life easier for them, and good marketing is all about making your customer's life as easy as possible.

4 The more items you put in a direct mail package, the more often the potential customer has to say no. Stickers, scratch cards, certificates, envelopes within envelopes, all promote involvement. The important rule is to be consistent – everything should have a common theme.

5 The most brilliant ideas are frequently the most simple. Charities are particularly good at this, faced as they frequently are with making minimal budgets stretch as creatively as possible. The asthma charity, who included a narrow drinking straw through which prospects were invited to breathe as they read the mailing (to simulate what an asthmatic attack felt like), provides a particularly impressive example of this.

CASE STUDY **10.4**

Direct marketing for cynics

Ogilvy and Mather Direct is one of the top direct marketing specialists in Europe. An offshoot of the famous Ogilvy and Mather agency, its tradition of creativity, fed by careful research, is something very much in keeping with the kind of approach laid down by David Ogilvy himself in books like *Confessions of an Advertising Man* (1964).

One of O&M Direct's most innovative clients is American Express. But the agency faced a tough challenge with a recent drive to recruit new card-members. It was targeting an audience who looked fine in terms of socio-economic profile, but who had already ignored two letters brimming with enthusiasm about the benefits of carrying the card. The positive, upbeat tone was simply flowing off them like water off a duck's back. The third mailer took a risk. It empathised with the mood of the target audience by playing to their doubts and cynicism about card membership. The envelope carried the message: 'I'd been planning to cancel my American Express Card. Luckily I had it stolen first...'

Not what you would call the hard sell, and not very flattering about American Express. But inside the envelope was a letter explaining that this particular card holder was glad he hadn't cancelled the card because when it, and the rest of his luggage, was stolen, he had so many emergency benefits to fall back on as a result of membership. The mailing worked where a more wide-eyed account of the joys of the card had failed.

Questions

1 How far do you think that successful marketing communication needs to match the mood of its recipients?

2 Being cynical is a risky strategy. How might it work for the following products or services?
 – Car rental.
 – House purchase.
 – Dry cleaning.

Source: Cramp, 1995.

Legal, decent, honest and truthful?

The British system of control of advertising and promotion (as with many other professions) works by self-regulation. The Advertising Standards Authority, set up in 1962, is the body that polices all British advertising in non-broadcast media. Television and radio advertising are policed by the Independent Television Commission and the Radio Authority. The ASA re-routes many complaints addressed to it in the first instance to the appropriate body.

The ASA protects not only the interests of the consumer by ensuring fair dealing, but also the credibility of advertisers themselves. Although funded by a levy on all advertising expenditure, it is entirely independent both of the industry and of the government. It states as its primary objective 'The promotion and enforcement throughout the UK of the highest standards of advertising in all media so as to ensure in co-operation with all concerned that no advertising contravenes or offends against these standards, having regard *inter alia* to the British Code of Advertising Practice.' Prospective advertisers need, therefore, to take account of the standards the ASA sets for advertising and sales promotion.

These are set out in a combined document available from the ASA. The codes specify that advertising and sales promotion be legal, decent, honest and truthful. Furthermore they should be undertaken with a sense of responsibility to the consumer and society, and adhere to principles of fair competition in business.

The ASA has no powers of legislative enforcement itself. Instead it will refer complaints about breaches of the law to the appropriate body, eg the Trading Standards Department.

The ASA has got teeth, however, in the shape of the support that advertisers, agencies and media owners have pledged to it. A publisher can be warned not to accept advertisements that have not satisfied its requirements. In the vast majority of cases breaches of the code are accidental. Most advertisers and agencies value the free and confidential advice which the ASA gives, and demonstrate this by checking their creative material with the ASA before publication.

As well as responding to complaints from the public and requests from the industry, the ASA carries out about 150,000 spot checks itself each year. It keeps a special watching brief on certain areas, including alcohol, health-related products and environmental claims.

In 1990, a typical year, the ASA received 10,000 complaints. A third were re-routed to the appropriate authority, a third were classed as frivolous complaints and a third were taken up and dealt with direct. Decisions are published in the ASA's Monthly Report, which is circulated to the media industry. If a complaint is upheld, which is frequently the case, the advertiser is asked to withdraw or amend the advertisement. If the advertiser's response is unsatisfactory, sanctions are applied.

Broadcast advertising is dealt with by the ITC for television and Radio Authority for radio. Advertisement scripts need to be cleared before production with each body, and then the finished commercial needs to be seen and approved before it goes on air. This is a highly effective screening process, although it is very hard work for those involved! Recent advertisers whose work has been rejected as unsuitable for television include the ice-cream manufacturer Haagen-Dazs (some of whose very adult ice-cream work was deemed too steamy for the screen) and Unilever, whose original campaign for the UK launch of the brand *I Can't Believe It's Not Butter* was thrown out because of its possibly confusing effects. Each of these companies used the rejection of their work as a public relations theme. Perhaps, after all, there is no such thing as bad publicity!

CASE STUDY **10.5**

Controversial advertising gets talked about

The ITC innocently approved a quirky television commercial for the soft drink, Tango, in 1991. The ad, cast in the form of a spoof sports video (complete with enthusiastic commentary and expert opinion) featured a rewind and slow motion playback sequence as a consumer, refreshed by his draught of Tango, had his ears boxed by a character dressed in orange. The ad was the first in a very original and salient campaign which has achieved extremely high levels of recall.

It also achieved very high levels of complaint. Within a few days of its first appearance on ITV, the ITC was being flooded with calls from all over the country. Most came from head teachers of schools reporting that their pupils were being injured or distressed by other children in the playground belabouring them about the head. In a couple of instances this had led to cases of perforated eardrums. When asked what had happened, the tearful reply was usually 'I've been Tango'd'.

The effect of the ad could hardly have been predicted. It certainly was not spotted as potentially dangerous either at script or finished commercial stage. To prevent further injury or distress the ad was immediately withdrawn and a re-cut version substituted with a less aggressive approach from the character in orange.

Advertisers can consciously set out to shock – and some of Tango's more recent advertising has attracted criticism for connecting soft drinks with fetishism. Perhaps the most famous example of deliberately shocking advertising dates from Spring 1992 when Benetton unleashed its notorious United Colors of Benetton press and poster campaign on the UK. Only a few months previously its national poster campaign featuring a new-born baby had been withdrawn after a national outcry as to its lack of taste. The new campaign featured powerful documentary photographs depicting disturbing aspects of contemporary life (an AIDS victim dying in the arms of his family, a blazing car, a soldier brandishing a human thigh bone, and two refugees from a flood disaster).

A spokeswoman for the ASA commented that publishers might be reluctant to run the ads because they dealt with 'violent or tragic situations which could cause offence and distress'. Direct action was taken by the militant AIDS pressure group Act-Up who objected to what they saw as 'blatant Aids profiteering'. It invaded the Oxford Circus branch of Benetton and scattered armfuls of sweaters from the shelves all over the floor.

But the campaign was a publicity coup par excellence. A columnist in *The Independent* ruefully calculated that the press coverage it had generated was worth about £550,000, and that excluded all the prime time television news and current affairs exposure it had earned. Given that Benetton's entire 1991 UK ad spend was only £600,000 this was quite a bargain. It guarantees, if nothing else, that the brand name will still be in people's minds long after they have forgotten what all the fuss was about.

Questions

1   Is there a foolproof way of spotting potential problems in advertising (given that nobody anticipated any problems with Tango)?
2   Advertising does not take place in a vacuum. Discuss this idea with reference to the case examples.
3   The ASA will act on relatively few complaints (eg the Benetton baby poster was withdrawn after a record 600 letters had been received – a tiny fraction of the millions of people who saw it). How does this affect its ability to act authoritatively?

Summary

This chapter has looked at advertising – the most visible form of promotional activity for most mass-market consumer goods marketing. Direct marketing is gaining ground on it as, encouraged by advances in technology and discouraged by the rising costs and possible inefficiencies of traditional advertising, many traditional advertisers are experimenting with reaching their customers direct. The prevailing economic climate is forcing a promotional rethink for many marketing organisations keen to integrate their promotional activities rather than keeping them in separate compartments.

Key concepts

Advertising: any form of paid-for media communication designed to inform and influence existing or potential customers.

Advertising to Sales (A/S) ratio: the ratio between the sales value of a product or service and the amount of its advertising budget. Frequently used as a guide to how much to spend on advertising.

Body copy: the words, other than headlines, of a press advertisement.

Broadcasters Audience Research Board (BARB): the UK research body that commissions and publishes regular television viewing information for advertisers and programme makers.

Commission: traditionally the basis of advertising agency remuneration, a percentage of the purchase price of media (usually 15 per cent) which is returned to them by the media owner.

Copy: the words of an advertisement, or (more generally) advertising material of any sort.

Corporate advertising: advertising that promotes a company rather than an indivudual product brand.

Cost per thousand (CPT): the cost of reaching 1,000 of your target audience. Used as a yardstick to compare value for money in media.

Coverage: how many people in your target audience have been reached by your advertisement at least once.

Database: at its simplest, a list. Usually used to mean lists stored on computers.

Direct marketing: activity that develops and exploits a direct link between an organisation and its customers.

Frequency: the number of times your advertisement reaches your target audience.

Integration: the drive to co-ordinate promotional activity instead of regarding each element of the promotional mix as a separate tactic.

Media: literally means 'ways' – the vehicles such as press, television or posters that carry advertising.

Semiotics: a theory of communication that stresses the creation of meaning in messages by their recipients.

Share of voice: the proportion of advertising accounted for by your advertising in its product category in a specified period.

Television Rating Point (TVR): a measure of advertising achievement, a rating point is one percent of your target market seeing your advertisement.

Unique Selling Proposition (USP): the feature, unique to any successful long-term product, that differentiates it from any of its competitors.

SELF-CHECK QUESTIONS

1 Integrated marketing is:
   a An approach to marketing communications that values customer acquisition above customer retention.
   b Using communication to affect opinion rather than behaviour.
   c Marketing to organisations rather than individual consumers.
   d An approach to marketing communications that seeks to get the various communication disciplines working in harmony.
   e An approach to marketing that is led by technology.

2 Hierarchy of effects models:
   a Are an accurate description of what goes on in the communication process.
   b Are particularly useful when dealing with organisational hierarchy.
   c Suggest that consumers are taken through distinct stages from behavioural to cognitive to affective effects by communications.
   d Suggest that consumers create their own meanings for communications.
   e Suggest that consumers are taken through distinct stages from cognitive to affective to behavioural effects by communications.

3 Brand image advertising:
   a Sells the functional benefits of the product or service.
   b Surrounds the product with an aura of associations.
   c Was invented by Rosser Reeves.
   d Is not good for frequently-purchased items but fine for luxuries.
   e Is not as effective as more rational advertising methods.

4 BARB stands for:
   a British Audience Research Board.
   b Broadcast Advertisng Research Body.
   c Broadcasters Audience Research Board.
   d Broadcast Advertising Report Bulletin.
   e British American Research Body.

5 The Advertising Standards Authority:
   a Deals with complaints for all British advertising media.
   b Can only act in response to a complaint from a member of the public.
   c Charges for its services.
   d Has no powers of legislative enforcement.
   e Is a government funded agency.

Which of the following are true and which is false?
   6 All advertising activity is meant to have a direct effect on sales.
   7 Advertising agencies are responsible for paying bills to media owners, even if their clients default.
   8 Acount planners in advertising agencies prepare estimates for how much the advertisements will cost to produce.
   9 Drip advertising goes on continuously but at a low level.
  10 Circulation is always higher than readership.

Discuss the following
  11 If consumers are selective in their attention to advertising, what is the point of using mass media?
  12 Creativity in advertising is all about selling things – discuss.
  13 Argue a case for a large advertiser to make more use of direct marketing to consumers.
  14 Compare and contrast the strengths and weaknesses of any two of the following media (using examples as appropriate):
     a radio
     b posters
     c press.
  15 In an increasingly fragmented media environment, has self-regulation for advertisers got a future?

Further study
....

Books

Ogilvy, David (1983) *Ogilvy on Advertising*, Pan.

Anything by David Ogilvy is worth a look, and this title has the advantage of being lavishly illustrated.

Douglas, Torin (1985) *Complete Guide to Advertising*, Macmillan.

An excellent, well-illustrated text.

White, Rod (1993) *Advertising: What it is and how to do it*, 3rd edition, McGraw Hill.

Two more authors to look out for are David Bernstein and the irrepressible Winston Fletcher. They both write very readable accounts of what working in advertising is really like.

The Institute of Practitioners in Advertising (IPA) publishes excellent case studies of effective advertising each year called 'Advertising Works' in conjunction with NTC publications. These offer very useful practical insights.

Bird, Drayton (1993) *Commonsense Direct Marketing*, 3rd edition, Kogan Page.

On direct marketing, this book is hard to beat as a single recommendation (although some readers may find it too 'hands on').

Holder, Roger (1991) *The Direct Marketing Textbook*, Croner.

Roger Holder who heads up the Institute of Direct Marketing (a body committed to the wider understanding and use of the medium through training and education) has written this very useful book.

Journals

Admap
Published monthly, is accessible and authoritative – offering an excellent selection of informed articles about advertising practice.

Campaign
The UK advertising industry's 'house magazine' – a weekly dose of gossip interspersed with thoughtful articles and features.

Media Week
A very useful weekly for keeping up to date with developments in the world of advertising media.

References
· · · · · · · · · · · · ·

Advertising Standards Authority (1995) *8th British Codes of Advertising and Sales Promotional Practice*, available free from Brook House, 2–16, Torrington Place, London WC1E 7HN (Tel: 0171 580 5555).

Caulkin, S. (1993) 'Everybody's soul mate strides on', in *The Guardian*, Finance Page, 3 July.

Cramp, B. (1995) 'The art of bonding', in *Marketing*, 21 September, pp. 32–6.

CHAPTER **11**

Promotion–selling, sales promotion and public relations

Objectives

When you have read this chapter you will be able to:

▶ Identify the contribution made by direct selling, sales promotion and public relations to the strategic marketing communications effort.

▶ Plan a sales call.

▶ Appreciate the human resource elements of the sales process.

▶ Recommend sales promotion responses to a variety of marketing situations.

▶ Differentiate between public relations and other forms of marketing communications.

▶ Apply the main public relations techniques to a selection of marketing problems and understand the basis for their evaluation.

Introduction

In the previous chapter we looked at the general area of communication theory with particular respect to advertising and direct marketing. Now it is time to review three further techniques that complete the integrated marketing communications package for successful organisations: personal selling, sales promotion and public relations.

We might picture these activities layered in a kind of pyramid, with public relations at the base and selling at the apex, literally the sharp end (see Figure 11.1). But they interact in an effective promotional mix to the point where it is difficult to say which layer takes precedence, and the likely mix will vary from organisation to organisation. As with the techniques in Chapter 10, the emphasis in the 1990s is towards the integration of these various disciplines into a seamless process of mutual communication between an organisation and its customers or partners.

Selling

Selling is interpersonal activity that completes a marketing exchange in terms of the transfer of ownership of a good or service. It can take place between any combination of groups and individuals. Selling is an essential part of the

figure 11.1
A promotional pyramid?

marketing mix. In a sense, selling is what everything else leads up to. Without a customer there is no business, and without selling there are no customers. Even in situations like self-service retailing, selling is going on. Instead of people doing the selling, interior design is taking on the job. Whether it is the bright airy ambiance of Sainsbury, or the discreet wooden panelling of a gentlemen's outfitter, retail appearance is capturing the attention of a prospective customer and convincing him or her that these particular products offer benefits more effectively and efficiently than the competition. Furthermore, those products would not be there at all were it not for the fact that a salesperson had sold them to a wholesaler or a retailer in the first place.

The importance of selling

Selling has long been seen as the poor relation of marketing. Definitions of marketing as a business philosophy often contrast the advantages of the marketing concept against sales-led thinking and production-led thinking (see Chapter 1). The selling concept is seen by Kotler (1991) as a management orientation that fears the customer will not buy enough of the organisation's output unless a concerted promotional effort is made. As we have argued in Chapter 10, it is highly unlikely that people can be persuaded to buy what they do not want. Customer-led approaches work much better.

But this should not blind us to the fact that marketing needs both production (product quality) and sales (customer service) at the very heart of its activity. Companies that boast marketing excellence, such as Marks and Spencer or IBM, recognise the central importance of selling. Indeed, their selling operation is like a microcosm of marketing itself. Far from trying to load unwanted goods on to unsuspecting customers, these companies start by interpreting the needs of their customers and end by fulfilling them through personal service.

Much of the literature on selling dwells on closing individual sales. It is as if the writers or sales trainers expect the relationship with the customer to end with the sale, casting customers as only so many stepping stones on the way to organisational success. On the contrary, Levitt (1986) points out that even if companies see their part of the bargain ending in the sale, for their customers it is the beginning of the relationship. They have become customers by acquiring the product or service. Even the language of selling, which talks about closing the sale, has an air of finality about it that belies the reality of successful selling. Companies like IBM see their sales relationships as ongoing. In a high-tech product field like information technology or office automation the relevance of after-sales service should be clear as advances in software lead to continuous improvement. But the way successful companies approach selling is based not so much on their product field as on the conviction that looking after existing customers is as important, if not more important, than winning new ones.

So, far from the stereotypical foot in the door merchant immortalised in cartoons and situation comedy, the successful sales person is likely to be someone who works hard to understand customer needs, fulfils those needs appropriately, and takes the long view. At the same time, customer empathy has to be combined with commercial vision. The sales representative has to be precisely that, representative of the company's interests in the mutual relationship.

So development of skills such as time management and presentation technique are essential to maximise the effectiveness of the scarce resource represented by time available for selling.

Planning a sales call

Personal selling is the most expensive form of promotion, as well as being the most powerful. No other technique accommodates the range of feedback the customer can give a sales person, allowing direct negotiation and customisation of the offer. But because of the power of the technique, its use needs to be carefully planned. The kind of wastage that is taken for granted in impersonal forms of promotion such as advertising cannot be tolerated in selling. It is only to be expected that a large percentage of the audience seeing a television commercial will not be in the market for that particular product or service. But selling cannot afford to be anything less than 100 per cent relevant to its audience all of the time.

We will address the issue of salesforce management a little later in the section. First let us follow the stages a sales person will go through in planning and carrying out a sales visit. This encounter with the customer need not be face to face. The same broad considerations apply to selling over the telephone (although of course the opportunities for visual communication are severely limited in such situations). What matters is the personal nature of the encounter – facilitated by comprehensive research and preparation before the event, convincing presentation during the sales call, and assiduous follow-up.

There are six main stages involved in planning and carrying out the personal selling process, as follows.

Stage 1 Prospecting

This is in many ways the most important part of the entire process. By identifying people who are likely to be interested in what you have to offer, selling becomes more efficient and successful. Screening out inappropriate customers at this stage will save much wasted effort and time later on.

As in direct marketing, it is often the case that existing customers will be the source of additional leads. Other useful sources include:

▶ competitors
▶ exhibitions
▶ government information
▶ mailshots
▶ newspapers and journals
▶ professional and trade associations
▶ suppliers
▶ trade directories.

DID YOU KNOW?
Personal financial advisors are among the most avid readers of the births, deaths and marriages columns in their local newspapers. Births often signal the need for school fees planning, deaths can result in the need for investment advice, and marriages create the opportunity for mortgage, life assurance and pension planning as couples contemplate their future together.

The importance of each type of source of leads will vary from industry to industry. But once possible customers have been identified, they have to be scrutinised to ascertain their suitability. This process, known as lead qualification, can involve gathering information about their size, creditworthiness and potential. Information here will tend to be qualitative, but a certain amount of quantitative data may be available in the shape of annual reports, company literature and the financial press. For business-to-business sales people, just finding out who is the best person to approach in the organisation is often one of the most confusing and frustrating parts of the operation. The same job title often covers widely differing functions in different companies. To confuse matters further, in most organisational buying situations responsibility for the purchase will be spread among several people (as discussed in Chapter 3).

ACTIVITY **11.1**
....

Information sources

List the key information sources to which you would refer if you were prospecting for the following sorts of customers (please be as specific as possible):

1 Prospective students for a college of further education.
2 Donors for a charity dedicated to funding bone cancer research.
3 Season ticket buyers for your local football team.
4 Potential sponsors for the Royal Opera House, Covent Garden.
5 Subscribers to a new magazine devoted to archery.

Stage 2 Approach

Just as the immediate objective of a job application is to secure an interview, so this stage of the sales planning process focuses single mindedly on gaining personal access to the decision maker. Research is very important here. The kind of information sought falls into two types. There are objective facts about the company, its recent performance, its own customer base. But there is also what might be known as subjective information to do with company style, the way decisions are made, even the personal interests and characteristics of the people with whom you will be dealing. The unique strength of selling is, after all, its personal quality. Attention must therefore be paid both to the strictly functional and the more human aspects of the encounter.

Gaining the opportunity to get through to the targeted individual can be a challenge. Some secretaries are like brick walls and will fend off approaches with ruthless efficiency. With the growth in person to person media (e-mail and the increased number of direct telephone lines are two recent developments) this is becoming less of a problem, but there is still no substitute for tact and determination. Lead qualification should have eliminated all those apparent prospects who are not in a position to take advantage of what you have to offer. So painstaking explanation of the relevance of your product or service to the targeted organisation should eventually pay dividends.

Stage 3 Presentation

This is the hoped-for culmination of the hard work and research that have gone into the first two stages. The sales presentation provides the chance to enjoy the undivided attention of the prospect while you put your case. Visual impressions are extremely important, so appropriate dress code and grooming must be observed. In international business transactions there is the added complication of different styles of business etiquette. This varies from the formal quasi-rituals that accompany business in Japan, to the casual back-slapping approach of some American companies. These cultural norms can be learned and adopted without too much trouble. But there are other aspects of business etiquette that constitute more of a problem. The expectation in some countries of business gifts that amount to little short of bribery can cause severe ethical difficulties for companies used to plain dealing.

> **DID YOU KNOW?**
>
> *First impressions are important. Communication starts as soon as you walk into a room. This underlines the importance of careful planning as to the kind of visual impression you need to make in a particular situation.*

For all its weaknesses as a detailed account of what happens in advertising, the AIDA model discussed in Chapter 10 provides an excellent template for a sales call. Having a model in mind helps the sales person to keep control of the encounter in a way that avoids wasting valuable selling time or imposing for too long on the valuable time of the customer. Here is how the AIDA model can be applied to the structure of a sales call, either in person or on the telephone:

- ▶ *Attention*: this can be gained by as simple a device as a friendly greeting. Often an attention-getting device can be used, such as a visual aid or a model or sample. Giving your counterpart in the negotiation something to hold and/or look at can focus both your minds on the matter in hand.
- ▶ *Interest*: here we come to a fundamental principle in selling. Focus on the benefits. This entails engaging the customer's interest in what you are selling by allowing him or her to appreciate its relevance to their needs. Questions to diagnose the customer's sphere of interest are vital here. The temptation is always to dwell on product features (company perspective) rather than the benefits (customer perspective). An inexperienced computer sales person might be carried away with the amount of memory that a new machine has as a feature. The customer is only likely to be interested in the fact that it will be able to store more information. Engaging the customer's interest will require careful judgement as to what the appropriate benefits are in each case. This question should be easy to answer because of the research involved in preparing for the sales call.
- ▶ *Desire*: this is when interest is personalised directly to the prospect. Dramatising the benefits to the customer involves seeking their co-operation in the process through questions. Open questions are particularly important in sales presentations at this point. They allow you to empathise with the customer and to produce genuine responses to the needs articulated. Another way of promoting interest to desire is to give the customer the opportunity to convince themselves of the desirability of the product. Test driving a car, using a software package for a limited trial period or taking an introductory flying lesson are all ways in which desire can be confirmed.
- ▶ *Action*: the outcome of the encounter needs to be clear. It may not always be immediate purchase. At the very least the sales person should aim to come away with valuable information from this kind of engagement with a customer. It may mean an order next time. But the prime

objective of a sales call is a sale. In a real sense this is part of the service. The customer can actually be helped to resolve the purchase by a tactful and supportive approach.

Although an overall structure is always necessary, different situations call for different approaches to presentation format. Working in a mechanised and repetitive environment, telephone selling requires more formal discipline than working person to person over a longer period of time. Thus the use of a script for telephone selling can help maximise the effectiveness of the time spent on each call, and ensure that nothing is left out. Far from shoehorning a caller into a manipulative relationship, a telephone selling script, if used properly and conceived correctly, can actually guarantee levels of customer service. More apparently spontaneous approaches lack such consistency.

At the other end of the scale is the diagnostic, consultative selling process, where the encounter follows its own route. The skills required from the sales person here are no less active, but consist of careful listening and conscious analysis of the customer's needs. It is important to keep sufficient control of the situation to ensure that the dialogue remains relevant to the problem in hand. Swift thinking and a high level of product knowledge are essential for success here. The technique is best suited to markets where the sales function is combined with a high level of technical expertise such as industrial chemicals or telecommunications.

Stage 4 Handling objections

Using the terminology 'handling objections' is misleading insofar as it puts the sales person and the customer in an adversarial role. Negotiation is a more helpful expression here. It recognises that there are two sets of interests which the sales process must reconcile into one outcome. The negotiation is a two-way process in which there will be give and take. Having said that, there are aspects of the relationship between buyer and seller that resemble a kind of game. It is therefore best to be aware of them and have a sense of how to cope with this side of the process.

What are often called psychological objections are various internal sorts of resistance to being sold something. It may simply be that the timing of the call is inappropriate. The customer may have had a bad day. There may be a feeling of antipathy with the sales person, or it may just be that the customer is phased by having to commit themselves. Listening skills are important here, especially the ability to probe behind the external objection. If, for example, it turns out that you are dealing with the wrong person after all, it may be in your interest to curtail the sales call and wait for an opportunity to make the right contact later.

Logical objections are easier to deal with insofar as they are objective. The price may be too high, or some technical aspect of the product may be less than clearly understood. The way to deal with this aspect of negotiation is to ask questions. By questioning, it may even be possible to take the customer through his or her objection to an answer of their own devising. Objections to price can be resolved by concentrating on value, or misunderstandings as to function can be resolved by further demonstration. It is important to take objections of whatever sort seriously and respectfully. The last thing you want to do is to argue with the customer. Arguments create winners and losers, and put distance between buyer and seller. Working towards mutual understanding, on the other hand, creates a win/win scenario.

Stage 5 Closing

Again, the term 'closing' sits uncomfortably with a view of selling as a strategic function. It sounds too final, as if the process is complete and the door can be shut on the relationship. In fact, good closing skills are part of the professionalism that sales people offer as a service to their customers. Making the sale means that the customer's immediate problem has been solved. They are in the market for something, be it advertising, a new car, an order for a new product. Moving them to purchase absolves them of that immediate need and takes that particular job off their list of things to do.

Nevertheless it can be difficult to get to the point where the sales person asks for the order. This may be due to a number of reasons. Culturally the British are uncomfortable with being explicitly commercial in their relationships, although in the US and elsewhere in the world this is not such a problem. A more deep-seated reason may be the anxiety a salesperson inevitably suffers about failure and rejection. Quite apart from the personal disappointment this causes, there is also the sense of the enormous investment in time and preparation the sales call will represent. While things are still in the process of negotiation, there is still hope. The fear is that moving to a conclusion may decide events adversely.

Developing a conscious technique to cope with this delicate stage of the negotiations is therefore desirable. Sales training manuals offer many solutions. One piece of oft-repeated advice is to watch for buying signals. It may be that the kind of questions the customer asks lead naturally to the order. Spontaneous positive comment on the product or service can signal readiness to purchase. Body language becomes more relaxed, and often the customer will move closer to the sales person. A number of popular closing techniques can be brought into play at this point to tie up the deal, as follows:

1   *Ask for the order*: Simple and straightforward, this consists of requesting the order directly. Pen and order form can be useful props here: 'Why don't you fill this form out right now and it can be yours today?'
2   *Trial close*: A number of techniques share the function of establishing how near the customer is to the point of purchase. For example the 'alternative close' consists of asking a purchase-related question (eg whether the customer wants delivery now or next week). This flushes out the decision without a direct approach, and can therefore be used to keep the negotiation in play: 'Will you be paying by cheque or credit card?'
3   *Assumptive close*: Here the salesperson makes the positive assumption that the customer has said yes, and concentrates the negotiation on some less central aspect of the deal. As with the straightforward request, the appearance of pen and order form can be used to confirm this assumption

in due course: 'So we're really only talking about whether you want electric or manual windows on the car.'

4   *Allocative close*: Allocation, or the sharing of an over-demanded product between keen customers, is one of the functions of a salesperson in an expanding market. The allocative close puts it to the customer that there is a shortage of the product or service, and that therefore speed of purchase is of the essence to avoid disappointment: 'I'll phone the warehouse to check, but we should still have just enough in stock for you to get delivery next week if you order now.'

5   *Summary close*: Another straightforward device, this simply consists of the salesperson summing up all the points made about the product, all the answered objections and all the benefits (often with the use of visual aids or graphics) and asking for the order. The momentum of such a close can be irresistible: 'It's got all the things you need, it's on special offer this week, we stock it in purple, we can have it to you by Friday. Now if you can just sign this, we can go to lunch!'

Stage 6 Follow up

Estimates vary, but even the most conservative suggest that it is five times cheaper to do business with existing customers than it is with new ones. It therefore makes a lot of sense to nurture relationships, and sales people are in an excellent position to do this. Checking on delivery dates, keeping the customer informed if there are any changes to plan, contacting the customer after delivery in order to establish if everything is satisfactory are all ways in which the salesperson can use his or her front-line position to consolidate a relationship and win future business. Personal management software is making it easier to keep regular contact with a customer database by the power it offers to flag up appointments that need to be made or phone calls that need to be placed to keep in touch.

Sometimes follow-up is part of the product or service being sold. For example, computer equipment sales will tend to include training and consultancy as part of the package. But even if there is little or no service content in the offer itself, as in the case of office consumables such as stationery, good sales people will concentrate on keeping customers as much as on creating them. A good personal relationship with a customer can give a salesperson an unshakeable competitive advantage over other companies, and make business more of a pleasure.

Motivating and managing the personal selling process

An organisation's salesforce is usually its largest single marketing communications expense. As such it needs careful management. Unlike impersonal promotional tools like advertising or sales promotion which operate through the media, direct selling involves people. The salesforce therefore needs a different kind of management from other areas of promotion, drawing heavily on human resource management ideas.

We can divide the salesforce management process into three main tasks: the three *S*s of Strategy, Structure and Support.

Salesforce strategy

The organisation's marketing plan will break down into a number of complementary strategies to be implemented by its various divisions (see Chapter 12). Salesforce strategy will support clear objectives governing volume sales, revenue targets and market-share targets. For individual salespeople these objectives mean the setting of specific goals. These goals may cover any or all of the following:

- *Call frequency*: the number of times sales visits are made.
- *Growth*: the amount of development expected from existing customers.
- *New business*: the year-on-year increase in worthwhile new accounts.
- *Profitability*: the target for allowable discount.
- *Quota*: the volume of sales of each product carried.

The immediate targets for individuals in the front-line salesforce need to be realistic. There is the additional human resource consideration here that because of the motivational power of objectives, some sophistication may be called for in their setting. For example, volume targets might be set at three thresholds: minimum, probable and possible. This is especially important when performance is linked to remuneration, as we shall discuss later.

Salesforce structure

The second major area for salesforce management decisions is how the complex resource of the salesforce is best organised. There are three main approaches here, which are often reflected through into the organisation of the marketing department as a whole (see Chapter 13).

Geographical structure

The basic idea of the salesforce territory is a logical response to the needs of companies whose products are in wide distribution, as in the case of a nationally-available grocery line. One salesperson is responsible for each territory. This means that there are no clashes between rival salespeople from the same company and that the customer has one simple point of contact with the organisation. The difficulty with this approach, however, is that a variety of different account sizes and types within the same area may reduce the efficiency of the individual salesperson's efforts. There is also the need for constant review of territory size as the business environment is a dynamic one.

Customer-type structure

This would appear to offer the most marketing-oriented solution to structuring the salesforce. After all, we are used to the idea in marketing that the customer should be at the centre of our thinking. Wrapping the salesforce round different customer types is therefore an attractive idea. It puts segmentation into practice. In certain markets it makes sense because of the concentration of certain types of customer in particular areas. But more usually this approach has the disadvantage that customers of the same salesperson can be widely dispersed, making it hard to provide a high level of personal service at an economic cost to the company. About half of the typical salesperson's time is spent travelling, so the disadvantage of increasing this inefficiency becomes apparent.

Product-line structure

At first sight this approach seems to contradict many of the ideas on which marketing is founded. Marketing adopts the customer's perspective rather than the organisation's. In other words we should stress benefits not features. Customer needs rather than the available products ought to be the starting point in marketing decisions. But in spite of this, a product-based structure for a salesforce may offer the right solution in certain markets. Where a high level of technical expertise is demanded of the salesforce it may be the only way to provide the specialisation the customer will demand.

In fact most salesforce structures will have elements of each of these three approaches. A large fast-moving consumer goods salesforce structure is illustrated at Figure 11.2. The pyramid starts at the level of the individual sales rep working his or her territory. Their work will involve managing accounts of a minimum size, and devoting time and attention to growing the most promising ones. Although they are each highly autonomous they will report to sales managers, and take part in team meetings on an area-by-area basis.

The next level up, the area sales managers, will motivate and direct the territorial sales staff, convening regular meetings and acting as a channel of information to and from the higher echelons of management. They will have direct sales responsibilities themselves for larger accounts.

The next line of management begins to blur the distinction between geographical and customer-type organisation. These regional account managers (RAMs) have line management responsibility for area sales managers (ASMs), but also deal with significant accounts that need constant personal attention. Retail groups often have a regional bias, and this kind of customer offers a great deal of potential for personalised promotions whereby significant volumes of stock can be moved in the context of a special offer. RAMs will be based in regional offices with administrative support.

National account managers (NAMS) are the aristocrats of the salesforce. Not only do they drive the best cars but they control the company's business from

figure 11.2

Salesforce structure for a national fast-moving consumer goods company

head office with the largest customers in the country. As well as being prestigious, these customers are very hard to deal with because of the level of power they command. As we have seen in Chapter 9, being delisted from a retail giant like ASDA or Sainsbury's can mean losing access to a very large slice of your customer base overnight. NAMs are under intense pressure to do business with the retail barons on terms advantageous to their company. They have strategic input to sales and marketing plans and communicate directly to the board via the sales director.

Bestriding this pyramid like a mighty colossus, a charismatic sales director is a considerable advantage to an organisation. His or her visibility and dynamism set the tone for the rest of the operation in what can be a very gruelling and competitive field. Credibility and leadership are at a premium here. Not only will the director motivate and inspire from the top down, but he or she will also fight for resources for his salesforce at board level – often in competition with colleagues arguing the merits of other forms of promotional expenditure.

Floating apart from this structure in Figure 11.2 is an example of a product-specific salesforce being used in tandem with the other two approaches. In this case it is a specially bought-in temporary salesforce from a broking company whose services have been engaged to launch a new product. The decision to hive off this activity from the main salesforce might be taken for a number of reasons. The product might, for example, be the result of a recent merger or acquisition and so not fit into the portfolio of products they are already selling. It might not be clear how the time and resource costs of carrying the new product might impact on the support the salesforce can give to their existing ranges. Or it might just be that, for political reasons, it is considered best to give the launch an independent chance of success.

Salesforce structure is the result both of planning and evolution. As will be clear from our discussion, there is no universally-applicable model. Instead a flexible and responsive approach that takes into account the need to adapt to changing market conditions is most likely to offer success.

Salesforce support

Of the three Ss this is the one that raises most operational issues. There are five interlocked areas to cover:

▶ Recruitment.
▶ Training.
▶ Remuneration.
▶ Motivation.
▶ Evaluation.

This is the area where sales management draws most upon human resource management. As we shall see, however, the peculiar nature of the selling function throws up certain emphases unique to this area of management.

Recruitment
In any service environment the quality of the people involved is paramount. Sales is no exception. In spite of this there are plenty of dubious sales job adver-

tisements in any newspaper. Many of them feature unlikely-sounding OTE (on-target earnings) figures, or mouth-watering testimonials. There is an almost religious avoidance of the use of the word sales. Such ads testify to a very high turnover of recruits, many of whom will have been far from suited to the real task of selling.

Companies with a real commitment to their customers are identifiable by their commitment to attracting the right kind of sales staff. Big money promises are less important than the training and development they can offer in a structured career. Instead of wanting to attract a continuous stream of sales-fodder, they are interested in selecting only those candidates who are likely to succeed in the long term.

Training

As we have seen in our review of how to plan and carry out a sales call, natural abilities can usefully be enhanced in order to maximise personal effectiveness. The number of different tasks involved in a selling role offer plenty of scope for training input:

▶ Time management is essential in order to maximise the effectiveness of the limited number of selling hours available in any day.
▶ Product knowledge needs to be constantly updated to keep pace with technical developments and customer expectations.
▶ Presentation and negotiation skills also need to be honed to perfection.

Because of the amount of reporting back and administration involved in controlling business with multiple clients, salespeople need to be very well versed in order processing and distribution systems. The amount of training investment necessary to an effective salesforce is one of the reasons why selling is such an expensive promotional tool.

Remuneration

Staff costs are the main item of expenditure in any salesforce management set-up. The way that salespeople are rewarded reflects the individual nature of their jobs. The kind of performance-related pay that has gradually caught up with the majority of managerial and even professional jobs in the 1980s and 1990s has long been a feature of salesforce remuneration.

Systems vary from company to company. One extreme is the commission-only sales job, where apart from an initial investment in product and sales training, the recruit is left unsupported. Income depends entirely on perfor-mance. At the other end of the scale is the salary-only sales person. Typically an employee like this will have a job description that includes responsibilities other than selling. Indeed, selling may not even be the most important part of what they do.

The majority of cases, however, feature a mixture of commission and salary. The trick is to get the balance right. Too heavy a dependence on commission, and variations in the salesperson's monthly amount may lead to instabilities elsewhere in his or her life. Instead of being performance enhancing such uncertainty can have negative consequences. But balanced against this is the feeling that different levels of achievements among the salesforce ought to be recognised by different levels of reward. Remuneration arrangements need to be informed by the kind of realism that we have noted as an aspect of objective setting in the strategic input necessary to salesforce management.

Motivation

Part of the problem with too heavy a reliance on commission is that it fails to take into account the classic work of Herzberg (1966) into motivation. Herzberg's research found that money was what he called a hygiene factor. Such factors need to be present in sufficient quantities to make a job tolerable – like office environment, proper lighting, ease of access, etc. But in themselves he found they were less powerful in enhancing performance than the factors he called motivators. These are things like status, interesting work, praise and peer esteem.

Most successful sales people are self-motivated high achievers who thrive on stress. Their job means a high level of autonomy as they spend a great deal of time working on their own. Thus their need for motivation is different from the kind of motivation traditionally expected from managers. Sales managers can help their staff best by providing clear objectives and structuring what can appear to be dauntingly complex requirements. This kind of leadership is best given by example. Again we are reminded of the essentially personal nature of the selling process.

As an alternative to direct financial inducements, yet providing the simplicity of a common currency of reward across the salesforce, a number of major companies use an annual competition as an incentive for their salesforce. Performance is judged against agreed criteria and the winners are feted with appropriate recognition at the annual sales conference. As a form of sales promotion this can motivate the salesforce to get behind a particular brand and boost its volume or distribution in a particular year.

CASE STUDY **11.1**

Inventive incentives

Companies keen to reward and recognise contribution to their sales success can choose from a range of incentives. But which ones are the most effective and what kind of system can optimise long-term relationships with staff?

There are a number of problems with straight cash as a reward. Such bonuses tend to be perceived as part of the general pay packet, and can lead to bad feeling if they are withdrawn. Furthermore money gets sucked into paying for things like the gas bill rather than on something specific. Vouchers have the advantage that they get saved up to be spent on something special. £25 worth of vouchers is a much more appealing prospect than the equivalent in cash for most people.

The voucher industry is estimated to be worth £500 million a year in the UK – although this is a very approximate figure. But vouchers need careful targeting to the right socio-economic group. If a voucher only works with one retailer, for example, a member of staff may feel pigeonholed into one group when he or she aspires to another. Marks and Spencer remains the most popular choice, however. It heads the list of three times as many people as its nearest rival.

In spite of the danger of typecasting its employees, Norweb has settled on Argos vouchers as the basis for a successful long-running incentive scheme called the Ambassador Service. Non-sales staff are encouraged to generate leads for the sales force in the areas of heating systems, cookers and other appliances. Each introduction generates points that are increased with every sale made. The scheme draws non-sales staff into feeling that they are very much part of the company, and brings home to them how people's jobs depend on one another. Norweb sales staff have their own incentive schemes alongside the Ambassador Service, but consider the leads generated internally on the scheme are a lot higher quality than those that come from advertising activity.

Vouchers for travel are particularly popular, as this can mean that families or partners can be part of the celebration. European destinations, particularly France, Germany and Spain, are enduringly popular. Hong Kong has had a sudden surge of being fashionable as an incentive travel destination towards the aspirational end of the market.

Questions

1   What kind of research might a company carry out before deciding on the most appropriate kind of incentive to offer its sales force?
2   Vouchers have a number of advantages over cash as an incentive. Discuss their disadvantages.
3   What factors do you think contribute to the popularity or otherwise of an incentive travel destination?

Adapted from: Derrick, 1994; Miles, 1992.

Evaluation

Selling is one of the most accountable jobs in the marketing repertoire. As will be clear from the list of objective areas in the section on salesforce strategy, there is no shortage of performance indicators by which to judge the achievements of individual salespeople. The merciless measure of statistics can be applied to call frequency, sales against targets, sales against previous periods or in comparison with colleagues' performances. The profitability of sales efforts can be calculated in terms of return per call, and how accounts have grown or shrunk during the year.

This is a hard standard to be judged by, and can lead to insecurity and the temptation to massage figures. On the other hand it provides an objective source of feedback which can be used by the sales manager and the sales person to improve performance.

Sales promotion
....

Sales promotion is promotional activity designed to enhance the speed or volume of purchasing response. It operates through adding value on a temporary basis to a product or service in order to provide an extra incentive to purchase. It can be directed at consumers, distribution intermediaries, salespeople, or any combination of the three.

In the trade press sales promotion is often referred to as below-the-line expenditure. This is to differentiate it from media advertising expenditure, on which commission is payable (see Chapter 10 for a fuller explanation of this).

The imaginary line of the expression is drawn to separate expenditure that is commissionable from that which is not.

Sales promotion often works better when combined with advertising. Indeed, in certain markets (such as petrol) the sales promotion can provide the central platform for advertising messages, because there is little else to say about the product to differentiate it from the competition. Advertising agencies sometimes refer to specific advertising in support of a sales promotion as scheme advertising, reserving the term theme advertising for the mainstream, long-term brand building campaign.

Sales promotion comes of age

DID YOU KNOW?

Traditionally there has been little love lost between sales promotion companies and advertising agencies: 'In 1981, US manufacturers spent 60 per cent more on promotions than on advertising, and distributed 1,024,000,000,000 coupons. Bloody fools.' (Ogilvy, 1983)

Sales promotion, rather like sales itself, has tended to suffer from an image problem. As the head of one of the biggest advertising agencies in the world, David Ogilvy saw sales promotion agencies as his direct competitors for a share of the client's marketing budget. It is instructive to note, however, that from the 1980s onwards, more and more advertising agencies (including Ogilvy's own) have been absorbing sales promotion businesses. This is not just a sign of the integrated times. It is a tribute to the increased credibility and maturity of the sales promotion industry itself.

The main reason for sales promotion's image problem stems from the necessarily short-term nature of the kind of activity involved. Because the added value (of whatever sort) needs to be clearly seen as something above and beyond what is normally available, the life of any effective promotion rarely exceeds three months. As a result there has been a temptation to see promotional activity of this sort as tactical rather than strategic.

Sometimes the result has been activity that has no relevance to the core brand proposition, or whose timing has been less than optimum in relation to advertising. There has even been the fear, particularly with respect to price-based promotion, that the activity can undermine long-term marketing effort for the sake of a short-term jump in sales.

But in the 1990s, sales promotion has come of age. More money is now spent on sales promotion than on advertising (although this figure includes money spent directly on funding discounts and allowances to retailers). Consumer sales promotions are thriving in some pretty surprising places. Even quality newspapers like *The Times* and *The Independent* are finding that their up-market readers respond well to essentially the same kind of bingo games that led the circulation battles of the tabloids in the 1980s. There are a number of reasons for the boom:

▶ Crowded markets offer shoppers an unprecedented number of products. Sales promotion can endow them with a temporary sparkle.
▶ Powerful retailers have put pressure on manufacturers to work harder. More promotional activity is one response to this.
▶ Advertisers frustrated by rising costs, media clutter and patchy coverage of their target audiences are moving more money from above the line media advertising to below the line sales promotion.

▶ Senior marketing decision-makers have grown up with sales promotion as a technique. It now has board level credibility.

▶ The quality of the people working in the industry itself has improved and there has been a move towards greater professionalism.

▶ Technology (scratch cards, printing processes, packaging and point-of-sale display) has favoured the growth of creativity.

▶ The legal climate governing games of chance is becoming relaxed, leading to a boom in instant win promotions.

For all these steps forward, however, sales promotion has suffered some notable reverses in the public mind. Any industry that depends so much on novelty will inevitably suffer the difficulties associated with doing things for the first time. Pioneers, as they say, get scalped. Sales promotion history is littered with some spectacular wrecks, all the more embarrassing for being so deliberately visible.

CASE STUDY **11.2**
· · · · · · · · · · · · · · · · · ·

Great sales promotion disasters of our time

It's not often we get a chance to pity the poor marketing whizz kid, but here are a few of the most legendary sales promotions from hell...

Hoover free flights

Customers spending £100 or more on Hoover products qualified for two free flights to Europe or the US. Sounds like a good deal? A lot more people than Hoover expected thought so. As well as flooding the market with second-hand vacuum cleaners for the foreseeable future the promotion resulted in law suits, media vilification, the departure of three senior managers and a £19 million provision to cover costs. American parent company Maytag ended by selling the European Hoover operation to Candy in 1994 at an £80 million loss.

Cadbury's Creme Eggs

A classic from 1984. Inspired by the success of puzzle-picture books like Kit Wright's *Masquerade* (containing clues to the location of a buried golden hare), Cadbury's buried 12 £10,000 golden eggs at secret locations around Britain. About 100,000 enthusiastic treasure hunters dug large holes in the English countryside, many blithely ignoring the competition rules which stated that none were buried on private land, National Trust property or at ancient monuments. Some venerable sites still bear the scars. After intervention from the Environment Secretary, Cadbury's blew the whistle on the promotion with six eggs to go. Apart from the embarrassment, however, the £750,000 promotion led to record egg sales.

Mercury

Aiming to kick start the consumer market for mobile phones, Mercury offered customers buying its One 2 One mobiles from November to Christmas 1994 unlimited free calls on Christmas Day. So many people took up the offer that the entire system jammed. In spite of the fact that many callers couldn't get through, the company revealed afterwards that at least 20 people had hogged the phone for more than 12 hours during the yuletide yammer-in.

Pepsi in the Philippines

One to rival Hoover – but on the other side of the world. Pepsi offered a million pesos (a modest £26,000) to anyone finding a bottle top printed with the magic number 349. Due to a computer error, however, no fewer than 800,000 such bottle tops were in circulation. The potential payout was £19 billion. After a 3 am crisis meeting Pepsi management agreed to pay £13 to each winner – but withdrew the offer £8 million later. Factories and lorries were attacked, there were two fatalities, thousands of lawsuits and a legacy from which it will take years to recover.

Questions

1   The Hoover Free Flights disaster has been blamed on 'groupthink' – the tendency of people in organisations not to question decisions. Suggest ways in which this tendency might be reduced.
2   Is it possible to predict consumer uptake of sales promotions with any accuracy?
3   If you were a Pepsi manager in the Philippines, how might you have tried to deal with the lottery run?

Source: Denny, 1994.

The role of sales promotion

Within its general remit of increasing the speed or intensity of purchasing response, sales promotion can help solve a number of specific marketing problems.

Prompting trial

For new products or reformulated existing products, sales promotion can tempt new or lapsed consumers to give a product a chance.

Increasing loyalty

To confirm consumers in their purchasing habits by encouraging multiple purchase.

Widening distribution

Prompting more retailers and wholesalers to stock a product either by offering them a direct incentive or through making the product demonstrably more attractive to the consumer through the promotion.

Increasing display opportunities

Rather than looking for extra volume as a direct result of the promotion, the marketing department may use it as a platform to refresh salesforce, trade and consumer interest in the product. Particularly in a market like confectionery, where 70 per cent of purchases are made on impulse, display is an essential factor.

In order to work most effectively sales promotion needs to enhance existing brand values as it solves these tactical problems. An inappropriately-conceived piece of activity can waste management time and confuse the customer into the bargain.

Sales promotion techniques

From the variety of sales promotional tools available, many can serve a number of different marketing ends. This allows established brands to offer their customers variety in the format and style of promotional activity; a considerable bonus given that an important part of the rationale for sales promotion is to provide a new perspective on the product.

Some of the most popular techniques, with some notes on their use, are as follows.

Advertising allowance

This is a sum of money paid by a manufacturer to a retailer or wholesaler on the understanding that it will contribute to joint advertising activity. This kind of approach is noticeable at Christmas, for example, when some major retailers publish catalogues or run substantial television advertisements detailing special offers. Manufacturers will usually have co-funded this activity. The definition of what constitutes advertising activity, however, can be rather loose. Often the allowance is merely a device for transferring extra margin to a powerful retailer.

Competitions

These can be used to generate salesforce, trade and consumer interest. The best response levels are achieved by the simplest ideas. Competitions like Spot the Ball, usually featuring the words 'Using your skill and judgement', are very popular because entrants recognise that very little skill and judgement are in fact needed. They are very nearly lotteries and, as such, find little favour with the small but vocal group of people whose main hobby is doing competitions. 'Compers', as they style themselves, have their own magazines and jargon. Avid for EFs (entry forms) and POPs (Proofs of Purchase), they despise what they see as skill-free contests. They are, however, a very small minority of anyone's market.

Coupons

Enormously flexible, these offer savings to consumers when redeemed against the purchase price of a particular product. Consumer-choice coupons allow the consumer to decide which pack size to use the coupon against – the largest savings being attached to the largest sizes. Manufacturers are at loggerheads with many major retailers over the problem of malredemption whereby some stores allow coupons to be used against purchases that do not include the product in question. Technology is providing the answer to this in the shape of machine-readable coupons which will only work in combination with specific bar-codes when scanned at point of sale. A further recent development is the retailer-specific coupon issued to storecard customers. These not only guarantee secure redemption, but their use can be tracked to individual customers.

Dealer loaders

These are promotional gifts to wholesalers and retailers to encourage them to take on more than their usual stock levels of a promoted line. The old sales adage 'stock pressure sells' relies on the fact that if a wholesaler or retailer has a lot of stock, there is the immediate incentive for them to sell it more quickly.

Display allowance

This is a sum of money or free stock given to a distribution intermediary in order to guarantee a special display. This amounts to buying shelf space in prime locations, such as at gondola ends (the end of a fixture where shoppers will notice a featured product as they turn their trolleys).

Free gifts/trial

As the name implies, this involves giving something away with a purchase. In the 1960s plastic daffodils were all the rage with soap powder. These days the gift is more likely to be connected with the product (eg special glasses with whisky) and used as a branding device. Free trial can involve attaching sample packs to a purchased product, dropping free samples through selected letter-boxes, or using coupons.

Free draws/free mail-in

These are basically a free raffle. The magic words 'no purchase necessary' absolve them from the legal restrictions attached to lotteries (a form of regulated gambling) where no skill or judgement comes into participants' chances of winning. Conversely, as we have seen, virtual lotteries such as spot the ball-type competitions are absolved from these same legal restrictions by insisting that skill and judgement are part of the competition. They are practically the same as free mail-ins, but tied to a purchase.

Instant win promotions

These have proved highly popular with manufacturers in the 1990s. Again, the chance to enter without purchasing the product must be available (although the conditions in the small print usually specify that free entry will be limited to one per envelope sent to the competition address). This seems to be obeying the gambling regulations in the letter rather than in the spirit, but many in the marketing industry would argue that such legislation is now outmoded due to changing social mores. The advantage of such promotions is their simplicity. The disadvantage is that there are a great deal more instant losers than there are instant winners, so careful thought needs to be given to the creative side of the promotion and the number of prizes involved.

In-store promotions

These are any promotional activity that takes place in, and is exclusive to, a retailer. Merchandising, competitions, sampling, and free draws are popular examples. Such activity benefits from the active support of the retailer.

On-pack promotions

These are any promotion whose details are communicated entirely on the packaging of the product. Because of the pressure on selling space in retail outlets it is virtually impossible to place manufacturers' promotional leaflets. Packaging and printing technology have facilitated the move to on-pack communication. In spite of the complications this presents in terms of stock control and materials purchasing, the special packaging often gives the manufacturer the chance to jazz up familiar packaging with attention-grabbing flashes.

Personality promotions

This uses real people, frequently models in fancy dress, mounting a particular drive. In the 1960s cigarette companies used it a lot. These days it is more common with newspapers and specialist foods. It is often used in conjunction with sampling and can create considerable goodwill. The cook-in sauce brand *Chicken Tonight* has established an advertising campaign around the idea, using consumers as the personalities rather than paid models.

Reduced price offers (RPOs)

These have the advantage of being simple and effective. They can be used to gain extra display impact if the offer is communicated on-pack by a colourful flash. Used too often they soften prices and put margins at risk in the entire sector. In spite of this they are popular with frequently-purchased, low-priced goods.

Re-usable container premiums

These are good for products packaged in glass or metal. The customer can be persuaded to trade up to a larger size than normal by limiting the storage jar or tea caddy to a larger pack. A further advantage is that the branded item will remain in the kitchen for some time after the promotion, perhaps encouraging product loyalty.

Sampling

This involves giving away small amounts of product. It is very powerful – the product sells itself to the consumer. But it is extremely expensive. Coupons that may be redeemed against a new product are less expensive because they will not be subject to 100 per cent use. They are less effective as a result, however.

Self-liquidating premiums (SLPs)

Here an exclusive item of branded merchandise is offered to consumers at little more than cost price. The benefit for the manufacturer is that the promotion should cover its costs. There are significant financial risks involved in the set-up costs, however. An economic quantity of the goods needs to be available from the chosen supplier, and sensible reorder quantities need to be on call at short notice. This can be difficult to get right. Quality problems or delays will impact directly on the reputation of the brand rather than the supplier. However, if things go well, the benefit for the consumer is an unusual item offering good value and positive brand associations. Such promotions inevitably require the use of intermediaries such as handling houses to deal with response and process applications.

CASE STUDY **11.3**

Promoting into the 21st century

High technology is revolutionising the sales promotion industry in the same way that it has revolutionised the distribution of goods and services. Electronic point-of-sale (EPOS) scanning, credit card companies, retailers and financial services companies are converging to target consumers with greater accuracy and effectiveness than has ever before been possible.

ASDA has installed the Check-out Saver system in all 185 of its scanning stores to target, print and dispense coupons at point of sale. These instant print coupons come in four types:

▶ Competitor coupon (eg for a rival brand of washing up liquid when another is bought).
▶ Cross category coupon (eg for a salad ingredient when mayonnaise is bought).
▶ Own-user coupon (eg money off next purchase as a loyalty booster).
▶ Retailer coupon (eg to encourage trial of a new service from the store itself).

Redemption rates are very high compared to other forms of couponing. Own-user coupons aimed at straight rebuys, for example, reach levels of 50 per cent. Cross category, perhaps unsurprisingly because of the potential time lag involved, average out at 4.5 per cent.

Even infrequently purchased products such as shaving foam (say, every three months) can be effectively targeted with coupons generated electronically. The received wisdom about infrequently purchased goods used to be that they were not appropriate targets for couponing. By the time the next purchase happened, the coupon would have disappeared. A system trialled in the US takes care of this by identifying the shopper from his or her credit card number and storing the information that a coupon will be required about 10 weeks hence. Thus the machine spits it up at the check-out just as the consumer's original can of foam is about to run out – in time for it to influence the next purchase decision.

As well as credit card companies, banks and building societies are jumping aboard the couponing bandwagon. Britain's 18,000 automatic telling machines (ATMs) are being targeted as dispensing points for £20 note-shaped retail vouchers. In the scheme, piloted in 1994 by Aimmedia an innovative marketing services company, retailers pay £375 per week per machine to have their coupons fed into the 1.5 billion transactions that are carried out through ATMs each year. Aimmedia has even developed a geographical targeting system based on shop locations to indicate the machines each retailer should be in.

Questions

1   Competitor coupons yield a redemption rate of 10 per cent according to the Check-out Saver research. Is this more or less than what you would expect, and why?
2   Targeting coupons so personally might have some negative side-effects (eg people might feel that their privacy was being invaded). How would you as a retailer or manufacturer deal with this potential problem?
3   If you were Aimmedia, how would you go about establishing a price to retailers for ATM use?

Adapted from: Massey, 1994.

Strengths and weaknesses of sales promotion

The main advantages of sales promotion as a technique are as follows.

Something for nothing

The great strength of sales promotion is that it offers something for nothing. This stimulates a positive attitude to the product among consumers and intermediaries.

Short-term effectiveness

This tips customers over the edge of the decision to buy, thus leading to immediate sales increases.

Flexibility

Sales promotion can address a number of different marketing problems. The absolute costs and lead-times involved are frequently less daunting than for other kinds of marketing communications.

It is most effective in certain situations. For example, when launching a new product, sales promotion can prompt early trial. It can be used to communicate a major product improvement, a new pack size or variant. Used in the trade it is excellent for increasing distribution (via incentives to middlemen). Dealer loaders such as free gifts can persuade channel intermediaries to accept much higher levels of stock than they might otherwise, thus bringing forward business. This increases cash flow and, by flooding the distribution channel, effectively crowds out the competition. Used in tandem with advertising, sales promotion can be very effective at increasing the impact of commercial messages.

The drawbacks of sales promotion are as follows:

Temporary effects

By their very nature these are short lived (usually less than 90 days). It is therefore very difficult to get strategic messages about your brand across by sales promotion alone.

Cost effectiveness

At first sight this looks like one of the attractions of the technique. However the need to support sales promotion with other techniques (scheme advertising, salesforce support, public relations activity) means that the real cost of a promotion can exceed its apparent budget by some way.

Lack of continuity

The 'one-off' dominates sales promotion as a technique. Only a few are recurring. The pressure to be original negates the economies of scale that might be possible from a long-running advertising campaign.

Too much activity can make a product look busy, although this depends on the size and traditions of the product and consumers' expectations. There is some evidence to suggest that continual cut-price promotion devalues the brand in the eyes of consumers. There is certainly a growth in the number of deal-prone customers who switch brands promiscuously in search of the cheapest alternative (see Chapter 8).

So sales promotion is best avoided as a technique on established brands with no improvements to tout. It cannot, on its own, restore the fortunes of brands in the decline stage of the product life-cycle. There may be more effective ways of supporting brands in markets where sales promotion is the norm (such as pre-sweetened breakfast cereals). But being first in with a new sales promotion idea may give you an edge, however temporary. Heavy price promotion offers short-term benefits to the consumer, but falling margins may deter participating companies from making the kind of investment in quality necessary to long-term consumer satisfaction.

In spite of its apparently tactical nature, it is essential to integrate the planning and timing of sales promotion activity across the range of a company's products or services to maximise its support for the sales effort. This involves looking at least a year ahead at timing, techniques, geographical areas, brand co-ordination, synergy with planned advertising and the need to create selling support material.

ACTIVITY **11.2**

Selling sales promotion

Taking the role of a new business executive in an established sales promotion agency, prepare a five-minute presentation to a new client who has not used the medium before. The client is one of the following (please choose whichever one you prefer):

1   Your college or business.
2   Your local crime prevention officer.
3   A new sports centre.

Public relations

A cynical view of public relations might describe it as applied conviviality to keep bad news out of the press and free advertising in. It is yet another marketing communications technique with an image problem in some quarters. But for a more comprehensive, and more useful, definition we can turn to the words of the Institute of Public Relations (IPR) definition. This bills it as 'the deliberate, planned and sustained effort to establish and maintain mutual understanding between an organisation and its public'.

In fact you could extend the definition of public relations to cover every aspect of an organisation's interaction with its customers – even the marketing exchange process itself: 'The loudest message from the one to the other is performance, the loudest message from the other to the one is purchase' (Bernstein, 1974).

We shall concentrate on how companies can manage public relations within their promotional mix to help achieve specific marketing communications tasks.

Public relations in the strategic mix

Companies are free to choose whether or not to advertise, do direct marketing, run a salesforce or use sales promotion. But they have no choice about public relations. Public relations happens whether you like it or not. The only choice is whether to manage the process, or let things drift along by themselves.

Companies that let things drift along are nevertheless still sending out messages. Product performance, packaging, what the reception area looks like, even the way the telephones are answered are beaming images to customers, employees, stakeholders, competitors and suppliers.

It makes sense to make a conscious effort to manage public relations. But it is a historical fact that practically all in-house PR departments have arisen from a crisis, rather than from planning. A company faced by a takeover threat, for example, suddenly realises that it matters very much indeed what people think about it. The confidence of City institutions can save its independence. The sudden threat posed by a contamination scare, an industrial disaster or a management gaffe, can precipitate a programme of damage limitation. The best-prepared organisations are the best at weathering such storms. Companies in the 1990s have learned, if not from their own experience then from that of others, the value of a programme of pro-active public relations.

DID YOU KNOW?

A misguided sense of humour can be an expensive attribute for a company chairman. In 1991 Gerald Ratner quipped to an Institute of Directors conference that some of his jewellery chain store earrings sold for less than the price of a Marks and Spencer sandwich, but that they probably wouldn't last as long. Later in his speech he described a £4.95 decanter as 'complete crap'. The resulting public relations debacle (not helped by the recession) wiped £122 million off the share price of the company, closed 330 stores and led to 2,500 job losses including Ratner's own two years later.

A further factor in the increased use of public relations as a marketing tool is its perceived cost effectiveness. Advertising growth has slowed down in the first half of the 1990s as public relations expenditure has increased. Perhaps less enlightened companies expect PR to do their advertising on the cheap, and have therefore switched money from one budget into another. They are, however, two very different techniques, as Figure 11.3 shows. But there is evidence that public relations budgets are more likely to withstand the pressure of a recession.

Unlike advertising, which tends to flourish only in positive economic conditions, public relations is a wise investment in good and bad times. Second, the absolute costs of public relations are less than those of advertising. Cost-cutting managers feel there is more fat to trim off their relatively substantial advertising appropriations. If a reduction of £50,000 means cancelling 5 per cent of the planned advertising or 80 per cent of the planned PR programme, there are persuasive grounds for retaining the latter unscathed.

Public relations techniques usually involve a third party standing between the organisation and its audience. Usually this is a journalist, whose work is facilitated by a PR professional with information and material. In the case of a PR technique like sponsorship, the third party will be the event, institution or individual whose reputation is being used as a way of getting a brand's message across. Techniques such as advertising and sales promotion offer organisations precise control of the content and presentation of their messages. They reach the public direct through paid-for media exposure. With public relations the messages are dependent on third parties.

This can give public relations greater credibility than advertising. Particularly for a service, whose benefits are more difficult to convey than those of a tangible product, an expert's endorsement can work better than direct communication. We are more likely to trust a travel writer than an advertisement on the subject of an untried holiday destination, for example.

figure 11.3
**Public Relations vs.
Advertising**

Public relations	**Advertising**
● Informative	● Persuasive
● Background	● Foreground
● Editorial	● Identified sponsor
● Gratis	● Guaranteed
● Credible	● Biased
● Once only	● Repeatable

This leads us to another difference between public relations and the other marketing communications disciplines. No other technique places the same emphasis on dialogue. In spite of the amount of research that goes into its creative development or campaign analysis, advertising tends to be a one-way process. Public relations, on the other hand, implies dialogue. Any worthwhile programme begins in research to find out what an organisation's publics are thinking and saying. This is why the IPR definition stresses 'mutual understanding'. Good public relations involves a lot of listening.

CASE STUDY 11.4

Perrier in peril...

The 1990 benzene contamination scare that hit Perrier (then leading the UK mineral water market with 60 per cent share) is a classic of successful PR crisis management. The key to the whole exercise was an emphasis on dialogue, complemented by lightning reaction and a sureness of policy.

On 10 February small traces of the cancer-inducing chemical benzene were detected in a sample of Perrier by scientists in North Carolina. It transpired, eventually, that the source of the contamination had been a mistake by an employee at the Vergeze plant, who had splashed a bottling machine accidentally with the wrong cleaning fluid. Nevertheless, there had been several product scares in the recent past. Perrier, like a number of other large companies, had prepared a contingency plan to cope with sabotage or contamination. That very afternoon, the US company announced the withdrawal of stocks from shop shelves for safety tests.

The following day Perrier UK and its PR agency Infoplan met to agree action. A customer hotline was set up, receiving 1,700 calls on the first day. Testing in the UK revealed traces of benzene. By Wednesday 14 February, Valentines Day, UK stocks had joined the 40 million bottles withdrawn world-wide at a cost of £20 million. The trade were contacted personally by phone, hand-delivered letter, or fax. The UK chairwoman, Wenche Marshall Foster, instead of holding a press conference, gave 20 individual interviews to key UK journalists over a period of 24 hours. Infoplan's strategy of person-to-person contact spared the Perrier directors the ordeal of having to face a barrage of questions under television lights. Panicky press conferences can result in television pictures of directors under pressure in a crisis. The Perrier approach led to a greater concentration on the actual information available instead of a 'scare' angle with emotive pictures.

By the end of the first week of the crisis the brand looked to be weathering the storm. The number of calls to the Infoplan line had dropped to 1,000 a day – some of them from customers congratulating the company on its responsible policy. The French government had OK'd the recommencement of bottling operations after checks at Vergeze, and the UK Department of Health had offered the public assurances that there was no health risk involved in drinking the water.

Already the company was planning the UK relaunch of the brand with Infoplan and advertising agency Leo Burnett. Brand advertising over the years had emphasised Perrier's slightly quirky personality with gently humorous puns on the word 'eau'. The come-back advertising drew on this heritage of goodwill by adopting a jauntily confident tone. Posters were planned that assured the consumer that Perrier was now 'Eau K', and a television ad was shot that greeted viewers with the message 'Helleau Again'. Shops received stocks of the specially labelled 'new production' at the beginning of April – a mere six weeks after the crisis had struck.

Questions

1   Perrier's behaviour has been held up as a text-book example of how to handle a crisis. How might other companies learn from their experience?
2   What are the advantages and disadvantages of press conferences compared to individual interviews?
3   Perrier's return was heralded by humorous advertising. What alternative approaches might it have taken?

Adapted from: PR Week, 1990.

Strengths and weaknesses of public relations

The advantages of public relations as a promotional technique are as follows.

Coverage

It reaches people who are difficult to reach through advertising, either because they consciously avoid it or because they simply don't see much of it (like AB men or young people, both of which groups are notoriously difficult to reach through traditional advertising media).

Economy

The visible costs are considerably less than those of advertising. While the two techniques can hardly be compared on a like-with-like basis, this nevertheless looms large in what clients say about it. Administrative costs and time over-heads can be heavy, though.

New products

Editorial public relations is particularly effective in support of new products, especially in the business-to-business sector where trade press can generate extensive coverage of the market.

Services

Third-party endorsement means that unfamiliar products or intangible ser-vices can be described more extensively and credibly than if they were merely being advertised.

The disadvantages of public relations are as follows.

Difficulty of control

Because of PR's reliance on third parties, exact details of message content, pre-sentation or even appearance cannot be guaranteed.

Reliance on news values

The kind of repetition used in other forms of promotion is difficult. Sustaining a theme requires particularly careful planning and management.

Evaluation

Effectiveness is difficult to gauge in any promotional technique. But public rela-tions campaigns offer a particular challenge. Pre- and post-campaign qualitative research is expensive, and relying on measures like editorial column inches is crude and subjective. The issue of evaluation is dealt with at greater length towards the end of the chapter.

Editorial PR techniques

The concept of 'publics' implies that different audiences will have particular preferences when it comes to how messages are mediated. In some cases the best way may be through a direct approach. Receptions, conferences, exhibitions are all tools that come under the heading of public relations. More often, however, because of the size of the publics you need to reach, the media will come into the equation. Knowing how to deal with the media and, in particular, how to write effective press releases, is a core skill in PR.

ACTIVITY **11.3**
....

Mapping publics

Draw a diagram mapping the six most important publics of an organisation or individual of your choice. How does this diagram help you to establish the most appropriate media or techniques for reaching the publics indicated? How might it help you to select appropriate messages in each case?

Journalists are busy people. Effective editorial PR aims to make their lives as easy as possible. One way of doing this is to be able to spot an angle to a story that is likely to interest readers, listeners or viewers. A second necessary skill is the ability to communicate the idea briefly and coherently in a press release. The most important knack to acquire, though, is an appreciation of what makes news.

DID YOU KNOW?

That news values haven't changed much in the last 100 years? 'When a dog bites a man that is not news, but when a man bites a dog that is news' (Charles Anderson Dana, 1882).

What makes a story?

The simple answer is anything. But a brief glance through a local or national newspaper reveals that the stories they contain hang on some particular hook. Journalists are trained to look for what is newsworthy in a story. It needs to contain at least one of the following elements:

- ▶ action
- ▶ conflict and debate
- ▶ unusualness
- ▶ local interest (for local media)
- ▶ human interest
- ▶ topicality
- ▶ relevance to a national issue (eg a soap opera, politics, scandal, the Lottery, Christmas, etc).

Different papers have different approaches to news. Some are very serious, others mix heavyweight stories with quirkier tittle tattle. The same is true for radio programmes and television. The skill lies in matching a story or an angle with an appropriate outlet. After all, the media need an endless supply of material to fill their column inches or broadcast minutes, so there is no shortage of opportunity; but it needs to be the right kind of material.

Although this chapter uses the terminology 'press release', what is said about printed media does not always hold true for broadcast. Action is very important to television. Sound is important to radio. As with creative choices in advertising, a sensitivity to the strengths and potential of media is important in PR – and can enhance coverage of the target publics by maximising exposure across a number of media.

Another thing to bear in mind about the media is the deadline. As new technology tightens its grip on the traditional world of the newspaper, the time between receiving a news item and its publication is shortening. But the best story in the world is still no good to a journalist if it arrives too late to be used. Having clear policies can help a company minimise the delay in releasing news – especially in the case of a crisis where speed of reaction is essential.

Writing a press release

> I keep six honest serving-men
> (They taught me all I knew);
> Their names are What and Why and When
> And How and Where and Who.
> > Rudyard Kipling, *The Elephant's Child*

Good press releases bristle with facts, preferably in the first one or two sentences (the lead as journalists call it). What is happening? Who is involved? Where is it taking place? When is it happening? and Why is it happening? These questions are as important for the launch of a new product as they are for a summit conference of world leaders or a major sporting event. The first couple of sentences of your release are crucial to the success or failure of what follows. They will be being scanned by an extremely busy journalist. On them depends whether the press release ends up on the desk for further investigation, or in the bin.

Another good reason for starting with the essential facts is that sometimes editors print press releases without changing them, except for cutting them. Traditionally editors cut from the bottom. So the less important details should go into later paragraphs. This tradition has affected the way newspaper stories are written. Almost invariably, the reader can pick up the main point of the story (with the essential information) from the first paragraph of each news item.

The rest of the release should include supporting facts and details. If there is a personality involved in the story, it is a good idea to include a substantial quote. This means the journalist can select a few words to give his or her story a personal stamp. It is essential to provide a number for further information at the end of the release.

As in any other sort of marketing relationship, customer care is important when dealing with journalists and editors. Press releases can demonstrate this by catering for the needs of the journalist's own customers (by having news value). The more immediate needs of the journalist or editor can be catered for by following their professional conventions:

- ▶ Dates and other factual details should be exact and full to avoid misunderstandings. The release needs to be double checked for accuracy. Getting things wrong makes both the issuer and the journalist look inept.
- ▶ Production details are important. Wide margins, double spacing, one side of the paper only... all these apparently aesthetic features actually affect how easily a press release can be used by a journalist.
- ▶ Brevity is the soul of wit, especially in a press release. It's useful to remember that one side of double-spaced A4 fills about six column inches in most newspapers (that's only about 150 words).
- ▶ Facts, not opinions, count. Opinions are for the journalist to form. Press releases that go over the top about the qualities of a product will be dismissed as an attempt to get free advertising.
- ▶ Simplicity pays dividends. The average reading age of the Great British public is lower than you think!

The feature article

This is when a PR practitioner offers an editor a complete article on a particular subject. It can be reprinted as it stands or rewritten slightly by another journalist. The advantage is that it allows an issue to be treated in depth. The disadvantage is that such articles need to stand on their own two feet as editorial matter. They will tend to be useful as background material, but less so in support of specific products or services.

Visuals

The problem with press releases is that journalists can make of them what they like. This may not always accord with the issuer's interests, although it makes a good story. The beauty of pictures is that they are easier to control (in general) and have much more immediate impact than the written word. As with feature articles, publications frequently accept an organisation's own pictures. And, again, customer care is important here. Because of the format of newspapers and magazines certain types of picture work better than others. Close-ups, upright images rather than sideways ones (ie portrait not landscape), people close together, people doing something that is easily understood. These are all characteristics of typical press photographs.

We live in an increasingly visual culture, dominated by television and video. So photographs are a very natural way of communicating. The main problem is keeping a supply of fresh ideas coming. At one stage, for example, no share flotation was complete without a photocall of abseilers descending the company HQ wall. This was, at least for a while, a good way of making a pretty dull event visually exciting. Banal as it may seem, pictures involving hats, children and animals (sometimes all three) are enduringly popular. And, despite changing attitudes, young women with 'nice smiles' tend to be seen as a safe bet as well.

The video release

The ability to think in pictures is essential to securing time on television news programmes. This has been extended in recent years by organisations who supply video material to news programmes, thus saving the considerable cost of originating images to put over the words. Amnesty International is one of the most successful non-profit organisations to employ this technique. Its promotional campaigns highlight the plight of people whose stories would not normally make the news agenda, but by supplying video material it can often gain priority with television editors desperate for visuals.

DID YOU KNOW?

The American PR consultancy Hill and Knowlton was instrumental in getting American troops involved in the Gulf War. Retained by the Kuwaiti government, their emotive video releases told a very direct and selective story of the build-up to the conflict. In the absence of other video material from the region, their freely-supplied images dominated US television coverage and exerted a crucial influence on popular opinion.

The broadcast interview

Journalists, especially in the broadcast media, are keen to combine topicality and human interest via the technique of interviews. There is a burgeoning industry in media training for senior personnel from organisations like major companies and the police in order to optimise their performance in what can sometimes seem like a gladiatorial struggle.

Radio and television interviews can be very intimidating for the inexperienced. As with all media it is essential to consider the special opportunities they present. For example, radio news bulletins tend to be very short, so simplified messages work best. Complex arguments should give way to one main point. The growth in popularity of the soundbite, a conveniently sized quote that can be worked into a news report, is a symptom of this.

For longer interviews, the object of the presenter will be to make entertaining programming. He or she will want to sound confident and in control. A positive manner on the part of the interviewee is therefore a real help. Whether the interview is to be recorded or is going out live may affect the best kind of answers to the questions posed, especially if the information might go out of date quickly. Life can be made easier for the interviewer by being briefed in advance with some written material about the product or organisation in question. To ensure their programme goes smoothly, most presenters will brief their subjects in advance on the shape the interview is to take.

Managing and evaluating public relations

Public relations can be carried out by an internal department, an external agency, or a mixture of both (the most common arrangement). When dealing with an external agency, the management of the relationship is an important element to get right for both parties. As with advertising agencies (see Chapter 10) the relationship will be the result of a period of courtship, cemented in agreed terms of business covering the following areas:

► Exclusivity (so the agency does not face competition in its territory or to its business, and the client does not have to share its services with a competitor).
► Scope of the services offered.
► Systems for approving and authorising work undertaken.
► Copyright and property responsibilities.
► Confidentiality.
► Fees and terms of payment. These are usually in the form of an agreed monthly fee called a retainer, supplemented by charges for expenses and

services bought on the client's behalf such as printing or copyright fees. Such expenditure will usually be marked up to offer the agency an agreed profit margin.

▶ Legal liability.

The areas covered are very similar to those governing relationships between advertising agencies and their clients. The payment method is different, however, in that public relations is a below-the-line expense. The media commission on which many advertising agencies still base their income does not form part of the picture.

The outline programme for the services to be offered to the client will also be agreed and updated at regular intervals. Such programmes will cover the background and objectives of the activity, and delineate the key messages that the programme will seek to communicate. Precise target audiences, the PR techniques to be used and budgets for the projected activity are also established and agreed as a result of this process.

As with advertising, client/agency meetings are a central technique in managing the PR process. The cycle of activity requires regular update meetings to report back on achievements and monitor media and other activity. Usually on a monthly basis, these are supplemented with quarterly or six-monthly planning meetings which respond to changing external conditions and trends. They are also an opportunity to evaluate the success of the activity carried out in the longer term.

Commonly-used measures of success include the following.

Cuttings book

A subjective measure, perhaps, the client needs to be satisfied with the amount of press coverage that can be demonstrated from a period of activity. While many PR practitioners condemn the comparison of their art to advertising, they often refer to how much their column inches or broadcast minutes would have cost to buy. Certainly a fat cuttings book can enhance a client's 'feel good' factor about PR.

Strategic messages

Key words and phrases are agreed and the success of the campaign is gauged by their appearance in editorial matter. For example, the campaign relaunching Dr Barnardos as Barnardos in 1988 resulted in gratifyingly frequent occurrences of certain key phrases such as 'shedding its Victorian "orphan" image' in press reports. This technique has the advantage of linking targeted media coverage closely to strategy, but it also means that the messages themselves have to be realistic. Also, the key words must be well conceived. John Major's ill-fated 1994 'Back to Basics' campaign became a public relations disaster.

Market research

In an ideal world this would be the best way of evaluating PR effectiveness. The relevant key audiences would be sampled and polled before, during and after the activity. The major weakness with such an approach is its cost, which limits its use to the largest organisations.

Numerical targets

Influenced perhaps by the quantified media research that advertising agencies can invoke, this attempts to introduce a similar kind of rigour to PR. The requirement to register an agreed number of 'hits' certainly provides a measurable objective. But the problem is that numbers may not be the right currency in which to measure the quality of the activity.

Whatever the methods of evaluation used, the setting of realistic and clear objectives is the cornerstone of this kind of promotional activity.

Summary
••••••••••

This chapter has concluded our introductory survey of the main promotional tools by looking at selling, sales promotion and public relations. Selling is at the sharp end of business, when a customer transaction is finalised in a mutually satisfactory way. In spite of the differences in perspective between selling and marketing, selling is a vital part of the marketing process. Sales promotion is a support activity designed to make selling more effective. It is a flexible technique covering a number of approaches and applications. Finally, public relations aims at creating the right kind of environment (both inside and outside a company) for sustainable success. It actively manages the messages sent out by a company, usually with the assistance of third parties such as journalists.

Key concepts
••••••••••••••••

Below the line: promotional expenditure that is not commissionable (see Chapter 10). Commonly used to differentiate sales promotion expenditure from media advertising.

Closing: bringing a sales interview to the point of purchase.

Commission: a remuneration scheme whereby a salesperson is rewarded with a percentage of the value of achieved sales.

Feature article: a non-news story in a paper or magazine.

Hygiene factor: according to Herzberg (1966) a condition necessary to satisfaction in the workplace, but not necessary to increased performance.

Lead: the first couple of sentences of a press release or article.

On target earnings (OTE): expected, rather than guaranteed, earnings of a salesperson, taking into account commission and bonuses.

Prospects: potential customers. They need to be qualified by careful research.

Public relations: the management of mutual understanding by an organisation with its publics.

Sales promotion: promotional activity designed to increase the speed or volume of transactions.

Scheme and theme: two types of advertising: scheme is in support of a particular promotion, theme is general brand advertising activity.

Stakeholder: an individual or group with an interest in an organisation.

VNR: Video News Release

Self-check questions

....

1 The six stages of the personal selling process consist of:
   a Prospecting, listening, arguing, handling objections, negotiation and closing.
   b Prospecting, approach, presentation, handling objections, closing and follow-up.
   c Approach, attention, interest, desire, action and follow-up.
   d Prospecting, presentation, punctuality, process, physical evidence and people.
   e Prospecting, approach, problem-solving, handling objections, probing and promising.

2 The allocative close:
   a Assumes that the customer has said yes.
   b Is a straightforward request for the order.
   c Puts it to the customer that there is a shortage of the product.
   d Sums up each point agreed in the presentation and ends with a request for the order.
   e Offers the customer a discount if he or she will agree the sale.

3 The salesforce management process can be divided into the three Ss of:
   a Subterfuge, structure and suspicion.
   b Strategy, structure and support.
   c Stratification, structure and stasis.
   d Situation, selling and sustenance.
   e Structure, stability and strategy.

4 Personality promotions:
   a Exploit psychological weaknesses in consumers' personalities.
   b Use models, often in fancy dress.
   c Are never used in conjunction with sampling.
   d Are an example of above the line expenditure.
   e Are a recent addition to the sales promotion repertoire.

5 Public relations can have greater credibility than advertising because:
   a It is planned and sustained.
   b It is more cost effective.
   c It uses third-party endorsement.
   d It is for products not services.
   e It uses video news releases.

Which of the following are true and which are false?
6 Successful selling aims to look after existing customers as much if not more than winning new business.
7 Questions can be a useful way of diagnosing a customer's sphere of interest.
8 Good salespeople always talk a lot.
9 Most successful sales promotions last for a minimum of three months.
10 Good press releases are full of honest opinions.

Discuss the following

11 Salespeople are born not made.

12 'Everyone lives by selling something' (Robert Louis Stevenson, 1850–1894)

13 Sales promotion has no future as a form of strategic communication.

14 Public relations is an unethical imposition on journalists trying to present an objective view of the world to their audiences and readers.

15 The future of editorial public relations lies with the video news release.

Further study
•••••••••••••••••

Books

Bernstein, David (1984) *Corporate Image and Reality*, Reinhardt.

An excellent and articulate account of public relations on a corporate level.

Carnegie, Dale (1992) *How to Win Friends and Influence People*, Cedar Books.

There is a lot of farsighted wisdom in this book and it is has the advantage of being extremely readable.

Cummins, Julian (1993) *Sales Promotion*, 2nd edition, Kogan Page.

A good treatment of sales promotions.

Mazur, Laura and White, Jon (1995) *Strategic Communications Management*, Addison Wesley.

Plenty of up-to-date examples and some very thoughtful commentary.

Moss, Danny (Ed) (1990) *Public Relations in Practice: A Casebook*, Routledge.

A wide variety of fascinating examples of public relations at work.

References
••••••••••••••

Bernstein, D. (1974) *Creative Advertising*, Longman.

Denny, N. (1994) 'Law of the bungle', in *Promotions and Incentives*, October, pp. 26–30.

Derrick, S. (1994) 'Paper promises', in *Marketing Business*, September, pp. 37–8.

Herzberg, F. (1966) *Work and the Nature of Man*, World Publishing Co.

Kotler, P. (1991) *Marketing Management: Analysis, Planning, Implementation and Control*, 7th Edition, Prentice Hall International.

Levitt, T. (1986) *The Marketing Imagination*, Collier Macmillan.

Massey, A. (1994) 'Hi-Tech Promotions', in *Marketing Business*, May, pp. 35–8.

Miles, L. (1992) 'Supplementary benefits', in *Marketing Business*, September, pp. 41–4.

Ogilvy, D. (1983) *Ogilvy on Advertising*, Pan.

PR Week (1990) 'Bridge over troubled waters holds steady', 19 April, pp. 4–5.

CHAPTER 12

Strategic marketing management–planning, organisation and control

Objectives:

....

When you have read this chapter you will be able to:

▶ List the major generic strategies available to marketers in a range of competitive situations.

▶ Justify marketing planning as a business discipline and use a selection of analytical frameworks.

▶ Prepare and present an outline marketing plan, with provision for evaluation and control.

▶ Identify a range of common marketing organisational structures.

▶ Determine and apply measures of marketing effectiveness.

Introduction

....

Strategy is the overall vision of how an organisation's purposes are to be fulfilled. The word has its roots in a Greek word meaning the activity of generals. The traditional outcome of such activity was stratagems – ploys and ruses to win a battle, and eventually the war. Marketing strategy sounds a more civilized process, but the outcome is the same. In the commercial battlefield you may be fighting competitors, indifference or inertia – but a sound strategy is the key to long-term victory.

Throughout this book we have emphasised an important distinction between strategy and tactics. The original meaning of tactics (another Greek word) was the arrangements made for individual battle. We use the term to mean the day-to-day implementation of plans to achieve long-term aims. It's helpful to think of strategy as being like a principle (the way we do things) and tactics being like the practices based on that principle (what we do).

In the real world of business we can talk about two ways in which strategy comes about. The first is called deliberate strategy, the conscious pursuit of objectives through deliberate plans and their execution. The second is called emergent strategy, when a company falls less consciously into a way of doing things. Emergent strategy can, of course, be recognised and consolidated into deliberate strategy by evaluation and control. (See Figure 12.1.)

Furthermore, there are levels of strategy at work in an organisation. The governing principle of operation is the corporate strategy. It is long term, concerned with the overall direction of the organisation. Corporate strategy is expressed in terms of the organisation's mission (and we will look at the subject of the mission statement later in this chapter, at the beginning of the section on planning). In an organisation that places the customer at its centre, the corporate strategy will be imbued with the marketing philosophy. Within this

figure 12.1
Levels of strategy

overall framework, and supporting it, is the functional marketing strategy (along with the other sets of functional strategies, financial, production and human resource). Marketing strategy will be more specific and practical than corporate strategy, although customer orientation will link them.

Later in this section we will review a number of common strategies that can be identified in the way companies achieve their aims. Formulating strategy requires the kind of helicopter vision that is one of the characteristics of good marketing. Rather than seeing the organisation from the internal perspective of day-to-day operations, the strategist steps back and tries to see things from outside just as the marketer tries to see things from the customer's point of view.

Searching for differential advantage

The key to success in a competitive environment is to maintain an advantage over rival firms that gives customers a reason to choose you. There are as many possible sources of this kind of advantage as there are dimensions of a business that are relevant to the customer. This creates considerable scope for discovering and developing them. The advantage may be lodged in the organisation's own capabilities, in the product or service, or in the nature of the relationship with the customer. Here are some examples of differential advantage in each of these three categories which have already been mentioned in this book:

▶ *Organisational capacity*: Benetton's computerised warehousing capacity gives it an edge in restocking swift-selling lines, so that customers can get the clothes they want, when they want them.
▶ *Product or service*: First Direct's telephone banking lines are staffed by human beings rather than machines 24 hours a day, so account holders receive personal service whenever they call.
▶ *Nature of the relationship with the customer*: *Reader's Digest* can target existing customers with offers it knows will be of interest because of purchase behaviour already logged.

The concept of differential advantage is similar to the classic idea of the unique selling proposition described in Chapter 10 as the basis of effective promotional communication. Marketing strategy aims to uncover and enhance differential advantage to the long-term benefit of the organisation.

Strategic options
....

The search to establish differential advantage can take a number of directions. Businesses can take some guidance in this area from the findings of the long-standing American project known as PIMS (Profit Impact of Marketing Strategy). Originated in the 1960s by the American company General Electric, the project was brought under the aegis of the Harvard Business School in the 1970s. Participating firms submit regular confidential information on the market conditions under which they have been operating, together with their performance in competitive and absolute terms. Most of the firms involved are large manufacturers (services are under-represented in the sample) but a significant proportion are active internationally. The project aims to discover which strategies are most profitable in which situations. Although its findings are not above reproach because of the causal links they assume, the following broad patterns have emerged (Buzzell and Gale, 1987):

▶ The single most important contribution to long-term competitive success comes from the quality of the product or service on offer.
▶ High market share means high profitability. Economies of scale, return on investment and the efficiency of marketing expenditure all increase with the size of market share.

These findings confirm the received wisdom of marketing that success breeds success. Traditional marketing strategy has always put a great deal of emphasis on building market share, in the belief that establishing a brand's position in the purchasing habits of a large volume of consumers must be good for its long-term profitability. The pricing strategy of penetration pricing discussed in Chapter 8 values market share above immediate revenue in support of this principle.

Market share-related strategy

Kotler and Armstrong (1994) sum up the kinds of strategy available to a firm as a function of its share of the market. They split the options four ways to suit the four kinds of competitive position that a firm can occupy: market leader, market challenger, market follower and niche player.

Market leaders
Market leaders are, as we have seen, likely to be the most profitable and therefore most powerful competitors. But they also have the most to lose. Their available strategies either defend what share they already have – this is made easier by the economies of scale that they enjoy – or they aim to expand their business, either by increasing share or by increasing the overall size of the market itself.

CASE STUDY **12.1**
....
Kit Kat Konquers Kompetition
In the highly competitive confectionery market, Rowntree's Kit Kat is the biggest single brand. It faces intense competition from a number of able challengers, but maintains its pre-eminence through following a confident strategy of:

▶ Defending share through aggressive merchandising and advertising combined with unique product quality.

▶ Increasing share by innovative sales promotion and highly competitive pricing and distribution policies.

▶ Expanding the total market by concentrating not only on Kit Kat as a confectionery brand, but also as a grocery line.

Questions

1 Which of Kit Kat's competitive advantages do you consider to be the most sustainable, and why?

2 How do you continue developing new ways of promotion and distribution for a mature product? Can you give examples from markets other than confectionery?

3 One of Kit Kat's perceived strengths as a brand is that it exists as an important brand both in confectionery and grocery markets. What problems might this present?

Market challengers

Market challengers are the number two brands in each market. Often they will direct their competitive activity at smaller companies rather than at the dominant player, quietly growing share as a result. Confronting the market leader is unlikely to be successful. A flanking strategy is often more successful. This borrows military terminology to describe an attack on the side of the army rather than head-on. It assumes that the market leader will be so preoccupied with its main business that it may leave parts of the market undefended. In the 1980s, for example, the relatively tiny Apple computers took on the might of IBM and won in the personal computer market, because the larger company had not realised the potential of the business. IBM was so busy defending its predominance in the mainframe computer market that it took a while to recover from the challenge.

DID YOU KNOW?
Robert Townsend, author of Up the Organisation (1979), made a virtue of being a market challenger when he was head of Avis in the 1970s. Because Avis were number two to Hertz in the car rental market his advertising assured customers that 'we try harder'.

Market followers

This group of companies are nowhere near the market leaders, but have found themselves a comfortable position and are therefore not keen to rock the boat. By careful market segmentation and an intelligent use of distinctive competences, such companies can maintain impressive profits. In spite of the price wars raging among their national counterparts, local newspapers in the UK provide an example of a market that is controlled by no more than half a dozen major companies. Instead of fighting each other, they actively manage their business so that the existing shares of the market are maintained whenever publications change hands.

Niche players

By selecting a precisely defined market segment that is too small to be of interest to a major competitor such companies can establish very lucrative businesses if they are content with low volume. Their success suggests that the correlation between market share size and profitability works best at either end of the scale – leaving the middle ground to less profitable businesses. However, niche marketing, like market following, may not be a sustainable option. As soon as the major players notice the profits to be made there is a strong possibility that they will move in with their superior fire power. The growth of UK independent record labels in the late 1980s established a niche in the music industry that led the major labels to launch their own pseudo-independent labels. These were able to back their artists with promotion and distribution that the original niche players could not match, leading to the 'defection' of several 'Indie' bands to the major labels.

Product/market strategies

Another way of looking at strategic options is to move away from market share and look at how an organisation relates to its customers and its offerings. Igor Ansoff, who pioneered the treatment of strategic management as an academic discipline in the 1950s, identified four strategic options based on the firm's orientation to its markets and its offerings (see Figure 12.2).

The first strategy, increasing sales of an existing product in an existing market, is known as penetration. As we have seen earlier, this can be a credible choice for market leaders keen to expand their business without excessive risk to existing share. Market penetration, as it is known, can be illustrated by brand leader Kellogg's Corn Flakes. Its promotional campaigns to persuade lapsed users to come back into the fold 'Have you forgotten how good they taste?' represent an attempt to increase usage by the existing market.

The next strategy is more risky, involving taking an existing product and putting it into a new market. Mars pioneered the fun-size sector in the grocery trade in the early 1980s by repackaging its existing product in a new format that would appeal to the family shopper. The needs of such a shopper differed markedly from those of the core Mars buyer, purchasing confectionery for themselves. Fun size appealed to those buying for others, perhaps as a children's treat or something to put into lunch boxes. The market sector expanded rapidly to the point where, in the 1990s, practically all of the major countlines

figure 12.2
**Ansoff's Growth
Vector Matrix**

	Existing	New
Existing	Market penetration (eg Kellog's Corn Flakes)	Product/service development (eg Rolo bar)
New	Market extension (eg Mars fun size)	Diversification (eg Sony)

Markets / Offerings

have a fun-size incarnation available in supermarkets. This strategy is known as market development, and carries a medium level of risk.

The third option is product development. This is more risky than market development because the absolute costs of entry are usually higher. A product or service new to the organisation is offered to an existing market. BIC, who sell disposable pens, lighters and razors with great success, tried to introduce a line of disposable perfumes in the late 1980s. The introduction was a marketing disaster. The kind of exclusivity and personal imagery that people associate with perfume was missing from this kind of presentation. Customers who were happy with disposables in their other purchases could not accept the format for perfume. On the other hand, representing an existing product in a new format (like the Rolo Bar, pioneered successfully in 1994) can rejuvenate interest in a brand from lapsed users.

Ansoff's final option is the most risky of all – although it offers compensatingly high rewards for those prepared to wager the high stakes involved. This is when an organisation diversifies, bringing new products and services to new markets. The double unfamiliarity here can provide the recipe for expensive failure. But an organisation with a sufficiently clear strategy can make a success of the process. The media industries provide some good examples of diversification. Sony, up to the late 1980s a manufacturer of consumer electronics hardware, took the step of becoming a producer of associated software at the end of the decade with its purchase of CBS. This acquisiton brought it new products in unfamiliar markets. Recording artists such as Michael Jackson and Bob Dylan became part of Sony's stable of talent, although George Michael was not so easily absorbed. As well as its audio catalogue, CBS's treasures included blockbuster films and television series. Should Sony the equipment manufacturer launch a format incompatible with other manufacturers' products, the possession of such a bank of material might guarantee its success – giving Sony an invaluable competitive advantage. But even the best laid strategic plans can be fouled up by circumstances. Sony's acquisition of CBS has given it a useful new revenue stream, but its launch of the mini-disc format has been stalemated by economic recession.

In Chapter 9 we looked at the patterns of potential conflict in distribution channels, identifying their directions as horizontal (between parallel channels) and vertical (along the same channel). We can use the same terminology to describe the direction of diversification in related industries (or integration as it is known). Vertical integration is when an organisation like a publishing company buys into the industry that feeds it (eg a paper mill) or into the industry it feeds (eg a bookselling chain). In the example here, the purchase of the paper mill would be called backward integration (moving back up the supply chain) and the purchase of the bookseller would be forward integration (moving down the chain, closer to the final customer).

Horizontal integration is when companies buy into organisations that parallel their own. Rupert Murdoch's acquisition of both the *Sun* and *The Times* as part of his News International group clearly brought him two very different products addressing different markets. But they are both at the same stage of the newspaper business horizontally. The media industry arouses political sensitivities because of the role that newspapers and broadcasting have in keeping the electorate informed in a democratic society. 'Cross-media' ownership has thus aroused wide objections. In another industry such integration might pass unnoticed as the inevitable struggle for greater efficiencies, leading to lower prices and better service for the consumer.

Terry's Chocolate Orange gets squeezed harder

Kraft Jacob Suchard acquired Terry's of York in 1993. High on its agenda was a revaluation of the brands in the company's portfolio, including the famous Chocolate Orange. The existing market for Chocolate Orange was seen to rely too closely on gift-purchase and seasonal business at Easter and Christmas. The Orange needed to be unpeeled to give it access to new segments.

The process involved a fundamental rethink of the brand's format. A core assumption had been that the confectionery needed to be orange-shaped, which effectively limited its usage occasions to the narrow range mentioned above. This straitjacket was abandoned as Terry's, advised by their design consultancy Design Bridge, explored the possibilities of new formats for the product. The process of selection involved scoring candidate products on texture, consistency, size, indulgence and impulse. This rigorous process eliminated ideas that would not have filled the brand's criteria. Among them, surprisingly, were ideas that had at first seemed quite appropriate but that did not score on appropriate attributes in research.

The result is that in 1995 the Chocolate Orange brand covers ten different items including treats, everyday products, products for sharing, using as informal gifts and eating oneself, cakes, countlines, boxed gifts and drinks. Each of these product forms has been carefully assessed against the original brand proposition in order to establish its credibility with consumers.

Questions

1   How might you research the acceptability of new formats for leading products in the following fields?
    – Clothes washing detergent.
    – Breakfast cereals.
    – Malt whisky.
2   Acquiring brands is a popular way to buy into profitable markets. What kind of difficulties do new brand owners face?
3   Terry's Chocolate Orange has a very potent advertising heritage. What risks does expansion into new formats carry, and how might they be minimised?

Adapted from: Lawder & Sholl, 1995.

Competition-based marketing strategies

The dominant voice in strategic thinking for the 1980s and 1990s has been that of Michael Porter, a Harvard professor whose diagnosis of strategic options focuses on the idea of competition between firms in mature markets (the situation in which most marketing strategy now takes place). Rather than wavering indecisively in the market-place, Porter (1980) recommends that a firm deliberately takes up its stand on one of three strategic platforms:

▶ *Cost leadership*, where it concentrates on its ability to exercise economies of scale in a number of different market sectors by investing heavily in technology to enable it to beat its rivals on price.

▶ *Differentiation*, where it concentrates on product quality to justify a premium price (thus generating more profit).

▶ *Focus*, where it devotes its efforts to servicing a narrow range of customers or segments rather like a niche marketer (with the same risk that too much success in growing the market will inevitably attract larger competitors).

Any of these three generic strategies should create the kind of differential advantage that will give a customer a reason to go to that particular supplier rather than a rival. We can illustrate the three positionings from the refined (but intensely competitive) world of classical music CDs.

CASE STUDY **12.3**
· · · · · · · · · · · · · · · · · ·

CD competitive strategy

Cost leadership is the strategy adopted by Tring International (whose pricing policies are looked at in Chapter 8). It has joined forces with the Royal Philharmonic Orchestra to record and release a projected series of 200 discs of the basic classical repertoire beginning with 20 releases in 1994. Using the latest in bit mapping digital technology it is able to offer superb sound quality to consumers for less than £5 a disc.

Differentiation is the strategy adopted by Deutsche Grammophon. Its core business concentrates on full-price recordings by top flight international stars and orchestras. It is confident that record buyers will be prepared to pay up to £15 a disc for this kind of quality.

Focus is the strategy adopted by Harmonia Mundi. This label specialises in early music – a category running from medieval times to the eighteenth century. Its full price recordings appeal to a segment of the market for their carefully researched authentic performances.

Of course, the picture is not quite this clear. Deutsche Grammophon, like most of its major label rivals, operates a budget label (Classikon), and an early music label (Archiv) as two thriving sub brands. But the general shape of the industry corresponds to Porter's prescription fairly well.

Questions

1　Porter's model describes the CD industry fairly well. How might it be used to help predict what will be happening five years from now?

2　How can labels like DG ensure that their budget offerings do not erode the 'value' of their full-price recordings?

3　How far is a budget positioning ever likely to be appropriate for a classical music label?

Marketing planning
· ·

Why plan?

For something that appeals to common sense, planning meets with more than its fair share of resistance. When confronted by the need to plan, people in organisations often claim to be too busy, or too cynical, or think it's not their job, or protest they don't have enough information. These are all understandable objections, but they do not absolve anyone of the responsibility of planning. As somebody once said, 'To fail to plan is to plan to fail.'

Put simply, planning is the process of trying to match an organisation's capabilities to the opportunities around it. Looked at in those terms planning and marketing are very similar. Marketing attempts to satisfy external demand by understanding it, and making it the justification for an organisation's activity. This requires answers to a number of key questions.

What business are we in?

This is the basis of an organisation's mission statement, the cornerstone of corporate strategy (and therefore a key determinant of marketing strategy). It is a question that needs to be asked on a regular basis. Otherwise the organisation will sink naturally into a state of self-maintenance, oblivious of the changing external environment. The answer to the question defines the customer and the nature of the relationship sought.

A good example of an organisation that asks this question regularly is the Royal Mail. Its mission statement, the result of careful analysis and rigorous thinking, is condensed into very few words: 'At Royal Mail our mission is to be recognised as the best organisation in the world distributing text and packages.'

This statement reflects several decisions about what sort of business the Royal Mail is in. Evidently it is international. Its definition of its service as 'distributing text and packages' suggests two separate streams of communication – one information-oriented, one to do with physical distribution. Underlying this precise account of what the organisation does is a visionary commitment to excellence, indeed to being 'the best'. And the importance of the customer's point of view is implied in the aspiration `to be recognised'. The measure of success the Royal Mail is looking for has its roots in customer satisfaction. Having made these decisions the organisation can then go about implementing them and communicating them without fear of confusion or contradiction. A mission statement gives everyone confidence that they are going in the right direction to fulfil the purpose of the organisation.

This is not to say that organisations may not change their purpose. In the 1970s Dr Barnardo's (as it was then known) had to face up to the fact that its traditional role of looking after parentless children was becoming outmoded. Its Victorian heritage of institutional care was no longer relevant. But another need had taken its place – helping disadvantaged young people through training and support. Recognising a new need, it changed its mission accordingly and remains a highly effective organisation.

Non-profit organisations like Barnardo's need an even clearer idea of what business they are in than commercial enterprises. The sink-or-swim criterion of profitability is an unambiguous indicator of success, at least in the short term. To measure success in the voluntary sector is a much more complex process, as we shall see in Chapter 14.

So the first step in marketing planning must be to identify and articulate the mission of an organisation. Is it appropriate and realistic? Does everyone in the organisation subscribe to it (what is known as goal congruency), or are there differences that need to be resolved?

Where are we now?

Having decided on the mission, the next question determines what stage the organisation has reached. The answer to this question requires research and analysis. Where information is not available, informed estimates must be made. One of the advantages of planning is that it forces us to make our assumptions explicit. There are four areas to look at: internal capabilities and external opportunities, competition and business analysis (taking a strategic view of customers and markets).

Internal capabilities and external opportunities

Planners have evolved structured ways of looking at the current situation of an organisation. One of the simplest and most effective of these is called SWOT (strengths, weaknesses, opportunities and threats) analysis. We have looked at this form of analysis in Chapter 2 in connection with the marketing environment. Revisiting the concept allows us to hone its use in a way that maximises its relevance to planning.

Strengths and weaknesses tend to be internal, and to do with the past or the present. Opportunities and threats tend to be outside the organisation, and to do with the future. When naming strengths and weaknesses it is essential to assume the perspective of the customer. It may be that the organisation sees efficiency of manufacturing process as one of its strengths. Unless this efficiency is passed on to consumers as superior product quality or lower prices it is unlikely to be of any relevance. Researching customer needs is dealt with at length in Chapter 3 on marketing research. It is important to check the relevance of the organisation's offerings to its customers on a regular basis. Usage and attitude surveys, or brand standing research, can help elucidate the true strengths and weaknesses of an organisation.

Often it may appear that the same aspect of an organisation may be both a strength and a weakness depending on how you look at it. This is not a very helpful finding in practical planning and signals the need for further analysis. Breaking down the aspect into its component parts will usually reveal a more useful pattern in this case. It helps to be as specific as possible. Another aspect of effective SWOT analysis is to prioritise. Ranking entries under each heading into an order of importance throws up the key issues facing an organisation. This can then feed into the formation of appropriate objectives.

Opportunities and threats: STEP factor analysis

Looking at opportunities and threats brings us to another useful check-list for analysis of the environment outside the organisation. This is called STEP factor analysis. It is discussed at length in Chapter 2 describing the socio-cultural, technological, economic and political environments in which an organisation's activities take place. As with SWOT analysis, the framework has to be used intelligently to avoid confusion about what is relevant. Prioritising aspects of the external environment helps reveal the main opportunities and threats facing the organisation.

Competitive analysis

A more customised vision of an organisation's external environment can be gleaned from scrutinising the competition it faces. Here we are still looking outside the organisation, but at the more immediate environment in which it operates. Michael Porter, whose ideas on generic strategy we have briefly reviewed earlier in this chapter, has contributed a useful model for this purpose, known as the 5 forces model. (See Figure 12.3.)

Porter's approach concentrates not only on the immediate rivalry among existing firms in the market-place, but recognises four further competitive pressures. These are:

▶ The threat of new entrants to the market who may change the rules of competition.
▶ The power of suppliers.
▶ The power of buyers.
▶ The threat of substitutes.

The model can be illustrated by looking at the UK retailing environment in the 1990s. Chapter 9 introduced the concept of multiple grocers – chains like Tesco and Sainsbury's who are locked in a fierce battle for share of the grocery market. This is the industry rivalry part of the model. The power of suppliers, the manufacturers of branded goods, appears to be on the wane. The power of buyers, consumers like ourselves, is also limited due to our lack of organisation (although groups of consumers can unite on issues such as the Greenpeace-sponsored boycott of Norwegian seafood over whaling issues in 1993). The threat of substitutes (other types of grocery shopping or even growing or hunting one's own food) has been minimised by the major multiples' careful market segmentation and positioning. They are aiming at the motorised customer, to whom time and convenience is as important as value for money.

There is, however, the threat of new entrants who may change the rules of engagement by introducing new formats for shopping. A successful recent

figure 12.3
Porter's '5-forces' model

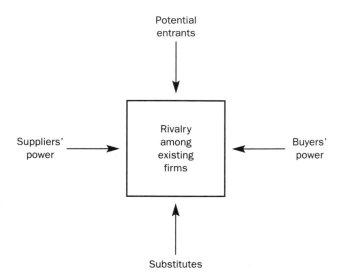

format in the United States is the warehouse club – like a cutprice cash and carry for consumers. The opening of the first branch of the US warehouse club CostCo in Thurrock in 1993 was resisted bitterly through the courts by a number of large retailers. In the event the format has not taken off in the UK in the same way as it has in America. British customers are more cautious, and are not prepared to buy in the bulk sizes the clubs need to trade through to maintain volume.

Competitive analysis helps firms understand their position relative to customers and suppliers, encouraging them to apply the full range of marketing tools to develop sustainable advantage. Distribution, for example, becomes as important as promotion in this kind of competitive framework, even though traditional marketing thinking has tended to underrate its importance.

Business analysis

As well as scrutinising its internal characteristics, and external settings (both wide-angle through STEP and narrow focus through competitive analysis), an organisation needs to examine its business activities itself. Portfolio models are useful here. We have already discussed the role of the Boston Consulting Group's portfolio model in Chapter 6, in relation to a firm's management of its product range. The model can also be applied to other aspects of its operations – groups of products, factories, divisions, international markets. All of these can be termed strategic business units (SBUs) and be subjected to classification as stars, cash cows, problem children and dogs. Recognising their position relative to one another in terms of their contribution to cash flow (or its equivalent in a non-profit organisation) can help decide appropriate strategies to maximise their value to the organisation as a whole.

Another useful matrix is the General Electric Business Planning Grid, from the same remarkable company that brought us management by objectives and the PIMS database (see Figure 12.4). This aims to refine on the rather crude information inputs of the BCG (the brute measures of rate of market growth and relative market share). In their place it puts composite measures requiring a degree of judgement on the part of the planner. One axis plots market attractiveness and the other plots competitive business strength. Part of the challenge of using this matrix sensibly is to identify what, in a firm's sphere of operations, constitutes market attractiveness. Common features are size, rate of growth, number of competitors, susceptibility to change or regulation, and so on. Some of these will be more important than others depending on the markets concerned. Similarly, the attributes required for competitive business strength will vary from industry to industry. What the model lacks in simplicity is made up for in the way it forces plannners to quantify and test their assumptions.

The resulting matrix divides into nine sectors. SBUs falling into those occupying the top left-hand three merit investment, those in the middle are less of a priority, those in the lower right-hand three need to be looked at with a view to halting their drain on company resources.

While planning frameworks in general, and portfolio models in particular, are useful tools, their use needs to be tempered with caution. A brief summary of the strengths and weaknesses of such tools is as follows.

Strengths

▶ Check-lists mean that nothing gets left out.

▶ Frameworks help the organisation look at itself dispassionately, and take the customer viewpoint.

▶ Models facilitate shared information and test assumptions.

▶ Models access accumulated experience from a wide range of industries.

Weaknesses

▶ Accurate information is difficult to establish and input satisfactorily.

▶ Models may be based on inappropriate experience (eg service industries are under-represented and growth markets are no longer the norm).

▶ Misdiagnosing the position of an SBU on a matrix may lead to costly mistakes.

▶ Implementing recommendations to divest or harvest an SBU can have dire social consequences in job losses and factory closures.

Where do we want to go?

The various forms of analysis covered should identify some key issues about the way an organisation is going. In turn this should facilitate the formation of some definite objectives, to steer the enterprise to where it wants to go. In order to be useful objectives need to be SMART:

▶ *Specific*: raising sales by ten per cent is better than raising sales. And raising sales in a particular section of the market (for example through cash and carries or through multiple grocers) helps focus effort effectively.

▶ *Measurable*: the outcomes being sought by the objective need to be quantifiable. If the effect of marketing effort is not measurable in some way it is impossible to learn from experience and to control the implementation of a strategy. Measures of success need to be considered at the same time as the objectives are set.

▶ *Achievable*: there is no point in setting an objective if it cannot be achieved. Careful analysis of all the factors that might contribute to the achievement of an objective, weighed against all the factors working against it, can help to flush out objectives whose time has not yet come.

▶ *Relevant*: the objective needs to be related to the issues identified in the situational analysis. The fewer objectives there are, the more chance there is of achieving them. Prioritising the most important ones is essential.

▶ *Time-related*: marketing takes place in the real world, and time is an inescapable factor. Marketing objectives need to take this into account, especially as speed becomes more important in establishing differential advantage. Being first into a market has traditionally carried benefits (hence the emphasis on innovation which is discussed in Chapter 7), but a time frame for the achievement of any kind of objective helps to focus the effort and resources necessary.

ACTIVITY **12.1**
• • • • • • • • • • • • • • • •

Objectionable objectives?

Consider the following objectives. How do you rate them and how might they be improved? Measure them against the SMART criteria and reword as necessary.

1 Increase brand awareness and expand market share.
2 Increase sterling sales by 10 per cent in two years.
3 Make every child a wanted child.

Forecasting

In order to render objectives more credible, planners have to be able to envisage the future. This is not the scientific discipline it sometimes appears to be. Forecasts are not judged by how accurate they are, but by how useful they are. They can help create greater cohesion among the managers of an organisation as assumptions are exposed and a common vision of the future is established. The value of the exercise is not whether things turn out exactly as expected, but whether you can anticipate major problems before they get the better of you.

There are six commonly-used methods of forecasting. They can be divided into quantitative methods and qualitative methods.

Quantitative forecasting methods

Extrapolation
This is simply taking a statistical trend and extending it into the future as if it were a line on a graph. So, if your business in the 1970s was in selling vinyl long-playing records, extrapolating the trend in the increase in sales of pre-recorded cassettes would have led you to the conclusion that LPs were on the

way out. This kind of technological substitution is often depicted by what is known as an 'S' curve (see Figure 12.5). The line is not straight, as the rate of substitution of one technology by another is gradual to begin with, accelerates, and then slows down again as the available market saturates.

Leading indicator
It may be that you can anticipate increases in sales of your product or service by watching a related product or service. The price and availability of paper, for example, is a useful leading indicator for book sales. An overall drop in share prices or a rise in interest rates is a commonly accepted leading indicator of the level of economic activity of a country, hence the prominence given to such information in news and current affairs.

Model building
This forecasting technique aims to include all the main factors that will influence an organisation's costs and sales, and assemble them in a logical way that recognises their interdependence. Even though computer power and statistical information have enabled some very complex models to be built, their sophistication should not disguise the fact that they are judgemental in the relationships they include and assume.

Qualitative methods

Scenario building
Pioneered in the 1970s by Shell, this technique assumes that it is impossible to forecast the future. Instead it presents managers with a number of alternative visions of what may happen. Confronted by possible futures, managers can break free of their conventional expectations and prepare for the unexpected. One result of the technique has been Shell's decentralisation in advance of its competitors to match an increasingly fragmented world market.

figure 12.5
'S' curve

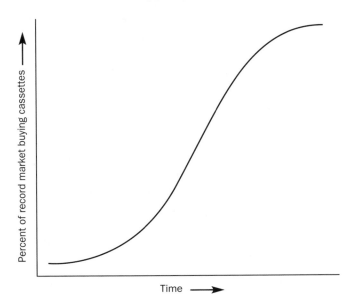

Delphi technique

Named after the oracle in ancient Greece where expert advice was always available, this technique collects forecasts individually from a panel of experts. The forecasts are then collated and replayed back to the experts, who then have another shot at a more concerted forecast. The result is a kind of consensus of what is likely to happen. The experts concerned may be sales people, managers, customers, consultants or academics.

Judgement

Probably the most important forecasting method, and one that the other methods can make better but not replace. Marketing is, after all, human activity and so a humanistic, intuitive judgement based on sound experience is central to effective forecasting.

Not all of these techniques will be feasible or relevant for all organisations. They neither eliminate the risk of business failure, nor do they guarantee success. Too heavy an emphasis on them can lead to what has been called analysis-paralysis, where the company is so busy contemplating the choices available to it that it becomes incapable of snatching the initiative. But appropriate analysis on a regular basis is a sure sign that an organisation is externally-oriented, seeking ways of providing customer satisfactions more effectively and efficiently than its competition.

How do we get there?

Functional strategy

This part of the process is all about finalising functional marketing strategy. As we have seen, this needs to support the corporate strategy articulated in the mission statement and overall direction of the company. The role of each marketing mix element in achieving the objectives needs to be assessed. Pricing strategy, as we have seen in Chapter 8, can be focused on one of four main areas: income, volume, market share and societal. Skill and experience will guide the marketing planner to the most likely strategic alternative in order to achieve the objectives in view.

Tactics

The functional strategy needs to be broken down into time-related, costed actions. Time and money are scarce resources, and a line has to be drawn between what you need (given the nature of the task) and what you can afford. Assumptions on costs and trends need to be worked into this thinking. The appropriateness of the organisation for carrying out plans successfully is a crucial issue which we will examine in greater detail later in this chapter. Executive responsibility needs to be assigned, and control and review mechanisms put into place. A useful aid here is a Gantt Chart, which maps out month by month what work is to be done and by whom (see Figure 12.6). Potential bottlenecks are clearly predicted in this simple visual format. Gantt charts are helpful psychologically. Like many other planning tools they can help share information quickly and effectively, and keep everyone's attention on the task in hand.

figure 12.6

Gantt Chart

Objective	description	Time period
1		
2		
3		
4		
5		
6		
7		
8		
9		
10		
11		
12		

JAN   FEB   MAR   APR   MAY   JUNE

Writing the marketing plan

One of the advantages of marketing planning is that it allows the organisation to agree and communicate its programme of action internally. The main instrument of this communication is a written marketing plan. The precise format of the plan will vary from one organisation to another, but it will usually cover a year's activity, and represent the finalisation of longer-range plans (usually three-year and five-year plans, which can take full account of the environmental trends brought to light by STEP analysis). Planning becomes easier and more meaningful as a process once it is established as a continuous cycle.

The main presentation components of a written marketing plan are as follows:

1   *Executive summary*: a short synopsis of the rationale, implementation and costs of the plan designed to provide an instant overview for executives who need to know what the plan contains but do not need detail.

2   *Mission statement and business strategy*: this should provide a context for what follows in terms of the organisation's overall direction and aims.

3   *Situational analysis*: this section presents the findings of the SWOT, STEP and competitive analyses which we have reviewed earlier in the chapter. Detail of the analyses themselves is best consigned to an appendix. The main body of the report should be reserved for what is important. From this the key issues that emerge should be stated. What are the main opportunities that face the organisation, and what threats does it need to overcome to take advantage of them?

4   *Statement of marketing objectives*: these objectives should fall naturally out of the key issues identified in the situational analysis. Their number should reflect what can be realistically achieved in the planning period, so they will reflect the highest priorities of the organisation.

5   *Marketing strategy*: this statement of functional strategy should relate the role of each element of the marketing mix to the achievement of the objectives.

6   *Marketing tactics*: detailed plans with timings, costs, and responsibilities. This is likely to be the bulkiest part of the plan itself, following on from the strategies to their implementation over the course of the planned period of activity.

7   *Controls and evaluation*: the plan should make it clear what measurements are implicit in its objectives. It should specify how and when these measurements are to be applied to evaluate the success of the plan in its various stages, and the mechanisms for corrective action as necessary. This aspect of marketing planning is dealt with in greater detail later in the chapter.

Marketing organisation

An organisation is a collection of individuals and resources who are united in the conscious pursuit of a common purpose. Concepts like planning and strategy are part of our conception of organisation, as they provide and articulate the unifying purpose that binds the organisation together. How effectively and appropriately the organisation is structured will therefore determine its success in achieving its purpose.

There are a number of ways of organising for marketing in a company. In Chapter 11 we looked at several options for organising a salesforce, a promotional decision that has much in common with human resources management. The conclusion reached there, that there is no one blueprint for a successful sales operation, can be transferred to marketing organisation as a whole. It is necessary to understand the strengths and weaknesses of a number of alternatives to cope with a changing customer environment.

Some Japanese companies have dispensed with marketing departments altogether. Their very literal interpretation of marketing is that it is everybody's business, so it should not be hived off into a separate management function. However, even though they may not have the M-word in their job title, senior executives in such organisations will have responsibilities for determining customer needs and wants and integrating the organisation's efforts towards satisfying them.

Marketing organisation will be a function of the overall organisational culture prevailing in an enterprise. Centralised cultures work by what is known as top down management. Policy and aims are decided by top management and handed down to the organisation itself to be implemented. Decentralised cultures, on the other hand, work by a bottom up management policy whereby major decisions are delegated to active managers themselves. Both approaches have their advantages. With a centralised approach lines of communication are clear and marketing plans are readily implemented. It works well in a packaged goods environment, where quality can be built into the product at the manufacturing end of the chain. Decentralisation facilitates innovation and flexibility, but can create confusion in marketing policy and blur accountability. It works well in a service environment, where autonomy at the point of delivery to the customer can make all the difference to repeat business.

The issues are most clearly observable in international marketing. Choosing whether to standardise a company's offerings throughout its markets (symptomatic with centralised management) or adapt them to individual market conditions (a decentralised management ploy) is an ongoing dilemma for many organisations. Some highly effective international marketing companies manage to derive the best from both worlds, with structures that combine centralised corporate strategy with delegated marketing strategy.

CASE STUDY **12.4**

Hair today...

In the late 1980s Sunsilk diagnosed a problem in its Saudi Arabian market. Research revealed product formulation and value for money as positive attributes, but imagery and packaging needed updating to restore the brand to its positioning as the first choice for beautiful hair. Both local management and centralised Unilever strategists guided its relaunch.

Local management's input included the choice of new variants available (including yogurt, a reflection of the exotic hair care tastes of the target market) and the packaging initiative of adorning the revamped labels with illustrations of women with beautiful hair of the type appropriate for each variant.

Central strategy input included the adoption of a flip-top closure (a universally popular alternative to screw-tops) and an advertising format that portrayed a reference figure coming to the aid of a woman worried about a hair care problem. The formula had worked well in North America. There the television treatment featured a well-known hair stylist working on a Baywatch-style film-shoot. One of the bikini-clad beauties is close to tears as her hair goes to pieces. He takes her aside, presses a bottle of Sunsilk on her, and soon the scene is re-shot to everyone's joy and satisfaction.

Bikini-clad beauties were unacceptable as subject matter in an Islamic country, as was the idea of a male reference figure advising on hair care. So while local management accepted the centralised advertising approach, the execution was adopted to a Saudi Arabian scenario. Out went the beach shoot. Instead the situation was an engagement party for a beautiful young woman. She too was close to tears, afraid to show herself because her hair looked a mess. The reference figure became her prospective mother-in-law (a figure of some authority in Saudi Arabian culture), whose recommendation of Sunsilk turns anxiety into exhilaration as the young woman greets her fiancé.

Questions

1 Local and central decision-making worked together well in this relaunch. Are there any types of decision that should only ever be local and only ever central?
2 What kind of assumptions might you have to challenge in transferring a television campaign from one international market to another?
3 Changes such as packaging design are not always welcome in local markets. How, as a central strategist, might you 'sell' the idea of change to a local manager?

Major alternatives for organising the marketing function

If marketing management is to fulfil its role of co-ordinating and integrating an organisation's customer orientation, it needs to work closely with other departments. It is essential that marketing makes itself felt throughout an organisation.

Marketing-oriented companies can be identified by the presence of people with marketing experience at the highest levels of management, as well as by the lines of communication between marketing and other departments. Less genuinely marketing-oriented firms may well have marketing departments, but will limit their role to one of strictly functional responsibility for promotion and selling. Whatever a company's commitment to marketing, however, its marketers have the job of internal marketing as well as dealing with external customers. In other words, marketing departments need to establish the customer's place at the heart of the organisation through training and development, clear communication, reliable systems and explicit professionalism.

As for the marketing department itself, there are three major organisational influences: by function, by products and by customer.

Organising by function

Functional organisation divides the marketing task into its separate constituents – advertising, research, market intelligence, market forecasting and so on. Executives responsible for each function report to marketing management. The structure is straightforward and clear, and suits the need of organisations with a unified product line and a centralised culture. Business to business marketers often find it an appropriate structure because they tend to specialise in one type of product or service, and the boundaries of their markets are clearly defined. (See Figure 12.7.)

figure 12.7
**Functional
organisation**

Organising by product

Fast-moving consumer goods (FMCG) companies often have a number of different products or groups of products in their overall portfolio. This diversity encourages them to make product rather than function the unit of organisation, as the circumstances faced by one set of products may be quite different from those faced by another group in the same company (see Figure 12.8). Product-based organisation has the disadvantage of proliferating numbers in marketing departments. The 1990s have seen much painful delayering of organisations as businesses have slimmed in order to retain their profitability in recession. Product-based marketing departments have seen some casualties as a result. But, for all its expense, this kind of organisation permits a great deal of flexibility in responding to the particular demands of different product markets.

The brand manager

Product-based organisation has been responsible for the creation of the classic marketing role of the brand manager. The brand manager is usually someone

figure 12.8
Product-based organisation

relatively young in the organisation whose responsibility is to look after the brand as if it were their own business. As the personal advocate of the brand within the organisation they are responsible for making things happen in the process of maintaining and improving long-term profitability. There are few more testing forcing-grounds for business talent, as the brand manager has to have a finger in every pie in the organisation.

Brand management is not without its critics, however. There follows a brief account of its good and bad points.

Good points

▶ Provides the brand with a personal advocate inside the company.
▶ Developmental role for future senior management.
▶ Regular turnover of brand managers provides a stream of fresh ideas and energy.

Bad points

▶ Expensive and labour intensive.
▶ Brand managers have a great deal of responsibility but less authority than more senior staff.
▶ Short-term involvement by brand managers (who may only spend two years on the brand before moving on) can be detrimental to the long-term health of the brand.

> **DID YOU KNOW?**
> *The brand manager first appeared on the organisational horizon in 1927 when Camay, then a fledgling soap brand, was not performing satisfactorily for Procter and Gamble. A young man called Neil H. McElroy was given the task of looking after it. Under his tutelage Camay prospered and so did McElroy – he eventually became president of the company. Brand management proved so effective that it spread to other P&G brands, and soon other fmcg companies were imitating it. Some 85 per cent of consumer goods companies now use brand managers in their organisation. (Dibb et al., 1991)*

The value of products and services is vested in their brand personalities. For all the debate about brand management, it has the enduring appeal of being an appropriately personal way of managing these valuable assets.

Organisation by market

Firms whose businesses are concentrated in a number of different markets, geographical regions or customer types will organise themselves accordingly (see Figure 12.9). Dividing a marketing department between consumer and industrial markets, for example, is an intelligent response to the different kinds of channels, product sizes and pricing decisions involved in each. This is especially the case in different national markets, where a considerable portion of marketing time is occupied by the management and recruitment of intermediaries unique to each market. It is also becoming more important to organise by customer type in response to the growth of retailer power discussed in Chapter 9. Companies operating in the packaged grocery sector need to pay special attention to servicing the demands of these powerful customers. This requires allocating marketing and sales executives dedicated to servicing their needs, as in the sales force structure outlined in Chapter 11.

figure 12.9
Market-based organisation

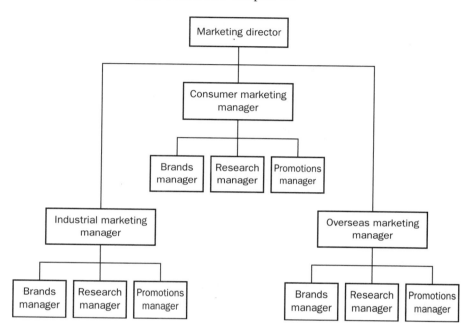

CASE STUDY **12.5**

Shuttle shuffle

Eurotunnel's marketing organisation has been through a number of incarnations. In October 1994, as the launch of Le Shuttle approached, the single post of sales and marketing director was split into two, one either side of the channel. Neil Cooper (UK operations director) moved from London to Folkestone as UK sales and marketing director. His continental counterpart was Jean Paul Courant, previously sales and marketing director for the entire group. His new role was based in Calais.

The Folkestone HQ had managers responsible for customer services, passenger sales and general marketing. Calais was organised on geographical rather than functional lines, with managers for France, Germany, Holland and Belgium. Two pan-European functions survived the restructuring. One combined research and brand marketing, the other competition and pricing. Overseeing both sides of the channel was commercial director Christopher Garnett (brother of politician Virginia Bottomley). He explained the new structure ensured that 'all activity is focused on meeting early targets from each of the key markets'. The restructuring was announced a week after the disastrous press launch of the Eurostar train in October 1994, when hundreds of increasingly sceptical journalists were held up for over an hour because of technical problems with the new train.

Christopher Garnett had joined Eurotunnel from the ferry company Sealink in 1991. His strategy for the tunnel emphasised speed and convenience. Research revealed that UK customers had concerns about claustrophobia, terrorism and rabies. So Garnett's UK launch advertising featured lovable cartoon characters to lighten the tone. By contrast the French campaign featured the likes of Napoleon and Winston Churchill giving the tunnel their approval in a celebration of Gallic engineering.

Six months after the restructuring Christopher Garnett, known for his infectious optimism, had left the company. His departure was part of a second shake up after a year of problems with delays in equipment and safety approvals. Sir Alastair Morton, Eurotunnel's outspoken co-chairman, acknowledged a long-term debt of £7 billion on the project and named 1995 as the 'make or break' year for the tunnel.

The new order saw the roles of finance director and chief operating officer rise to greater prominence. The jokey cartoon ads gave way to a more sober approach. Neil Cooper was replaced in the UK by separate marketing and sales directors, both internal appointments. The marketing director came from Le Shuttle Holidays, and her sales counterpart moved up from UK sales manager. The continental organisation remained in place. With 70 per cent of traffic coming from the UK, uniting the roles of sales and marketing in one post had proved impractical. However, external observers suspected the moves reflected a lack of confidence. Ian Wild, a transport analyst with BZW, commented: 'You could look at the bright side and say Eurotunnel is an evolving company. Its objectives are changing rapidly and so you should expect restructuring. But one would have hoped that those responsible for the launch of the service were competent enough to run with it once it's off the ground.'

Questions

1 Do service industries such as travel have different organisational requirements from manufacturing industries?

2 How useful do you think a managerial background with a ferry company would be for a senior manager in Eurotunnel?

3 Comment on the public relations threats and opportunities presented by restructuring an organisation. How might they be managed to its advantage?

Sources: Batchelor, 1994, 1995; Lane Fox,1994; Teather, 1995.

Matrix organisation

Function, product and market influences often feature together in the make-up of a pragmatic, adaptive marketing structure. A company that organises mainly according to function could have a further grouping within it dedicated to product innovation, drawing its membership from various functions. This would be a combination of product and function organisation. Similarly, most fmcg companies, while organising their marketing departments on product group lines, will organise their sales departments on customer types. This kind of multi-stranded organisation is known as matrix organisation. Its advantages are that it allows flexibility and innovation. Its disadvantages are that lines of responsibility are not always clear, creating conflict and inefficiency. However, compared to the tall hierarchies of the traditional centralised organisation (where layers of management report up functional lines to senior decision-makers) it can be less expensive and more responsive to customer demands.

Marketing control

There is many a slip between cup and lip, according to the proverb. Part of the marketing function is to monitor the successful implementation of marketing plans, and to take corrective action if necessary.

Monthly checks: sales by period

The most obvious way of doing this is to assess performance against objectives on a regular basis. Most manufacturing companies divide their year into sales periods of four weeks each (making a thirteen-period year). Meetings between sales planning and marketing at the end of each period provide a means of updating planned sales with actual sales. Price moves by competitors, promotional activity, unforeseen price increases, even factors like the weather, can all affect demand and therefore the level of stocks in distribution channels. Production planning needs to be tailored to how things are going – making more if sales are exceeding expectation, and cutting back if the reverse is true in order to save on inventory costs. The need for remedial action may be clear – whether a burst of promotion activity brought forward to support a drooping brand, or the delaying of a price increase to make the product better value.

The 'Z' chart

A very useful format for graphing the periodic sales progress of a brand in a way that focuses on long-term trends rather than short-term blips or seasonal distortion is the 'Z' chart (see Figure 12.10). This involves the plotting of three lines (or 'curves' as they are known). When the chart is complete, after a year of observation, the three lines are joined in a way that resembles a 'Z', hence the name. The lines are as follows:

▶ *Moving annual total*: calculated by adding the current sales period's total sales to those of the periods for the last 12 months. This reveals long-term trends in the brand's performance very well.
▶ *Periodic sales*: sales for each period are graphed on a monthly basis. This helps diagnose seasonality and other short term peaks and troughs.
▶ *Cumulative periodic sales*: this curve moves diagonally up the chart from left to right, connecting the parallel lines of the 'Z'. Compared to the target curve this can be a very revealing indicator.

figure 12.10
'Z' chart

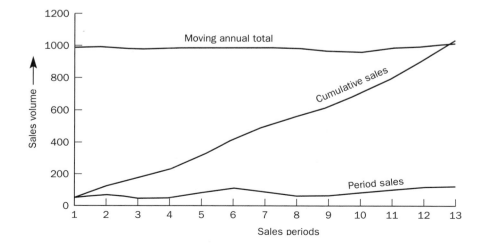

A picture of success?

Using the following periodic sales data, draw a 'Z' chart for year 3 and comment on the overall trends it reveals:

Sales period	Sales (tonnes) by four-week period:		
	Year 1	Year 2	Year 3
1	1,200	1,210	1,200
2	1,210	1,210	1,200
3	1,300	1,250	1,200
4	1,200	1,200	1,000
5	1,100	1,100	900
6	1,000	1,010	1,000
7	1,000	900	900
8	850	900	850
9	900	850	850
10	1,000	850	950
11	1,300	1,200	1,100
12	1,250	1,200	1,150
13	1,100	1,000	1,000

Retail audit

Another regular source of control feedback for FMCG companies is the retail audit. This is a service provided by a specialist research company who sends its researchers into a sample of retail outlets in order to gauge the sales rate of the products in a particular market. Subscribers to the service are given regular presentations updating them on the position of their brands relative to the competition, and even the levels of availability of their brands to shoppers by outlet. This information can be used to diagnose distribution problems in time to put them right.

Annual checks: brand review

On a less frequent basis, the brand review (already discussed in Chapter 10) provides an opportunity for the marketing department to assess the health of its brand from a number of longer-term indicators such as annual market share, sales, profitability, promotional activity and qualitative research. This can assist the formulation of action plans to put the brand back on its strategic track.

Each of these control activities can be flowcharted to reveal common stages. Performance standards have to be set in order to gauge whether or not they are being achieved (hence the importance of careful objective setting). Information systems have to be sensitive and timely in order to show up variances from plan. Diagnosis has to be accurate – it can be counterproductive to cure the wrong ill. And responsibility for the improvement needs to be clearly delineated and followed up. (See Figure 12.11.)

figure 12.11
Control process loop

Marketing audits

Marketing as a function in the 1980s got a reputation in some quarters for extravagance, especially in the booming years of promotional expenditure in the early part of the decade. Nevertheless, it is as subject to external or internal audit as any other business process. An audit is a systematic and rigorous examination of systems and their effectiveness. Because the marketing environment is ever changing, external marketing audits carried out by independent consultants are good practice every three to five years to reassess the relevance of the organisation and its procedures.

In an effective marketing organisation a less formal kind of audit should be an ongoing part of the general orientation towards planning and organising with the customer in mind. It will contribute to the kind of situational analysis we have discussed as fundamental to the marketing planning process, particularly in terms of a relevant SWOT analysis.

Summary
....

This chapter has looked at some of the main strategies used by marketing companies to achieve their objectives, placing marketing planning in the context of organisational activity.

Key concepts
....

Centralised/decentralised organisation: alternative management styles where decisions are taken by top management (centralised) or delegated to those responsible for implementation (decentralised).

Cost leadership: strategic use of economies of scale to undercut competition on price.

Delphi technique: forecasting method involving a panel of expert opinion.

Differentiation: generic strategy that concentrates on non-price factors.

Extrapolation: predicting the future by assuming that past trends will continue.

Flanking: strategy that avoids head-on confrontation to concentrate on an undefended section of a competitor's business.

Focus: generic strategy that aims at a particular niche market.

Leading indicator: a trend in one area of the economy that can be used to predict changes in another.

Marketing audit: an objective check on the systems and activities of a marketing operation.

Matrix organisation: an organisation that is structured on two or more principles (eg by function, product, market).

Mission statement: a verbal distillation of an organisation's corporate strategy.

PIMS: Profit Impact of Marketing Strategy, a long-running research project that aims to relate profitability to a number of alternative marketing strategies.

S curve: graphed line representing change that starts slowly, accelerates and slows down again.

Scenario building: forecasting technique that presents a number of radically alternative visions of the future.

Strategic Business Unit (SBU): a component of an organisation's business structure.

Strategy: the principles on which activity is founded.

Tactics: the day-to-day activities resulting from strategy.

'Z' chart: a graph representing sales as moving annual total, periodic actual and cumulative.

SELF-CHECK QUESTIONS

1   Corporate strategy is:
   a   Decided by functional marketing strategy.
   b   Reactive to short-term competitive activity.
   c   The framework for functional marketing strategy.
   d   The implementation of plans to achieve long-term aims.
   e   More specific and practical than marketing strategy.

2   Which of the following statements are not true of market challengers?
   a   They often direct their competitive activity at smaller firms.
   b   They tend to use penetration as a way of expanding their existing business without excessive risk to market share.
   c   They carry out flanking activity.
   d   They have a vested interest in the status quo.
   e   Their success suggests that high profitability is a consequence of either very high or very low market share.

3   PIMS stands for:
   a   Profit Isolation from Market Saturation.
   b   Product Impact of Marketing Solutions.
   c   Profit Impact of Marketing Strategy.

    d Projected Implications for Marketing Science.

    e Positional Intelligence in Motivational Situations.

4 Which of the following forecasting techniques are quantitative rather than qualitative?

    a Scenario building.

    b Model building.

    c Extrapolation.

    d Leading indicator.

    e Delphi technique.

5 Put the following elements of a marketing plan into the order you would expect to find them in the written document:

    a Tactics.

    b Situational analysis.

    c Controls and evaluation.

    d Strategy.

    e Statement of objectives.

Which of the following statements are true and which are false?

6 The overall organisational culture prevailing in an enterprise will be a function of its marketing organisation.

7 Top down management has the advantage of allowing important decisions to be delegated to those who will implement them.

8 Departments structured on a functional basis can often work well in business-to-business marketing.

9 Brand management gives a lot of power but relatively little responsibility to comparatively junior managers.

10 Retail audit services can expose weaknesses in distribution.

Discuss the following

11 To fail to plan is to plan to fail.

12 The key to differential advantage lies in product quality.

13 How can small companies defend themselves against aggression from larger rivals? Illustrate your answer with examples.

14 Forecasting is all about persuading other people of your vision of the future.

15 The brand manager is an endangered species, not worth preserving.

Further study
· · · · · · · · · · · · · · · ·

Books

Ansoff, H. I. (1961) *Corporate Strategy*, Penguin Books.

The man who put business strategy on the academic agenda in the 1950s – and still highly relevant.

McDonald, M. (1988) *Marketing Plans: How to prepare them how to use them*, Heinemann.

Professor McDonald, a marketing director of Canada Dry before he entered academia, has established himself as the doyen of British marketing planning.

Ohmae, K. (1985) *The Mind of a Strategist*, Penguin.

Valuable cross-cultural view of strategic thinking.

Porter, M.E. (1980) *Competitive Strategy: Techniques for Analyzing Industries and Competitors*, Free Press.

A densely argued, enormously influential book which set the business agenda for a decade.

Sun Tzu (1994) *The Art of War*, Wordsworth Classics.

An ancient oriental treatise on warfare which Professor John Saunders uses instructively in his article 'Marketing and competitive success', in Baker, M. J. (Ed) (1987) *The Marketing Book*, Heinemann, pp. 10–28.

References

Batchelor, Charles (1994) 'Softly softly approach – The French enlisted history-makers to market the Channel Tunnel, but UK advertising has had to be coaxing and humorous', in *Financial Times*, 10 February, p. 18.

Batchelor, Charles (1995) 'Commercial Director leaves Eurotunnel after shake-up', in *Financial Times*, 7 March, p. 20.

Buzzell, R. D. and Gale, B. T. (1987) *The PIMS Principles: Linking Strategy to Performance*, Free Press.

Dibb, S., Simkin, L., Pride, W. M. and Ferrell, O. C. (1991) *Marketing: Concepts and Strategies*, European edition, Houghton and Mifflin.

Kotler, P. (1988) *Marketing Management: Analysis, Planning, Implementation and Control*, 6th edition, Prentice Hall.

Kotler, P. and Armstrong, G. (1994) *Principles of Marketing*, 6th Edition, Prentice Hall International.

Lane Fox, Harriet (1994) 'New marketer for Eurotunnel', in *Marketing*, 27 October, p. 7.

Lawder, P. and Sholl, S (1995) 'A consumer-built path to better brands', in *Journal of Brand Management*, (2) 6, June, 356–64.

Teather, David (1995) 'Eurotunnel hits confidence low', in *Marketing*, 23 March, p. 1.

CHAPTER 13

International marketing

Objectives

When you have read this chapter you will be able to:

▶ Explain the major operational and theoretical differences between domestic marketing and international marketing.

▶ Assess the opportunities offered by the international marketing environment.

▶ Justify the selection of international markets and recommend appropriate entry decisions.

▶ Analyse product, price, promotion and distribution strategies in an international context.

▶ Apply basic marketing planning techniques to international business.

Introduction

Almost one-third of all industrial investment is aimed at markets overseas (Gilligan and Hird, 1989). Some businesses, such as electronics and cars, are international by nature. The high stakes involved in their research and development programmes necessitate international markets. There simply are not enough domestic consumers in any one country to make the game worthwhile. Other industries, which have started off on a purely domestic footing, have had to seek customers elsewhere in the world for a variety of reasons. Certainly the trend is towards more and more marketing taking place on an international footing, which has led to a growing interest in the whole area of international marketing theory and practice.

International marketing takes place across national boundaries. It embraces the activities of a range of companies from exporters (who remain based in one country) to transnationals or multinational companies (MNCs) whose operations and management span the world. A truly international company will display the following characteristics:

▶ Product planning, manufacturing and research and development in several countries.

▶ A wide distribution of sales volume throughout a number of markets.

▶ A mix of nationalities at senior management level.

International marketing involves risks and uncertainties that are many times greater than those facing a company operating in only one national market. There are a number of reasons why companies are prepared to overcome these difficulties and extend their marketing activities. Among the most common are the following:

▶ Adverse economic conditions at home prompt the search for new markets abroad. The fine-arts sector in Eire targets Europe and North America rather than the tiny domestic art market, encouraged by marketing schemes sponsored by the An Chomhairle Ealaion (Arts Council of Ireland).

▶ A product's life-cycle needs extension (see Chapter 6). The Volkswagen Beetle ceased production in Europe in the early 1980s. It has now been reincarnated in South America as the 'Fusca', produced in Brazil and Mexico. It is one of the most popular cars in a market more interested in reliability than comfort.

▶ The avoidance of domestic competition. UK confectionery giant Rowntree faced a highly competitive but stagnant domestic market in the 1980s. This led it to attempt to buy a presence in the United States of America through acquiring several American businesses outright. In the event it failed to make the breakthrough for which it was looking, and had sold the businesses again by the end of the decade.

▶ The search for economies of scale. To reap the full benefits of investment in manufacturing plant, companies may be spurred to expand into markets that might otherwise have gone unconsidered. Cadbury's Wispa, which involved the commissioning of a £12 million plant in the early 1980s, needed to think in terms of European markets from the outset.

▶ The need to get rid of excess stocks. International marketing's equivalent of clearance pricing (see Chapter 7) is an activity called dumping. Excess stock of a particular product is cleared on to another country's market at very low prices in order to liquidate capital. There is no long-term ambition to enter the market – it is just a hit and run exercise. Countries try to protect their domestic marketers from this destabilising phenomenon with legislation.

▶ Historical accident. Being in the right place at the right time is often cited as the reason behind one of the most successful international brands of all time – Coca Cola. US forces took the drink with them wherever they went in World War Two. An aggressive distribution policy on the part of the brand itself guaranteed that the footholds thus created would be exploited. As a result, Coke's red and white livery is one of the most immediately recognisable marketing devices anywhere in the world.

Whatever motivates a company to market its goods internationally, the differences between such marketing and domestic activity need to be understood and planned for. Figure 13.1 summarises some of the main points of divergence between international and domestic marketing.

As we shall see in the material that follows, international marketing is even more difficult to get right than domestic marketing for the following reasons:

▶ It places greater stress on environmental analysis.
▶ It makes more searching demands on a company's planning and control systems.
▶ It requires a more extensive repertoire of marketing and business skills (languages, treasury, law, etc.).

figure 13.1
Domestic vs. International marketing

Domestic marketing	International marketing
• Main language	• Many languages
• Dominant culture	• Multi-culture
• Research relatively straightforward	• Research complex
• Relatively stable environment	• Frequently unstable environment
• Single currency	• Exchange rate problems
• Business conventions understood	• Conventions diverse and unclear

▶ It presents a greater diversity of manufacturing decisions (eg location of factories).

▶ It demands higher risks in terms of investment and market entry.

▶ It creates particular problems for debt-collection and payment methods

▶ It offers less accumulated marketing experience and wisdom on which to draw.

DID YOU KNOW?

The simplest things can land you in the soup in international marketing. Campbell's Soup, a market leader in North America, lost $30 million in Britain because UK consumers could not understand why the cans were so small and dismissed them as poor value. On its abortive 1960s launch, the company failed to get the message across that the soup was concentrated and required dilution with water.

The international environment

As we have seen in Chapter 2, marketing responds to a number of variables in the external environment: socio-cultural, technological, economic and political. These variables present threats and opportunities to the firm, which need to be recognised and assessed. Because of the complexity and unfamiliarity of the international environment, successful international marketing requires vigilant attention to environmental factors. The process of scrutinising the business environment on a systematic basis is known as environmental scanning. Some of the most important issues for international marketers to consider are as follows.

Socio-cultural factors

Culture is a set of learned behaviours that unite a group of people, often along national lines. Language, education, religion, lifestyle, taboos, norms and values are some of the areas that culture embraces. Culture affects not only the way people define their wants and needs through consumption, it also influences the way they work and do business together. Clearly, for firms who are serious about international marketing, cultural sensitivity is paramount.

Coming to terms with it involves change. Dietary norms in certain countries mean that food products often have to be reformulated for export markets to avoid forbidden ingredients such as pork derivatives. Such adaptation is relatively straightforward compared to the kind of difficulty people from different cultures can find in working together. English managers tend to be pragmatic and informal. French managers, on the other hand, are trained to be far more analytical in the way they approach problems, and are expected to justify their solutions with argument and evidence. While both approaches work well in isolation, they can lead to misunderstanding and antagonism when combined. Mughan (1993) suggests that companies adapt best to cultural difference by:

▶ *Self-analysis*: recognising the situation from the customer's point of view and adapting behaviour accordingly.

▶ *Cultural training*: particularly for personnel working with counterparts from other countries or dealing direct with distributors or customers.

▶ *Recruitment*: the shortest route to widening the culture of an organisation is through direct recruitment in the international labour market. As we have noted, one of the characteristics of most international companies is the presence of a range of nationalities in its senior management.

Technological factors

Consumer needs and wants are bound up with technological infrastructure. The kind of fuel used for cooking, for example, will affect the type of oven, the choice of pan and utensil, even the sort of food cooked and the frequency of meals. The kind of transport used for getting to work will affect choice of garments and accessories. Instead of being the isolated events on which individual companies concentrate their marketing, consumers' choices are part of a whole pattern of consumption.

So the level of technology in a country will dictate appropriate product and service responses to consumer needs. Other aspects of marketing activity will also need to reflect this. Telephone-based market research, for example, is not much use in countries where levels of telephone ownership are low. The availability and scope of advertising media will affect the planning and execution of promotional strategies. Distribution channels are extremely sensitive to technology. It may well be that a company has to rethink its entire approach to distribution in a new geographic market because the kind of systems on which it relies in its original market are not available.

Technology is a central factor in business-to-business marketing as well as consumer marketing. Different telecommunications standards have presented substantial difficulties to marketers even within the same continent. There has been a move to harmonise this and other aspects of business technology, but progress in such attempts is only as fast as the slowest member of the group. Initiatives from the European Union have helped speed up and co-ordinate technological harmonisation, which is a potential source of significant competitive advantage for European companies trading elsewhere in the world.

Economic factors

The potential of a market is governed by the number of likely customers it contains, and their ability (and willingness) to spend. Measures such as per capita income are often available, but can conceal enormous disparities between rich and poor in some countries. Evenly distributed income makes for better marketing prospects in a number of middle-income purchases such as consumer durables. Other yardsticks for purchasing power across the population include ownership rates of durables such as motorcars, the balance between urban and rural population, and the prevailing rate of inflation. It can be useful to look at Gross National Product (GNP). This figure is particularly relevant to the potential for industrial marketing. As ever with statistics from a number of sources, there can be problems with continuity of information and difficulties in comparing like with like.

Market size can also be assessed from the existing levels of activity in the sector in question. Are there domestic producers to provide competition, and how many other firms are already exporting? A very low level of activity might suggest that the opportunity is not yet ripe. Local firms may provide competition disproportionate to the quality of their offerings because of their control of existing distribution channels.

Fluctuations in currency exchange rates can wreck the soundest international marketing strategies, but they also provide attractive short-term opportunities in markets such as tourism. Visitor traffic to Europe from North America depends not only on the cultural and recreational delights awaiting tourists, but crucially on the standing of the dollar among international currencies. In 1985 a dollar bought ten French francs, making Paris a very attractive destination. Three years later American tourists were a much rarer sight on the Champs Elysees, as their currency now bought only five francs.

On a corporate level such fluctuations can mean the difference between profit and loss. Deciding when to buy and sell in the various markets in which a multinational company is involved is a high-risk, 24-hour responsibility. The international financial environment, accelerated by the spread of near-instantaneous computer-based information systems, has never been more volatile. This is one of the key differences between international marketing and domestic activity, but as well as increasing the risks involved it can offer significant windfall profit opportunities.

Political factors

Success in international marketing contributes to the balance of trade in the domestic economy by helping a country to sell abroad more than it buys in from other countries. When this balance is positive the domestic environment for business growth is much enhanced. As a result, governments tend to intervene in international marketing by assisting their countries' industries to make sales abroad, and by placing obstacles of various kinds in the way of prospective importers.

Governments are also under pressure to assist in alleviating unemployment and stimulating economic activity. Many countries actively court foreign investment, providing tax concessions and support of various kinds to persuade international companies to site their manufacturing units in depressed areas. This is true not only for production industries but also for service economies. Eire has had considerable success in establishing itself as a location for making films, aided in no small measure by favourable exchange rates between the dollar and the Irish punt. Nevertheless, an enlightened policy offering generous tax incentives as well as a pro-active attitude to attracting film-makers, has helped Eire make the best of its largely non-industrial economic heritage.

On the other hand, political conditions can cause severe difficulties for international marketers, even to the point of having to withdraw completely from a market (as did Coca Cola from India) or write off an entire operation (as did Chrysler in post-revolutionary Iran). The reaction to potential instability is to reduce the commitment of the company's relationship to the country. It may mean, for example, withdrawing direct manufacturing facilities in favour of a safer, but less profitable, exporting strategy. Some industries, such as mineral exploitation, do not have this option by their very nature. The host government's ultimate sanction here is expropriation – the confiscation of the assets of the industry involved (with or without compensation). Instances of this have declined from the 1970s to the 1990s, but it remains a possible sanction, as Nigeria proved in the late 1980s when it confiscated the assets of a number of Western oil companies.

Less severe measures invoked by governments in order to protect their domestic industries include the following:

▶ Quotas to limit the numbers of goods allowed in.
▶ Duties like a special tax on imports (which then makes them non-competitive on price).
▶ Non-tariff barriers such as product legislation which means that expensive adaptations need to be made before the item is legally saleable in the host country.

CASE STUDY **13.1**

Doing business with the Bear

Life for entrepreneurs in the emerging market economies of Eastern Europe is rather like the Goldrush. Russia has been catapulted into the capitalist system almost overnight, providing Western marketers with unprecedented opportunities. Seemingly limitless natural resources, a large and skilled labour force, and consumers avid for Western goods spell what seems like marketing heaven. On the other hand, a thriving organised crime milieu (business executives are regular murder victims), extensive corruption, and a widespread insistence on dealing exclusively in cash act as a restraint upon foreign investors. Former Eastern Bloc countries Poland, Hungary and Czechoslovakia have stolen a march on their erstwhile communist master. Their new market economies are developing painfully fast, aided by the kind of legal and financial institutional framework and banking system that Russia lacks.

Being a consumer in Russia has its challenges. There is only a quarter of the retail floor space per shopper available in Britain, and most retailers insist that their customers queue three times: once for service, once to pay and finally to collect the item. Some companies, like the French dairy products giant Danone, have found the answer in setting up their own outlets (often within other shops) with dedicated staff and cash handling. Muscovites have developed a taste not only for McDonald's (one of the most popular restaurants in the city) but also for fresh yoghurt, a previously unheard-of delicacy. Danone is not alone in establishing its own base in a difficult retail terrain. Mars has built a $70 million chocolate and petfood factory outside Moscow, and Allied Lyons is investing half that much in an ice-cream making plant. Local production reduces a company's vulnerability to import tariffs, acts as a hedge against currency fluctuations and can provide significant economies.

Pepsi Cola was an early pioneer in the Russian market, opening production in the 1970s under a joint venture arrangement (sharing the investment with a local firm at the instigation of the then communist government). While this has given it an early foothold in the cola market, quality problems due to the vagaries of local producers have dented the brand's image. Coca Cola, who followed Pepsi into Russian production in 1993, has been able to do so more on its own terms – positioning its brand as a premium foreign product as opposed to the familiar 'Russian' Pepsi.

Foreign brands are seen as highly desirable by Russian consumers who are prepared to pay more for them. In spite of a price difference of 66 per cent over local brands of detergent, Procter and Gamble has managed to occupy 70 per cent of Moscow shelf-space (an indication of its popularity). This has been generated in no small measure by the ready availability of television advertising to foreign companies. It is something like five times cheaper to reach one per cent of your target market point (one TVR – see Chapter 11) in Russia than it is in France at 1995 prices.

Questions

1 What sources of information might companies thinking of investing in Russia use to gauge the available opportunities?

2 Local production reduces a company's liability to import tariffs. What disadvantages does it bring?

3 How sustainable is the price premium of foreign brands in Russia?

Adapted from: *The Economist*, 18 March 1995; Rubython, 1994.

International marketing research
....

As we have seen in Chapter 4, marketing research reduces risk and aids effective decisions. For the international marketer, the research task of listening to the customer in a planned and systematic way is made more difficult by the unfamiliarity of the environment in which the research is conducted.

Secondary, or desk research, uses published sources of information such as censuses, directories or reports. International organisations such as the OECD, International Monetary Fund (IMF) or European Union (EU) can provide useful statistics at a general level. However, in individual markets systematic research towards this kind of material may be in its infancy, preventing the detection of meaningful trends. In countries with a history of political instability, there may be large gaps of information. Problems of comparability of data between countries also dog the secondary research effort. How to define a particular sector and what to recognise as significant information are decisions that need to be taken carefully and applied consistently.

Primary research, where a company unearths information for the first time, is also vulnerable to special difficulties in the international context. Research methods that might be taken for granted in Western countries may prove culturally inappropriate in others. Survey methods that assume literacy and education levels, access to telephones, or even willingness to respond to questions, frequently need to be reassessed in the light of international conditions. Like advertising agencies, who are realigning themselves as transnational groupings in order to parallel their clients' promotional needs, market research agencies are facing the challenge of international market research by establishing international networks. Such research agencies can offer their clients local knowledge without losing a global perspective.

Other sources of market intelligence include national trade associations and chambers of commerce (or their equivalents). However unscientific it might appear, there is no substitute for personal visits to the targeted country to get a feeling for the customer and competitor environment. International trade shows and exhibitions are particularly useful in this respect, and are one of the most widely-used techniques of information gathering for international marketing. One of the key characteristics of marketing across national boundaries is the length of distribution channels. Intermediaries such as agents and foreign distributors can provide very valuable information. While what they offer in the way of research is anecdotal, their appreciation through experience of what is important and relevant should never be underestimated.

ACTIVITY **13.1**
··················

EU information

The EU has established over 300 'European Documentation Centres' around the UK. These centres are regularly updated with documents originating from the European Commission and Parliament. Most of them have a direct bearing on conditions for international marketers in the Single Market. Find out the location of your nearest EDC (it may even be in your university library) and visit it to familiarise yourself with its resources.

Market selection
··························

The process of selecting and targeting markets in international business is broadly the same as that described in Chapter 5. The criteria that govern what is a viable market segment discussed there are common to international market segments, but are particularly important when it comes to the areas of accessibility and actionability.

Accessibility means that customers can be reached with promotion and distribution. Market segmentation frequently identifies consumers with similar needs and aspirations across a number of national boundaries. A woman business executive living in Paris will have more in common with a working woman living in Turin than with a housewife in rural France. But reaching urban women with a promotional campaign that runs in precisely the same kind of media throughout Europe may be impossible because of differences in coverage between countries. Either the campaign execution or the limits of the segment will have to be adjusted in order to make the segment as a whole accessible.

Actionability means that the number of customers is of an order that can be dealt with by the organisation. International market segments are often attractive to firms because of the sheer number of consumers involved. This can tempt firms to enter markets on which they have no hope of making an impact, leading to their subsequent withdrawal. A common reaction to this problem for firms anxious to expand into new markets is to form alliances, either with other firms in the domestic market or with similar enterprises abroad. While seeming to turn the idea of competition on its head, this form of co-operation means that new market segments become feasible without affecting existing relationships.

Segmentation, and the targeting that follows, take place against a constantly shifting background of market dynamics. Certain areas in the world grow in attractiveness to certain marketers while others decline. Kenichi Ohmae (1985) was one of the first marketing writers to point to the domination of world markets by what he called the Triad – the three major world players of Europe, America and Japan. But the situation is capable of turbulent change. The rapidly-developing countries of the Pacific Rim (in particular Singapore, South Korea, Hong Kong and Taiwan) are going through a period of unparalleled economic growth. While income is still unevenly distributed throughout their populations, their increasing prosperity has created a market of consumers hungry for Western luxury brands to reflect their rising status. As a result names like Burberrys and Ralph Lauren feature prominently in Singapore shopping arcades, and jobs in the aerospace industry are being lost by America to Taiwan. As industrial sectors have grown in these countries, agriculture has decreased in importance. This alters the mix of goods and services required in the business market, creating opportunities in information technology and construction among other areas. Finally, the governments enriched by their nations' developing prosperity are providing Western armaments suppliers (many of them from the former Soviet Union) with rich pickings from swelling defence budgets.

As well as spotting the areas of growing demand for a particular product or service, the process of market selection needs to take into account the kind of trading environment that prevails in the segment under consideration. While liberalisation of trade, deregulation and privatisation have been world-wide trends in the 1980s, there has been a compensating response from regional trading blocks organising themselves against the depredations of economic invasion. Much of the impetus behind the establishment of the European Union, for example, has been from fear that otherwise the member countries will see their domestic industries shrivel as American or Japanese multinationals run riot. A frequent response to the establishment and growth of trading blocks is the phenomenon of insiderisation (Preston, 1993). This is when companies seeking a presence in a protected market will aim at a co-operative strategy involving joint-ventures with domestic firms, or the foundation of a subsidiary company providing jobs and tax revenues within the host economy. The UK car industry provides several examples of this pattern.

Finally, competition is an important consideration when deciding on which segments to target. Growing sectors attract entrants who can quickly crowd out competitors who have insufficiently well-defined offerings. Market selection therefore requires careful consideration of the unique advantages of the company's offering to its prospective customers.

ACTIVITY **13.2**

Environmental forces

List the main environmental forces (socio-cultural, technological, economic and politico-legal factors) that have led to the adoption of the following products by consumers in the UK in the last 30 years:

▶ Ground coffee.
▶ Bottled mineral water.
▶ Dried pasta.
▶ Luxury continental biscuits.
▶ Mexican lager.

Market entry decisions
••••••••••••••••••••••••••

Market entry is perhaps a misleading term for the way in which firms interface with their international customers. It gives the impression that such decisions are taken deliberately by companies free to choose between a number of alternatives. In fact, many companies fall into international marketing almost by accident. They find they have already made their entry into a market by the time they come to consider the best way of relating to it. Usually the nature of their relationship with their international customers will evolve with their business. It may be that, as with distribution patterns (see Chapter 9), a firm will use more than one method of accessing international business.

The various ways we shall review here range from low-risk, low-commitment indirect entry methods to high-risk, high-commitment direct entry methods, as illustrated in Figure 13.2. While some firms may move from one end of the spectrum to another as the importance of their international business develops, this is not always the case. Jumps can be made from exporting to direct manufacturing for political reasons before they make sense commercially. Nissan's establishment of a UK manufacturing base in the 1980s came at a time when the company's share of the British car market was still relatively weak. The long-term justification for the move was the advent of import restrictions connected with the coming European Single Market. Conversely, companies can move back along the spectrum from high commitment to low commitment for pragmatic reasons. The withdrawal of Coca Cola and IBM from India in the 1970s came about because of political pressure to allow host-country control of the companies rather than from commercial failure. Finally, some of the most successful international marketing operations are franchise based. In other words the level of commitment of the parent firm is focused exclusively on a low-risk strategy as part of the business system it runs at home and abroad. There is thus no room for evolution to a more committed posture.

As with all strategic choices, the higher the risk the higher the likely rate of return. The option chosen depends on the firm's willingness and ability to commit its resources, managerial, financial and operational. Naturally the firm's ambitions and size will influence how it orients itself to its target markets. Many of the kind of disciplines on distribution strategy we have observed in Chapter 9 also come into play for international market entry decisions. The kind of product or service involved, whether the firm is operating in the consumer or industrial sector, and the level and nature of competition, will all be contributory factors in choosing the best method of market entry. In most cases the most lucrative but economically binding method is to manufacture the product direct in the market concerned. This operational decision is one of the hallmarks of the truly international firm, carrying with it the advantages of

figure 13.2
**Market entry
methods**

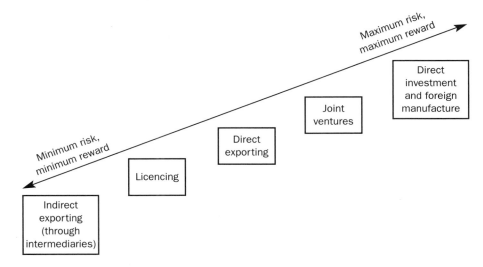

proximity to customers and a range of stakeholders which includes host-country employees. Most companies' experience of international marketing, however, starts with indirect exporting.

Indirect exporting

Exporting, whether indirectly (involving the services of other companies to sell the product in the foreign market) or directly (where the firm deals direct with its overseas customers), assumes that production takes place in the home market. Products end up in export markets through a number of routes.

The least active, on the part of the manufacturing firm, is when a buying organisation from another country sources its product for sale in the foreign market. Domestic purchasing of this sort is becoming increasingly frequent as companies try to benefit from the price differences present in various markets. Import record shops are a good example of this kind of activity happening on a small scale. The dedicated fan is prepared to pay a premium for a recording available in the US which the record label has decided not to release in Europe.

A more active posture towards the issue of exporting is to use the services of an export management company. Sometimes this is an independent organisation who will handle export arrangements for a number of clients, like a functional distribution intermediary. Like advertising agencies the management company will have several accounts competing for its attention, and the range of services and expertise offered will vary from one company to another. The kind of things likely to be offered will be purchasing, shipping, financing, and negotiation of foreign orders. The establishment of the Single European Market has led to a rise in the number of small- to medium-sized enterprises (SMEs) from Britain seeking access to mainland Europe. For them, export management companies can act as fixers, setting up contacts and accelerating their acquisition of foreign market knowledge. Alternatively, a company can set up its own subsidiary export management company, as in the case of Unilever in the UK which has a division called Unilever Export. This enables a diverse range of the company's brands to access the expertise of a central export service – creating economies of scale similar to the ones provided to their clients by independent export management companies.

As we have seen, international marketing sometimes involves unexpected alliances rather than competition between firms. Piggybacking is an example of how different companies can share resources in order to access foreign markets more effectively. What happens is that a firm with a compatible product (known as the rider) pays to get on board the distribution system already operated by a firm active in the foreign market (known as the carrier). As a result, the rider gets access to an instant network of outlets, and the carrier can add more value to its activities by offering its intermediaries a greater product range.

Licensing

Licensing is the offer of a brand name, process or trade secret in return for a royalty or fee. It is a frequent method of entry in the drinks market. Budweiser, for example, is made in the UK under licence from the US brewing giant Anheuser-Busch. Interestingly the beer has a premium positioning in the UK as a lager for trend-conscious yuppies. In America, on the other hand, it is very much a working man's beverage. While licensing offers many advantages as a low-risk and cheap method of accessing income from foreign markets, it offers little control and can create problems in the longer term. The licensee, having developed expertise with the product, can sometimes start manufacturing an alternative offering dangerous competition. Licensors (the granters of licences) therefore have to keep devising innovations that increase their licensees' dependence on them in the relationship. This drive towards innovation is clearly visible in the software market, where products such as Windows 95 have been criticised for being new for the sake of innovation rather than for any clear benefits available to existing users.

Direct exporting

Direct exporting involves the manufacturing firm itself in the task of distributing its products in the foreign market. In this respect it is treating its foreign customers as it would its domestic ones: choosing agents and distributors, and directly supporting their efforts. Expensive and time-consuming as this is, it offers greater control and profits than relying on intermediaries. There are the additional advantages of more immediate market intelligence and an enhanced experience curve. As a strategy it suits business-to-business marketing very well in the area of capital equipment such as printing presses or packaging machinery where there is a high degree of specialisation and a limited number of customers and suppliers.

DID YOU KNOW?

Coca Cola's non-US business accounts for 80 per cent of its total income. In many of its markets it is manufactured under licence. The secret recipe is still stored in a safe in Atlanta Georgia, and known only to three people. Exclusivity is guaranteed by the fact that Coca Cola supplies the syrup concentrate for the drink, with dilution, aeration and bottling taking place in the host country. Even though a large number of licensees are involved, product standardisation as 'the real thing' is assured.

Joint venturing

Joint ventures offer another example of co-operative rather than competitive operations in international marketing. A foreign company and a domestic company join forces, either by buying into each other or establishing a third jointly-owned enterprise. Complementary strengths facilitate success together which would elude each company on its own. Sometimes, as in the case of pre-glasnost Russia, a joint venture is the only way a foreign firm can gain a toe hold in the market. The resulting arrangement is often fraught with problems, as Pepsi Cola found to its discomfort with its pioneering operation in Russia. The number of joint ventures in the automotive sector in the 1990s has increased with liberalisation of trade in the former Eastern bloc, as European and US car manufacturers struggle to decrease costs and grow market share at the expense of their Japanese competitors. But even these voluntary arrangements are subject to difficulties that reveal themselves in the longer term. If the foreign partner wants to standardise aspects of its offering in line with global policy, the domestic partner may object. As a result, joint ventures tend to have limited life-cycles. They work best in sectors where there is a high degree of local adaptation rather than in industries with a monolithic approach to their markets.

Foreign manufacture

In many situations some form of manufacturing in the host country may be the only way of accessing a new market. Although many companies may therefore be forced into this posture, it has many advantages over the alternatives. There is a clear sense of commitment to the local market, and the speedy availability of parts and spares provides a crucial source of competitive advantage against other suppliers. Finally, being on the scene directly allows a company to detect changes and developments in the external environment quickly enough to be able to plan round them effectively.

CASE STUDY **13.2**

Today a garage, tomorrow the world...

Hewlett Packard, the US computer manufacturer, has deliberately adopted foreign manufacturing as a strategy from the outset. Founded in 1939 by American engineers Bill Hewlett and Dave Packard, the firm used a clapperboard garage as its original premises. But in spite of its humble origins, HP has always seen the world as its market.

Its flexible approach to production in several countries has allowed it to reap the rewards of the combination of cheap facilities and specialist skills as they become available on the international scene. Furthermore it has pioneered the concept of strategic alliances with other firms such as Canon with whom it competes in certain markets, but co-operates in others. Hewlett Packard sees its policy of geographically-dispersed manufacturing units as fundamental to its ongoing commitments to local and international customers.

Questions

1 Tom Peters and Robert Waterman in their famous book *In Search of Excellence* (1982) extolled HP's culture of decentralised decision-making. In a world industry, what problems might this create for the company?

2 Do you feel that strategic alliances work against the consumer's interest by interfering with competition, or are on balance a good thing?

3 Geographically dispersed manufacturing is one sign of this company's customer centredness. What other evidence might you look for?

The extent of the host country's participation in the process of foreign manufacture can vary from superficial assembly to research- and development-led innovation. At the superfical end, products can arrive in bits (completely knocked down, or CKD) and be reassembled in what are known as screwdriver plants, a name that denotes the level of manufacturing skills required. The idea here is to avoid import controls aimed at finished products. As a manufacturing policy, foreign assembly is usually merely a tactical response to protectionist measures.

At the other end of the scale is the kind of direct manufacturing investment that distinguishes the truly committed transnational company. While this kind of strategy is very popular with host country governments keen to grow their economic manufacturing base, it can also be perceived as economic colonialism. Care needs to be taken that the firm is contributing to its host economy as well as benefiting from the relationship.

The international marketing mix

Marketing, as we have seen in Chapter 1, is a business philosophy that puts customers at the centre of an organisation's thinking. This philosophy does not change, whether the marketing is carried out in one country or several. However, the task aspects of marketing – the management functions involved – do need to be tailored to the international environment. Reviewing the four elements of the marketing mix from an international standpoint highlights the major differences involved.

Product

Product is the fundamental component of any marketing mix. Promotion, price and distribution all take their cue from the basic offering to the consumer. There are good business reasons for trying to make a standard product acceptable to as large a number of customers as possible. Thinking back to the material on market segmentation in Chapter 5, we can reflect that a segment's size is one of the key criteria in deciding its attractiveness. International segments are certainly sizeable, but are rarely as homogeneous as marketers might wish. There has to be a trade-off between the ideal economies of the one-product-suits-all approach of the truly global marketer, and the adaptation to individual tastes that complicates the production operations of most international suppliers.

DID YOU KNOW?

Although UK Smarties eaters will only find eight standard colours in their tubes, the sweets are produced in a total of 15 colours because of the complex product standards and dietary laws in the various markets in which they are sold throughout the world.

Standard or differentiated?

Some products are more amenable to a standardised global approach than others. Typically, areas like sporting goods, office and industrial equipment, toys and computer games are standardised. Food, on the other hand, in spite of its central importance in fmcg marketing, is highly culturally conditioned. There are exceptions to this general principle, of course. Chewing gum and soft drinks seem to have little trouble crossing borders, but office equipment manufacturer Xerox encountered early resistance to its copiers in the UK when it was found that the machines were too large to get through British office doorways (narrower by several inches than their American counterparts). It must be admitted, moreover, that companies like McDonald's, who are feted for their global approach to their markets, provide evidence, on closer inspection, of considerable pragmatism in different countries. The truly global brand may be condemned to be an eternal gleam in a marketing manager's eye rather than a reality on the supermarket shelf. Consumers are, after all, a highly unpredictable bunch. Their needs are in a state of continuous evolution – a fact that drives the product life-cycle (see Chapter 6). It could be argued that by the time a company has standardised its products to a global simplicity, its consumers will have moved on.

Product life-cycle and NPD

Products and services, like their users, have life-cycles. As we have seen, profit levels vary at each stage of the cycle. Keeping a positive cash flow in the long term requires a company to make sure that its portfolio of products is in the right combination.

Moving into a new market with an established product can give it a new lease of life, but in the competitive marketing environment of the 1990s companies need to extend their products swiftly if they are not to be forestalled in foreign markets by competitors

CASE STUDY **13.3**
· · · · · · · · · · · · · · · · · · ·

Good ideas travel well

Imitation is one of the sincerest forms of flattery. It has also provided one of the most productive sources of new product development in international marketing as companies adapt successful ideas from one market into another. Polo Mints, for example, were launched in the UK in 1948 as a direct imitation of the successful American product Lifesavers. Lifesavers, still a very successful product in the US, are so named because of their resemblance to tiny lifebelts. Rather than concentrating on the ring in the UK, however, Rowntrees has traditionally focused their advertising and branding on the hole. The kind of imitation that led to the birth of Polo would be a whole lot more difficult in the 1990s, as it is now possible to protect the shape of a product as well as its trademark under copyright law.

Questions

1   Apart from copyright law, how might a manufacturer in one country protect its ideas from imitation by a foreign rival?
2   Can you think of any other examples of 'me too' brands on an international scale?

New product development keeps a company in touch with the evolving needs of its customers. Certain international markets, known as lead markets, contain a higher than average number of consumers who respond well to innovation (see Chapter 3 on buyer behaviour). A presence in these markets is essential for the producer who wants to keep abreast of ideas and emerging technology in its product field. If you are a consumer electronics company, for example, you have to be active in the chaotically innovative Japanese market in order to be able to plan effectively for the slower markets of the West.

CASE STUDY **13.4**

Croissants crisis?

Cereal giant Kellogg's is a keen international marketer with a mission to have the world wake up to a bowl of corn flakes. This has meant a flexible approach in several of its fledgling markets. The French, for example, are not renowned for their appetite for breakfast. If anything it will be a croissant and a cup of coffee, often consumed at a bar on the way to work. Corn flakes have been slow to catch on, and research suggests that something like 40 per cent of the minority group of French corn flake consumers douse them in warm milk instead of the cold milk essential to their crisp presentation. To counter this trend, Kellogg's French advertising has illustrated the cereal with milk in a clear jug rather than the opaque ceramic jug used for the hot milk in café au lait.

Asian consumers are another target for Kellogg's activities. To its standard range of corn flakes and wheat flakes, the company has added a special product in India: Basmati flakes. Almost half the world's population lives in Asia, so this kind of adaptation is worth contemplating for Western companies keen to recruit them as new customers. As in France, the Asian way to start the day is at odds with standard notions of breakfast cereal. Breakfast in Asia tends to be hot, soft and savoury rather than cold, crunchy and sugared. Indeed, initial reactions from Asian consumers to Kellogg's products included using the cereals as snacks to be eaten straight from the box like crisps or crackers. Nevertheless, between 1991 and 1995 Kellogg's has managed to double its volume of exports into the 30 or so Asian countries with which it trades.

Questions

1 Food is one of the most culturally sensitive of all product groups. Which kinds offer international marketers the best opportunities in the short term?
2 What kind of distribution strategy might Kellogg's adopt to complement the approach it is making to consumers in France and/or Asia?

Adapted from: Berkowitz et al., 1989; Bridge, 1995.

Branding

An important contribution in adding value to a product is made by branding. As discussed in Chapter 6, a brand is the identity of the product – its distinctive personality. While the basis for the brand identity must lie in the product's quality and performance, it can be extended into a communication separate from the product itself. Kotler and Armstrong (1994) make a useful distinction between the utterable brand (a name like Persil or Guinness) and the unutterable brand (a symbol, logo, colour scheme, or even the typeface in which a brand name usually appears).

International branding works best on the unutterable level – although even here elements like colour can have an unexpected cultural significance. White, for example, denotes mourning in some Eastern societies; green is popular in Muslim countries, although its use for packaging materials is considered bad form in Egypt where it is the national colour; red and black are avoided in some other African countries. A number of popular international logos use a combination of yellow and red – including McDonald's and Shell. In fact Shell has revamped its logo in the late 1980s in order to eliminate the word 'shell', and now relies exclusively on the stylised shell symbol in its distinctive colours. This eliminates the problems of pronunciation and translation that accompany international attempts at utterable branding.

The attraction of reputable brands to international consumers is such that a thriving trade in counterfeit goods has developed, and continues to develop, especially in product fields like fashion goods, publishing, computer software and cosmetics. It could be argued that the very existence of pirated goods indicates a marketing failure on the part of the genuine manufacturers. After all, if their own marketing mix is on target there should be no room for imitations.

ACTIVITY **13.3**

Country as brand

Country of Origin (COO) influences the perceived quality of a product. But such perceptions are often subjective. Working in pairs write down your product type/ quality expectations (three adjectives at most) with the following countries of origin. Do this exercise individually at first and then compare your list with that of your partners. What, if any, differences are there, and what does this reveal? Do your expectations change, for example, with product type? Are any of them based on actual experience as a customer?

▶ Ireland.
▶ New Zealand.
▶ Japan.
▶ Germany.
▶ UK.
▶ Korea.
▶ China.
▶ Finland.
▶ Italy.
▶ America.

DID YOU KNOW?

What's in a name?

The annals of international marketing are full of unfortunate examples of brandnames that don't travel. Here are a few classics:

▶ *Vauxhall's Nova didn't go down too well in Spain, where the name literally means 'doesn't go'.*

▶ *Amorous types asking for Durex in Australia might find themselves in a sticky situation, as it is a brand name there for a kind of adhesive tape.*

▶ *Thirsty French consumers can refresh themselves with a soft drink called 'Pschitt', while their neighbours in Germany can purchase loopaper called 'Bum'. Neither brand seems set for launch in the UK.*

▶ *Volkswagen was somewhat taken aback when its British distributors gave the thumbs down to a new top-of-the-range model in 1994. Its name means chariot of kings in Persian, but to British ears the 'Sharan' sounded like the sort of car that would come with furry dice as standard.*

Pricing

As we have seen in Chapter 8, pricing decisions are governed by competition, production costs and company objectives. International pricing decisions need also to take into account exchange rates, the difficulties of invoicing and collecting payment across borders, and company policy towards its activities in each market.

Designing methods of invoicing and payment that are proof against all the vagaries of international trade has proved impossible, in spite of progress towards the standardisation of documentation. It is prudent to allow for a level of unrecoverable debt when setting price levels.

Tariffs and purchase taxes may have the effect of making imported goods expensive compared with host-country alternatives. The international marketer either absorbs the difference (sacrificing profit to remain competitive), or sacrifices volume in the hope of obtaining a premium positioning. In the long term the only way to get round the problem, however, is to lobby the host-country government and perhaps move to a different form of relationship with the market. Some multinational companies who have subsidiaries in other countries use a technique known as transfer pricing to minimise the effect of tariff barriers when possible. Tariffs are usually levied at a percentage of the price of a product. Transfer pricing involves selling-on goods to subsidiaries within another country at a price deliberately set as low as possible to attract the minimum taxation. The resale price to the end-user can then be set at a more realistic level.

Another way of avoiding taxation, and hedging against the deleterious effects of currency fluctuations is to abandon money altogether and trade direct in goods and services. This form of international barter is known as countertrade. According to the OECD, this form of trade accounts for five per cent of world trade as a whole, and up to 35 per cent of trade involving lesser developed countries and Eastern Europe where hard currency is in short supply (Bennett, 1995).

Companies active in a number of markets are at liberty to charge different prices for the same product in different markets (perhaps subsidising one with profits from another). The most extreme example of this practice is called dumping – when goods are off-loaded at uncommercial rates just to get rid of them. Charging a substantially lower price in a nearby country can cause the embarrassing phenomenon known as parallel importing. This is when an entrepreneur from the higher-price market imports large quantities of the goods from the low-price country and sells them cheaper than the official import. In the UK this has happened in markets as diverse as pharmaceuticals and soft drinks, but price harmonisation in the EU is making it less feasible.

A final aspect of pricing in international marketing is the question of exactly what is included in the price paid by a distribution intermediary taking title to goods. Freight and insurance costs need to be paid, and all parties to the agreement need to be clear on whose responsibility this is. This need has spawned a technical vocabulary of pricing terminology known as incoterms (defined and updated by the International Chamber of Commerce). Here are some of the most common incoterms explained:

▶ *FOB (Free On Board)*: the price includes loading on to a ship at a specified port in the exporter's country, but after that the cost of freight is the buyer's responsibility.

▶ *CIF (Cost, Insurance and Freight)*: the exporter is responsible for the cost of freight and insurance for the goods to a named destination in the importing country.

▶ *CPT (Carriage Paid Too)*: this is similar to CIF above, but the buyer has responsibility for insuring against loss or damage to goods.

Promotion

This is one of the most interesting and challenging areas of international marketing, particularly sensitive to socio-cultural, technological and political factors. The international marketer's 'holy grail' of a global approach to the brand is nowhere more visibly evident than in international advertising. Unfortunately great advertising ideas do not always cross national boundaries.

CASE STUDY **13.5**

Tearing their hair out

When Procter and Gamble launched its combined shampoo and conditioner Wash 'n 'Go in post-glasnost Poland in the early 1990s the television advertising formula that had worked wonders elsewhere in the world fell flat. To some extent the sheer volume of advertising impact the company could afford on the recently liberalised television channels created levels of awareness that were counterproductive. Polish viewers began to be suspicious of something they were seeing promoted so heavily. Rumours started circulating that the product was actually damaging to the hair and sales fell off sharply.

There was also a problem with the creative treatment itself. Post-campaign research revealed that the locker-room ambience that Western viewers recognised as sophisticated and sporty, reminded Polish viewers of the factory changing-room. The creative approach was hastily altered. Out went the lockers. In came a well-known Polish gymnastic star going through a vigorous routine and finishing with an endorsement of the product. This appeal to Polish national pride went a long way to rehabilitating the brand's fortunes in Poland. The original strategy had, however, badly dented its original sales curve.

Questions

1 How can manufacturers resist the dangers of cultural dissonance in promotion?
2 Wash 'n 'Go appears to have been overpromoted through excessive TV advertising weight. Discuss ways of determining an appropriate weight of advertising (TV ratings – see Chapter 10) for a new market.

Adapted from: 'Europe Express', BBC2 1992.

Technological factors affect the choice of promotional media in foreign markets. Many domestic brand managers anticipate that replicating their domestic promotional plans in foreign markets will be sufficient. But there is little point in extending a successful print campaign to a country where print technology or magazine coverage is not competent to carry it off. As media empires grow through diversification and vertical integration this is becoming less of a problem – but it still presents difficulties to advertisers wanting to stage something as simple as a poster campaign using the same copy in a number of European countries. Panel sizes in the UK (where posters account for about five per cent of media expenditure) and France (where they account for 12 per cent) are different.

Exhibitions are a very important promotional medium for the international marketer, especially in the business-to-business field. It may be that a firm makes no use of this medium at all in its domestic business – so getting expert advice on the choice and use of trade shows is important. Such gatherings provide very useful first-hand contact with potential customers, and competitors, even if orders do not emerge immediately.

Regulation on what is and is not permissible in advertising varies greatly from country to country, although harmonisation in this field is another aspiration of the EU. It is hard enough, as the Wash 'n' Go example suggests, to find a formula that is culturally acceptable across national boundaries. But such an ad might not be permitted at all in certain countries because it features a woman in a state of undress. Legal restrictions on the use of direct marketing (involving as it does the computer storage of personal information) and sales promotion (things like free offers are banned in certain countries) make truly standardised promotional approaches very difficult across an international campaign. While the economic advantages of size and synergy are highly desirable, even global advertisers such as Benetton and Marlboro need to balance homogeneity of strategy and flexibility of execution in local markets.

Distribution

Making a product or service accessible to the maximum number of customers at the minimum cost is a challenge to the international marketer. The temptation is to concentrate on those aspects of the chain nearest to the manufacturer rather than see the process from the customer's point of view. This is neglecting to give logistics (working back from the customer) as much importance as physical distribution (working from the manufacturer to the customer).

Distribution channels between nations are chosen with a number of considerations in mind: the value and type of product, the cost and speed of alternative methods of transport, the ease with which a channel can be managed. Once inside the country itself, however, the channel is more difficult to influence. The company needs to adapt its practices to local opportunities. In the West retailing patterns have emerged that assume that shoppers have access to cars and do their main shopping at intervals of a week or so. Elsewhere in the world shopping is a more frequent activity, and the amounts bought are smaller. These differences work their way back through the entire system. Countries like India have elaborate distribution systems, with goods passing through a lengthy chain of wholesalers before reaching the final customer. The distribution systems of Japan are so complex as to represent a challenge to foreign goods marketers every bit as difficult as an import tariff. The nature of Japanese retailing is dealt with in Chapter 9 on distribution.

Using local agents and brokers who are familiar with the opportunities offered by such complex systems is the key to managing this difficult area. A large part of export management time is taken up by their careful recruitment, support and review.

International marketing planning
•••

As we have seen in Chapter 12, planning is the systematic and continuous attempt to match a company's capabilities to the opportunities presented by its environment. It involves establishing the aims of the organisation, the analysis of its present position and the establishment of a programme of action to carry out the aims. Companies active in the international sphere need to be clear on what they are doing and why, so planning is particularly important for them. Their planning procedures will follow the basic template outlined in Chapter 12. However, the extended nature of their organisations makes the implementation of agreed plans difficult. Head office can have a very different perspective on the direction of the business from a local company, for example.

Many successful multinationals have developed a planning culture that allows strategy to be developed centrally, but implementation through short- and medium-term plans to be taken care of locally and regionally. Even with this kind of approach, however, international marketing planning is still rife with difficulties. Here are some of the main problems:

> Sketchy market intelligence limits the quality of the information on which planning is based.
> There is a scarcity of experience and theory available to international marketers.
> Many of the models available to planners have been developed from experience with fmcg markets in a domestic, usually North American, context. Too literal an application of them may have a distorting effect.

DID YOU KNOW?

Parker Pens blotted its copy book in the 1980s when central management decided to streamline product models, advertising and packaging. In the space of two years it rationalised products by 80 per cent and imposed a unified advertising campaign on its markets in 150 countries. Local management felt ticked off by such a high-handed approach. As a result it was a disaster. Facing virtual bankruptcy the company reverted to a more devolved (if expensive) approach and market share immediately recovered.

International business theory

International business has attracted some influential thinkers. One of the most far-reaching theorists has been Michael Porter of the Harvard Business School, whose work on international competition has helped set the planning agenda for the 1990s. He argues that companies operating in the international environment can gain competitive advantage from concentrating on what he calls the value chain. This is the sequence of operations in production and marketing through which products and services pass. Performing these stages better than competitors can give a company the edge. A key factor here is the geographical location of each stage of the chain – playing to a country's particular strengths.

David Ricardo

Porter's thinking is reminiscent of the ideas of the very first theorist of international trade, the classical Scots economist David Ricardo (1772–1825). Ricardo developed a theory of what he called comparative advantage in which he argued the benefits of trade between nations on the grounds of efficiency. It is easy, he argued, to make good wine in Portugal because of the natural resources of that country. So rather than struggling to make indifferent wine in England, it makes better sense to import. In return the importing country can offer what it has comparative advantage in – eliminating inefficiency and making greater wealth available to all.

Attractive though Ricardo's ideas are, they do not take into account the conditions of market turbulence in which international companies operate. As we have seen, rapid change is a characteristic of many international economies. This means that sources of comparative advantage may change. Taiwan was a low-wage economy making cheap shoes in the 1980s. It is now becoming a world player in aerospace and technology, threatening jobs in traditionally high-skilled economies elsewhere in the world.

Life-cycle

Another influential theory of international trade that acknowledges the idea of change is the idea of the trade life-cycle. Advanced in the 1960s by the American theorists Vernon and Wells, this traces a process that starts when a country targets a foreign market for its exports. The establishment of a new market for the product spurs production by native producers. The final stage is when the original exporters face competition themselves from imports. The Japanese car industry is often pointed to as a prime example of this. Japan, originally a market for American cars, is now a major player in the American car market itself. In broad terms the theory is a credible one. But as life-cycles of products become ever shorter, its reliability as an aid to planning is questionable.

Business gurus like Tom Peters (1987) maintain that the only response to the chaotic international environment is to abandon strict planning in favour of a flexible approach. But even such a pragmatic prescription acknowledges that some kind of objectives are necessary. Planning pays, even if plans have to be changed. The process itself keeps the organisation focused on its purpose. This is no mean feat in the shifting international environment as business attitudes move from the ethnocentric (seeing a firm's operations as extended from its domestic base) to the geocentric (accepting the world itself as the primary market).

Summary
. . . .

This chapter has illuminated the main ways in which international customers offer the marketer a specialised set of challenges in planning and operations. For all the difficulties involved in the management of product, price, promotion and place in international trade, marketing across borders is setting the business agenda for the twenty-first century.

Key concepts
. . . .

Comparative advantage: theory propounded by David Ricardo (1772–1825) maintaining the utilitarian benefits of international trade.
Culture: learned behaviour specific to a group of people.
Exporting: manufacturing goods in one country, but selling them to customers overseas.
Expropriation: confiscation of a firm's assets by a host government.

Gross National Product (GNP): the total domestic and foreign added value claimed by residents.

Host country: a country where international marketing operations take place.

Incoterms: standard terminology for international marketing agreed by the International Chamber of Commerce.

International marketing: marketing activity that crosses national borders.

Licensing: a low-risk form of market entry whereby the owner of a product or idea allows another company to use it in a foreign market in exchange for a royalty.

Non-tariff barrier: obstacle to international marketers from a non-fiscal source (eg product safety legislation).

Pacific Rim: the collection of newly-industrialised countries around the Pacific.

Quota: a non-tariff barrier that limits imports to an agreed percentage of the market.

Tariff barrier: a financial tax on imported goods.

Value chain: the processes whereby raw materials are converted into a finished product offering to the consumer. Its effectiveness can be enhanced by an international context.

SELF-CHECK QUESTIONS

1 Which of the following features of a company does not constitute proof of its involvement in international marketing?
   a A mix of nationalities at senior management level.
   b A wide distribution of sales volume throughout several different countries.
   c Product planning, research and manufacturing in a number of countries.
   d Exporting activity on a small scale.
   e Foreign distribution intermediaries.

2 Which of the following aspects of marketing management have no greater importance in international marketing than in domestic marketing?
   a Environmental analysis.
   b Planning and control.
   c Product quality.
   d Manufacturing decisions.
   e Invoicing and payment.

3 Which of the following consumer characteristics is least affected by cultural factors?
   a Language.
   b Education.
   c Values.
   d Spending power.
   e Hair type.

4 Rank the following market entry methods in order of their potential risk:
   a Direct exporting.
   b Foreign manufacturing.
   c Licensing.

    d Joint venturing.

    e Foreign assembly.

5 OECD stands for:
    a Organisation of Economic Coordination and Development.
    b Overseas Export Coalition Directorate.
    c Open Export Channels Directive.
    d Organisation for Economic Cooperation and Development.
    e Overseas Economic Criteria Development.

Which of the following are true and which are false?

6 Joint ventures are an effective form of long-term market presence.

7 Sporting goods, office equipment and computer games offer manufacturers opportunities to standardise their products.

8 Lead markets contain a higher than normal number of innovation-prone customers.

9 Unutterable branding is preferred by global marketers.

10 The theory of international trade life-cycle holds that the final stage of the cycle comes when exporters are faced with competition in the host country from domestic manufacturers.

Discussion

11 What advice would you offer a small- to medium-sized business aiming to enter a new international market?

12 Promotional management is one of the most difficult areas of international marketing. Why is this, and what precautions can companies take to avoid pitfalls in this area?

13 Discuss the problems presented by international market research. Are they different in kind from those presented by domestic research?

14 With international marketing assuming an ever greater importance, what qualities will marketing managers require in the 21st century that their predecessors lacked?

15 What ethical problems are raised by companies from the developed world expanding into third world markets?

Further study
••••••••••••••••

Books

Paliwoda, S. (1993) *International Marketing*, 2nd edition, Heinemann.

Some very good bits, and has the advantage of being written from a UK perspective. But also contains rather a lot of technical information to plough through.

Preston, J. (Ed.) (1993) *International Business: Text and Cases*, Pitman.

A valuable collection of specially written articles and recent case studies which provides a lot of information and context for international marketing students.

Terpstra, V. and Sarathy, R. (1994) *International Marketing*, Dryden Press.

A deservedly popular text-book which handles the subject in a well-structured format with interesting examples. In spite of the fact that this is a 'European edition' it is still rather American in tone (although perhaps that should recommend it further as being international itself).

Journal

Levitt, T. (1960) 'Marketing Myopia', *Harvard Business Review*, (38) 4, July/August, pp. 45–56.

Much reprinted and referred to, this article got the ball rolling on 'global marketing' but is valuable for its visionary insights into marketing on a more general level as well.

References
··············

Bennett, R. (1995) *International Marketing: Strategy, Planning, Market Entry and Implementation*, Kogan Page.

Berkowitz, E. N., Kerin, R. A. and Rudelius, W. (1989) *Marketing*, 2nd edition, Irwin.

Bridge, R. (1995) 'Asians give West food for thought', in *The Times*, 11 May, p. 27.

Europe Express (1994) Channel 4 Television, 16 August.

Gilligan, C. and Hird, M. (1989) *International Marketing: Strategy and Management*, Routledge.

Economist (1995) 'Selling in Russia: The March on Moscow', 18 March, pp. 87–90.

Kotler, P. (1988) *Marketing Management: Analysis, Planning, Implementation and Control*, Prentice Hall.

Kotler, P. and Armstrong, G. (1994) *Principles of Marketing*, 6th Edition, Prentice Hall International.

Mughan, T. (1993) 'Culture as an asset in international business', in Preston, J. (Ed.) *International Business: Text and Cases*, Pitman, pp. 78–86.

Ohmae, K. (1985) *Triad Power*, Macmillan.

Peters, T. (1987) *Thriving on Chaos*, Knopf.

Porter, M.E. (1990) *The Competitive Advantage of Nations*, Free Press.

Rubython, T. (1994) 'The ultimate investment', in *Business Age*, April, pp. 81–82.

Terpstra, V. and Sarathy, R. (1994) *International Marketing*, 6th edition, Dryden Press.

CHAPTER **14**

Wider applications of marketing

Objectives

When you have read this chapter you will be able to:

▶ Apply basic marketing principles to a wide range of situations.

▶ List the differences in emphasis between marketing a tangible good and a service.

▶ Tailor a marketing programme towards the needs of an organisational customer.

▶ Recognise the role of marketing in not-for-profit bodies, such as charities and cultural institutions.

▶ Describe the basic rationale and techniques of internal marketing.

▶ Appreciate the background and characteristics of the emerging concept of relationship marketing.

Introduction

This final chapter looks at some of the ways the marketing concept has been extended to cover areas other than the profit-oriented fast-moving consumer goods environment. We will examine marketing practice in services, non-consumer markets, and non-profit organisations (some of whom can be openly hostile to the idea of commercial exchanges). We will also look at the growing area of internal marketing, whereby organisations are improving their ability to satisfy external customers by encouraging their own employees to see each other as customers. We will end with a brief account of relationship marketing, an important development in the way marketing is being understood in the 1990s.

Extending the boundaries of marketing

Marketing, as is argued in Chapter 1, is a way of increasing an organisation's success by concentrating on customers as the justification for its existence. Instead of being inward looking, a marketing-oriented organisation is recognisable by its external focus. Evidence for this comes from how it sees its mission, how information is gathered and shared, and whether decisions are made with the customer in mind. Experience suggests that organisations (of whatever size or purpose) who adopt this kind of approach enjoy long-term success. Organisations who neglect it tend to go to the wall.

Marketing as an established discipline evolved in post-war America in fast-moving consumer goods industries. At first, marketing experts tended to be housed in advertising agencies – acting as consultants to a number of clients. Then more and more manufacturing companies decided to create their own in-house departments. By the 1960s marketing was a widespread practice on both sides of the Atlantic for consumer goods manufacturers. Soon companies selling to other businesses and organisations also started reaping the benefits of marketing.

The 1970s saw the spread of the marketing approach to the service sector, spurred by deregulation and increasing competition. Service industries do not produce a tangible product for a customer to own and use, but an intangible service where the benefits are transferred directly at the time of purchase. For example you don't 'own' a haircut (service) in the same way as you own a hat (product) – but you can derive the benefit of looking smart from either. As we shall see, services create a new set of challenges for marketers but the basic principles of branding and customer focus remain the same as in product marketing.

To complicate matters further, some services have a cultural problem with marketing. At one stage in their history, institutions like banks and insurance companies would have rejected the idea of advertising and sales promotion as unprofessional. Having swallowed their misgivings they are now among the most innovative practitioners of branding, customer care and direct marketing – although their adoption of marketing has not been without its problems.

DID YOU KNOW?

In 1986 professions like law and accountancy were allowed to advertise for the first time in the UK. Some of their early attempts were a little shaky, such as the major accountancy firm who launched an ad featuring a soap powder box flashed with the message 'New Improved Tax Advice!'

In the late 1970s organisations in the non-profit sector began to explore the potential of marketing to increase their effectiveness. Charities, schools and colleges, health services, the arts and public sector organisations started to try out the vocabulary of customers, price and product. The 1980s saw the UK lead body for marketing, the Chartered Institute of Marketing (CIM), alter its definition of marketing to acknowledge the goal of satisfying customer demand 'efficiently' as well as 'profitably' – a recognition that there is more to organisational effectiveness than making money.

The growth of marketing in non-commercial contexts has continued. To some extent this has reflected a political environment that has seen market forces as the natural arbiter of what is possible (or even desirable) in society. But it also testifies to the versatility of customer focus as a successful operational principle. Non-profit marketing has become increasingly sophisticated and earned itself a new prominence on marketing's professional agenda. In its 1995 mission statement the CIM names 'improving the performance of "not for profit" and public sector organisations' as a central policy towards the year 2000. On the other side of the Atlantic, Peter Drucker (1990) has written 'non-profit institutions are central to American society, and are indeed its most distinguishing feature'. He sees non-profit organisations as being at the vanguard of marketing's future development.

The principle that unites organisational, service, non-profit and commercial marketing is that they all involve exchange relationships. In other words, they can be analysed in terms of customers and providers who exchange consideration (not necessarily just financial, as we have seen in Chapter 8) for benefits. This kind of analysis opens the door to the application of marketing principles to facilitate all sorts of exchanges and to increase the value of the exchanges to the mutual benefit of those involved.

CASE STUDY **14.1**   **World Wide Fund for Nature**

In 1978 George Medley, a senior executive from Glaxo, the international pharmaceuticals group, left the company after 20 years in industry. He had been head-hunted by a very different kind of organisation, the World Wildlife Fund (WWF) a charity with an income of £800,000 a year. By 1990, after a name change and a refocusing of its aims, the World Wide Fund for Nature was earning £20 million a year.

One of George Medley's first actions as head of the organisation was to gather senior staff together for a strategic planning session where they addressed the question of their mission. What kind of an organisation were they? The consensus was that they existed to conserve species in the natural world, but there was no clear idea on how the money required was to be raised. In effect, Medley's leadership turned the WWF from being a conservation organisation into being a fundraising operation. As a result it now provides the financial resources to support a wide variety of environmental projects around the globe.

The 1980s were the decade when most of the population woke up to green issues in a big way. But the WWF was not just riding a wave of popular interest in the environment. Under its new 'business culture' it deliberately introduced carefully costed direct-marketing programmes in order to recruit donors. The cost of establishing 100,000 new donors in 1991 was calculated to be £2 million – an average of £20 per donor. But WWF's research told it that its donors stayed with it for an average of 11 years donating a total of £400 each. This meant that it could expect to break even on the cost of recruitment for each new donor in a period of 12 months – a remarkably quick pay-back period in any business. In spite of this, however, many other charities would look very warily at the costs being risked in this operation.

Questions
1 Do you think this shift in the way that the WWF sees what it does has meant it has changed its objectives?
2 If you assumed responsibility for the WWF in the 1990s, how would you go about promoting it, to whom, and why?
3 What kinds of marketing exchanges are taking place in the following organisations?
   a A young offenders institute.
   b A hospice for the terminally ill.
   c The National Gallery in London.

Source: Business Matters, 1992.

Services versus products
....

The UK service economy is now outstripping its manufacturing economy in its value and the number of people employed in it. Service marketing has, therefore, assumed a new importance for marketing theorists. Although the basic principles of marketing a service are the same as those involved in marketing a tangible product, there are important differences in emphasis. Services have characteristics that separate them from products in a number of practical ways. Customers are in the market for benefits, and have little interest in whether those benefits are sourced from physical goods or services. Yet marketers need to understand what makes services different in order to present them to maximum advantage. Four widely recognised differences between services and products are as follows.

Intangibility

Unlike products, which can be handled and owned, services are intangible. They are experiences rather than objects. This means that potential customers cannot inspect or try out a service before purchase in the same way they might test-drive a car. The effect is to make promotion crucially important in service marketing. Communicating the benefits of what is on offer in a way that is accurate, attractive and credible is essential. Very often this means that techniques such as public relations (where a third party endorses the service) or word of mouth (where its reputation is spread by dedicated customers) have a more important role to play in promotional mixes for services than they do for products. We are likely to respond positively to a restaurant critic giving a good rating to the local Tandoori, even though we may take its advertising with a pinch of salt.

Another problem stemming from intangibility is that prices are difficult to set and justify in service industries. Customers cannot compare like with like in the same way they can compare physical products to assess their relative worth. So pricing needs to be carried out in a way that inspires customer confidence in the value of the offer. The perceived risk in buying a service is typically higher than in buying a product, so pricing needs to be explicitly linked to assurances of quality.

A further consequence of intangibility is the opportunity it creates for what are known as ancillary products. These are products that have a value from their association with the main offering. Tourism and the arts are essentially intangible services, but they are increasing their earnings through exploiting tangible merchandise such as apparel, books and recordings. These tangible products are reflections of the service experience which accompanies them.

DID YOU KNOW?
In Covent Garden's Royal Opera House shop, music buffs can buy not only recordings and videos, but a wide range of operatic gifts including Barber of Seville marmalade.

Inseparability of production and consumption

Products are bought and used by consumers some time after manufacture. Services, on the other hand, are bought and consumed at one and the same time. This casts the customer in a more active role than is usually envisaged in marketing exchanges. The customer is more like a partner in the production process. As a result the conditions under which the service is delivered need to be carefully considered. This is why banks and building societies pay so much attention to the design and layout of their branches. People need privacy and individual attention in transacting their personal financial affairs. They need to feel confident in the service provider, as well as comfortable in carrying out their side of the process. Easily-completed forms, queuing systems that minimise wasted time, even a relaxing colour scheme with appropriate fixtures and fittings can all provide sources of competitive advantage for financial institutions because of this.

Another consequence of inseparability of production and consumption in services is the importance of the element of place, or distribution. Making services available to people when and where they need them has been the impetus behind the growth of direct insurance and telephone banking. Theatre, opera and ballet companies often seek to extend their audiences by touring or playing in venues not normally associated with artistic performances.

Services are either administered directly by real people (such as physiotherapy), or mediated through technology of some sort (such as a CD-ROM-based information system). Whichever is the case, inseparability of production and consumption means that customers tend to associate the service with the person or machinery providing it. The result is that service providers need to pay special attention to the highest standards of customer care.

Heterogeneity

This is a long word for a simple concept – the impossibility of comparing like with like in services. Heterogeneity simply means 'differentness'. With products such as tins of baked beans, the manufacturing emphasis is on standardisation of production. One tin of Heinz Beans should be much the same as another tin of Heinz Beans to maintain consumer satisfaction with the brand. With services, on the other hand, the precise nature of what is being offered will depend on each transaction. No two visits to the doctor are ever quite the same, even though the benefit of improved health is the offer in each case. Sometimes the differentness of the service is key to the benefits involved. No two news broadcasts contain the same information, but every news broadcast offers the same benefit of keeping its audience up to date with events.

The consequence of heterogeneity for service marketers is to force them to be more active in explaining their advantages over competitive offerings. People in the market for life assurance or investments, for example, find it difficult to make sense of the choices available to them because there are so many imponderables. Different schemes offer different combinations of advantages and disadvantages. Sales advisors can play a crucial role in suiting the policy or scheme to the individual buyer.

Another consequence is the importance of umbrella branding. The power of a brandname like Rentokil, or a device like Lloyds' famous black horse, may well reassure an uncertain buyer in a confusing market. As a result, corporate advertising and public relations are particularly important in the service sector.

Perishability

Like the issue of intangibility, this is a fundamental source of difference between products and services. Many products are subject to perishability, as witnessed by 'best before' markings on grocery products. But even highly perishable products have got some kind of shelf life during which they can be stored if not sold immediately. This is not the case with services. If an airliner departs with unsold seats, those seats will remain unsold forever. Synchronizing supply and demand is a perennial dilemma for service marketers.

Pricing is an area where this is particularly apparent. Differential pricing, where different prices are charged for services at different times of the day, week or year, is a common response to the need to flatten out demand to meet availability (as we have seen in Chapter 8). So theatregoers seeing a show early in the week will tend to pay less than theatregoers attending the more popular weekend performances. Similarly, the notorious complexities of fare structures on rail or air journeys reflect the need of those industries to recoup high fixed costs by maximising seat occupancy.

Here is a brief check-list of some of the main practical marketing consequences of service characteristics:

1   *Intangibility*:
    – An emphasis on promotion (especially public relations with third-party endorsement).
    – Higher perceived risk by consumers, so pricing needs to be linked with assurances of quality.
    – Opportunities for ancillary products.
2   *Inseparability of production and consumption*:
    – Customers participate in services, they need to feel confident and comfortable.
    – Distribution focuses on when and where the service is needed.
    – Customers identify service providers with the services themselves, so a high standard of customer care is essential.
3   *Heterogeneity*:
    – An emphasis on selling as a way of explaining comparative advantage in a confusing market-place.
    – Umbrella branding to reassure customers.
4   *Perishability*:
    – An emphasis on synchronizing supply and demand.
    – Pricing techniques to maximise uptake across time.

Modelling service provision

Chapter 6 looked at how we can analyse product offerings through looking at different levels: core, tangible, extended, and so on. Services can be usefully subjected to this kind of analysis, but marketers can also benefit from more specific attempts to model the way their services are produced. An influential approach, the Servuction model, has been proposed by Bateson (1987). It takes its name from the conflation of the two words 'service' and 'production' (see Figure 14.1).

The model emphasises the active role of the customer in producing the service *with* the service provider, rather than just passively accepting it. Services take place as a result of co-operation. The Servuction model explains

figure 14.1
Servuction model

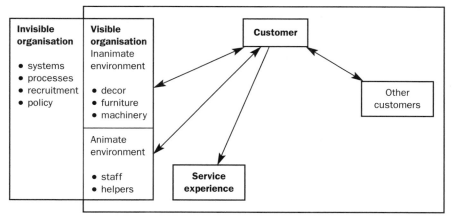

Adapted from: Bateson (1987).

the production of the service as the result of the customer's interaction with three other forces:

1   The invisible organisation (the service-provider's internal systems and processes).
2   The visible organisation, consisting of the people (animate environment) and physical conditions (inanimate environment) which mediate the service. and
3   Other customers.

The role of these three components may vary from one situation to another. Other customers, for example, may be very important if the service is a theatre performance or a football match where audience reaction is part of the atmosphere. However, in an individual medical consultation, other customers will not feature at all.

The Servuction model leads to a number of useful conclusions about service marketing. Here are some of the most important:

▶   The active role of the customer means that if the way the service is provided changes, the customer needs to be educated into a different way of consuming. This can make it difficult for some service organisations to develop beyond a certain level of operations, as they risk confusing or disenchanting their existing customers.
▶   Mistakes made in services are much more difficult to conceal than problems on a production line for physical goods as they happen in the full gaze of the customer. Systems need to be in place to deal with customer feedback.
▶   Customers have a set of expectations when they approach a service encounter which some researchers have called a 'script'. For example, we all know (or dread) more or less what is going to happen when we visit the dentist. If the service provider departs from the kind of role the script expects, the customer becomes uncomfortable and dissatisfied. Staff training and internal communication thus assume a central role in service marketing.

Three more 'Ps'

These differences in emphasis between marketing services and marketing tangible goods mean that we can add three more 'Ps' to the four we have dealt with in previous chapters. As well as product, price, promotion and place, service marketers can manipulate the elements of people, process and physical evidence.

People

Even though services can be administered mechanically (as in the case of an automated telling machine dispensing cash), people are involved in the vast majority of service situations. Profitable retailers, for example, concentrate on customer service in order to move the locus of competition away from price cutting. Investing in training and delegating decision-making authority to customer-facing personnel are ways in which the quality of the personal aspect of service can be enhanced.

Process

Designing systems with customers in mind is essential to successful service delivery. A useful analogy with product marketing would be in the area of packaging. What might seem to a manufacturer to be a secure or economical form of packaging may strike a consumer as difficult to get into or tacky. Services need to be easily accessible and conveniently presented. In a service situation such as car rental or hotel booking, clear and easy procedures can provide a source of competitive advantage.

DID YOU KNOW?
Hotel chain Trust House Forte has streamlined its booking procedure to allow customers to book accommodation anywhere in the UK through dialling only one number. To add to its marketing effectiveness, the number is also used as a branding device: 40 40 40.

Physical evidence

The engineering of an appropriate physical environment for the delivery of the service is a way of compensating for its intangible nature. The distribution issue of atmospherics (mentioned in Chapter 9) is particularly important here. Assurances of quality and reliability can be conveyed through decor and furnishings. Uniform is another common expression of branding intangibles through tangible physical evidence. As well as promoting the corporate identity of the organisation, uniforms are a way of reassuring the customer of the roles and competence of service providers.

Non-consumer marketing

A significant proportion of marketing activity is directed not at consumers, but at organisations, industries or other businesses. As with services marketing, the fundamental principles do not differ from standard marketing. However, organisational needs are different from consumer needs. What organisations do with products (the mode of use) is different from what consumers do. Organisations tend to turn what they buy into goods and services for others, rather than using them directly for their own benefit. This affects the way in which products and services are marketed to them. We can use the structure of the traditional marketing mix to illuminate the main differences between organisational and consumer marketing.

Product in organisational marketing

Reliability is paramount in the minds of people carrying out purchasing for their organisations. Not only does the ability of their organisations to satisfy customer needs depend on the quality of the goods or services they buy, but their own professional success as buyers is tied to making the right decisions.

DID YOU KNOW?
Fear is the key, at least in organisational purchasing. Rarely invoked in consumer advertising, the fear appeal underlies one of the most famous advertising slogans in the history of industrial marketing: 'Nobody ever got fired for buying a Xerox'.

The kind of classification process that can be applied to consumer goods and services can be extended to cover industrial goods and services, as we have seen in Chapter 6. Organisations buy three kinds of goods and services: materials and parts that they process into their own products, capital items that are used to conduct the process, and supplies and services that maintain or facilitate the process.

Industrial marketers need to be aware of the different kinds of buying behaviour associated with these different categories. For example, buying decisions about supplies and services such as those used for maintenance, repair and operating (MROs) will tend to be low-involvement. At the other end of the scale are items of capital expenditure. These evoke protracted and high-involvement decisions on the part of their purchasers. Marketing capital goods such as installations (eg factory machinery) usually means a direct relationship between manufacturer and customer, with technically literate salespeople negotiating and advising on the right purchase.

As we have seen in Chapter 3, buying behaviour differs between consumer and organisational markets. Webster and Wind's classic 1972 study of the way people in organisations buy divides the roles involved in organisational purchasing into five main types (see Figure 14.2). Some of these roles may be shared by the same person, depending on the situation.

Users tend to start the ball rolling on a purchase by demonstrating or articulating a need. The opportunity exists, therefore, for industrial marketers to appeal direct to them in order to flag their brands as the obvious solution (a path taken by a number of IT manufacturers).

Influencers act as reference points for others, while buyers are the professional purchasers – conducting negotiations with a number of suppliers in order to get the best deal for the company. Their interests and priorities may be different from those of the users.

Deciders are those who can say yes or no to the purchase. As budget holders, they need to be confident in the decisions of their staff. This confidence

figure 14.2
Organisational buying behaviour

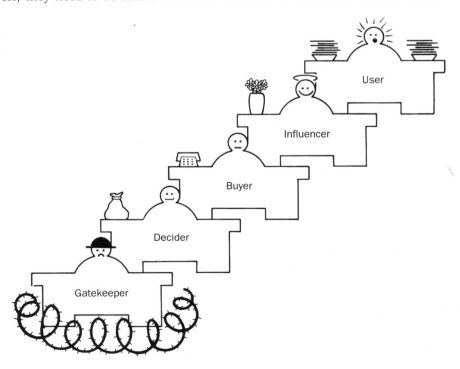

can be enhanced by suppliers' branding activities. Finally, gatekeepers (such as determined secretaries) can make or break a supplier's marketing efforts by their capacity to allow or deny access to people within the organisation.

Industrial marketers spend time researching and envisaging the different motives and needs of each participant in the decision making unit (DMU). The most important part of the process, however, is the organisation's own customer base. Canny industrial marketers sell 'through' the company in a way that guarantees that the benefits they are offering match the company's needs. In this way, successful industrial marketers are able to become more like business partners than suppliers to their customers.

Price

Price in organisational marketing is, generally, less important to customers than in consumer marketing. There are exceptions to this – such as the office stationery market, where competition between a number of very similar suppliers drives down prices. Also, negotiation on price (as one of a number of factors surrounding purchase) is far more common in industrial marketing than in consumer marketing. However, because of the need for industrial products to perform reliably and exactly, price is often a secondary issue in purchases of capital items. Their cost can be spread over a period of time (hence their capital status). Finally, the specialised nature of certain types of equipment market means that some manufacturers have very little competition on price – leaving purchasers little alternative.

Some pricing tactics are peculiar to organisational marketing. Contractors bidding for a new construction project, for example, will submit tenders for the work based not only on their own projected costs but also on what they expect their competitors will be bidding. Such 'sealed bid' pricing, where prices are submitted to buyers in confidence, relies on the bidders' ability to read the market. It can have some surprising results.

DID YOU KNOW?
Central Television bought its broadcasting franchise from the UK government in 1993 with a sealed bid of £6,000 per year? Central had no competition, and got away with the minimum specified by the rules. Yorkshire Television, on the other hand, offered £43 million per year – over £20 million more than its nearest rival – for its franchise. It has been argued that this was one of the reasons that led to its merger with Tyne Tees Television a year later.

Place

Distribution decisions in organisational marketing are subject to a wide variety of influences. Capital equipment and certain types of raw materials are frequently bulky and dangerous. This places pressure on the physical distribution operation, and explains why distribution channels connecting buyers to sellers in these markets are often very short.

Traditionally, industries have tended to concentrate in particular areas because of the proximity of energy supplies, raw materials or labour. In England the ceramic-producing potteries surround Stoke on Trent in Staffordshire, and the Black Country of the West Midlands is known for its legacy of heavy industry. California boasts 'Silicone Valley', although information technology as an industry has the capacity to site itself more flexibly than manufacturing industries.

Time as a distribution variable is extremely important in industrial marketing. Manufacturers faced with the opportunity cost of lost output will pay a premium for prompt delivery. Industrial buyers try to insure themselves against discontinuity of supply by using a group of suppliers rather than just one. This is not so much to encourage competition on price as to make sure they are not left high and dry. With developments like just-in-time manufacturing (discussed in Chapter 9), the trend is for suppliers and buyers to become more closely involved in each other's planning.

DID YOU KNOW?

Just-In-Time manufacturing is no proof against natural disasters. The Kobe earthquake in Japan in 1994 threw road and rail transport into disarray. As a result, the many manufacturing companies in the area who rely on just-in-time inventory systems had to shut down with the loss of millions of yen. With higher stock levels they would have been able to absorb the temporary gap in supply.

Promotion

This is one of the major areas of difference between organisational and other forms of marketing. A typical consumer promotional mix will feature a large advertising spend, with extensive use of sales promotion, some public relations and relatively scarce use of personal selling. Industrial marketing tends to reverse the trend. Personal selling, because of the complexity of the decision-making unit, is essential. And, because there are fewer buyers in the market than in consumer marketing, the emphasis is on protecting and retaining existing business.

Public relations, through the thousands of specialist magazines and journals that service UK trade and industry, is another key ingredient. Sales promotion of the consumer kind is relatively rare, but exhibitions are a key promotional resource (particularly for international business marketing). Printed material and publicity, carefully placed by direct marketing methods, are far more important than media advertising. In spite of this, business-to-business accounts are highly prized by advertising agencies who find that the wide range of services their clients require (exhibitions, conferences, brochures, etc.) provides a continuous stream of profitable work.

CASE STUDY **14.2**

Gillette – the sharp edge of industrial sales promotion

Marketers in the office stationery sector are faced with the problem that users, an important part of the decision-making unit, don't tend to associate products like paper clips or window envelopes with any particular manufacturer. So long as the materials do their job, the user is happy. But unbranded products make profitable marketing very difficult – especially in a market sector that is already very low-involvement.

Manufacturers whose interests extend to branded consumer goods therefore have an advantage. Gillette, for example, not only makes shaving products but is also active in stationery. It owns three major pen brands – Parker, Waterman and PaperMate – and the correcting fluid brand Liquid Paper.

1995 promotional support for Liquid Paper sales into the office market exploited the attractiveness of its other brands to create interest in the promoted products. Gillette realised that the vast majority of office managers responsible for stationery purchases were female, so tailored its offer towards them. Stationery buyers ordering promotional packs of Liquid Paper Multi Fluid received a free Gillette Sensor for Women razor, worth over £4 at retail prices.

PaperMate pens were supported with a less gender-specific promotion. Twelve-packs of selected PaperMate writing instruments carried application forms for a free cinema ticket voucher redeemable for two proofs of purchase. The object here was to introduce more excitement into a routine purchasing decision. As Gillette UK marketing director Chris Rhodes commented: 'The office is not the world's most exciting environment, so we were trying to stir things up. If you get it right, you get a great deal better effect; an impact far out of proportion to the expense.'

Questions

1 How hard should manufacturers try to brand low-involvement products for organisational markets?
2 Suggest a sales promotion idea for each of the following business-to-business products:
   a Personal computer disks retailing at £6.99 a packet of ten.
   b Office cleaning services (a year's contract worth £15,000).
   c A new type of laminated glass for the construction industry.
3 What kind of ethical problems might a company encounter using sales promotion to access organisational markets?

Source: Clarke, 1995.

ACTIVITY **14.1**

You the user

Think of three of the 'organisational' purchasing decisions you are affected by as a student or as an employee. They could be in the areas of furniture, interior or exterior decoration, audio-visual equipment, stationery, catering or a number of other areas depending on your circumstances.

1 Which people in your organisation fulfilled the roles identified by Webster and Wind in the buying process?
2 How could you as a user exert more influence in the buying process?
3 What advice would you give to a salesperson selling to your organisation or college in order to get past gatekeepers?

Not for profit marketing

At first glance, marketing and profit seem to be interdependent as notions. However, marketing has proved an effective approach in the non-profit sector among organisations devoted to causes other than commercial gain (eg charities, health, social welfare, education and the arts). Marketing's association with big business means that some managers in non-profit organisations still treat it with suspicion. Common objections are as follows:

▶ *Marketing is unnecessary*: the advantages of good health or a sound education should be self-evident.
▶ *Marketing is wasteful*: it consumes scarce resources that would be better applied direct to the organisation's mission.
▶ *Marketing is manipulative*: its reduction of human transactions to buying and selling is demeaning.

These misgivings are understandable. But they tend to be caused by imperfect or misunderstood marketing rather than the effective application of genuine marketing principles. Marketing is a way of using scarce resources to maximum effect by agreeing on a focus for an organisation's activities: the customer. Rather than existing to serve their own ends, organisations need to find their justification outside themselves. In this sense, non-profit organisations need customers just as much as commercial organisations do. It is essential for them to articulate who their customers are, and to shape their efforts towards them.

Many non-profit organisations are therefore embracing marketing principles as a way of making themselves more effective in a competitive environment. However, just as organisational and services marketing display different emphases from fmcg marketing, so non-profit marketing has its own set of features. Again an analysis along the lines of the four Ps is a useful way of highlighting these.

Product

Most non-profit organisations are providing services – so what we have said about service marketing earlier will hold true for them. Their services link them to their users in a different way from commercial organisations, however. Instead of 'customers', organisations working in the social welfare sphere prefer the notion of 'clients'. This emphasises a more equal relationship between those who are helping and those being helped, as well as implying a professionalism on the part of the helpers which puts them on a par with firms like lawyers and accountants. Ted Levitt (1986) described products as 'problem solving tools'. Non-profits see themselves as empowering their clients to help themselves, rather than spoon-feeding them with pre-packaged benefits.

This means that sometimes the notion of what a customer wants is less relevant to effective non-profit marketing than what a customer needs (even though this sounds like marketing heresy!). A local authority housing unit, for example, may refuse requests for trivial repairs from its tenants (frustrating their short-term wants), but provide the facilities for them to carry out such repairs themselves. The money saved can be used to delay rent increases – satisfying the genuine long-term need for cheap accommodation (Harrow and Shaw, 1992).

Price

Although many charities make a charge of some sort for their services, pricing in the non-profit sector tends to be below cost. Prices to the target market are subsidised by fundraising or government grants. This makes the management of non-financial price factors even more important in the non-profit sector than in the commercial sector. Someone going to the subsidised theatre in the UK, for example, will pay on average half of the true cost of a ticket. But there will be other elements of price – inconvenience, the conventions to be observed at the theatre, the attention to be paid, etc. Some of these aspects of price are integral to the experience. Others can be reduced by action on the part of the theatre. Clear signage, well-trained staff and a user-friendly atmosphere can reduce the non-financial price of a theatre visit by putting unfamiliar customers at their ease.

Voluntary organisations exact a price from their supporters in return for the benefits of involvement. This price can be financial, such as a donation, or expressed as a gift in kind such as unwanted computing equipment. By making it easier for their supporters to donate (by promoting payroll giving and other tax-efficient arrangements) charities can soften their financial prices in the same way that commercial organisations offer flexible payment schemes.

Time, given on an individual basis by many thousands of volunteers who participate in the work of the group, is perhaps the single most common form of price paid by a voluntary organisation's supporters. Again, the deterrent impact of such pricing can be reduced by action on the part of the organisation. Arranging for volunteers to staff a charity shop on rotas of short shifts rather than for full days is one way of doing this.

DID YOU KNOW?

Research carried out for the Charities Aid Foundation at the beginning of the 1990s shows that one in four people in the UK give nothing at all to charity in the course of a calendar year. The majority of donations come from the ABC1 socio-economic groups, mainly from those aged over 40. This is true even for charities with a youthful, trendy image. Meanwhile the number of new charities grows at a seemingly inexorable pace (at over 300 a month).

Place

Non-profits have the same need as commercial organisations to make themselves available to customers as and when required. Because so many of them are active in the service sector, the timing of their provision is very important (given the intangibility and perishability of services noted earlier in the chapter). Drop-in centres and telephone advice lines are two ways in which voluntary groups commonly administer their services in an attempt to strike the right balance between convenience to the customer and cost to the organisation.

CASE STUDY **14.3**
· · · · · · · · · · · · · · · · · · · ·

A playbus for the elderly

Age Concern Wakefield District (ACWD), one of almost 1,000 local groups working under the Age Concern England umbrella, has pioneered an original way of taking its services to isolated elderly people in West Yorkshire. Age Concern exists to increase the quality of life for older people. One way of doing this is to encourage them to organise social activities for themselves by facilitating the formation of neighbourhood groups. If there are good transport facilities and an obvious venue, such as a village hall, this is a lot easier.

ACWD's catchment area, however, features a wide spread of elderly people in the semi-rural districts outside the main conurbations of Pontefract and Wakefield. Not only do these potential clients not live near a convenient venue, but the rationalisation of public transport that happened in the 1980s meant that bus services that had connected them to the cities and towns were disappearing.

ACWD's solution was to take itself to its clients through a scheme called 'Mobile Age Concern', or MAC. The organisation acquired and converted a single-decker bus to form a mobile centre that could be taken out and parked in a number of locations selected for their potential to form groups. The results have been very encouraging. In 1989 bus 'members' wrote and published a book of reminiscences about life in the Wakefield district, organised an exhibition and worked on a tapestry together. The bus has also been used for outings, parties and games. In one location, bus users raised money from raffles to buy a proper china tea service for on-board refreshment. Once the bus has served its purpose as a focus to establish a group, the idea is to quietly withdraw and let the group carry on under its own steam so that the process can be repeated elsewhere.

Questions

1   After the scheme had been running for two or three years some of its users started referring to MAC as the 'Bingo Bus'. ACWD was not very happy about this as it felt that games of bingo – though popular – were not a very effective use of the resources of the organisation. Do you share this view, and what would you recommend ACWD do?

2   A potential problem with the scheme was that groups might see the bus rather than each other as the focus of their activities. How might you prevent this from happening?

3   A number of voluntary groups working in other fields visited ACWD to learn from its experience with MAC. What would be the advantages and disadvantages of this form of distribution for the following sorts of groups?:
  ▶ Citizens Advice Bureau specialising in debt counselling.
  ▶ Playscheme for children aged 3–5.
  ▶ Teaching English as a second language to Muslim women.

Promotion

Non-profits tend to have much smaller promotional budgets than their commercial counterparts, with an attendant reliance on public relations rather than paid-for advertising to get their message across. What advertising and printed publicity they do use, however, needs to be carefully conceived so as not to risk being counter-productive. Donors are unlikely to be impressed by publicity material that looks too expensive if it is pleading the case for urgent financial support.

A second consideration non-profits bear in mind with particular sensitivity is the moral dimension of imagery. Environmental pressure groups and charities will invariably use recycled materials for their literature. Charities working with the developing world or with disadvantaged people will studiously avoid stereotyped imagery portraying their clients as beggars. There is often a tension, especially in fundraising publicity material, between the emotional imagery which gets people to sit up and donate and the stereotypical imagery which voluntary groups are at pains to avoid.

DID YOU KNOW?
In the early 1990s the children's charity NCH (National Childrens Homes) took a decision to use illustrations and cartoons in its advertising rather than photographs to avoid the impression that it was 'faking' reality in its posters. For obvious reasons the real victims of child abuse could not be photographed, so the charity had been using child models – but it decided that even this was potentially misleading and best avoided.

ACTIVITY 14.2

Stereotypes

Charities are extremely sensitive about avoiding stereotypical or negative imagery in their promotional work. While commercial advertisers are coming round to this view, how people are depicted in advertising tends to look like wishful thinking (especially against the editorial matter in which it usually appears). This activity requires you to search a magazine or newspaper looking for an advertisement (for either a commercial or a non-profit enterprise) featuring a photograph of someone.

1 How might the impact of the advertisement change if, instead of photography, the graphic technique used was illustration or cartoon?
2 Do you think the depiction of people in advertising ought to be more representative or less representative of society as a whole?
3 When (if ever) might it be useful to use stereotypical imagery in promotional material?

CASE STUDY **14.4**
....

Greenpeace reveals all...

In 1995 the Advertising Standards Authority censured several pieces of advertising by charities and environmental pressure groups for making misleading claims that might lead to unnecessary alarm among consumers. One celebrated example was Greenpeace's press advertisement that bore a full-frontal male nude (actually an Italian renaissance sculpture) with the challenging headline 'You're not half the man your father was'. The body copy revealed that chemical dumping in our seas was causing sperm count to dwindle and 'willies to shrink in size'. The members of the Authority criticised Greenpeace for not being able to substantiate this claim, leading to the withdrawal of the advertisement. Greenpeace admitted to having made a bit of a cock-up, but pointed out that if it waited for irrefutable scientific proof about every issue it raised, it would be rendered completely impotent.

Questions

1 How controversial can a non-profit afford to be? Can you think of other deliberately shocking advertisements from pressure groups or charities that you have found impressive?
2 Should the ASA apply the same principles to an organisation like Greenpeace (trying to raise an issue) as it does to a large company like Procter and Gamble (trying to sell a product)?
3 The link between cigarettes and lung cancer had been known about for over a year before the news was broken to the market in the 1960s (while the results were painstakingly rechecked). Comment on the ethics of this course of action.

Internal marketing
....

Non-profits such as the ones we have mentioned are often dedicated to selling an idea rather than a physical product. Many commercial companies have woken up in the early 1990s to the need for selling ideas like their mission and objectives. Their target audience is not just external, however, but internal: their employees themselves. No matter how convincing a company's marketing mix, the deciding factor as to whether it can clinch regular repeat business is its people. Customer service, innovation, and commitment to quality all stem from the workforce. Internal marketing is an extension of the marketing concept that treats an organisation's employees as its internal customers, recognising their essential role in its external marketing success.

This approach impacts on organisations at three levels. First, at a basic policy level, internal marketing holds that it is no use having a mission and values unless they are communicated to staff. The development of a distinctive organisational culture, almost like an internal brand, is key to this process. Second, on the strategic level, internal marketing spreads ideas and techniques for how a company does business. Quality programmes, cost-saving exercises and team building are common strategic routes to success. Their establishment as strategic paths depends on a company's ability to enthuse its staff by satisfying their motivational needs like any other group of customers. Finally, on a tactical level, internal marketing can facilitate day-to-day operations like training (especially in customer service), recruitment and relocation.

The basic shift in perspective that internal marketing seeks to introduce is for employees to see themselves as linked to external customers by a series of marketing relationships inside the company. They are encouraged to see each other as suppliers and customers in this chain. This has the effect of allowing staff who are relatively remote from customer contact to realise that their contribution is vital to the ability of the company as a whole to compete effectively. The concept of the internal customer is usually embedded in a total quality scheme such as the Post Office's 'Customer First' initiative. Employees throughout the company are provided with the techniques to improve their service to each other and, by extension, to the final customer. Because the ideas come from themselves, the workers have ownership of them and their own customer needs (for job satisfaction and pride in their work) are satisfied.

The techniques of internal marketing revolve around effective communication. Information about the organisation is central to this – business gains, future developments, memorable details and news. Communicated via techniques such as cascade briefings (where employees are briefed in groups before passing on the information to further groups of employees), this kind of information can make each member of a company an invaluable ambassador to the external world. Second, the importance of marketing itself needs to be explained to workers throughout the organisation. Companies like Nestlé Rowntree send staff from all functions on marketing courses in order to impress upon them the reasons behind decisions and working practices that may seem illogical from a non-marketing viewpoint. This has the result of gaining a company-wide acceptance of the rationale of marketing, with consequent gains in effectiveness.

Finally, internal marketing can be used to help allay the effects of crises – whether potential or actual. Well-briefed employees give credibility to the reactions of a company faced with serious adverse publicity. Observers will believe them. Indeed, a well-managed crisis can have a lasting beneficial effect on a company through uniting the workers in a kind of Dunkirk spirit that survives after the crisis has blown over.

Internal, like external, marketing is a process. In other words it continues progressively. We can identify four main stages of development in this process – from the beginnings of an effective internal marketing approach to the maturity of a company buzzing with effective internal communication:

1 *Instruction*: this level of internal marketing aims to let employees know exactly what is required of them to get the job done. In spite of making them secure in their objectives, it is largely one-way communication. As we

shall see, fully developed internal marketing is a two-way process, recognising the mutuality of any marketing exchange.

2   *Information*: at this level of internal marketing the employees not only understand what they have to do, but why they have to do it. Training and communication develop staff through providing a business context for their decisions. Segmentation is as important here as in any other marketing activity. Different groups of staff will have different needs and attitudes.

3   *Involvement*: the third level of internal marketing development is when the employees are actively involved. The company can access their enthusiasm and ideas, and in return the staff benefit from seeing their creativity rewarded and having a stake in the company's success. Involvement depends on the commitment of senior management to make it work.

4   *Participation*: the fourth and rarest level of internal marketing is when employees genuinely take part in decision making by the firm as a whole. Tom Peters (*Business Matters*, 1991) tells the story of an American sausage factory where hourly-paid workers actually prepare capital investment proposals and are involved in all aspects of running the company. It might sound utopian, but it has the effect of improving profitability.

CASE STUDY 14.5

Lloyds: an inside job

Today's financial services market is crowded and sluggish due to the recession and fall in consumer confidence. This increases the pressure on banks and building societies to get their internal marketing right. In 1991 Lloyds Bank began an internal marketing drive to turn itself from a hide-bound institution into a dynamic, customer-driven operation.

Lloyds' repositioning coincided with some very difficult changes for staff – restructuring, redundancies and a review of payment systems. The research that the bank carried out prior to launching its internal marketing showed, unsurprisingly, that the staff were confused, demoralised and distrustful of what managers told them.

The bank's response was to invite a senior investigative journalist from outside the company to prepare a report on what was happening to Lloyds, and where it was going. The objectivity of the report gave it credibility with staff who might not have believed the same information direct from the company. The report started the ball rolling on a continuing process of research, feedback to staff and action. Issues covered to date include changes to appraisal schemes and training, the setting of performance standards and value for money (VFM) measures.

The company itself has learned useful lessons from this experience. It now places a new emphasis on local communication of head office policy. Face-to-face briefings between branch managers and their staff, supported by overhead slides and notes from head office, are replacing the centralised communication culture that had placed too great a reliance on impersonal technology to get its message across.

Questions

1   List five points on which you can measure the effectiveness of internal marketing.

2   Do the internal marketing needs of a service provider such as a bank differ markedly from those of a company producing tangible goods? What might the main differences be?

3 Widespread redundancies have been a feature of the banking and building society industry over the last decade as it has restructured in the face of increasing competition and the impact of technology. As a local branch manager faced with the problem of briefing your 12 staff on a likely ten per cent cut in jobs over the next two years, prepare some notes for a ten-minute presentation. How might you apply the AIDA model to this? (See Chapter 10.)

Source: Mitchell, 1994.

Relationship marketing
••••••••••••••••••••••••••

Concepts like the product life-cycle and the Boston Consulting Group Matrix (discussed in Chapter 6 on product) remind us that marketing takes place in a dynamic environment. Just as products and services need to be adapted and invented to cope with changes in demand, so ideas tend to change their emphasis over time in order to explain and predict events. Marketing itself as an idea is no exception to this condition of evolution.

Most of the marketing ideas we have covered in this book have been proved to work in growth markets where there is still room for expansion. Most consumer goods and service markets are now mature, leaving little room for growth. Much of the emphasis in contemporary marketing activity is on customer retention to defend share.

Traditionally, however, marketing's four Ps of product, price, promotion and place have been seen as ways of generating transactions that (it is hoped) will create a continuing relationship with customers. The relatively recent theoretical concept of relationship marketing has evolved to describe an alternative approach, where the marketing mix is seen as supporting a relationship with the customer in which the transactions may take place (Berry, 1983).

Christopher and McDonald (1995) argue for a view of the market as a network of value-laden relationships. These include not only the relationship with the customer, but with wider groupings who influence and sanction exchanges – such as suppliers, existing customers (whose good opinion can create new customers) and internal markets (such as those described in the previous section on internal marketing).

In a sense there is nothing new about relationship marketing. Successful marketing, as an anonymous wag once quipped, involves 'selling things that don't come back to people that do'. The long-term perspective is one of the things that differentiates the marketing concept from the selling concept (as discussed in Chapter 1). But relationship marketing as a concept allows us to consider the widest possible field of potential marketing activity that is still relevant to building profitable business. Philip Kotler (1986) has coined the term 'megamarketing' to describe a strategic approach to relationships beyond those of the immediate customer and supplier. He illustrates his case with examples describing how major national contracts are won not only because of quality and performance factors, but also because of political nous on the part of the victorious companies.

No man is an island, according to the seventeenth-century poet John Donne. We certainly do not act in isolation as customers. Our behaviour is influenced by the experience and advice of others. We talk about products like cars and food. We talk quite a lot about marketing activity such as advertising as well. Relationship marketing recognises this. By widening its focus to include the other complex influences on an organisation and its customers, it provides a useful template for marketing thinking and innovation as we near the end of the twentieth century.

ACTIVITY **14.3**

Marketing networks

The relationship marketing concept pays attention to nurturing relationships not only with customers directly but with a number of other groups whose influence or activities have a bearing on marketing and purchasing activity. These include reference groups, distributors, employees and suppliers.

DID YOU KNOW?
Leeds-based brewer Joshua Tetley runs 1,000 pubs in the UK. Recognising the importance of relationship marketing in a very direct way it launched the '100 Club' – a staff incentive scheme that rewarded employees who knew at least 100 customers by name. When the scheme was launched there was some scepticism in the company as to whether anyone would qualify. The outcome exceeded all expectations. Some 500 employees knew 600 or more of their customers by name, and the leading club member knew 1,200.

1   Map out the important groups in each of the four categories mentioned for the following companies:
    – An automotive manufacturer such as Rover Cars.
    – A financial institution such as Lloyds Bank.
    – A multinational corporation such as Nestlé.
2   Try to find an order of priority between the groups in each case. Is their relative importance the same or different depending on the type of company or industry?
3   What kind of promotional messages do these companies already send out to the various groups covered?

Summary

The purpose of this chapter has been to discuss and illustrate the wider applications of marketing into areas such as services, non-consumer marketing, non-profit organisations and internal marketing. We have ended with a brief look at relationship marketing. All of these versions of marketing correspond to the basic marketing principles outlined in this book, but each has its own set of special emphases in practice.

Key concepts

Ancillary product: a product, such as a souvenir, sold alongside another product or service.

Animate and inanimate environment: the human (animate) and mechanical or physical (inanimate) environment in which a service is delivered.

Charity: an organisation (in UK law) that exists to do one of four things: the relief of poverty, the advancement of religion, the advancement of education, or any other purpose considered charitable. Therefore Eton school is a charity, but Greenpeace isn't.

Customer script: the set of role expectations with which a customer approaches a service.

Exchange relationship: a basic unit of marketing, whereby something is given and received between parties to the relationship.

Internal marketing: marketing activity that treats the people inside an organisation as customers.

Non-profit sector: organisations who exist for reasons other than commercial gain.

Pressure group: an organisation with a point to make in a democratic society.

Relationship marketing: a concept that emphasises the importance of keeping customers as opposed to getting customers.

Service characteristics: characteristics that distinguish services from tangible products such as intangibility, inseparability of production from consumption, heterogeneity and perishability.

Servuction: a model of service provision that emphasises the customer's role as partner in the process.

Stereotype: an unchanging (and therefore hackneyed) image. The origin of the expression is a printing term meaning an inflexible printing plate.

SELF-CHECK QUESTIONS

1 Marketing has been adopted by organisations such as schools, hospitals and charities to achieve which of the following objectives?
   a Increase profitability.
   b Reduce costs.
   c Widen earning potential.
   d Maximise efficiency.
   e Maximise effectiveness.

2 Services differ from products in a number of ways. Which of the following are commonly acknowledged to be service characteristics?
   a Intangibility.
   b Imperishability.
   c Inscrutability.
   d Heterogeneity.
   e Heterosexuality.

3 Industrial products fall into which of the following groups of three main categories?
   a Materials and parts; capital items; consultancy.
   b Mechanical material; investments; corporate resources.
   c Machine parts; installations; inventory.
   d Material and parts; capital items; supplies and services.
   e Material goods; invisibles; supernumerary supplies.

4 Common objections to marketing from managers in non-profit organisations include which of the following?
   a Marketing is unnecessary.
   b Marketing involves charging for things.
   c Marketing is wasteful.
   d Marketing is manipulative.
   e Marketing involves stereotypes.

5 Place the following stages of development of internal marketing in order of progression:
- **a** Participation.
- **b** Information.
- **c** Involvement.
- **d** Instruction.

Which of the following are true and which are false?

6 Customers are fussy about whether benefits are mediated by services or products.

7 Opportunities for ancillary products are created by the intangibility of services.

8 According to Webster and Wind (1972) deciders are members of a DMU whose role is to negotiate with suppliers.

9 Geographical concentration is a feature of many industrial markets.

10 Relationship marketing concentrates an organisation's efforts on finding customers.

Discuss the following

11 The reason for falling church attendance in the UK is poor marketing.

12 Industrial salespeople are a different breed from consumer salespeople.

13 The secret of successful service marketing lies not in a firm's marketing department but in its recruitment and training function.

14 Internal marketing is just another attempt at mind-control by management.

15 Relationship marketing is fine – unless your customers value their privacy.

Further study
∙∙∙∙∙∙∙∙∙∙∙∙∙∙∙∙∙∙

Books

Bateson, J. (1987) *Managing Services Marketing: Text and Readings*, Dryden Press. *An excellent collection.*

Christopher, Martin, Payne, Adrian and Ballantyne, David (1991) *Relationship Marketing*, Butterworth Heinemann. *A useful text.*

Druce, Rosalind (1990) *The Marketing Handbook*, NEC/Channel 4. *A short but practical guide to non-profit marketing.*

Hague, Paul and Jackson, Peter (1994) *The Power of Industrial Brands*, McGraw-Hill. *An accessible book to the non-consumer field, which in spite of the volume of activity that takes place under business-to-business or organisational marketing, is still relatively neglected.*

Hill, Elizabeth, O'Sullivan, Catherine and O'Sullivan, Terry (1995) *Creative Arts Marketing*, Butterworth Heinemann. *Covers the fascinating world of arts marketing with a highly practical focus.*

Kotler, Philip and Andreasen, Alan (1991) *Strategic Marketing for Non-Profit Organisations*, Prentice Hall. *A substantial, highly influential tome.*

Palmer, Adrian (1994) *Principles of Services Marketing*, Kogan Page.

Peters, Tom (1988) *Thriving on Chaos*, Pan.
A good starting point in studying internal marketing.

References
••••••••••••••

Bateson, J. (1987) *Managing Services Marketing: Text and Readings*, Dryden Press.
Berry, L. (1983) 'Relationship Marketing', in Leonard L. Berry, G. Lynn Shostack
    and Gregory D. Upah (Eds.) (1983) *Emerging Perspectives in Services Marketing*,
    Proceedings of the American Marketing Association, Chicago, pp. 25–8.
Business Matters (1991) 'An Audience with Tom Peters', BBC2 TV.
Business Matters (1992) 'The Giving Business', BBC2 TV.
Christopher, M. and McDonald, M. (1995) *Marketing: An Introductory Text*,
    Macmillan.
Clarke, S. (1995) 'Go Write Back', in *Promotions and Incentives*, September, p. 64.
Drucker, P. (1990) *Managing the Non-Profit Organisation*, Butterworth Heinemann.
Harrow, J. & Shaw, M. (1992) 'The manager faces the consumer', in Willcocks,
    L. and Harrow, J. (Eds.) *Rediscovering Public Services Marketing*, McGraw Hill.
Kotler, P. (1986) 'Megamarketing', in *Harvard Business Review*, March/April,
    pp. 117–24.
Levitt, T. (1986) 'Differentiation – of Anything', in his *The Marketing Imagination*,
    2nd edition, Free Press.
Mitchell, A. (1994) 'The Message not the Media', *Marketing Business*, November,
    pp. 21–4.)
Webster, F. and Wind, Y. (1972) *Organisational Buying Behaviour*, Prentice-Hall.

Answers to self-check questions

Chapter 1
•••••••••••••

Multiple-choice

1 e Marketing-led firms recognise that without customers they have no reason to be in business!

2 b The functional role of marketing extends beyond the task of promotion: it encompasses analysis, strategy, tactics (of which promotion is one, but 'product', 'price' and 'place' are also important) and management.

3 d Only firms that embrace all three of these can be described as adopting the marketing concept: they are prerequisites to 'creating and keeping profitable customers'.

4 d Organisations that emphasise 'getting the sale' are in danger of losing out when it comes to building long-term relationships with customers.

5 a When organisations keep an eye on what is going on in the world outside, they are in a better position to anticipate changes in demand and to react to them.

True / False

6 True. Income will probably determine the quality and style they can afford and age is likely to influence their functional needs: young single people in their first homes may value style while those with young children may be looking for durability.

7 True. Retailers are the most common type of intermediary used to get grocery products from the factory to the consumer.

8 False. The purpose of marketing control is to identify any departure from the plan to enable corrective action to be taken if necessary.

9 False. Marketing principles are relevant to all organisations that have customers

10 True. The concept of internal marketing, although quite new, is helpful in encouraging organisations to integrate their efforts in improving service levels.

Discussion

11 A firm might adopt a sales orientation if it is concerned with 'making the sale' but isn't too worried as to whether its customers are satisfied with their purchases. This may occur if the product being sold is unlikely to be a repeat purchase. The examples of double glazing, fitted kitchens and encyclopaedias are given in the text. It could be argued that financial services salesmen have also been guilty of adopting this approach to selling pensions, which are a good example of a one-off purchase. The discovery of large-scale mis-selling of private pension plans throughout the whole industry (to members of corporate pension schemes who would have been better off staying in their company schemes) has led to regulation to force the companies concerned to compensate the victims of their hard-sell. The question of whether the approach is excusable depends, perhaps, on one's ethical stand point. One might be persuaded that it is excusable particularly as governments use it to attract voters in elections! As to whether or not it is desirable, the fact that bad word-of-mouth travels faster than good is a sufficient deterrent for most businesses, whose interests are usually better served by a more customer-focused ethos.

12 The most commonly cited fifth 'P' is that of *people*, though this can be thought of as an integral part of the product, rather than a separate element of the marketing mix. Particularly in service industries, employee performance has a direct influence over the way the customer experiences the product. 'Processes' and 'planning' are other additions that are some-times made to the marketing mix, but it could be argued that this is inappropriate, as manufacturing processes are primarily the responsibility of the production function and planning is a central activity and not just a marketing tool. Nonetheless, people, processes and planning can all affect demand for an organisation's products, and marketing orientated firms will consider them all with customer needs in mind.

13 Public utilities such as British Gas, the water companies and the electricity companies are in very similar situations as other industries in that they depend on satisfied customers for continued revenues and profits. It is in their own interests to attempt to 'create and keep profitable customers'. If they do not, they are vulnerable to either takeover bids or liquidation (though the government would almost certainly intervene if there were any threat of this.) They may also be subject to price controls if governments perceive them to be failing to deliver a fair deal to customers. Only in situations of pure monopoly, where consumers have no choice (and are unlikely ever to have any choice) as to whom to buy from might it be possible for public utilities to ignore the marketing concept. Even then there is a risk that the environment will change and leave the business in jeopardy (as in the case of Krosno Glass).

14 There is an argument that universities should be 'product' orientated, providing courses that are believed to be *worthwhile* rather than responding to demand for places. This may be a reason for the government's willingness to pay higher fees for students on science-based courses rather than arts-based courses. Universities themselves may be tempted to be 'production' orientated, and strive to be more efficient. They may accept large numbers of students to increase their revenues in order to cover their fixed costs, even if this has a negative impact on the quality of the student experience. A 'sales' orientation may be evident during Clearing, when places need to be sold to students to make courses viable, even if they do not match the students' ambitions or qualifications very well. But the best institutions recognise that there has to be a balance between their own objectives and the needs of the student if they are to thrive and maintain their good reputations in the market.

15 While the marketing mix for toothpaste and political parties is likely to be very different, the application of the other principles of marketing will bear remarkable similarities. Both toothpaste manufacturers and politicians have to understand their environments and the ways in which they are changing, and they are likely to use market research (or opinion polls) to help them do this. Both are likely to identify key target markets and attempt to present themselves in a better light than the competition (or opposition), though there is some debate as to whether their target markets comprise 'citizens' or 'customers' (the latter being arguably more passive than the former). They will prepare plans (or manifestos) that will give direction to their activities and attempt to use limited resources in the most effective way possible to increase their market shares (or share of the vote).

Chapter 2
· · · · · · · · · · · ·

Multiple-choice

1 e These types of competitors are in the same industry but are not trying to gain business from exactly the same customers, so they are only competing indirectly.

2 c Both of these can enable suppliers to charge high prices which businesses may have no choice but to pay.

3 e Patents are one of the ways in which innovators are rewarded to compensate them for their research and development costs.

4 c Action should be taken at this stage, but the type of action will depend on the nature of the environmental change.

5 e When inflation threatens an economy, governments may raise interest rates to dampen excess demand and break the price/wage increase spiral.

True / False

6 False. Although their price brackets may be similar, consumers will use different decision criteria as the two purchases meet different consumer needs.

7 False. These decisions will affect levels of customer service, and are therefore of interest to marketers.

8 True. This is a heavily branded market with highly differentiated products that their producers hope will be perceived as unique by their customers.

9 False. Demographics are concerned with the size and composition of populations, over which businesses have virtually no control.

10 True. Innovation can be triggered by new needs and wants in society, but can also lead to changing values and lifestyles.

Discussion

11 As a communication tool, the Internet offers opportunities to a wide range of industries who wish to provide information to customers. When the problems of security coding are ironed out, it has the potential for enabling credit card transactions to take place too and has been described as providing a 'virtual market-place'. (Perhaps one day it will be possible for us to browse through supermarket shelves from the comfort of an armchair, push a few buttons to order the goods we want and then have them delivered to the door or collect them from a warehouse.) Those who currently supply information in different ways may be forced to re-assess their operations and consider new ways of meeting their customer needs: will e-mail reduce the volume of postal traffic, and will the trade press be spurned by advertisers?

12 In an oligopoly a business feels some protection from new entrants, as the few large firms in the industry tend to deter them by heavy expenditure on promotion to reinforce the popularity of their brands, or investment in capital goods which make them highly efficient. They are, however, vulnerable to the activities of existing competitors, particularly on pricing strategy. Firms fear losing market share if their prices are higher than their competitors, so a price cut by one firm tends to be followed by all the others. This can ultimately lead to reduced profit margins in the industry as a whole unless cost savings can be made by improved efficiency.

13 Tobacco companies have diversified out of purely tobacco product manufacture; they are mainly conglomerates now, selling financial services, cosmetics and food products as well as tobacco. By creating a portfolio of products they have protected themselves from the decline in tobacco sales being experienced in many Western markets following extensive publicity about health risks over the past 30 years. They have also made efforts to penetrate foreign markets, particularly some less developed countries where the consumption of tobacco is still buoyant, consumer and government health concerns are less aggressive and taxation less punitive. More recently, they have attempted to stop the decline in consumption in Western markets by cutting prices (a move that seems to have worked: for the first time since the early 1960s the American cigarette market has stopped shrinking (*The Economist*, March, 1995)).

14 The big supermarkets have a very high share of the grocery retailing market. Consequently, if food manufacturers wish to reach the mass market in the UK, they must persuade the big retailers to stock their products. But the big retailers buy in bulk, so they insist on very low prices. Also, they will only stock products if they are sure that consumers will buy them, and will resist all but the most successful brands. Supermarkets also buy unbranded products which are then given their own label and placed to compete with branded alternatives on the shelves. If they are not satisfied with their supplier, they can change without the end-user customer even knowing that there is any difference in the product. Marks and Spencer uses the second of these strategies only. All of its products are bought unbranded, and given its own name, St. Michael. This enables it to choose its suppliers carefully and dispense with those that do not meet its exacting quality standards.

15 Traditional university and college students are recent school leavers in their late teens and early twenties. A dip in the birth rate will therefore reduce the size of the school-leaver market some 20 years later and can create recruitment difficulties for educational institutions unless governments intervene by introducing policies that encourage greater participation in further and higher education. Strategies that target mature students are one response to this problem. By recruiting across a wider age-band, educational institutions are less exposed to the more intense competition for students that can otherwise occur. Another response is to engage more aggressively in head-on competition. Some universities have increased their marketing budgets substantially, and now include TV advertising among the promotional techniques they use to recruit more 18–21 year olds.

Chapter 3
. . . .

Multiple-choice

1 c Income, education, wealth and occupation are the most commonly used, with occupation being the easiest to identify.

2 b Derived demand is the term used to describe the fact that businesses only buy products and services because consumers or other businesses demand their products and services.

3 b A straight rebuy is a purchase class in organisational buying.

4 e Children are unlikely to be initiators, deciders or buyers in this product category, though they may influence the decision and will almost certainly use the product!

5 c Recession occurs when there is a down-turn in demand in the economy, leading to lower levels of business.

True / False

6 False. Modified rebuy situations usually require new information sources so that established purchasing habits can be reviewed.

7 False. Personal characteristics such as personality, buying style and risk tolerance will all influence decisions.

8 True. Consumers refer to the behaviour of peers to ensure that they themselves will remain accepted members of the group.

9 False. It is likely that consumers will use commercial as well as personal and public sources of information for this type of decision.

10 True. MOSAIC and ACORN are both systems that attempt to relate lifestyles to post-code districts.

Discussion

11 Evidence suggests that advertising has little impact on consumer perceptions of a product at the time it is actually seen; however, if it is creatively presented it may be subject to selective retention that can increase the likelihood of a consumer trying the product. After trial, advertising can be more influential still. When consumers who have seen products advertised actually sample them, they are more likely to be favourably impressed, having been positively influenced by the expectations that the advert has planted (Mitchell, 1994).

12 Central purchasing is likely to be the most efficient means of procurement for products that are required throughout a large organisation and for which discounts can be negotiated from suppliers for large quantities. Company car fleets, for example, are usually purchased centrally in big companies and stationery supplies are often ordered on an annual contract. Products required by only one division of an organisation, or those that are technically complex or specifically related to a particular production process, may be more effectively purchased at local level where the product knowledge is greatest. In these situations, the role of a central buyer may still exist, but simply to process the transaction rather than make an informed input into the decision-making process.

13 The decision-making process for a critical purchase, such as a house, is likely to involve a sizeable decision-making unit. The initiator could be a parent, whose job has been relocated, but the decision to move and which house to buy may be influenced by children, parents, building societies and professional experts such as surveyors and solicitors. In a family unit, the final decision is likely to be a joint one by the adults of the household, but the transaction itself is likely to be conducted in conjunction with a mortgage lender who will provide some of the money for the purchase.

14 Social class is a construct that cuts across many other determinants of consumer behaviour, including income, education, wealth and occupation. In days gone by (and in some countries today) social classes were relatively easy to identify or measure as these four features often ran in parallel, with the wealthiest members of society having been educated for the longest and getting well-paid jobs in the professions. But changes in social structures have altered this pattern and made it very difficult to classify social groups in this way. In the future, an examination of lifestyle is likely to give a better indicator of the beliefs, values and purchasing behaviour of different sub-groups of society.

15 Just like consumers, organisational buyers are likely to investigate four sources of information:

▶ Their own experience of previously buying computers (were they reliable?, did they deliver on time?, was the back-up service adequate?).

▶ Opinions of others, particularly other members of the decision-making unit who may be experts in this field.

▶ Public information, including reports in computer magazines and the trade press. These provide a relatively unbiased perspective on the alternatives available.

▶ Promotional literature, and also face-to-face interaction with salespeople who can provide product feature information.

Chapter 4
·············

Multiple-choice

1 b The others are not available within the organisation itself, but can be obtained from other sources (note, however, that even a customer database is an external source of data if it is purchased from a list-broker rather than generated internally).

2 c Respondents are being asked to place their views on a scale, hence the term 'scaled question'.

3 b The frequencies of response to each question are the summation of the responses of all individuals in the sample; further statistical analysis can be undertaken when the frequencies have been calculated.

4 d This is the only objective that implies a general investigation rather than more specific description or the need for experimentation.

5 d Focus group discussion should be led by a trained moderator who can orchestrate the debate around key issues of relevance to the objectives of the research.

True / False

6 False. There may be no need to conduct any primary research if the answers can be found in the secondary data.

7 False. Randomness means that the sample is more likely to represent the views of the whole population, so fewer respondents are needed.

8 False. Qualitative research does not even try to be statistically reliable. It seeks to identify attitudes, feelings and motivations, rather than to measure their occurrence.

9 True. Data are simply facts and figures, whereas information is produced when these facts and figures are interpreted with reference to the objectives of the research.

10 False. It isn't possible to compare the two for reliability. They are likely to be used in different circumstances and for different purposes; their reliability will depend on their appropriate use in the right circumstances to achieve specific objectives.

Discussion

11 Buying syndicated research is a very useful way of obtaining market information that would otherwise be unavailable. It can be particularly useful when it would be too expensive for a single firm to undertake the research individually, as in the case of regular large sample consumer surveys such as the TGI. The findings of the research are, however, publicly available to all the competitors in an industry, so the strategic use of the findings to gain a competitive advantage is difficult. It is also possible that the research methodology, the nature of the sample or the timing of the research may not fit the information needs of the company very precisely, and that personalised *ad hoc* research is the only way of obtaining relevant information.

12 Before this question can be answered, more specific objectives have to be set so that data requirements can be identified. It is likely that the sample should contain both users and non-users of catering outlets to give a balanced view. You may choose a cluster sample, such as all the students from a particular year group or course, chosen at random from all the courses in your institution. For the most statistically accurate findings you could use a random sample from the list of all registered students. Alternatively, you could try a stratified sample, which selects groups of respondents in direct proportion to the number of male, female, full-time and part-time students. There is no hard and fast rule; the sample must simply be adequate to provide the information required with an acceptable level of accuracy.

13 Telephone surveys are useful in research where it is likely that the population is easily contactable by phone (so that the sample will not be biased). It is also a good way of reaching a geographically spread sample, when it would be logistically difficult to contact a balanced sample face to face. What is more, in comparison with face to face interviewing, this technique is both cheap and fast. These two factors contribute to the relatively heavy use of this technique in business-to-business research as opposed to consumer research.

14 The mean is useful for gaining an impression of the overall tendencies of the sample in a scaled question. When used in conjunction with the standard deviation it indicates the extent to which the respondents have similar views – the wider the deviation, the fewer the similarities between respondents. The mode indicates the most popular responses to a question. If there are two different, but equally popular, responses this implies that there are two distinct segments within the population under investigation. The median is simply the 'middle person's' response. The category into which this response falls can be thought of as the half-way point in public opinion.

15 'Paralysis by analysis' is an expression that refers to the way in which some organisations generate so much information that they are overwhelmed with facts and figures and feel unable to act on any of them. 'Data distress' is one example of this. Marketing information is only useful if it is a cost-effective way of improving decision-making and helping the organisation to achieve its objectives. It is not a substitute for action.

Chapter 5
•••••••••••

Multiple-choice

1 b While income *is* a demographic basis for segmentation, price is a *response* to the target market, ie part of the marketing mix.

2 c Although these systems use demographic and geographic characteristics to *analyse* the population, their findings enable marketers to *segment* the population on the basis of the lifestyle implied by these characteristics.

3 b When the different positions of their competitors are identified, organisations are better able to design appropriate competitive strategies.

4 b The number of competitors in different market segments is unlikely to have a major impact on the viability of a new market segment unless they subsequently adopt a head-on competition strategy.

5 d In this situation, avoiding the competition may not be a viable option.

True / False

6 True. Product differentiated marketing tries to find product versions that appeal to a wide range of people whereas multi-segment marketing strategies involve producing different products to reflect the different characteristics and needs of different groups within the total market.

7 True. This may take lots of different forms, and a number of examples are given in this chapter.

8 True. These concepts both imply a focus on a single market segment.

9 False. Figure 5.1 demonstrates how marketing mix decisions arise as a result of segmentation, targeting *and* positioning.

10 True. Segmentation based on purchase patterns such as this can be very useful.

Discussion

11 Demographic segmentation has been used extensively by soap manufacturers. For example, there are brands aimed at women (Lux and Camay), at men (Shield), at young people (Clearasil) and at babies (Johnsons). However, demographic segmentation is by no means the whole story. A further level of segmentation by benefit sought is apparent in each of these brands – namely good complexion, personal hygiene, prevention of spots, and gentleness. Other brands are not segmented on demographics at all, but focus on segments based, for example, on purpose of use (Fairy household soap), ease of use (liquid soap), natural ingredients (Body Shop), moisturising properties (Dove) or freedom from irritation (Simple).

12 Rotators need to be exposed to consistent promotional activity to maintain the standing of a brand in the eyes of consumers, encouraging them to select it above the others on their short-lists. Distribution should match, or better that of, the competition, but prices need not necessarily be lower, simply in an acceptable band. Deal-sensitive consumers are attracted by low prices, so price rather than brand should be emphasised in promotional messages. Distribution needs to be good, but these consumers may be willing to shop around to some extent in search of a bargain.

13 Store loyalty cards enable supermarkets to identify students and make them promotional offers that can be denied to other more affluent segments of their market. This makes the student segment more accessible and therefore more viable. The student market holds good potential for future business too, as this segment is likely to be more affluent than average in later life.

To attract the student market to its loyalty card scheme, Tesco launched a Student Clubcard which it promoted at 75 universities, and which required a lower minimum spend than its normal Clubcard.

14 Owner-managed businesses with limited resources competing against much larger companies tend to be the most successful niche marketers, particularly if they target small segments that are not viable for a larger competitor with higher overheads. Success produces a dilemma for these businesses. They are vulnerable to aggressive competitors if their market starts to grow, as they do not have a portfolio of markets to fall back on if they lose ground.

15 The answer to this can only be identified through research, and care should be taken to ensure that the market is a homogeneous one. Three common characteristics cited are 'error protection', 'number of functions' and 'ease of learning', but the most important of these might depend on the purpose of use. Home-workers may be willing to sacrifice ease of learning for a wide variety of special commands, but parents buying software for their children may rate ease of learning number one, followed by error protection. The two more important characteristics for each target market are the ones that should be placed on each axis.

Chapter 6
....

Multiple-choice

1 c It is intangible in that it does not offer physical benefits when the purchase is made, only reassurance, so it is part of the extended product, not the core or actual product.

2 d Stars need cash investment for promotional activities which will help them to extend their markets and sustain their market shares into maturity.

3 a

4 b Customers go through a very short decision-making process for convenience products. All the product categories except impulse products are likely to engage customers in longer deliberations.

5 c All the brand names given except Campari are associated with product lines as opposed to single products.

True / False

6 False. Saturation occurs at the maturity stage when no new customers enter the market.

7 False. The original equipment manufacturer is a major purchaser of components.

8 True. Under these circumstances 'dogs' have little long-term potential for profitability.

9 True. The intangible features are described as being part of the extended product.

10 True. Many supermarkets, for example, sell their own-brands as well as manufacturer brands.

Discussion

11 Groceries are usually categorised as staples, or FMCGs, as they are generally purchased on a regular basis, with a tendency for consumers to repeat purchase brands that they are happy with. But consumers may be tempted to 'shop around' when they buy a product class for the first time, or if they become dissatisfied with their usual brand, perhaps due to a new recipe which they don't like, or an increase in price. Speciality products might be sought as specific ingredients for recipes or, for example, if preferred foreign brands are not generally available except through delicatessens.

12 The aftermarket purchases for resale and repair, so potential buyers tend to be more numerous and smaller in size than OEMs. This means that buyers in the aftermarket usually have minimal buying power over their supplier, who can charge them prices that generate a reasonable profit margin. Suppliers to OEMs tend to rely heavily on the business from just a few customers and, in the face of hostile competition, are more likely to cut prices rather than risk losing business upon which their firms depend.

13 The product life-cycle for recorded music began with trumpet-shaped gramophone players and vinyl records. The market moved into growth, as the only alternative was live music which was not always convenient or practical. Records were soon joined and replaced by tapes and ultimately CDs, and the market has moved into a relatively stable period of what appears to be a long-term maturity. There are no signs yet that the market for recorded music is moving into decline. Tape cassettes, on the other hand, were not introduced at the very start yet have already passed through a growth phase (particularly during the expansion of in-car hi-fi and personal stereos), into maturity and more recently into relative decline since the launch of the CD format.

14 Although a question mark is a product that is failing to gain market share in a growing market, it may be worth sustaining. The environment may be changing, perhaps improving its future potential. Competitors may be passive, leaving the door open for a good promotional campaign to turn the tide. There may be potential for the product to thrive in a specialist niche, aimed only at a small segment of the total market. It could be that the question mark is an essential complement to another product line and serves to keep customers loyal by enabling the company to offer a full product mix. Finally, it may fill production capacity that would otherwise be spare, and therefore make a useful contribution towards overheads.

15 The two main reasons are risk and money. Whereas only 30 per cent of new individual brands survive, the figure is 50 per cent for brand extensions, which are supported by the corporate image and can reduce the psychological fears customers have of trying something new. Costs of promotion can also be lower. New brands can sometimes share the space purchased for their sister products or at least benefit from the media exposure of the family brand name.

Chapter 7
....

Multiple-choice

1 b Employees are *internal* sources of new product ideas, as they work for the organisation that will produce the new product.
2 e The product is 'dropped' too soon in the innovation process.
3 c Financial assessment takes places along with a marketing assessment at the business analysis stage.
4 b Opinion leaders are respected in society for their views and are unlikely to take the kinds of risks that innovators do in buying new products, so they tend to be early adopters.
5 e Trial is a typical part of the process people go through in adopting a new product.

True / False

6 False. It is known as a 'me-too' product.
7 False. It may start with a brainstorming session, but there are many other sources of new ideas too.
8 False. They are sometimes made at the concept testing stage, and usually at the product development and testing stage.
9 True. This is because test-markets are often impractical for the types of products and sales patterns experienced in industrial markets.
10 False. Laggards are the last group within a target market to adopt the product, but they get there eventually!

Discussion

11 Product line extensions are a relatively low-cost, low-risk way of providing consumers with more choice. It is a common route to NPD in recession when businesses are short of cash and more risk-averse. They are useful for filling a gap where a competitor could potentially enter, or where a competitor is strong and no one else is supplying that product. However, there are several drawbacks. Product line extensions do not always meet new customer needs, so may add unnecessary complexity to the market and incur higher costs for the business but fail to create any greater competitive advantage. Sometimes companies are diverted by product line extensions while competitors are getting on with the job of real innovation (as in the case of Coke, which was busy formulating a caffeine free variety while Snapple was being launched (Richards, 1995)).
12 There is no right answer here. It depends on circumstances. Drop-errors imply a missed opportunity. This is likely to be the more serious of the two for large organisations who can afford to take risks and fail from time to time (see Case study 7.1). It is a particular problem if the error allows new

competitors to enter or existing competitors to increase their presence significantly in a market. Go-errors are a big problem for organisations with limited resources who cannot afford to fail. Fear of them increases the hesitancy of smaller organisations to become involved in NPD.

13 The size and resources of the company are an important factor, as a global launch is very expensive. The nature of the distribution network is also important. It is rare to be able to launch a new product on a wide scale into a completely new network. The nature of the market is also a factor to consider. If 80 per cent of demand is likely to come from 20 per cent of the market, it is more sensible to concentrate on this proportion first. Finally, it will also depend on customer needs across geographical areas. A global launch is only sensible if customer needs vary little between areas.

14 Laggards are the last group to adopt a product; 84 per cent of the total market for a product is already using it by the time laggards come along, so the cost effectiveness of specifically targeting promotions at this group can be doubtful. It may be more appropriate to use reminder advertising, for example, which is aimed at retaining the loyalty of existing users but will overspill to the laggards who are likely to be influenced by the actions of others. Alternatively, if new and better products are already coming along by the time this group is ready to adopt, the promotional budget may be better spent on securing a foothold for the new products.

15 With me-too products, the business analysis stage is usually the starting point in the decision-making process, the idea and the concept having already proved successful in the market. Product development and testing, and a limited amount of market testing are also necessary, though it is unlikely that a test market will be cost effective.

Chapter 8
....

Multiple-choice

1 a, c and **e** These are all strategies that concentrate on earnings in the short term.
2 a, c and **e** Penetration pricing concentrates on buying volume, so the investment needs to hold out promise of a good return.
3 d and **e**
4 b.
5 c.

True / False

6 True. And it can mean that the cheapest product in a particular category is not the best selling choice.
7 True. However, there are exceptions, such as cigarettes and alcohol, where higher prices are used to limit consumption.
8 True. An example is the practice of selling consumer durables at near cost price in order to make money on warranties.
9 True. According to A.C. Ehrenberg's researches at least.
10 False. What the market will bear is more important in the long run.

Discussion

11 Consumers in the 1990s expect transparent dealings from manufacturers and service providers. Strong attention to public relations and a proactively ethical trading stance are two ways of assuring customers of good faith.

12 Distribution, product quality and promotion are all capable of softening the impact of price. But money is not the only thing that consumers exchange for benefits. Inconvenience, time, and energy are just some of the other non-financial price factors. By manipulating the other elements of the marketing mix to heighten consumer utility, sustainable competitive advantage can be created without sacrificing revenue.

13 Pricing decisions should never be taken in isolation. These three marketing areas offer plenty of scope for illustrating how price interacts with the other elements. Pricing services is, as we have seen in the chapter, a particularly delicate process.

14 While the tactic of the RPO might run the risk of cheapening a product's reputation, it is nevertheless a highly effective way of generating volume. The strength of any promotional idea, however, lies in its originality. Once price promotion becomes the done thing, manufacturers are in a very dangerous position. This can be a spur to greater creativity in promotional thinking, and an attempt to bolster brand values rather than simply cut price.

15 Price elasticity is important to know because it can help predict the effect of planned price changes. It can be learned only through careful observation over a number of years. Computer modelling can help to amplify the effects of such empirical observation.

Chapter 9
．．．．．．．．．．．．

Multiple-choice

1 Sorting, accumulation, breaking down bulk, assortment, convenience, promotion.

2 a While some common patterns emerge, distribution decisions need to be taken on a case-by-case basis, and regularly reviewed.

b Many buyers and sellers will use several different distribution systems at the same time (eg a retailer may use a traditional wholesaler and a cash and carry, depending on stock fluctuations and timing).

c Push promotion is aimed at the trade rather than at the consumer.

3 d They do, however, offer convenient opening hours.

4 e.

5 d.

True / False

6 True. Along with customers and product characteristics.

7 False. While it is common with luxury goods and expensive cars, exclusive distribution also applies to items like Body Shop cosmetics.

8 True.

9 False. The minimum is 100,000 square feet.

10 True. By reducing the amount of stock in the system, snags are exposed.

Discussion

11 Merchant intermediaries (such as retailers and wholesalers) actually buy and own what they resell, whereas functional intermediaries (such as agents and transport providers) are rewarded by commission or a fee. Merchants take more risk but can look forward to greater returns.

12 Intensive (eg batteries), selective (eg electric kettles) and exclusive (eg Porsche cars).

13 a A specialist discount retailer aiming for a monopoly in its category.

   b Confectioner tobacconist newsagent, like a traditional corner sweet and paper shop.

   c An independent grocer who allies with others in order to increase their buying power.

   d A go-between connecting buyers and sellers.

   e The range and amount of stock carried.

14 The Wheel of Retailing sees retailers as having a life-cycle whereby they start as discounters and then try to move up-market to a more profitable positioning. Meanwhile new discounters enter at the bottom of the market and the process renews itself.

15 Order processing, materials handling, warehousing, inventory management, transport.

Chapter 10
· · · · · · · · · · · · · ·

Multiple-choice

1 d Although technological advances (as in e) have facilitated its development.

2 e.

3 b David Ogilvy described it as a product's 'first-class ticket through life'.

4 c.

5 d.

True / false

6 False. Some of it is aimed at activity other than buying things, and some of it takes place on a corporate rather than product level where there is no obvious purchase to be made.

7 True.

8 False. This is the job of the production department.

9 True. As opposed to 'burst' which is shorter but more intense.

10 False. The reverse is true.

Discussion

11 This is becoming an increasingly vexed question as the opportunities for selective targeting presented by developing media become available. Cable and satellite TV channels may not offer vast numbers of viewers, but they can be a very efficient way of accessing otherwise extremely elusive audiences.

12 Sales may not be the immediate object of the advertising, but it remains true that an idea is being 'sold' to you every time you look at an advertisement. Perhaps finding some examples of advertising for non-commercial causes might help clarify an answer to this question.

13 Many large advertisers (Heinz and Nestlé among them) have made significant moves in this direction. To some extent it is sabre rattling against the large retailers (whose strangle hold on distribution is a danger to manufacturers) and to media owners (who need to be reminded from time to time that there are alternative ways of reaching the public rather than through their expensive vehicles.)

14 Radio and posters are surprisingly similar in a number of ways. Press is the odd one out here. As ever with advertising essays or discussion, examples are essential.

15 Self-regulation depends on there being a need for regulation itself in communicating with consumers. Some would argue that the market can take care of itself and does not need norms of good taste or fairness imposed on it. A medium addressing smaller and more self-assured publics does not have the same power to offend viewers, readers or listeners who have made a conscious choice to be their audience. On the other hand, advertisers are extremely sensitive about possibility of negative publicity – so might be reluctant to abandon any kind of controls.

Chapter 11
....

Multiple-choice

1 b.
2 c.
3 b.
4 b.
5 c.

True / False

6 True. In spite of the traditional idea of an adversarial sales encounter, successful salespeople are like business partners with their customers.

7 True. They are particularly important early on in the sales interview.

8 False. Good salespeople listen a lot.

9 True. Part of their effectiveness derives from their being temporary.

10 False. Leave opinions to journalists, but facts to the press release.

Discussion

11 Training is essential for salespeople to develop their potential and to keep in touch with ideas and techniques. However, most people would agree

that while there is no definite selling 'type', a successful salesperson needs to have the potential in the first place.

12 This quote, from a very commercially successful novelist, reminds us that selling is a basic human activity. Trying to convince other people of one's ideas in an argument is a selling job of sorts, as is going for an interview or having a date.

13 This might have been a widely held opinion 20 years ago, but the medium has matured into a highly regarded technique that can consolidate branding on a strategic level especially if integrated with other techniques.

14 PR is capable of abuse, like any other tool. But this view of it is too extreme. It is also naive to expect an objective view of the world from journalists, each of whom will have opinions and convictions that will inform his or her outlook.

15 The VNR is certainly a powerful device, but there is a discernible backlash against it from TV news editors for a number of reasons. One of the most important ones is that there are now a lot of VNRs being sent to newsrooms and so they can afford to be more choosy. On the other hand, technology seems to be driving us towards an increasingly visual culture, so perhaps the VNR or something like it in a digital set-up will be setting the agenda for the future.

Chapter 12
....

Multiple-choice

1 c Marketing strategy supports corporate strategy.
2 b this strategy is more in keeping with the behaviour of market leaders.
  d market followers are happy with the status quo, but challengers challenge by their nature.
  e niche marketers manage to get high profits from very low market share.
3 c
4 b, **c** and **d** But all methods of forecasting need to be combined with qualitative judgement.
5 b, **e**, **d**, **a** and **c**.

True / False

6 False. It's the other way round.
7 False. Top down (centralised management) has the advantage of giving clear instructions on decisions already taken.
8 True. Because of the concentration usually associated with industrial markets and product/service ranges.
9 False. Brand managers get a lot of responsibility without a lot of power.
10 True.

Discussion

11 Whether or not you agree with the pithy sentiment expressed here, it is certainly true that it would be very difficult to understand the concept of success without first having an idea of what it meant to be successful (ie objectives). Failure to plan means that success becomes impossible. However, it is a time consuming and challenging process, which diverts energy from the immediate task in hand.

12 Although this sounds as if it should be true, the chapter has provided examples of differential advantage sourced from two other areas as well – company capability and relationships with customers. There may well be more kinds of sources – again, examples of successful companies can help elucidate the principles involved.

13 There are a number of strategies available. The two most obvious ones, perhaps, are niching and flanking. Market segmentation is extremely important here.

14 In spite of its trappings of statistics and science, forecasting is a very approximate art. Therefore it needs to be done with confidence that your opinion (based on judgement and analysis) is valid. Scenario building, for example, works not because it is accurate, but because it allows a number of different visions of the future to be tried out.

15 Certainly the nature of the brand is changing, with the growth in retailer power and the developing technological environment. Brand managers are expensive, moreover, and many companies are seeking to downsize. However, it would be surprising if the function did not survive in some way because of its peculiar appropriateness to marketing.

Chapter 13
••••••••••••••

Multiple-choice

1 a The presence of a mixture of nationalities in management would be highly usual, but of itself it does not indicate involvement in international marketing.

2 c Product quality is a *sine qua non* of any kind of marketing, but the other aspects of marketing management are particularly problematic in the international environment.

3 c In spite of the fact that personal grooming is an intensely cultural phenomenon, hair type is something that we are born with and is therefore demographic rather than cultural. **d** is an arguable answer here, but studies show a high correlation between educational achievements and earning power.

4 c, **a**, **d**, **e** and **b**.

5 d.

True / False

6 False. Experience with joint ventures suggests that they are unlikely to remain stable in the long term.

7 True. All of these industries provide good examples of 'global' brands.

8 True. Manufacturers need to have a presence in such markets to keep abreast of developments.

9 True. Such branding eliminates the difficulties caused by language.

10 False. The final stage is when exporters face competition in their domestic markets from imports.

Answers to discussion questions

11 Small- to medium-sized businesses need, like any other business aiming at international markets, to be sure that there is a genuine opportunity out there. So research is necessary – especially on a personal basis. There is often much valuable information available from organisations such as chambers of commerce or trade bodies. In Europe, the SME has a privileged position in EU commercial legislation, so advantage may be taken of this. Partnerships with other companies are a good way of compensating for the disadvantages of size relative to larger competitors.

12 Promotional management is a difficult area at the best of times, but in the international context it presents peculiar difficulties. This is because of the cultural, technological and legal environments – all of which may be significantly different from country to country. There is no simple answer to this problem. Promotional managers should not assume that they can merely extend a successful domestic strategy to a new market without careful research. The growth of multinational agencies in the worlds of Advertising and Public Relations recognises this new need. Many multinational companies get good results through using local agencies who follow agreed overall strategies, but have a large amount of flexibility as to their detailed implementation.

13 Marketing research is more difficult to co-ordinate and carry out in the international arena. People in some cultures are not used to being asked questions about consumption. In this case confusion and unreliable data may result from an attempt to carry out the kind of research that would be straightforward in the domestic market. Secondary research, too, can be dogged by problems of continuity of data or its comparability with other data. This kind of confusion can extend to demographic statistics. For example, the population of Nigeria is thought by some analysts to be something like three times the official estimate. Like other marketing services, research is beginning to organisae itself on the lines of international networks. But the area is still fraught with difficulties.

14 The marketing manager of the 21st century will need to be more comfortable in a multicultural environment. Forward-thinking educators in the EU, for example, recognise the value of student mobility between countries in order to prepare them for this new challenge. This is the point of the various programmes run under the SOCRATES-ERASMUS scheme. Working, living and studying in a number of cultures – and being proficient in a number of languages – are all likely to be characteristics of employable graduates from the year 2000. As we have seen at the beginning of Chapter 13, International Marketing makes more searching demands than even domestic marketing. So the new breed of marketing manager needs to be in position to respond on each count.

Index